Consumer

Fifth Edition

Consumer Law in Scotland

Fifth Edition

WCH Ervine

Honorary Teaching Fellow, Dundee University School of Law

W. GREEN

 THOMSON REUTERS

First Edition	1995
Second Edition	2000
Reprint	2002
Third Edition	2004
Fourth Edition	2008

Published in 2015 by W. Green, 21 Alva Street, Edinburgh EH2 4PS part of Thomson Reuters (Professional) UK Limited (Registered in England & Wales, Company No.1679046. Registered Office and address for service: 2nd floor, 1 Mark Square, Leonard Street, London EC2A 4EG)

Typeset by Letterpart Limited, Caterham on the Hill, Surrey, CR3 5XL.

Printed in Great Britain by CPI Group (UK) Ltd, Croydon, CR0 4YY.

No natural forests were destroyed to make this product; only farmed timber was used and re-planted.

A CIP catalogue record of this book is available from the British Library.

http://www.wgreen.co.uk

ISBN: 978-0-414-01936-2

For Tomos

Preface to the fifth edition

This edition has required more revision than any previous new edition. This has principally been because of the Consumer Rights Act 2015, which has revised the law on the supply of goods and services, clarified the rights of consumers when purchasing digital content, consolidated the law on unfair terms, and introduced new enforcement powers. Other legislation has produced new civil remedies for victims of misleading and aggressive practices as well as updating of the regulations on distance and doorstep selling. These are welcome reforms that will benefit consumers. The same can hardly be said for the changes in what has become known as the "consumer landscape", the various organisations, public and private, that exist to promote the consumer interest. It is hard to disagree with the chief executive of *Which?* who described the proposals as a "shockingly ill-conceived plan". In Scotland the chief victim has been Consumer Futures, formerly known as the Scottish Consumer Council. It is sad to see the work and reputation of this excellent organisation that was built up over 40 years summarily discarded.

While the recent reforms of consumer law are to be welcomed their effectiveness will be affected by the problems of the trading standards service. Reductions in local government funding have seriously reduced its impact. A research report earlier this year, *The Impact of Local Authority Trading Standards in Challenging Times* found that most now operate with about half the number of staff that they employed five years ago and simply cannot provide the level of service that officers would like. Perhaps this will force consideration of new ways of organising the service in Scotland where 32 departments—many of which are quite small—may not be the best way to deliver an effective service.

While there have been many changes in consumer law and organisations in the last five years more changes are on the way. The Gill reforms of the civil justice system are about to take effect. Perhaps even more importantly, the devolution of more consumer protection functions to Scotland will result in further change.

It is, once again, a pleasure to thank those officials at government departments and many trading standards officers, as well as colleagues in the School of Law at the University of Dundee who have helped by answering my queries. As ever, the staff at W. Green have been efficient and helpful, in particular Ciara Daly, who saw the book through the production process.

PREFACE TO THE FIFTH EDITION

I have tried to state the law as at 24 March 2015, though it has been possible to refer to some later developments. In particular, I have anticipated the coming into force of the Consumer Rights Act 2015 on 1 October 2015.

Cowan Ervine
Dundee
July 2015

Preface to the fourth edition

In the preface to the third edition I observed that, in the light of a government consultation paper on consumer strategy, it was likely that a new edition would be needed sooner rather than later. This has proved to be the case, mostly as a result of legislative reform. Possibly the most important change in consumer law for 40 years, the Consumer Protection from Unfair Trading Regulations 2008, has transformed the way that trade practices are regulated. There have also been important reforms to consumer credit and the structure of consumer representation. More changes are promised. The Department of Business, Enterprise and Regulatory Reform is conducting a review of consumer law and the European Commission is reviewing its consumer *acquis*.

It is, once again, a pleasure to thank those officials at government departments and many trading standards officers, as well as colleagues in the School of Law at the University of Dundee who have helped by answering my queries. I should particularly like to thank David Hart, our law Librarian, for hunting down references, and Sarah O'Neill of the Scottish Consumer Council, who read Chapter 1. As ever, the staff at W. Green have been efficient and helpful, in particular Frances Reid Rowland, who saw the book through the production process.

I have tried to state the law as at March 24, 2008, though it has been possible to refer to some later developments.

WCH Ervine
Dundee
May 2008

Preface to the third edition

This edition appears after a shorter interval than that which divided the first and second editions. The rapidity of developments in the last four years has been such that the previous edition was becoming seriously outdated. Having remained dormant for several years after its enactment, Pt I of the Consumer Protection Act 1987 has produced a number of interesting decisions of which *A v National Blood Authority* seems to be the most significant. The Sale and Supply of Goods to Consumers Regulations 2002 have made important additions to the remedies available to purchasers of goods while *Clegg v Anderson* has given guidance on the meaning of satisfactory quality and underlined the primacy of rejection as a remedy for consumers who choose to avail themselves of the original Sale of Goods Act remedies. The House of Lords have had their first opportunity to consider the Unfair Terms in Consumer Contracts Regulations in *Director General of Fair Trading v First National Bank Plc.* The Enterprise Act 2002 has introduced super complaints and replaced the creaking procedure under Pt III of the Fair Trading Act 1973 with enforcement orders which have the potential to be much more effective. A white paper on the reform of consumer credit law appeared in December 2003 and to its credit the DTI has already begun to implement some of the changes foreshadowed though the details of these were announced too late to allow more than brief reference in the text. Just as final corrections were being made to the text of this edition the DTI published *Extending Competitive Markets: Empowered Consumers, Successful Business*, an important consultation paper on its consumer strategy for the next five years. No comment can be made on that document at this stage other than to encourage readers to study it and to note that it seems likely to ensure that a further edition will be necessary sooner rather than later.

Once again it is a pleasure to thank all those who have helped me. They include officials at government departments and many trading standards officers as well as colleagues in the Department of Law at the University of Dundee. I am also grateful to the staff at W. Green, notably Valerie Malloch and Rachel Cryer who efficiently saw the book through the production process.

I have tried to state the law as at May 7, 2004, though it has been possible to refer to some later developments.

WCH Ervine
Dundee
July 2004

Preface to the second edition

In the five years since the first edition there have been a number of developments in the field of consumer protection which have made it worth producing a new edition. Inevitably there have been more judicial decisions and legislation. In the latter area probably the most significant has been the revised Unfair Terms in Consumer Contracts Regulations 1999 which widen the range of organisations which can seek interdicts to prevent the use of unfair terms. Local government has been reorganised thereby altering the organisation of enforcement. Potentially the most significant development is the White Paper, *Modern markets: Confident consumers* published in 1999. This is the first White Paper to deal with consumer protection and to find any other official document of similar importance in this field one must go back to the *Molony Report* of 1962. The White Paper promises much, how much will be delivered remains to be seen.

Once again it is a pleasure to thank all those who have helped me. These include officials at various government departments, especially the Office of Fair Trading, and many trading standards officers. I am also indebted to colleagues in the Department of Law at the University of Dundee and the staff of the Law Library who have been unfailingly helpful. I am also grateful for the help and encouragement of the staff at W. Green.

I have tried to state the law as at April 6, 2000, though it has been possible to add some references to developments after that date.

WCH Ervine
Dundee
June 2000

Preface to the first edition

This book attempts to set out the law relating to consumer protection in Scotland. Consumer protection is a recent development and much of the law originates in statutes having application throughout the United Kingdom. While there are a number of good books on the subject they approach the area from the point of view of English practitioners. It seemed to me that there was scope for a book which stated the law in Scotland. Where the law is statutory there are often Scottish decisions interpreting it; and the common law still has an important role to play. In addition, the separateness of the Scottish legal system also has an impact.

The term consumer protection is not a precise one and there can be legitimate difference of opinion as to what material should be covered in such a work. My approach has been to deal with the protection afforded to private consumers of goods and services. It could be objected that even within that definition of the subject there are gaps. This is particularly true when considering the area of services where very little is said, for example, about the important topic of financial services. The answer to this criticism is purely pragmatic: space does not allow everything to be covered; and, in any event, there are excellent specialist works in this area.

Consumer principles are increasingly being applied to areas not normally associated with consumer protection such as the provision of services by the State. Consumer organisations have for some time been dealing with the operation of the courts, the social security system and education. A tentative look at this new aspect of consumer protection has been taken but once again constraints of space have dictated that it should be brief.

I am indebted to numerous people for their help. Over many years staff at the National and Scottish Consumer Councils and trading standards officers have been ready to answer my questions as have officials in various government departments notably the Office of Fair Trading. My colleagues in the Department of Law at the University of Dundee and in other departments, have been extremely helpful. Although with the passage of time there have been many changes in relation to advertising trade practices and the institutions of consumer protection it would not be right to omit mention of my debt to the editors of the *Stair Memorial Encyclopaedia of the Laws of Scotland* especially Mr Hamish McN. Henderson. Their assistance with my articles on consumer protection and advertising made work in those areas for this book much easier. Judith Pearson of the University of Aberdeen was good enough to read a draft of Chapter 9, and saved me from a number of errors. Needless to say, the errors in the work are solely my responsibility.

PREFACE TO THE FIRST EDITION

I have endeavoured to state the law as at January 5, 1995, though I have anticipated the coming into force on July 1, of the Unfair Terms in Consumer Contracts Regulations 1994, and it has been possible to incorporate some changes which took place after that date.

WCH Ervine
Dundee
July 1995

TABLE OF CONTENTS

CONTENTS

CONTENTS

CONTENTS

CONTENTS

TABLE OF CASES

TABLE OF CASES

TABLE OF CASES

TABLE OF CASES

TABLE OF CASES

TABLE OF CASES

TABLE OF UK STATUTES

TABLE OF ACTS OF THE SCOTTISH PARLIAMENT

TABLE OF UK STATUTORY INSTRUMENTS

TABLE OF SCOTTISH STATUTORY INSTRUMENTS

TABLE OF EUROPEAN LEGISLATION

1

CHAPTER 1

Background and Institutions of Consumer Protection

Consumer protection is essentially a modern topic. Indeed it is tempting to say   **1–01**
that it is a topic that dates only from the 1960s. Even in 1968 it was not
sufficiently well developed to merit a chapter in one of the leading Scottish legal
textbooks.[1] As in many other countries in Europe, North America and elsewhere,
the 1960s were certainly the beginning of a period of substantial development in
Britain in the field of consumer protection.[2]

It would be misleading, however, to give the impression that consumer   **1–02**
protection does not have a lengthy history. One of the oldest forms of consumer
protection is what would now be described as weights and measures legislation.
There are numerous examples of such legislation by the Scottish Parliament
dating from the Middle Ages. The Weights Act 1425 defined the standard stone at
15lb. Troy, 16lb. Scots, and under the Weights Act 1540 burghs were required to
keep one set of weights for buying and selling, implying that there was a
widespread practice of using one set of weights when buying and another when
selling. In the same year standard measures for barrels of salmon and herring
were instituted by the Measures Act 1540. The Measures and Weights Act 1587
appointed a commission to prepare a universal standard of weights and measures.
The results of its efforts appear as the second Measures and Weights Act 1587
that set out the "Mesuris and wechtis and the just quantitie thereof", while in the
Justices of the Peace Act 1661 it was laid down that all measures were to conform
with the measure of Linlithgow.

The Measures Act 1685 defined three barleycorns set lengthways as an inch,   **1–03**
12 inches as a foot, 36 inches as a yard, 37 inches as a Scots eln and 1,760 yards
as a mile. The purpose of this Act is stated as being

> "that there should be a fixed standard for measuring and computation of Myles [*sic*]
> and that the whole Isle of Britain should be under one certain kind of
> commensuration".

The foot so calculated was to be

---

[1] See Gloag and Henderson, *Introduction to the Law of Scotland*, edited by AM Johnston and JAD
Hope, 7th edn (Edinburgh: W.Green, 1968). Succeeding editions have had such a chapter.
[2] Sir Gordon Borrie, *The Development of Consumer Law and Policy—Bold Spirits and Timorous
Souls* (London: Stevens, 1984) p.2.

"the only foot by which all workmen, especially Masons, Wrights, Glasiers, and others are ordained to measure their work in all time coming, under the pain of ane hundreth pounds *toties quoties*".[3]

The importance of weights and measures was demonstrated by reference to them in the Act of Union, which provided that English weights and measures were to be used throughout the UK.[4]

1–04   The purity of goods is of cardinal importance to the consumer, and since the nineteenth century, legislation on this topic has continued to expand. In 1860 the "Act for Preventing the Adulteration of Articles of Food or Drink" was a mere 14 sections long.[5] This has gradually grown into a vast corpus of law of which the Food Safety Act 1990 is but the tip of a veritable iceberg of legislation, mostly to be found in statutory instruments.

1–05   The merchandise marks legislation, dating originally from 1862,[6] was the ancestor of the Trade Descriptions Act 1968 (now repealed), and was intended to control misleading claims about goods.

1–06   The legislation mentioned above has in common the fact that it invokes the criminal law as a means of consumer protection. Civil law had a much more limited role to play in protecting the consumer. It is sometimes said that the Sale of Goods Act 1893[7] was the first consumer protection statute of this type. Leaving aside the argument that in Scotland it may actually have weakened the consumer's position by importing alien concepts, it is difficult to see it in this light. True, it could be said to have benefited consumers in the sense that it clarified the law and made it more accessible, but, as one might expect in the age of laissez-faire, it left much scope to the parties to a contract to make their own bargain.

1–07   The role of the courts must not be forgotten. Theirs has not, on the whole, been a prominent role in protecting the consumer. However, *Donoghue v Stevenson*[8] has had immense importance for consumers, as for many other groups, and its reverberations continue to be felt. One might also regret that consumers or their advisers have not been more adventurous in invoking the principles of Scots law. On occasion clear invitations to do so seem to have been thoughtlessly ignored. For example, in *McKay v Scottish Airways Ltd*[9] Lord President Cooper seemed clearly to be pointing to the adoption of a reasonableness test for exclusion clauses, but this never seems to have been taken up by counsel in any later case.

1–08   While one must not ignore the ancient origins of some aspects of consumer protection, it was only in the 1960s that it came to have such prominence. If one were seeking an arbitrary point to use as the beginning of the modern era for

---

[3] I am indebted to the late Mr H McN Henderson, Deputy General Editor of the Stair Memorial Encyclopaedia, for drawing my attention to this material. For a comprehensive list of old statutes, see the general index to the Acts of the Parliaments of Scotland, Weights and Measures, A.P.S. xii 1232, 1233.

[4] See the Treaty of Union between Scotland and England 1707 art.XVII.

[5] For example, the Adulteration of Food and Drink Act 1860 (repealed).

[6] See the Merchandise Marks Act 1862 (repealed).

[7] Although the Sale of Goods Act 1893 was passed in 1894 it describes itself as the Sale of Goods Act 1893: see s.64 (repealed).

[8] *Donoghue v Stevenson*, 1932 S.C. (H.L.) 31; 1932 S.L.T. 317.

[9] *McKay v Scottish Airways Ltd*, 1948 S.C. 254; 1948 S.L.T. 402.

consumer protection, July 1962, the date of publication of the *Molony Report*,[10] would be appropriate. This report reviewed a wide range of consumer issues and advocated reform in many areas. The Trade Descriptions Act 1968 can be traced directly to its recommendations and many other legislative reforms were given an initial impetus by its conclusions.

In the five decades since the publication of the *Molony Report* much has been achieved. Legislation on consumer safety, exclusion clauses, consumer credit and various marketing practices has been enacted. Perhaps of more importance, an institutional structure (or consumer landscape as it has come to be known) was erected with the creation by the Fair Trading Act 1973 of the Office of Fair Trading, and the formation of the National Consumer Council which had a vigorous committee, the Scottish Consumer Council.[11]   **1–09**

In the same four decades the voluntary organisations which play such an important role have increased in importance and effectiveness. The Consumers' Association was barely eight years old when the *Molony Report* was published. It has developed into a dynamic organisation not only providing valuable information on products and services but also effectively lobbying for changes in the law. The Citizens' Advice Bureaux have expanded their network; and in a number of cities consumer groups have been set up under the aegis of the National Federation of Consumer Groups now merged in the National Consumer Federation.   **1–10**

The last two decades have seen important changes in the techniques employed to achieve the ends of consumer protection. Administrative control has become more prominent and, perhaps somewhat paradoxically, self-regulation has expanded. The advertising industry is the most striking example of control by self-regulation, but self-regulation has come to play a significant part in other areas such as package holidays, servicing and repair of electrical goods and the car trade. In the consumer White Paper *Modern Markets: Confident Consumers* published in July 1999, the Government indicated that they intend to place more emphasis on codes of practice as a way of improving trading standards.[12] The white paper was the first thorough review of consumer protection since the *Molony Report* over 30 years ago and has been followed by a number of reforms notably in consumer credit and trade practices, though like so many recent reforms this has been prompted as much by the need to comply with our European Union (EU) obligations. The Coalition Government published its consumer strategy *Better Choices: Better Deals—Consumers Powering Growth*[13] in April 2011. This aimed to create a simple, modern framework of consumer law across all sectors and was accompanied by a series of consultation documents published in autumn 2012. A draft Consumer Rights Bill was published in June   **1–11**

---

[10] Committee on Consumer Protection, *Final report of the Committee on Consumer Protection* (the Molony Report) (HMSO 1962) Cmnd.1781.

[11] Recently these were renamed *Customer Focus* and then *Consumer Futures* before being abolished in 2014.

[12] See Ch.4, Department of Trade and Industry, *Modern Markets: Confident Consumers* (The Stationery Office, 1999) Cm.4410.

[13] Department for Business innovation and Skills (BIS) and the Cabinet Office, *Better Choices: Better Deals—Consumers Powering Growth* (April 2011), *https://www.gov.uk/government/uploads/system/uploads/attachment_data/file/294798/bis-11-749-better-choices-better-deals-consumers-powering-growth.pdf* [Accessed 4 June 2015].

2013, which has become the Consumer Rights Act 2015. It represents the biggest overhaul of consumer law for decades. The Act sets out a framework that consolidates in one place key consumer rights covering contracts for goods, services, digital content and the law, relating to unfair terms in consumer contracts. In addition, the Bill: consolidates enforcers' powers to investigate potential breaches of consumer law; clarifies that certain enforcers (such as trading standards officers) can operate over local authority boundaries; and gives enforcers greater flexibility in the action they can take when dealing with breaches of consumer law.

1–12   As pointed out above, one of the most important developments in the protection of the consumer in recent years has been the creation of a structure of organisations dealing with the subject now commonly referred to as the consumer landscape. This landscape has recently been altered significantly. On 14 October 2010, the Coalition Government announced its intention to review the consumer landscape as part of a wider initiative to increase the transparency and accountability of all public bodies. The review had three objectives: to strengthen the front line of consumer empowerment and protection; to reduce the complexity of the consumer landscape; and to ensure that consumer services would be delivered more cost-effectively.

1–13   According to the Government, the number and character of consumer enforcement bodies was "confusing, duplicative and therefore inefficient, leaving consumers uncertain as to whom to turn for help and advice when things go wrong".[14] Whilst it acknowledged that there were many good things about the individual organisations it said that, taken together, they formed a complex landscape that could be difficult for consumers to understand and "this complexity and the lack of clarity about divisions of responsibilities have led to gaps in enforcement".[15] The government's proposals were set out in a consultation document[16] and its conclusions announced in April 2012, in *Empowering and Protecting Consumers—Government Response to the Consultation on Institutional Reform*.[17] These involved:

- The establishment of a new National Trading Standards Board (NTSB), to have responsibility for prioritising national and cross-local authority boundary enforcement in England and Wales. The NTSB is to be responsible for gathering important intelligence from around the country to combat rogue traders, and tackle priorities such as internet scams, illegal money lending and other enforcement issues that go beyond local authority boundaries. The Convention of Scottish Local Authorities (COSLA) has set

---

[14] House of Commons debate, 12 March 2013 c.60–61GC.

[15] House of Commons debate, 12 March 2013 c.60–61GC.

[16] BIS, *Empowering and protecting consumers—Consultation on institutional reform—Consultation on institutional changes for provision of consumer information, advice, education, advocacy and enforcement* (June 2011), URN 11/970 available online.

[17] BIS, *Empowering and Protecting Consumers—Government Response to the Consultation on Institutional Reform* (April 2012), *https://www.gov.uk/government/uploads/system/uploads/attachment_data/file/253701/bis-12-510-empowering-protecting-consumers-government-response-1.pdf* [Accessed 4 June 2015].

up a Scottish Consumer Protection National Enforcement Team (SCPNET) with a similar role in Scotland and is represented on the NTSB.[18]

- Citizens Advice Scotland (CAS) becoming the lead national, publicly funded consumer advocate and the main source of information for consumers about their rights.
- The Office of Fair Trading's (OFT) consumer law enforcement powers to be transferred entirely to local authorities' trading standards services. In effect, Trading Standards Scotland (TSS), under the guidance of Trading Standards Scotland (and in England and Wales) the NTSB, will take on primary responsibility for enforcing consumer law (taking on both local and national cases).
- The OFT's consumer law enforcement budget will be progressively allocated to the NTSB, and then on to local authorities trading standards services.
- The creation of a new Regulated Industries Unit working with the energy and postal services sectors and their regulators, replacing Consumer Focus.
- The Competition and Markets Authority (CMA) (which replaces the OFT) to continue to play to play a pivotal role in ensuring that markets are operating fairly and in the interests of consumers. The CMA retains responsibility for investigating and prosecuting cases that involve the Unfair Terms in Consumer Contracts Regulations and can also rely on consumer law powers in the context of market studies it undertakes.
- A new unit to be set up to share intelligence between the NTSB, the CMA, Citizens Advice Bureaux (CAB) and the Regulated Industries Unit which seems to be the Consumer Protection Partnership.

To properly understand the operation of consumer protection requires some knowledge of this structure and the next section of this chapter therefore deals with the organisations comprising it. At the time of writing it seems that we may not have seen the end of the rearrangement of the landscape as the Smith Commission recommended[19]—and the Coalition Government agreed—that consumer advocacy should be devolved.[20]

THE CONSUMER LANDSCAPE

Central Government and the Scottish Government

On May 12, 1999, for the first time for almost 300 years, a Scottish Parliament met in Edinburgh. This devolved Parliament was created by the Scotland Act 1998 (the Scotland Act) and has wide legislative competence. It can legislate within Scotland on all matters except those that have been reserved to the

1–14

---

[18] This was in line with the recommendations of an Audit Scotland report in 2013, Protecting Consumers, available from *http://www.audit-scotland.gov.uk/docs/local/2013/nr_130131_protecting_consumers.pdf* [Accessed 4 June 2015].
[19] The Smith Commission, *Report of the Smith Commission for further devolution of powers to the Scottish Parliament* (27 November 2014) para.72.
[20] *Scotland in the United Kingdom: An enduring settlement* (January 2015) Cmnd.8990, para.6.5. See Scotland Bill 2015 cll.43 and 44.

Westminster Parliament. However, many areas of consumer protection are among these reserved matters. The precise list is set out in the Scotland Act Sch.5, ss.C7–C9. The scope of these sections was discussed in *Imperial Tobacco Ltd, Petitioner*[21] in which the petitioner argued that ss.1 and 9 of the Tobacco and Primary Medical Services (Scotland) Act 2010 fell within them and thus were outwith the competence of the Scottish Parliament. Most of these are topics which have been the subject of UK-wide legislation. Section C7 is entitled "Consumer Protection" and covers the regulation of the sale and supply of goods and services and fair trading. Section C8 covers product safety and liability as well as product labelling, except in relation to food, agricultural and horticultural produce and fish. Section C9 covers weights and measures, units and standards of weight and measurement. Important as these issues are it should be noted that there are several important areas related to consumer protection which are within the competence of the Edinburgh Parliament. The exclusion of food, agricultural and horticultural produce and fish from the reserved matters in s.C8 has just been noted. It must also be remembered that the Scottish Parliament can legislate concerning the courts, and civil and criminal procedure. These areas impinge directly upon consumer protection. One has only to think of the importance of small claims procedure and the legislation on compensation orders for victims of crime in relation to consumer redress. Also, as we shall see later in this chapter, local government is a devolved matter. As much important enforcement work is carried out by local authorities, the Scottish Parliament and Government could have an important, if indirect, influence on consumer protection.

1–15   While the role of the Scottish Parliament and Government in consumer protection should not be overlooked, the government department with the greatest responsibility for consumer protection is the Westminster Department for Business, Innovation & Skills (BIS), (formerly the Department for Business Enterprise and Regulatory Reform (the BERR)), many of whose functions are carried out on a UK basis. The BIS is responsible for policy and legislation on trading standards, weights and measures, consumer credit and consumer safety. It is also responsible for funding consumer organisations such as Consumer Advice Scotland and the British Standards Institution. Competition policy, which is also relevant to consumer protection, is the responsibility of this department. These issues are the responsibility of a parliamentary Under Secretary of State, a far cry from the days in the 1970s when consumer affairs merited a minister in the cabinet. Where Scottish issues are involved the BIS will liaise with the Scottish Government.

THE COMPETITION AND MARKETS AUTHORITY

1–16   One of the most important organisations with consumer protection functions is the CMA a non-ministerial government department. It is the successor to the Office of Fair Trading which was created officially by s.1 of the Enterprise Act 2002 (the Enterprise Act) though it could trace its ancestry to the Fair Trading Act 1973, which created the post of Director General of Fair Trading. The CMA was created by s.25 of the Enterprise and Regulatory Reform Act 2013 subs.(3) of

---

[21] *Imperial Tobacco Ltd, Petitioner*, 2013 S.C. (UKSC) 153; 2013 S.L.T. 2.

which provides that "[t]he CMA must seek to promote competition, both within and outside the United Kingdom, for the benefit of consumers". The underlying purpose of the CMA would appear to be the same as it predecessors especially its immediate predecessor whose chief executive observed that "our goal is to make markets work well for consumers. Empowered and well-informed consumers act as a positive stimulus to competition between businesses".[22] In both cases the importance of combining consumer protection and competition law functions in the same organisation has been stressed as has been the importance of properly functioning markets not just for consumers but also for business and the wider economy.[23] The creation of the CMA is part of a wider institutional reform which also clarifies responsibility for publicly funded consumer activities and does not, as we shall see, have all the functions of its predecessor.

The CMA is run by a board which Sch.4 of the Enterprise and Regulatory Reform Act 2013 provides shall be composed of a chairman and no fewer than five other members appointed by the Secretary of State. One of these may be the chief executive of the CMA and that is the case at present as one of the members is Mr Alex Chisholm, the current chief executive. Members are appointed for terms of up to five years and may be reappointed. The current chairman is Lord Currie of Marylebone, an academic economist and founding chairman of Ofcom, the independent regulator and competition authority for the UK communications industries. In addition to the chairman and chief executive there are seven non-executive directors with backgrounds in law, business and consumer affairs and three executive directors. The role of the board is to decide the strategy of the CMA, set its priorities and plans, and be responsible for its performance. It is directly involved in decisions on individual market studies but would take enforcement decisions only on cases of strategic importance. **1–17**

The day to day operation of the CMA is carried out by the permanent staff of over 500 who are civil servants. The CMA will commence its first year of operation, 2014/2015, with a resource budget of £66.2m.[24] It does most of its work through multidisciplinary project teams based on the approaches employed by the OFT and Competition Commission which has been amalgamated with it. It has three groups, led by executive directors: enforcement; markets and mergers; and corporate services. These are supported by an Office of the General Counsel and an Office of the Chief Economic Adviser. The Office of the General Counsel and Office of the Chief Economic Adviser are responsible for the legal, economic, business and financial advice and analysis provided to case teams and inquiry groups.[25] **1–18**

As a result of the Government's wider institutional reforms, the CMA is a rather different organisation from the OFT. The majority of functions of public enforcement of consumer rights will be carried out by trading standards, working **1–19**

---

[22] See OFT, *Office of Fair Trading annual report and resource accounts 2006–2007* (The Stationery Office, 2007) (HC Paper No.532) (Session 2003/2004) p.7.

[23] For a fuller explanation of this approach see CMA, *Consumer Protection: Guidance on the CMA's approach to use of its consumer powers,* paras 3.6 and 7 CMA7, March 2014 available on CMA website.

[24] See *Competition and Markets Authority Annual Plan 2014/2015,* para.2.2 available at *http://www.gov.uk/government/organisations/competition-and-markets-authority* [Accessed 4 June 2015].

[25] A chart at p.19 of the document referred to in the previous note sets out the structure of the CMA.

in partnership with the CMA, which will have a clear focus on competition and markets. For this purpose, as well as its powers to address competition problems in a market, the CMA will have powers under consumer enforcement legislation to address features of a market which impact on consumer choice, even where competition is working well. The OFT's responsibilities for consumer advice and education have been transferred to the Citizen's Advice service.[26] The same order places responsibility for most business facing consumer education activities on Trading Standards. The OFT's role in relation to consumer credit has been transferred to the Financial Conduct Authority and its estate agency functions have been given to the a "lead enforcer", currently Powys County Council[27] trading standards service.

In addition to its general to promote competition, the Enterprise Act (as amended by the Enterprise and Regulatory Reform Act 2013) gives the CMA other general functions. Section 5 of that Act directs it to obtain and keep under review the information needed to carry out its functions effectively. Section 6 makes clear that the CMA may not only inform the public of the benefits of competition and give them information and advice about any of its functions but may also publish educational materials and carry out other educational activities. The CMA also advises government and public authorities on possible changes to the law relating to their functions.[28]

1–20   In addition to these general functions the CMA has various specific functions. While this chapter concentrates on the consumer protection functions of the CMA and it is not appropriate to give detailed consideration to its competition functions, it is important to note that a major part of its resources are devoted to the investigation of cartels, abuse of dominant market positions and mergers. This work is of the utmost importance for consumers. A recent practical example from the work of its predecessor, the OFT, resulted in total fines of £18.6 million being imposed on 10 companies for fixing the price of Umbro replica football kits in breach of the Competition Act 1998. Uncovering this cartel has led to direct benefits for consumers in the form of considerable reductions in the cost of these kits.

1–21   An innovation of the Enterprise Act is the procedure in s.11 for a "designated consumer body" to make a "super-complaint" to the CMA.[29] This creates a formal procedure by which consumer organisations can bring what they see as some failure in a market for goods and services that is significantly harming the interests of consumers to the attention of the appropriate regulator. It does not prevent anyone else complaining to the CMA but the advantage of being able to use this procedure is that it lays down a timetable for dealing with the complaint. Section 11(2) provides that the CMA must, within 90 days of receiving the complaint, respond stating how it proposes to deal with it. Only "designated" consumer bodies can make super-complaints and to achieve this status an

---

[26] See the Public Bodies (The Office of Fair Trading Transfer of Consumer Advice Scheme Function and Modification of Enforcement Functions) Order 2013 (SI 2013/783).

[27] Public Bodies (Abolition of the National Consumer Council and Transfer of the Office of Fair Trading's Functions in relation to Estate Agents etc.) Order 2014 (SI 2014/631).

[28] Enterprise Act 2002 s.7.

[29] Using powers in s.205 of the Enterprise Act 2002 the procedure has been extended to allow super-complaints to other regulators by the Enterprise Act (Super-complaints to Regulators) Order 2003 (SI 2003/1368).

organisation must "represent the interests of consumers of any description" and the other criteria set out in the *Super-complaints: guidance for bodies seeking designation as super-complainants* originally published by the Secretary of State for Trade and Industry. This guidance stresses the need for organisations to be independent, experienced and capable of drafting a formal super-complaint. The organisations currently entitled[30] to make super-complaints to the CMA are the Campaign for Real Ale Ltd, the Consumer Council for Water, the Consumers' Association (better known as *Which?*), the General Consumer Council for Northern Ireland, the National Association of Citizens Advice Bureaux and the Scottish Association of Citizens Advice Bureaux. Section 234(C) of the Financial Services and Markets Act 2000 gives designated consumer bodies the right to make a super-complaint to the Financial Conduct Authority (FCA) where they consider that there are features of a market in the UK for financial services that are or that may be significantly damaging the interests of consumers. The Act enables the Treasury to designate a body only if it appears to them to represent the interests of consumers.

Before these organisations were formally designated to make super-complaints   1–22
the system had been operating informally for some time and the OFT considered four super-complaints. The first about private dentistry was submitted by the Consumers' Association and resulted in a formal study of that market by the OFT's Markets and Policy Initiatives division. Its report[31] advocated various reform measures such as the provision of better information for patients and the relaxation of certain regulations relating to who could provide dental services. The National Association of Citizens' Advice Bureaux submitted a complaint about doorstep selling which has resulted in a full-scale investigation[32] and in December 2003 the Consumers' Association submitted a complaint about care homes. In May 2007 *Which?* submitted a super-complaint on restrictions imposed on providers of legal services in Scotland to which the OFT responded by recommending to the Scottish Executive and the legal professions in Scotland that they lift restrictions that could be causing harm to consumers.[33] *Which?* also initiated a complaint about excessive credit and debit card surcharges that has led to controls under the Consumer Rights (Payment Surcharges) Regulations 2012.[34]

Under Pt 8 of the Enterprise Act the CMA has important powers to discipline   1–23
traders who infringe certain domestic or European Community consumer protection legislation. These powers replace the powers under Pt III of the Fair Trading Act and the Stop Now Orders introduced by the Stop Now Orders (EC

---

[30] The Enterprise Act 2002 (Bodies Designated to make Super-complaints) Order 2004 (SI 2004/1517) as amended.

[31] OFT, *The private dentistry market in the UK* (2003) OFT 630.

[32] OFT, *Doorstep selling: A report on the market study* (2004) OFT 716.

[33] See OFT, *Response to Which?'s supercomplaint: Restrictions on business structures and direct access in the Scottish legal profession* (2007) OFT 946. This is also available on the archived OFT website, *http://www.oft.gov.uk/shared_oft/super-complaints/oft946.pdf* [Accessed 2 July 2015].

[34] Consumer Rights (Payment Surcharges) Regulations 2012 (SI 2012/3110).

Directive) Regulations 2001.[35] These powers that are shared with other enforcers are discussed in Ch.10 on the control of trading practices.[36]

1–24   The CMA also enforces some other consumer protection legislation which is discussed in other parts of this book. As we shall see, it plays a leading role in the enforcement of the new regime controlling unfair trade practices brought in to implement the EU's Unfair Commercial Practices Directive. It also has a leading role in the enforcement of the Unfair Terms in Consumer Contracts Regulations 1999.[37] It should be noted that these regulations and the Unfair Contract Terms Act 1977 will be replaced by provisions in the Consumer Rights Act 2015.

Local Government

1–25   Much of the day-to-day enforcement of consumer protection measures is carried out by local government. The reorganisation of local government carried out by the Local Government (Scotland) Act 1994 created 29 single purpose district councils in place of the two-tier structure of regions and district councils. The three island authorities also remain in existence. As the weights and measures authorities for their areas, these councils have statutory responsibility for the enforcement of much consumer protection legislation. They are responsible for the enforcement of weights and measures legislation, labelling and standards requirements of food and drugs, the Consumer Protection from Unfair Trading Regulations 2008 and the Consumer Credit Act 1974. This list includes only the better known pieces of consumer legislation which contain provisions impinging directly on everyday concerns. The enforcement of weights and measures legislation, for example, helps to ensure that the customer receives a kilogramme when they request that amount, or a pint of beer or a quarter gill as appropriate. They also enforce many other pieces of legislation as diverse as the Agriculture Act 1970, dealing with fertilisers and animal feeding stuffs, the Poisons Act 1972 and the Video Recordings Act 1984, to say nothing of many pieces of subordinate legislation often made under the European Communities Act 1972. One advantage of reorganisation has been that it has resulted in all the consumer protection functions of local government being carried out by one council. Previously, the regions were the weights and measures authorities and carried out the bulk of consumer protection work, while the former district councils had responsibilities in the field of food hygiene and the licensing of dealers in second-hand goods under the Civic Government (Scotland) Act 1982.

1–26   To carry out these duties the district councils have set up trading standards or consumer protection services. These are almost invariably located in larger departments, often termed environmental health and consumer protection departments, or even protective services departments. The use of the term trading standards service indicates the modern approach to the task which is seen as being neutral between traders and consumers. It recognises that the function of a trading standards department in ensuring fair trading is important not only to

---

[35] Stop Now Orders (EC Directive) Regulations 2001 (SI 2001/1422).

[36] Most of Pt II of the Fair Trading Act 1973, which created the Consumer Protection Advisory Committee, defunct these many years, has been repealed. Only those sections necessary to enforce the two remaining orders made under this legislation remain.

[37] For more detail see Ch.9.

consumers but also to those traders who meet their legal obligations. Those who do not trade fairly harm not only consumers but also those traders who act honestly.

The size of the larger Scottish regions meant that a service of considerable sophistication could often be provided. Strathclyde region was probably the largest regional consumer protection department in Europe. It was able to build up an impressive unit dealing with unlicensed money-lending. Lothian region's department had considerable success with specialist task forces, such as the vehicle enquiry team. As many authorities are now much smaller than the old regional authorities there must be concern about their ability to deal as effectively with some aspects of their functions as the regions were able to do. In 2012 15 of the 32 councils' trading standards had fewer than eight staff, five having fewer than five.[38] However, s.58 of the Local Government (Scotland) Act 1994 permits two or more councils to combine in providing services and trading standards functions could be provided on a joint basis.[39]

In addition to their statutory duties, trading standards services provide advice to traders on how to comply with legislation and some also provide advice to consumers. With the creation in the sheriff court of the small claims procedure which permits lay representation, some services have been accompanying consumers to court and acting as their advocates though pressure on local government budgets has endangered these schemes.

There has been a good deal of discussion recently about methods of regulation not only in relation to trading standards but also in many other areas such as health and safety and environmental protection. The Hampton Review[40] advocated a risk-based approach to regulation and included a set of principles for regulatory inspection and enforcement, based around risk and proportionality, as well as a major streamlining of regulatory structures. The Macrory Review[41] made recommendations aimed at ensuring that regulators have access to a flexible set of sanctioning tools that are consistent with the risk-based approach to enforcement outlined in the Hampton Review. In England and Wales these proposals were taken forward by the Local Better Regulation Office (now dissolved and it functions taken over by the BIS) created by the Regulatory Enforcement and Sanctions Act 2008. While the powers of the office do not extend to Scotland its influence has been felt here. In any event Pts 2–4 of the Act—to some extent—apply to Scotland. Part 2 makes provision for more consistent and co-ordinated regulatory enforcement by local authorities; Pt 3

1–27

1–28

1–29

---

[38] Audit Scotland, *Protecting Consumers* (January 2013) available at *http://www.audit-scotland. gov.uk* [Accessed 4 June 2015]. See also *The Impact of Local Authority Trading Standards in Challenging Times*, A research report commissioned by the BIS and the Trading Standards Institute, March 2015: *https://www.gov.uk/government/uploads/system/uploads/attachment_data/file/420218/ bis-15-139-the-impact-of-local-authority-trading-standards-in-challenging-times-r2.pdf* [Accessed 9 July 2015].

[39] At present the only example seems to be the arrangement under which Stirling Council provides trading standards services for Clackmannanshire Council.

[40] P Hampton, *Reducing administrative burdens: effective inspection and enforcement* (HM Treasury, 2005) available online at *http://webarchive.nationalarchives.gov.uk/20121212135622/http://www.bis. gov.uk/files/file22988.pdf* [Accessed 4 June 2015].

[41] Professor Richard B Macrory, *Regulatory Justice: Making Sanctions Effective, Final Report* (November 2006) available online at *http://webarchive.nationalarchives.gov.uk/20121212135622/ http://www.bis.gov.uk/files/file44593.pdf* [Accessed 4 June 2015].

provides for the introduction of a new expanded framework for regulatory sanctions by enabling ministers to confer new civil sanctioning powers on regulators in relation to specific offences; and Pt 4 provides for the introduction of a duty on regulators not to impose or maintain unnecessary burdens.

The home authority principle

1–30   The home authority principle is designed to avoid businesses that may have offices and factories in several different parts of the country receiving conflicting advice or being subject to differing interpretations of the law from various local authorities. The main feature of the principle is to prevent infringements by offering advice at source and by encouraging enforcement authorities and enterprises to work in liaison with a particular authority called "the home authority". This is the authority where the decision-making base of the enterprise is located and can be the head office, the factory, a service centre or the place of importation. The role of the home authority is to provide advice on policy issues, compliance with the law and adherence to standards and codes of practice. It is the link between enforcement authorities and originating authorities with whom they must liaise. Originating authorities are only relevant where an enterprise operates a decentralised structure and decisions may be made at a number of different places. It will monitor premises within its area at which goods or services are produced. It keeps the home authority informed about significant findings and, if there are problems, it will liaise with it to solve them.

1–31   Each local authority enforces the law in its area. Under the home authority principle when enforcement authorities detect breaches of the law they should consider consultation with the home or originating authority before embarking on detailed investigations or legal action. They should also routinely inform the home authority of enforcement action which they have taken.

Primary Authority scheme

1–32   The Primary Authority scheme enables a business trading across local authority areas to form a primary authority partnership with a single local authority in relation to regulatory compliance across all the local authority areas in which it operates. The scheme was created by Pt 2 of the Regulatory Enforcement and Sanctions Act 2008 and was amended by Enterprise and Regulatory Reform Act 2013. In Scotland, as a result of devolution, a local authority can offer a partnership only for the relevant functions that remain the responsibility of the UK Government. As we have seen above consumer protection is such an area.[42] Functions that have been devolved to the Scottish Government—for example, food standards, food safety and hygiene—are outside the scope of Primary Authority. Glasgow City has partnerships relating to fair trading with companies in the Arnold Clark and Peter Vardy car retailing groups. Through the partnership businesses receive advice on compliance from the primary authority which other local authorities who regulate it must follow. The intention is to provide a business with certainty and consistency and thus to reduce the burden and cost of

---

[42] See the Co-ordination of Regulatory Enforcement (Regulatory Functions in Scotland and Northern Ireland) Order 2009 (SI 2009/669).

regulation. The primary authority scheme is administered by the Better Regulation Delivery Office a division of BIS.

The role of COSLA

The COSLA is the national association of Scottish councils. It was formed in 1975 and exists to promote and protect the interests of the country's councils by providing a forum for discussion of matters of common concern. As a result of the UK government review of the consumer landscape in April 2012, the BIS entered into a partnership agreement with COSLA to provide a Scottish solution for a more effective consumer protection landscape. A national Scottish team known as Trading Standards Scotland (TSS) has been created bring together the existing national teams of Scambusters Scotland, the Scottish Illegal Money Lending Unit and the Scottish eCrime Unit. In January 2013 Audit Scotland carried out an audit of consumer protection in Scotland[43] and made several recommendations. Councils were advised to

> "ensure they have access to, and make use of, intelligence to help determine their local priorities, and contribute intelligence to information systems that support the work of other Scottish and UK councils, and the national teams".

It was also recommended that

> "COSLA and councils should ... work together to ensure strong national coordination for trading standards in Scotland that includes maintaining effective links with UK-wide arrangements, analysing intelligence to identify national risks [and] agreeing national priorities."[44]

In March 2013 COSLA established a national intelligence unit within TSS to manage intelligence for trading standards throughout Scotland. The Intelligence Unit works with a network of Local Intelligence Liaison Officers (LILOs) appointed by each Council across Scotland who gather local intelligence and log it onto the national (UK) Trading Standards Intelligence database, called Memex. A three year memorandum of understanding (MOU) and data sharing agreement has been created by the Head of the Intelligence Unit at TSS starting on 1 April 2014. This sets out how intelligence will be used to establish national priorities. Scotland will submit its national priorities to the UK Consumer Protection Partnership[45] to create UK national priorities.

The equivalent organisation for England and Wales is the NTSB with which TSS liaises. The NTSB was created by the BIS in April 2012 and consists of experienced trading standards officers.

1–33

1–34

---

[43] Audit Scotland, *Protecting Consumers* (January 2013) available at *http://www.audit-scotland.gov. uk/docs/local/2013/nr_130131_protecting_consumers.pdf* [Accessed 4 June 2015].
[44] Audit Scotland, *Protecting Consumers* (January 2013) available at *http://www.audit-scotland.gov. uk/docs/local/2013/nr_130131_protecting_consumers.pdf* [Accessed 4 June 2015].
[45] See below for more on this organisation.

The Chartered Trading Standards Institute

1–35   The Chartered Trading Standards Institute (CTSI) is the professional association of UK trading standards professionals who work in local authorities, business and consumer sectors and central government. Since April 2013, the CTSI has been responsible for facilitating the Consumer Code Approval Scheme previously operated by the OFT. The scheme is self-regulatory and aims to improve consumer protection by approving and promoting codes of practice, setting out the principles of effective customer care and recognising trusted traders. By voluntarily signing up to this approved code of practice, businesses can display the TSI-approved code logo, which allows consumers greater confidence in selecting a trader. The CTSI introduced the scheme on a self-funded basis. In April 2013, responsibility for providing business education was transferred from the OFT to the TSI apart from specific guidance for businesses where the OFT had conducted a market study or other in-depth analysis of business practices in a particular sector; and areas covered by the unfair terms legislation that are still dealt with by the CMA.

The Consumer Protection Partnership

1–36   The Consumer Protection Partnership (CPP) was formed by BIS in April 2012. It comprises BIS, the CMA, the NTSB, the TSI, TSS, CAB and CAS, the FCA, the Consumer Council for Northern Ireland, and the Department of Enterprise, Trade and Investment (DETI) (in Northern Ireland). Its primary purpose is to identify and prioritise areas where there is the greatest detriment to consumers. Partners will then agree and co-ordinate collective action to tackle such detriment, using all available tools at their disposal. The purpose of the CPP is to ensure that important issues do not fall between any gaps and that there is a "joined-up" approach to consumer issues.[46]

INDEPENDENT AND VOLUNTARY ORGANISATIONS

Consumer Advice Scotland

1–37   The Citizens Advice organisation is one of the largest volunteer organisations in the UK with over 20,000 volunteers. It was formed originally to provide advice to citizens during the Second World War. There are 61 local CAB in Scotland with 81 bureaux offices and over 250 advice points in Scotland, from the cities to the islands. There are over 2,500 volunteers as well as paid staff. 30 of the 32 local government districts in Scotland have CAB services. CAS is a registered charity which supports local bureaux by providing expertise on things like management and fundraising, resources such as IT support, tools and training to support advice

---

[46] For further information on this organisation see *Consumer Protection Partnership: Priorities Report 2013–2014: Report on the Partnership's work to date and future priorities* (November 2013) available on the BIS website, *https://www.gov.uk/government/uploads/system/uploads/attachment_data/file/252730/bis-13-1267-consumer-protection-partnership-future-priorities.pdf* [Accessed 4 June 2015].

giving, and help with running campaigns.[47] The citizens advice service helps people to resolve a wide range of problems covering debt and employment to consumer and housing. It provides a free, independent, confidential and impartial advice to everyone on their rights and responsibilities.

In 2013/2014 Scottish citizens advice bureaux helped people with a total of 887,000 issues from benefits to payday loans and housing to energy issues. Of these 289,652 were consumer issues of which 233,639 were dealt with in a Bureaux and 56,013 by Citizens Advice consumer helpline, a Great Britain wide service delivered in part by CAS from a call centre in Stornoway. CAB gives advice in a number of formats including face to face, telephone, home visits and email. In 2013/2014 it dealt with 177,000 issues for callers across Great Britain.[48]   **1–38**

The government's changes to the consumer landscape have resulted in the role of CAS being considerably extended. By April 2014, it had acquired responsibility for co-ordinating consumer education and advice, and consumer advocacy. In April 2012, CAS and its English equivalent took over from the OFT the running the government-funded consumer advice function, including the call centre Consumer Direct. This was achieved by the Public Bodies (The Office of Fair Trading Transfer of Consumer Advice Scheme Function and Modification of Enforcement Functions) Order 2013.[49] It also amended the payment of levies on gas, electricity and postal service industries to allow these industry levies to fund Consumer Direct.[50] In April 2014, Citizens Advice took on the functions of Consumer Futures (known as Consumer Focus until May 2013). Consumer Futures had been funded by a levy that BIS collected from companies that operate in energy and postal services and, in Scotland, water utilities. The same arrangements exist now that Consumer Futures is part of CAB and CAS.   **1–39**

The legislative source of these powers is found in the amended Consumers, Estate Agents and Redress Act 2007 (the 2007 Act). Before considering the functions of CAS it is important to note the definition of "consumer", "consumer matters" and "designated consumers". Section 3(2) of the 2007 Act defines a consumer for the purposes of the Act as "a person who purchases, uses or receives, in Great Britain, goods or services which are supplied in the course of a business carried on by the person supplying or seeking to supply them", and subs.(3) goes on to state that "consumer" includes both an existing consumer and a future consumer. Subsection (5) goes on to provide that "consumer matters" means the interests of consumers and any matter connected with those interests. It is to be noted that "consumer" is not limited, as it usually is in consumer protection legislation, to private individuals. It is wide enough to include anyone, including businesses.   **1–40**

As we shall see below, the term "designated consumers" is of importance. Section 4 of the 2007 Act defines them as consumers in relation to gas conveyed through pipes or electricity conveyed by distribution systems or transmission   **1–41**

---

[47] Citizens Advice Scotland is the operating name of the Scottish Association of Citizens Advice Bureaux, which is a company limited by guarantee and a registered charity (SC016637).

[48] See CAS, *ConsumerSnapshot* available at *http://www.cas.org.uk/publications/consumer-snapshot-0* [Accessed 4 June 2015].

[49] See Public Bodies (The Office of Fair Trading Transfer of Consumer Advice Scheme Function and Modification of Enforcement Functions) Order 2013 (SI 2013/783) art.2.

[50] Public Bodies (The Office of Fair Trading Transfer of Consumer Advice Scheme Function and Modification of Enforcement Functions) Order 2013 (SI 2013/783) arts 5 and 6.

systems, and consumers in relation to relevant postal services. The section also gives the Secretary of State power to add to this list and it is expected that consumers of water services in England and Wales are likely to be added when the functions of the Consumer Council for Water are transferred to the CAB.

1–42 Section 12 of the 2007 Act empowers CAS to investigate complaints made by or on behalf of designated vulnerable consumers. These are designated consumers as discussed above who will be considered "vulnerable" if the council is satisfied that it is not reasonable to expect that person to pursue the complaint on that person's own behalf. The explanatory notes to the Bill suggested that this,

> "might apply to persons who are unable to pursue a complaint by reason of a mental or physical disability, a lack of basic skills (such as literacy) or due to their personal circumstances (such as a recent bereavement)".

Both these powers are discretionary: the council is not obliged to take up these complaints. It may be that the councils will have difficult decisions to take on whether to exercise these powers given that their resources are likely to be limited.

1–43 Disconnection of gas and electricity supplies have been the subject of many complaints by consumers and s.13(2) of the 2007 Act provides that CAS "must investigate the complaint for the purpose of determining whether it is appropriate to take any action" to assist in reaching a satisfactory resolution. Also included are complaints by an electricity consumer against an electricity supplier in respect of the failure of a prepayment system. If it is, CAS must provide advice to the complainant, or make representations on behalf of the complainant to the person against whom the complaint is made.[51] Section 13(4) provides guidance on the circumstances in which CAS may refuse to take up a complaint. Two of these are that a regulatory body is under a duty to deal with it or that it would be better dealt with by some other dispute resolution process. Complaints that are frivolous or vexatious or have been subject to undue delay can be refused as can those where CAS considers that there are other compelling reasons why it is inappropriate to investigate.

1–44 It should be noted that where such complaints involve matters within the enforcement powers of the Office of Gas and Electricity Markets (OFGEM) or the breach of a licence which Ofcom could deal with, CAS has a duty to refer the complaint to them in most circumstances.[52] Section 16 gives CAS power to investigate any matter relating to the number and location of post offices.

1–45 A new task has been given to CAS by s.19A of the amended Consumers, Estate Agents and Redress Act 2007. This requires it, like the other consumer advocacy organisations, CAB and the General Consumer Council for Northern Ireland, to prepare, and keep under review energy consumer guidance.

1–46 To carry out its functions CAS has power to require certain persons to supply it with information. It is unlikely that these would need to be exercised in relation to the CMA or the regulators for gas and electricity, the Postal Services Commission or the Water Services Regulation Authority.[53] However, it is

---

[51] See Consumers, Estate Agents and Redress Act 2007 s.13(3).

[52] See Consumers, Estate Agents and Redress Act 2007 ss.14–15.

[53] See Consumers, Estate Agents and Redress Act 2007 s.24(3). Should a regulator fail to provide information CAS can, by virtue of s.25, refer the failure to the Secretary of State.

possible that there might be resistance from "any person who supplies goods or services in the course of a business . . . ". In that case CAS may apply to the Court of Session or the High Court in England and Wales for an order requiring compliance with the order.[54]

The Extra Help Unit

CAS has also taken over responsibility for the UK-wide Extra Help Unit from Consumer Futures. The Extra Help Unit is a team of telephone caseworkers based in Glasgow which helps people and micro-businesses throughout Great Britain who have complex energy or postal complaints. The Unit is not a public helpline. People can be referred to it by the Citizens Advice Consumer Helpline, their local politician, Ofgem or the Energy Ombudsman. The unit also provides an "Ask the Adviser" telephone service for advice agencies who need specialist support to help their clients.

1–47

Regulated industry consumer councils

A diminishing range of goods and services is provided for consumers by nationalised industries and also by industries subject to extensive regulation by government. These industries are statutory corporations invested with monopoly, or near monopoly, powers, and this makes it especially important that there should be scrutiny of their activities in the consumer interest. As the *Molony Report* noted "the evils of monopolistic control are not the exclusive prerogative of private enterprise".[55] The consumer interest in many of these industries has been represented by the creation of consumer or consultative councils. These bodies are discussed in Ch.7.

1–48

The Consumers' Association

The Consumers' Association, best known through its association with *Which?* magazine, was founded in 1957. In 1987 it became a charity and changed its name to the Association for Consumer Research, a private company limited by guarantee that is entitled to omit the word "limited" from its name. With effect from 1 April 1995 the name again became the Consumers' Association. This company carries on research, charitable and campaigning functions. It was prominent in the campaigns for the Unfair Contract Terms Act 1977, has vigorously campaigned on safety issues and recently has been prominent in the campaign against excessive bank charges. A subsidiary, *Which?* Ltd, now carries on the trading functions which consist primarily of publishing both books and magazines that, in addition to *Which?*, include *Computing Which?*, *Gardening Which?* and *Holiday Which?*. The Consumers' Association is financed by members' subscriptions, donations and fees for advisory services which it

1–49

---

[54] See Consumers, Estate Agents and Redress Act 2007 s.26.
[55] See the Molony Report, *Final Report of the Committee on Consumer Protection* (1962) Cmnd.1781, p.296.

undertakes and the trading profits of its subsidiary. In 2014 the Consumers' Association had over 800,000[56] members, and 1,480,000 subscribers to its magazines.[57]

The National Consumer Federation

1–50   The National Consumer Federation (NCF) was formed in 2001 by the amalgamation of the Consumer Congress and the National Federation of Consumer Groups. On its website it describes itself as "[a] leading voice for grass roots consumers and consumer organisations".[58] It encourages and co-ordinates the work of voluntary, independent local consumer groups, individual consumers and those who have an interest in consumer affairs through other organisations. It represents their views nationally. The NCF and the local groups are non-party political and non-profit making. The National Federation of Consumer Groups was established in 1963 to bring together local consumer groups which were first set up from 1961 with the encouragement of the Consumers' Association, publishers of *Which?*. Its individual membership scheme was introduced in 1977 for people who do not live near enough to a group. The Consumer Congress was a separate organisation, funded by government which organised an annual congress on consumer matters. Its members were mainly larger organisations, including trading standards departments, Age Concern and bodies representing disabled groups.

The British Standards Institution

1–51   The British Standards Institution, incorporated by Royal Charter in 1929, is an independent, non-profit making body which exists to co-ordinate the production of goods by devising, where possible, national standards. A "British Standard" sets out testing requirements, specifications or measurements with which a product should comply. Such standards are devised after consultation with representatives of manufacturers, distributors and users. Of particular relevance to consumers is the Consumer and Public Interest Strategic Advisory Committee (CPISAC), made up of senior representatives from consumer organizations consumers.

The Advertising Standards Authority

1–52   The Advertising Standards Authority Ltd (ASA) administers the system of self-regulatory control in the print, cinema and poster media. It is a company limited by guarantee whose directors are its chairman and council members. The chairman, currently Lord Smith, a former cabinet minister, is appointed by the Advertising Standards Board of Finance Ltd (ASBOF), an independent body created by the advertising industry. The ASBOF is obliged by its articles of association, before making any appointment, to consult with the BIS, and the appointment is also made in consultation with, and subject to the agreement of,

---

[56] *Which?*, *Commercial Review 2013/2014*, p.4.
[57] *Which?*, *Financial Review 2013/2014*, p.14.
[58] The National Consumer Federation, *http://www.ncf.info/* [Accessed 4 June 2015].

the existing members of the ASA council. The ASA articles provide that the chairman is not to be engaged in the business of advertising. It is the chairman who chooses the members of the council, normally totalling 12, of whom at least half must be independent. It is present policy to ensure that the proportion of independent to industry members remains at the maximum permissible level of two to one.

The functions of the ASA are to oversee the work of the Code of Advertising   **1–53** Practice (CAP) Committee in drafting and amending the British Code of Advertising Practice; to act as an appeal tribunal from the CAP committee from within the industry; to maintain a procedure for investigating complaints from members of the public; and to publicise the existence of the self-regulatory system of control. The ASA has been funded since 1974 by a surcharge of 0.1 per cent on the cost to the advertiser of advertisements other than those appearing in the classified columns of the press. The surcharge is collected by the ASBOF.

EUROPE

The European Union

As with so many areas of law, consumer protection is influenced by the UK's   **1–54** membership of the EU. Our accession to the EU (or the European Communities as it was then known) coincided with the development of its consumer policy and the creation of its consumer institutions. These institutions are described in Ch.2 (see paras 2–11 to 2–13).

Bureau Européen des Unions de Consommateurs (BEUC)

BEUC acts as the umbrella group for its members, 41 independent consumer   **1–55** organisations from 29 European countries. Its main task is to represent them at European level and defend the interests of all Europe's consumers. BEUC investigates EU decisions and developments likely to affect consumers, with a special focus on eight areas identified as priorities by its members: financial services; food; digital rights; consumer rights; sustainability; safety, health and energy. It has a secretariat with a staff of around 35 based in Brussels.

CHAPTER 2

European Dimension

2–01

An English judge once said memorably that EC (now EU) law was like an,

> "incoming tide. It flows into the estuaries and up the rivers. It cannot be held back. Parliament has decreed that the Treaty [of Rome] is henceforward to be part of our law".[1]

Like other areas of law, consumer protection is subject to this process and it is important to appreciate its impact. The EC and the EU have had an impact on the development of consumer protection law and policy in the UK. It is an impact that has produced benefits but can also be argued to have had disadvantages. In this chapter the origins and implementation of this policy are considered as well as its benefits and disadvantages.

2–02

In an economic community it is a remarkable irony that consumer protection has not had a high profile. There were only five references to consumers in the original treaty and, with one exception, the translation is probably not accurate. "End user" rather than "consumer" would probably be more appropriate. This, no doubt, is explained by the fact that the Communities were the result of negotiations which took place in the 1950s, well before consumer protection became the conspicuous issue that it did in the mid-1960s and 1970s.

2–03

The term "consumer protection" first appeared in art.100a of the Treaty of Rome, as a result of the Single European Act. This Act did not accord consumer protection the status of a separate policy of the EC in the way that environmental policy was recognised. That, however, was achieved by the Maastricht Treaty on European Union, signed in 1992, which added a Title XI on consumer protection to the original Treaty. This now appears in a slightly modified form in art.169 at the beginning of the consumer protection title, Title XV in the Treaty on the Functioning of the European Union (TFEU).[2]

LEGAL COMPETENCE OF THE EU

2–04

When looking at any legislative action of the EU it must always be borne in mind that the EC is not a sovereign state, and so one must always be able to point to some power in the EU treaties permitting the action taken. In the field of consumer protection there have, in the past, been some doubts on this score.

---

[1] *HP Bulmer Ltd and Showerings Ltd v J Bollinger SA and Champagne Lanson Pére et Fils* [1974] 2 All E.R. 1226, per Lord Denning at 1231.

[2] References to the Treaty in the rest of this chapter are to TFEU.

However, it has long been accepted that where the interests of consumers in health and safety have been at stake the EU has competence.[3] This could be justified by arguments based on the original art.30 (now art.28) which are implicitly accepted in the series of cases starting with *Cassis de Dijon*.[4] There had been a little more doubt about legislation dealing with the protection of the economic interests of consumers but, legally, it could be justified by pointing to art.2 of the original Treaty of Rome, which sets out the objectives of the treaty to create a common market and improve living standards. It was argued that differing national laws on advertising, contract terms and marketing practices impede the attainment of a truly common market, and that the improvement of the protection of the consumer is an aspect of a better standard of living. As Professor Bourgoignie has pointed out:

> "Improving the standard of living... could no longer be understood only in a quantitative way (increase in income and purchasing power of individuals) but also qualitatively, aiming to improve, in the widest sense of the term, the living conditions of European citizens."[5]

2–05   With the amendments made to the original treaty by the Single European Act and the Maastricht, Amsterdam and Lisbon Treaties the situation is now clearer. The starting point is art.4(1)(f) of the TFEU, which declares consumer protection to be one of the shared competences of the EU. "Shared competence" means that both the EU and its Member States may adopt legally binding acts in the area concerned. However, the Member States can do so only where the EU has not exercised its competence or has explicitly ceased to do so. One then turns to art.169 (using the new numbering following Lisbon), which contains the title on consumer protection. This amends this title which was originally inserted by the Maastricht Treaty. It provides in para.1 that:

> "In order to promote the interests of consumers and to ensure a high level of consumer protection, the Community shall contribute to protecting the health, safety and economic interests of consumers, as well as to promoting their right to information, education and to organise themselves in order to safeguard their interests."

2–06   These objectives are to be achieved by two means. The first is by art.114 (formerly art.95) measures relating to the internal market. Such measures can be adopted using the qualified majority voting procedures of the Treaty and must "take as a base a high level of protection". In addition, they will be attained by measures which support, supplement and monitor the policy pursued by the Member States. A further important paragraph of art.169 provides that "consumer protection requirements shall be taken into account in defining and implementing other Community policies and activities". Despite the fact that art.169 has an explicit new basis for consumer protection measures the vast majority use

---

[3] See Close, "The Legal Basis of the Consumer Protection Programme of the EEC and Priorities for Action" in Geoffrey Woodroffe (ed), *Consumer Law in the EEC* (London: Sweet & Maxwell, 1984).
[4] *Rewe-Zentrale AG v Bundesmonopolverwaltung fur Branntwein (Cassis de Dijon)* (120/78) [1979] E.C.R. 649; see paras 2–36 onwards.
[5] Thierry Bourgoignie, "European Community Consumer Law and Policy: from Rome to Amsterdam", 1998 6 Consum. L.J. 443, 444.

art.114. Very few use the other method, one of the few being the Directive on the indication of the prices of products offered to consumers.[6] It is also relevant to note that the Lisbon Treaty added art.12 TFEU, which places a duty on the EU to take consumer protection requirements into account in defining and implementing other EU policies.

The reference in art.169 to supporting and supplementing measures taken by Member States is a reminder that all of this is subject to the principles of subsidiarity and proportionality. This is now found in art.5 TFEU which states that "The use of Union competences is governed by the principles of subsidiarity and proportionality". This clause, which has been the subject of intense debate, is one of those provisions that can be used by opposing sides in an argument to justify their position. Lord Mackenzie-Stuart, a former President of the European Court of Justice (ECJ), went so far as to call it "gobbledygook" in a letter to *The Times*.[7]   **2–07**

As has been pointed out: **2–08**

> "The quest for a definition of subsidiarity is doomed to failure. It has become an intrinsic part of the debate on greater social, political and economic integration, and as such, will be subject to constant evolution, adapting to shifts in policy and opinion. It is a flexible but elusive concept, with the potential both to act as a dynamic for change and as a bulwark of the status quo. The priority for consumers is to ensure that it does not serve as a pretext to block proposals to improve consumer protection at Community level which might otherwise be neglected at national level."[8]

The important point to grasp, which art.169 supports, is that consumer protection is not just an optional extra for the Community. It is an essential feature of a single market. Such a market can be exploited by the unscrupulous who engage in fraudulent practices across national boundaries. This calls for action at EU level both in the interests of honest traders, who should be protected from such unfair competition, and consumers, who are entitled to protection of their interests. A failure to provide effective protection is bound to weaken consumer confidence and thus the success of the single market.   **2–09**

A difficult question is how to decide when action should be taken at Community level and when it should be left to Member States. In a communication to the Council and the European Parliament in October 1992, the Commission proposed three tests to assist in the application of the subsidiarity principle. These were "comparative efficiency", "value added", and "proportionality". In deciding whether there should be Community action the first two would involve the use of a number of criteria, such as whether there was a significant cross-border dimension, the effects on trade and competition, and the costs of taking action. The proportionality test would be used to ensure that action taken would be no more than necessary to achieve the desired aim. This would require consideration to be given to self-regulatory measures as well as legislation. In practice, these principles have not been much referred to by EU institutions. The   **2–10**

---

[6] Directive 98/6 of the European Parliament and of the Council of 16 February 1998 on consumer protection in the indication of the prices of products offered to consumers [1998] O.J. L 80/27.

[7] *The Times*, December 11, 1992.

[8] Leigh Gibson, "Subsidiarity: The Implications for Consumer Policy" (1993) 16 J.C.P 323, 336.

subsidiarity principle has been invoked on a number of occasions by the European Commission to justify not harmonising in an area. The Directive on Unfair Commercial Practices does not deal with taste and decency issues because these vary so widely among member states. They have rarely been of importance in ECJ judgments.

Institutional arrangements

2–11   The low status of consumer protection has often been reflected in the institutional arrangements in Brussels. As a result of a heads of state meeting in Paris in 1972 a directorate-general for environment and consumer protection was, for the first time, created in the Commission. After various changes of title the consumer protection functions were moved to a separate Consumer Protection Service with the intention that this service would influence the policies of all directorates which have implications for consumers. In 1995 consumer protection once again became the responsibility of a directorate-general (DG XXIV). In 1998 the mad cow crisis and other health concerns resulted in it being renamed the Directorate-General for Health and Consumer Protection, commonly referred to as DG Sanco.[9] This reflected the fact that its responsibilities and staff had been considerably increased as a result of the decision of the Commission to separate the services deciding policy on food and health from those responsible for questions of control that have been transferred to DG Health and Food Safety. Responsibility for consumer affairs is now located in the Directorate-General Justice and Health. The main consumer issues are located within Directorate E but Directorate A with responsibility for, amongst other policies, civil justice and contract law is also relevant.

2–12   At the same time as what is now the Directorate-General Justice and Health was set up, a consumers consultative committee (CCC) was created. The idea was that this body, consisting of representatives of national consumer organisations and trade union representatives, would be consulted by the commission on its consumer programme. In October 2003 it was renamed the European Consumer Consultative Group. In practice consultation is sporadic and, in any event, does not have the resources to be an effective commentator on policy issues.

Consumer protection programmes

2–13   It was in 1975 that the Community adopted its first programme for consumer protection[10] that set out to guarantee five basic consumer rights:

(1)   Protection of the consumer against health and safety risks.
(2)   Protection of consumers' economic interests.
(3)   Improvement of the consumers' legal position through advice, assistance, and the right to seek a legal remedy.
(4)   Improvement of consumer education and information.

---

[9] This acronym derives from the French name of the directorate: Santé et Protection des Consommateurs.

[10] Council resolution of 14 April 1975 on a preliminary programme of the European Economic Community for a consumer protection and information policy [1975] O.J. C92/1.

(5)   Appropriate consultation and representation of consumers in the taking of decisions affecting their interests.

In May 1981 a second programme along the same lines was adopted,[11] and ever since at regular intervals further programmes have been published. It cannot be said that a great deal was achieved by these early programmes. However, it must be remembered that there were considerable obstacles in the way of this. Until the Single European Act and the Maastricht Treaty there were doubts about the legal basis for consumer protection measures. Another formidable hurdle in the early years was the need for unanimity among the Member States before a measure could be implemented.

2–14

The more recent consumer programmes have shown a change of emphasis in part brought about by the treaty changes that have established the legitimacy of consumer protection as a community policy. The Commission's Consumer Action Plan 1996–1998[12] included new priorities. These were the protection of consumers' interests with regard to public services and financial services as well as in relation to the information society. It also alluded to the importance of sustainable consumption, assistance to the countries of central and eastern Europe to develop consumer protection policies and to Third World countries in order to improve conditions in relation to basic products.

2–15

The 1999–2001 plan[13] identified three areas as the main tasks for consumer policy. These were: a more powerful voice for consumers throughout the EU; a high level of health and safety for EU consumers; and full respect for the economic interests of EU consumers. The 2002–2006 document[14] noted that:

2–16

"European consumer policy is central to one of the Commission's strategic objectives, that of contributing to a better quality of life for all. It is also an essential element of the Commission's strategic objective of creating new economic dynamism and modernising the European economy."

The programme set out three objectives: the achievement of a high level of consumer protection; effective enforcement of consumer protection rules; and the involvement of consumer organisations in EU policies. In pursuit of the first objective the main initiatives were to follow up the issues on commercial practices addressed by the Green Paper on EU consumer protection and on the safety of services. The priorities for action under the second objective of effective enforcement were the development of an administrative co-operation framework between Member States and of redress mechanisms for consumers. The third objective, involvement of consumer organisations in EU policies, required a review of the mechanisms for participation of consumer organisations in EU policymaking and in the setting up of education and capacity-building projects. An evaluation of the strategy shows that its implementation achieved varying

---

[11] Council resolution of 19 May 1981 on a second programme of the European Economic Community for a consumer protection and information policy [1981] O.J. C133/1.

[12] Commission of the European Communities, *Consumer Action Plan 1996–1998*, COM (95) 519.

[13] Commission of the European Communities, *Consumer Action Plan 1999–2001*, COM (98) 0696–C4-0035/99.

[14] Commission of the European Communities, *Consumer Policy Strategy 2002–2006*, COM (2002) 208 final–2002/C137/02.

levels of success.[15] The EU strategy had more impact on the development of the national strategies of new Member States than the old and of the policies advocated more attention was paid to those on safety of goods and services and consumers' economic interest than those on financial services. Notable achievements for the Commission were the adoption of the Consumer Protection Co-operation Regulation[16] and the unfair commercial practices Directive.[17]

2–17   The current strategy document[18] emphasises the importance of consumers and consumer policy to the wider aims of the EU. Within that context it lists five priorities. These are to:

- increase consumer confidence in the internal market by establishing a uniform regulatory environment that is equally enforced across the European market and which effectively protects consumers;
- strengthen consumers' position in the marketplace by developing consumer education tools, the active support of EU consumer organisations, and their involvement in policy making;
- ensure that consumer concerns are taken into account in all EU policies;
- complement Member States' consumer policies; and
- collect consumer-related data to support the development of legislative proposals and other initiatives.

2–18   In May 2012, the Commission published a Consumer Agenda for 2014–2020, which replaces the Consumer Strategy for 2007–2013.[19] This agenda contains four main objectives:

- improving consumer safety so that consumers are protected from serious risks and threats that they cannot tackle as individuals;
- enhancing knowledge so that consumers can make choices, based on clear, accurate and consistent information; and
- improving implementation, stepping up enforcement and securing redress access so that consumers have fast and efficient ways of resolving disputes with traders; and aligning rights and key policies to economic and societal change so that consumers can access digital products and services easily, legally and affordably from anywhere in the EU.

---

[15] See Commission of the European Communities, *Review of Consumer Policy Strategy 2002–2006, Commission Staff Working Document accompanying EU Consumer Policy Strategy 2007–2013*, SEC (2007) 321.

[16] Regulation 2006/2004 on cooperation between national authorities responsible for the enforcement of consumer protection laws [2004] O.J. L364/1.

[17] Directive 2005/29 EC of the European Parliament and of the Council of 11 May 2005 concerning unfair business-to-consumer commercial practices in the internal market [2005] O.J. L149/22.

[18] Commission of the European Communities, *EU Consumer Policy strategy 2007–2013*, COM (2007) 99 final.

[19] Communication from the Commission to the European Parliament, the Council, the Economic and Social Committee and the Committee of the Regions: A European Consumer Agenda—Boosting confidence and growth, COM(2012) 225 final.

It is the last of these that indicates a change of emphasis. It links with the Commission's proposed Directive and Regulation on data protection,[20] which would reinforce the current EU data protection framework with a view to increasing consumer trust in the digital single market and in cross-border services.

ACHIEVEMENTS SO FAR

As this recital of the various Community programmes shows, there has been no shortage of good intentions towards consumers. To what extent have there been concrete achievements? In pursuance of its aim of promoting consumer protection the Commission has encouraged debate on the subject, an aspect of its work which should not be underestimated. The Commission organises or funds conferences and research projects throughout Europe for this purpose. This is probably of more importance in those parts of Europe where consumer protection is less well developed. It must be remembered that consumer protection has, until fairly recently, been more prominent in Northern Europe. However, there have been, and continue to be, benefits from this aspect of the Commission's work in the UK in general, and in Scotland in particular. The interest of the Commission in consumer redress influenced the creation of the small claims procedure in the sheriff court through both financial and moral support to the Dundee small claims experiment. Similar encouragement has been given to pilot projects in Belgium and Milan. More recently the Commission gave financial support for joint Scottish and Irish projects on in-court advice. The Scottish part of this project (which is still running) provides an adviser based in Edinburgh Sheriff Court.

2–19

Its interest in consumer redress was indicated in a communication from the Commission on "the out-of-court settlement of consumer disputes" and a recommendation on the principles applicable to the bodies responsible for out-of-court settlement of consumer disputes, often referred to as "alternative dispute resolution" (ADR).[21] This follows an earlier thought-provoking Green Paper on access to justice,[22] which stimulated discussion on a wide range of issues. Apart from the development of small claims procedures it raises the question of the use of group actions, which is a notable lacuna in the Scottish legal system. There are no practical methods by which those who are the victims of a common misfortune or fraud can band together to sue the perpetrator.

2–20

Another type of group action is sometimes referred to as the public interest action. This permits an organisation to take action in the public interest to stop some activity inimical to consumers. While available in some European jurisdictions, it is not available in the Scottish, or indeed the English, legal system. European influence may be beneficial here. Provision for such means of redress is contained in individual pieces of European legislation. As a result of the

2–21

---

[20] The General Data Protection Directorate, COM(2012) 10 final and the General Data Protection Regulation, COM (2012) 11 final, respectively.

[21] Commission of the European Communities, Communication on the out-of-court settlement of consumer disputes, COM (1998) 198.

[22] Commission of the European Communities, Second Commission three-year-action plan 1993–1995: placing the single market at the service of European consumers, COM (93) 378.

provisions of the Misleading Advertising Directive[23] and the Unfair Contract Terms Directive[24] it has been necessary to provide a version of this type of action. Initially, the Office of Fair Trading (OFT) was given powers to take action in some circumstances under these Directives. As we shall see later, in the case of unfair terms these powers have been extended to a range of other organisations. With the implementation of the injunctions Directive[25] there has been a further extension of this type of action. This directive addresses the problem of obtaining redress across national boundaries. This is a start and may accustom lawyers and administrators to a new idea. In time, it may be possible to develop a fully-fledged group action.

2–22   Given the desire to make the internal market a reality not just for business but for consumers and the fact that one of the perceived obstacles to this is concern about obtaining redress in cross-border transactions it is not surprising that the Commission has been taking action in this area. The European Consumer Centres Network (ECC-Net) has been set up at the initiative of the Commission. It is an EU-wide network designed to promote consumer confidence by advising citizens on their rights as consumers and providing easy access to redress, particularly in cases where the consumer has made a cross-border purchase. The network was created by merging two previously existing networks: the European Consumer Centres or "Euroguichets", which provided information and assistance on cross-border issues; and the European Extra-Judicial Network or the EEJ-Net, which helped consumers to resolve their disputes through ADRs using mediators or arbitrators. The aim of the European consumer centres is to provide consumers with a wide range of services, from providing information on their rights to giving advice and assistance with their complaints and the resolution of disputes. There is one centre in the UK in Essex and it is run by the Trading Standards Institute.[26]

2–23   Complementing this development on 11 July 2007, the European Parliament and the Council adopted a Regulation establishing a European Small Claims Procedure. It came into force on 1 January 2009. The aim of the Regulation is to simplify, speed up and reduce costs of litigation concerning small claims in cross-border cases by establishing a European Small Claims Procedure. This procedure applies in civil and commercial matters where the value of a claim does not exceed €2,000 (£1,465 at the time of writing), and will cover pecuniary as well as non-pecuniary claims. The Regulation also eliminates the intermediate measures necessary to enable judgments rendered under the European Small Claims Procedure in one Member State to be recognised and enforced in other Member States.

2–24   As part of its concern for safety the Commission has promoted the Rapid Information Exchange System (RAPEX). Under this system Member States notify the Commission's consumer protection service when they discover a dangerous product on their market, and the Commission in turn notifies other

---

[23] Directive 84/450/EEC of 10 September 1984 relating to the approximation of the laws, regulations and administrative provisions of the Member States concerning misleading advertising [1984] O.J. L250/17.

[24] Directive 93/13/EEC of 5 April 1993 on unfair terms in consumer contracts [1993] O.J. L95/29.

[25] Directive 98/27/EC of the European Parliament and of the Council of 19 May 1998 on injunctions for the protection of consumers' interests [1998] O.J. L166/51.

[26] The website is: *http://www.ukecc.net* [Accessed 8 June 2015].

Member States. EHLASS, the European Home and Leisure Accident Surveillance System, has also been promoted by the Commission. Under it Member States provide the Commission with statistics on home and leisure accidents involving products, to help identify areas where common action is needed.

In discussion of the achievements of EC consumer protection policy most attention tends to centre on its legislative achievements. Over the years a considerable number of measures have emanated from Brussels. In the early years progress was slow but it should not be forgotten that even in the very early years legislation that benefited consumers was passed. Various Directives whose primary aim was harmonisation of the common market also had the effect of improving consumer protection. Examples from this early period include legislation on the harmonisation of laws on classification, denomination, packaging and labelling of consumer goods as well as those on foodstuffs, animal health, pharmaceutical products, cosmetics and electrical home appliances. In the 1970s and 1980s more overtly consumer protection measures were adopted although the uncertainty over the legal competence of the EC in the area of consumer protection undoubtedly retarded progress. However, it is possible to point to a number of Directives from this period directly concerning consumers. Examples are those on the labelling of foodstuffs in 1978, the Misleading Advertising Directive of 1984 now amended by the Unfair Commercial Practices Directive 2005, the Product Liability Directive and the Door to Door Sales Directives of 1985, and the Consumer Credit Directive of 1986.[27]

2–25

As Professor Bourgoignie has observed,[28] most of these measures related to improving consumer information. It was only with the recognition in the EC Treaty itself of consumer protection as a community policy that more fundamental initiatives have been taken in the last 10 years. To quote Professor Bourgoignie:

2–26

> "Beyond solutions of an informational nature which aim to improve the quality of the consent which a consumer gives to his actions, the provisions of the Directives most recently adopted or proposed, seek to alter the very nature of consumer relationships by imposing new obligations, by confirming new rights and by prohibiting certain practices or behaviour."

Examples of such new directives are those on package travel, general product safety, unfair contract terms, timeshare, distance contracts, comparative advertising, consumer sales and guarantees, and the Injunctions Directive.[29] More recently the unfair commercial practices Directive was enacted and the consumer rights Directive has replaced the distance selling and doorstep selling Directives.

As has been suggested above, EU proposals can have a beneficial effect on domestic policy. Small claims is an example that has been cited. Added to that might be the control of unfair contract terms. Regulation of such terms has, since the passing of the Unfair Contract Terms Act 1977 (the 1977 Act), been quite

2–27

---

[27] Directive 87/102/EEC of 22 December 1986 for the approximation of the laws, regulations and administrative provisions of the Member States concerning consumer credit [1987] O.J. L42/48.

[28] Thierry Bourgoignie, "European Community Consumer Law and Policy", 1998 6 Consum. L.J. 443, 449.

[29] For details see relevant chapters.

effective. In many respects the Unfair Contract Terms Directive[30] duplicates that legislation. The importance of the Directive lies in the extensions which it makes to our law. This is discussed in more detail in the chapter on unfair contract terms and at this stage it is sufficient to point out two salient features. As mentioned above, the Directive requires organisations to be permitted to take action on behalf of consumers. Not only is this important in itself but, as has been argued above, it may lead to the recognition of a wider right to act in this way. The other point is more specific. The Directive applies more widely than the 1977 Act and, with its concept of good faith, introduces a potentially revolutionary tool into our armoury of legal weapons.

2–28   While benefits have undoubtedly been derived from the EU consumer protection policy, it is also possible to argue that it has had its disadvantages. There are those who consider that EU initiatives can be an impediment to the achievement of desirable reforms in the UK. The example usually given in this context is product liability. The debate on the need for reform was well advanced in the UK when a draft EC Directive was published. It may be argued that the desire to produce a detailed proposal put at risk the possibility of achieving any change at all.[31]

2–29   In addition to concerns about the content of some of the directives there has also been concern about the methods of implementing them and whether enforcement in this country is overzealous as compared with that in some other Member States. The UK can be said to have a good record in implementing EU proposals.[32]

2–30   It is sometimes said that the UK over-implements EU law, including single market Directives, in that on transposition it includes additional requirements or complexities that are not required by the Directive. Combined with this assertion it is not uncommon to find allegations that other Member States do not implement properly and adopt a less rigorous approach to enforcement.

2–31   The *Review of the Implementation and Enforcement of EC law in the United Kingdom* considered these issues. On the first point it "found little evidence to support the allegation that the United Kingdom deliberately adds requirements when transposing EC law". Where this did happen it was for two main reasons:

> "First, where EC Law has been integrated into existing United Kingdom law there is a tendency to carry over existing national provisions, [with] wider scope and tougher penalties than in other Member States... Second, the United Kingdom legal system is based on a tradition of precise drafting which aims to eradicate doubt in contrast with the purposive approach of continental jurisprudence on which EC law and that of other Member States is based."[33]

2–32   On the question of failure to implement properly in other Members States the same report found no evidence to suggest that other Member States have omitted

---

[30] See para.2–21, fn.24.

[31] See Gordon J. Borrie, *The Development of Consumer Law and Policy: Bold Spirits and Timorous Souls* (London: Stevens & Sons Ltd), pp.116–118. Doorstep selling might be another example.

[32] This is borne out by statistics, see Department of Trade and Industry, *Review of the Implementation and Enforcement of EC law in the United Kingdom* (July 1993), an efficiency scrutiny report commissioned by the President of the Board of Trade, in particular see Ch.3.

[33] Department of Trade and Industry, *Review of the Implementation and Enforcement of E.C. law in the United Kingdom* (July 1993), p.19 fn.1.

requirements of a directive though they noted that not all the Directives that they studied for the purposes of their review had been implemented in some other Member States.

It is not uncommon to hear complaints that enforcement is less stringent and more pragmatic in other Member States. The review considered this issue mainly in relation to a small number of case studies that it undertook. It concluded that it found "no evidence to support the assertion that United Kingdom enforcers were more highly qualified than those in other Member States". It went on to say that "simple comparisons of enforcement practice are not helpful in understanding deep seated differences in culture".[34] The review then goes on to consider the approach of the Sutherland Report.[35] While critical of some of the report's recommendations as overly bureaucratic it states:

> "Nevertheless, the basic thrust of the recommendations is sensible, and the call for a 'co-operative approach' to be taken to enforcement issues as the 'single most important way of reinforcing mutual confidence between Member States and the Commission' should build on the collaboration that enforcement authorities in all Member States are already developing."[36]

More recently the *Davidson Review* has largely confirmed the findings of the DTI review. It noted that "[g]iven the very large amount of EU-sourced legislation in the UK it is not possible, from examining a limited number of case studies, to draw definitive conclusions on the extent to which the UK may inappropriately over-implement European legislation".

However, it added that

> ". . . a number of factors indicate that inappropriate over-implementation may not be as big a problem in the UK—in absolute terms and relative to other EU countries—as is alleged by some commentators".[37]

ROLE OF THE EUROPEAN COURT

It must not be forgotten that the European Court of Justice (ECJ) has had a role in the development of the law relating to consumers. Much of this has been based on the exposition of art.30 (now art.28 TFEU) of the Treaty of Rome, which establishes the right of free movement of goods. There is also an equivalent in relation to services in art.59 (now art.49 TFEU). The theory behind this is that the

2–33

2–34

2–35

---

[34] Department of Trade and Industry, *Review of the Implementation and Enforcement of E.C. law in the United Kingdom* (July 1993) p.20.

[35] European Commission, *The Internal Market After 1992: Meeting the Challenge* (The Sutherland Report, SEC (1992)) 2044.

[36] Department of Trade and Industry, *Review of the Implementation and Enforcement of E.C. law in the United Kingdom* (July 1993) p.20

[37] Better Regulation Executive, *Davidson Review: Implementation of EU Legislation, Final Report* (HMSO, November 2006) para.8.

removal of barriers to trade between Member States benefits the consumer in permitting greater competition with the benefits that economic theory says will follow from that.[38]

2–36   According to the court, art.30 (art.28 TFEU) covers "all trading rules enacted by Member States which are capable of hindering, directly or indirectly, actually or potentially, intra-Community trade".[39] One of the best known examples of the application of the court's approach to art.30 is the *Cassis de Dijon* decision[40] where regulations governing the composition of alcoholic drinks that could be marketed in Germany were held to offend against European law. That case also demonstrated that there were circumstances where trade barriers could be justified. The court pointed out that:

> "[O]bstacles to movement in the Community resulting from disparities between national laws in question must be accepted in so far as those provisions may be recognised as being necessary in order to satisfy mandatory requirements relating in particular to the effectiveness of fiscal supervision, the protection of public health, the fairness of commercial transactions and the defence of the consumer."[41]

2–37   The scope for taking advantage of these exceptions on the ground of consumer protection is not great, as the case law shows. The court has frequently pointed out that where there are other ways of achieving the same end they should be used. The *German Beer* case[42] illustrates this point. Germany sought to argue that its beer purity laws, dating from medieval times, were justified on consumer protection grounds. The court pointed out that the objectives of the laws could be secured by labelling requirements which would also allow a freer market in beer with greater consumer choice.[43]

2–38   In the past few years the Court of Justice has been altering its approach in this area. In a series of cases beginning with *Keck and Mithouard*,[44] and including *Hunermund*[45] and *Clinique*[46] the court appears to be using a new definition of "measures having an equivalent effect". A distinction is being drawn between rules on the composition and presentation of products, and those restricting and prohibiting certain sales methods. The former are subject to the *Cassis de Dijon* controls but the latter are not regarded as measures having an equivalent effect. One particular problem that this new distinction throws up is that it leaves it unclear into which category advertising falls.

---

[38] For a detailed study of this area of EU law see Stephen Weatherill and Paul Beaumont, *EU Law*, 3rd edn (Harmondsworth: Penguin, 1999).

[39] *Procureur du Roi v Dassonville* [1974] E.C.R. 837.

[40] *Cassis de Dijon* (120/78) [1979] E.C.R. 649.

[41] *Cassis de Dijon* (120/78) [1979] E.C.R. 649, [8].

[42] *Commission of the European Communities v Germany (German Beer)* [1987] E.C.R. 1227.

[43] For a detailed discussion of this area, see Stephen Weatherill, "The Role of the Informed Consumer in European Community Law and Policy" (1994) 2 Consum. L.J. 49.

[44] *Criminal Proceedings against Keck and Mithouard*(C-267/91; C-268/91) [1993] E.C.R. 1-6097.

[45] *Hunermund v Landesapothekerkammer Baden-Wurttemberg* (C-292/92) unreported 15 December 1993 ECJ.

[46] *Verband Sozialer Wettbewerb eV v Clinique Laboratories SNC* (C-315/92) [1994] E.C.R. I-317.

FUTURE OF EUROPEAN CONSUMER PROTECTION

Consumer protection policy in the EU is at an uncertain stage. On the one hand   **2–39**
the Maastricht, Amsterdam and Lisbon Treaty changes appear to have enhanced
its significance. That must be balanced against the meaning given to subsidiarity
by some Member States who see it as a means to limit the ability of Brussels to
intervene in areas such as this. There does appear to be increasing realisation of
the importance of consumers to the success of the operation of the single market.
The Sutherland Report[47] made this point forcibly in pointing out that consumer
uncertainty was one of the major obstacles to the realisation of the internal
market and the point has been reiterated in the Commission's strategy documents
notably the current one.[48] If consumers have doubts about the quality of goods
from other Member States or their legal rights are obscure, they cannot be
expected to participate fully.

This was one of the most important factors behind the Commission's Green   **2–40**
Paper on European consumer protection published in 2001.[49] It argued that the
principal problem in guaranteeing consumer protection in the internal market lies
in the different national laws concerning commercial practices between
businesses and consumers. As a result neither businesses nor consumers are
taking full advantage of the potential of the internal market despite the
introduction of the Euro and developments in e-commerce. The Green Paper
argued that Community rules on consumer protection have not succeeded in
adapting to the natural development of the market or to new commercial
practices. The solution envisaged involved simplification of national rules and a
more effective guarantee of consumer protection.

The Green Paper put forward two methods of achieving simplification: the   **2–41**
adoption of new Directives or a framework Directive supplemented by a number
of targeted directives in specific areas. It should be emphasised that these
proposals dealt only with the protection of consumers' economic interests; health
and safety matters are not affected. The Commission's clear preference was for a
framework Directive that would harmonise the general rules on trading fairly
found in most EU states, though not the UK. This would not override sector
specific directives such as the unfair terms Directive but would provide a long
stop in those areas where there was no legislation or where the legislation did not
extend to some new practice. It was envisaged that some existing directives
would have to be revised and the framework directive would also be
supplemented by increased self-regulation.

This was an ambitious idea and one which has met with some scepticism.   **2–42**
Howells and Wilhelmsson argue that:

---

[47] European Commission, *The Internal Market After 1992: Meeting the Challenge* (The Sutherland
Report, SEC (1992)) fn.32.
[48] See para.2–18, fn.19.
[49] Commission of the European Communities, *Green Paper on European Union Consumer
Protection*. COM (2001) 531 final.

"EC consumer law is not yet sufficiently developed to protect the consumer, partly because the constitutional limits on Community activity in this area prevent the adoption of a comprehensive consumer policy."[50]

They go on to point out that references to moving from the minimal harmonisation approach of many existing directives to a policy of maximum harmonisation as the Green Paper seems to envisage has profound dangers for consumers. Minimum Directives that leave Member States free to make their own more protective rules might not have been agreed to in their present form if it had been thought that they might later become maximum directives. They also question whether the reliance of the Green Paper on information remedies and self regulation is in the interests of consumers. Following a period of consultation the Commission brought forward a draft Directive on unfair commercial practices[51] that was adopted in 2005 and has been implemented in the UK.[52] The Consumer Rights Directive is also a maximum Directive but fears that using this form would endanger longstanding rights resulted in it being reduced from its much more ambitious original draft. Whether the fears of critics will be realised it is too soon to say.

2-43   Two other potentially extremely important projects are in train. These are the review of the consumer *acquis* or body of EU consumer legislation and the Common Frame of Reference (CFR) project. The review of the consumer *acquis* aims to better achieve the Commission's regulatory goals by simplifying and completing the existing regulatory framework.[53] The CFR is a long-term project which aims at providing the European legislators (Commission, Council and European Parliament) with a "toolbox" or a handbook to be used for the revision of existing, and the preparation of new, legislation in the area of contract law. This toolbox could contain fundamental principles of contract law, definitions of key concepts and model provisions. It is based on the fact that the exchange of goods and services is governed by contract law. Problems in relation to using, agreeing, interpreting and applying contracts in cross-border transactions may therefore affect the smooth functioning of the internal market.[54] Perhaps the most important task facing the EU in the area of consumer protection is to ensure that a high level of protection is achieved not only through internal market measures but also—as art.169(2)(a) provides—by ensuring that it informs the other EU policies that affect consumers. These include agricultural, competition, transport, energy, taxation and public health.

---

[50] Geraint Howells and Thomas Wilhelmsson, "European Consumer Law: Has it Come of Age?" (2003) 28 E.L. Rev. 370.

[51] Commission of the European Communities, *Proposal for a Directive of the European Parliament and of the Council concerning unfair business-to-consumer practices in the Internal Market*, COM (2003) 356.

[52] Directive 2005/29/EC of the European Parliament and of the Council of 11 May 2005 concerning unfair business-to-consumer commercial practices in the internal market [2005] O.J. L149/22, implemented by the Consumer Protection from Unfair Trading Regulations 2008 (SI 2008/1277).

[53] Commission of the European Communities, *Green Paper on the Review of the Consumer Acquis*, COM (2006) 744 final.

[54] See Commission of the European Communities, *Second Progress Report on The Common Frame of Reference*, COM (2007) 447 final.

CHAPTER 3

Acquiring the Goods and Digital Content

This chapter deals with a number of issues connected by the fact that they relate to problems that may arise at the inception of the transaction. These will include questions such as: what sort of contract is it, legally speaking; when was it concluded; or what are the consumer's rights if it turns out that the person from whom the goods were bought was not the true owner? Other issues could be included at this stage such as the point at which a contract for the supply of goods is concluded. This topic has been omitted because it is fully covered in textbooks on contract and readers are likely to be familiar with the problems of distinguishing invitations to treat from offers and the rules of offer and acceptance. Contracts for the supply of goods or digital content are, in general, no different from other contracts and the general law of contract applies to them. **3–01**

Many of these contracts require no special formalities. However, as we shall see in Ch.8, those relating to credit must comply with certain statutory formalities to be valid. **3–02**

The law relating to the capacity of individuals was amended by the Age of Legal Capacity (Scotland) Act 1991 (the 1991 Act). As a result, a person of or over the age of 16 has capacity to enter into any transaction.[1] However, a person under the age of 21 may ask a court to set aside a transaction which was entered into while that person was 16 or over but under 18 years of age. The grounds on which this can be done are that the transaction was prejudicial. "Prejudicial"[2] means: **3–03**

> "A transaction which (a) an adult, exercising reasonable prudence, would not have entered into in the circumstances of the applicant at the time of entering into the transaction, and (b) has caused or is likely to cause substantial prejudice to the applicant."

This protection will be lost if the other party to the transaction was induced to enter into it by a fraudulent misrepresentation as to age or other material fact.

Children under the age of 16 generally have no legal capacity to enter into any transaction.[3] This rule could be inconvenient as such children do purchase goods, so the 1991 Act provides that they shall have legal capacity to enter into transactions "of a kind commonly entered into by persons of their age and circumstances" as long as this is "on terms which are not unreasonable". The purchase of things like sweets and comics by children under the age of 16 should **3–04**

---

[1] Age of Legal Capacity (Scotland) Act 1991 s.1(1)(b).
[2] See Age of Legal Capacity (Scotland) Act 1991 ss.3 and 4.
[3] See Age of Legal Capacity (Scotland) Act 1991 s.2(1).

not be open to challenge as a result. The same may be said of other purchases such as some sports equipment, computer software or recreational services. As the value of the goods or services rises and the age of the child diminishes it becomes more difficult to know what a child will be regarded as having capacity to buy.

TYPES OF CONTRACT FOR THE SUPPLY OF GOODS

3–05 A number of contracts can be used where goods are supplied to consumers. Perhaps the most common is the contract of sale which involves money being paid in return for goods. In addition, goods may be purchased on credit which might involve credit sale or conditional sale contracts, hire-purchase and hire or rental contracts. In addition, goods are sometimes acquired in return for vouchers and, less commonly by barter. At one time some of these contracts were regulated by different statutes and the legal consequences of these various forms could vary a good deal. The Supply of Goods and Services Act 1982 did a good deal to tidy up this unsatisfactory situation and the Consumer Rights Act 2015 (the 2015 Act) has taken things a good deal further. The first chapter of Pt 1 of the 2015 Act deals with the legal consequences of what are called collectively contracts to supply goods.[4] It is not quite a complete rationalisation of the area as the rules on the transfer of ownership are still left to the Sale of Goods Act 1979 (the 1979 Act).[5] However, it is a considerably clearer statement of the rules using modern drafting techniques. For example, related groups of sections are given headings making it easier to navigate through the 2015 Act. In Ch.2 of Pt 1 the first group is entitled *What goods contracts are covered?* and the second *What statutory rights are there under a goods contract?* This chapter will follow the headings that are relevant to it.

A contract to supply goods: what goods contracts are covered?

3–06 The scheme of this part of the 2015 Act is to define which contracts it deals with and then to set out what legal consequences follow in relation, for example, to the quality that can be expected (dealt with in the next chapter), when ownership is transferred and who bears the risk of something going wrong while the goods are being delivered and what remedies are available where a contract is broken. Section 1 points out that it applies only to agreements between a trader and a consumer whether the contract is written or oral or implied from the parties' conduct. To understand what this covers it is necessary look at the definitions of "trader", "consumer" and "goods" and then explain which types of contract are included in the term "a contract to supply goods".

3–07 A trader is defined in s.2 as

> "a person acting for purposes relating to that person's trade, business, craft or profession, whether acting personally or through another person acting in the trader's name or on the trader's behalf".

---

[4] See Age of Legal Capacity (Scotland) Act 1991 s.3(4).
[5] See Age of Legal Capacity (Scotland) Act 1991 s.4.

"Person", of course, is used in the legal sense of any entity recognised by the law so it covers not just individuals but companies and other organisations. Section 2(7) makes clear that "business" includes "the activities of any government department or local or public authority". This is a wide definition and, in addition to the obvious categories of traders, will cover not-for-profit organisations, such as charities, mutuals and co-operatives that often sell goods for profit. The reference to acting "through another person acting in the trader's name or on the trader's behalf" is a useful clarification of the law. Examples would be a trader that subcontracts part of a building contract or a company for which the employees make contracts with customers. In both situations it is the trader who is liable for proper execution of the contract.

Section 2 also defines "consumer" as "an individual acting for purposes which are wholly or mainly outside that individual's trade, business, craft or profession". This is wide enough to cover activities by businesses in some circumstances but will only apply to sole traders and partnerships governed by the Partnership Act 1890 as only "individuals", i.e. humans may be traders. This is more clearly expressed in art.2 of the consumer rights Directive, where there is a reference to "any natural person". That article does not make clear that some businesses can be regarded as consumers but this was the clear intention of the Directive as Recital 17 states that **3–08**

> "in the case of dual purpose contracts, where the contract is concluded for purposes partly within and partly outside the person's trade and the trade purpose is so limited as not to be predominant in the overall context of the contract, that person should also be considered as a consumer".

This might cover situations such as that in *R & B Customs Brokers Co Ltd v United Dominions Trust Ltd*[6] involving the purchase of a car for use both in the business and as the trader's family car.

For the purposes of this part of the Act "goods" means "any tangible moveable items, but that includes water, gas and electricity if and only if they are put up for supply in a limited volume or set quantity".

Essentially "goods" means anything physical that you can move thus excluding purchases of immovable property such as land or a house. However, the definition makes clear that goods can also include certain utilities (water, gas and electricity) but only where they are sold in a limited volume or set quantity. For example, gas sold in cylinders is covered but not gas piped into a home; and bottles of water are included but not water delivered through the mains. **3–09**

Which types of contracts are dealt with in this part of the 2015 Act? Section 3(4) states that such contract is one of a kind known collectively as "a contract to supply goods". There are four types of these contracts: a sales contract; a contract for the hire of goods; a hire-purchase contract; and a contract for transfer of goods. Section 3(5), makes clear these contracts include those involving the transfer of a share in the goods, whether between current owners or the owner of a share and a third party. We have already seen that there is a general definition of "goods"; s.3(3) goes on to exclude certain transactions that might otherwise come within the definition of a contract to sell goods. Contracts to supply coins or notes

---

[6] *R & B Customs Brokers Co Ltd v United Dominions Trust Ltd* [1988] 1 W.L.R. 321.

for use as currency are excluded though this does not cover sales of notes or coins as collectors' items. As with the 1979 Act goods sold under court orders, those intended to operate as a mortgage, pledge, charge or other security and gifts are also outside the ambit of this part of the 2015 Act.

The individual contracts to supply goods

Sales contracts

3–10   Section 5 of the 2015 Act defines sales contracts as those where a trader transfers or agrees to transfer ownership of goods to a consumer who agrees to pay the price. Ownership means "the general property in goods, not merely a special property". This "general property" is the right over goods that an absolute owner has in contrast to the more limited "special property" in a thing which means that a person can only put the item to a particular use rather than having absolute rights of ownership. The section, in line with the policy of clarifying the law, goes on to explain that this includes two common situations in addition to the obvious over the counter sale. The first is where a trader agrees to manufacture or produce goods for a consumer who agrees to pay the price. An example would be where a tailor produces a made-to-measure suit for a consumer. The other case is what are known as "conditional sales contracts" where goods are paid for in instalments and the trader retains ownership of them until the conditions in the contract have been met, whether the consumer has possession of the goods in the meantime or not. The point of this from the trader's point of view is that he or she has security for payment of the price as they are still the owners.

Contract of hire

3–11   As s.6 very clearly puts it:

> "A contract is for the hire of goods if under it the trader gives or agrees to give the consumer possession of the goods with the right to use them, subject to the terms of the contract, for a period determined in accordance with the contract."

Typical examples would be the short term rental of a hire car or DIY equipment. The same legal form can be used to finance a transaction where the lease is for a fixed period at a rent equivalent to the sale price of the goods and the cost of credit. These are often marketed by car dealers as car leasing or contract hire. As the section goes on to point out, it is to be distinguished from the common credit transaction of hire-purchase.

Hire-purchase

3–12   Hire-purchase agreements, defined in s.7, involve two conditions. First the goods are hired in return for periodical payments by the consumer and secondly ownership of the goods will be transferred to the consumer if the terms of the contract are complied with and the consumer exercises an option to buy or some other event set out in the contract occurs. The typical hire-purchase contract involves consumers paying a number of monthly or weekly instalments and one final, often quite small, optional payment whereupon they become the owners of the goods. The key point is that this form gives the trader a security for payment as the goods remain in their ownership until the final option payment is made. This looks very similar to the conditional sale mentioned above but as subs.(4) points out such a contract is not hire-purchase. The difference between them is that in conditional sale the buyer must become the owner on paying all the instalments whereas in hire-purchase, theoretically the buyer must exercise an option to purchase before becoming owner.

Contracts for transfer of goods

This final category of contracts to supply goods covers those where the exchange is not for money or, for any other reason, it is not a sales contract or a hire-purchase agreement. This would cover barter where one object is exchanged for another or the purchase of goods by means of vouchers. There used to be problems in this area as it was not clear if to barter extended beyond exchanges of objects to include cases where one side offered an object and cash in return for another object. As this was, and is, very common in the car trade where it is referred to as trading-in the question was of importance but is now only of academic interest.[7]

3–13

PRICE AND DELIVERY

Price does not usually give rise to problems in consumer sales. It is usually perfectly clear what the price is because it is marked on a ticket on the goods or on the shelf. The 2015 Act does not reproduce s.8 of the 1979 Act, which deals with situations where the price is not explicitly set out. This is probably because the price is one of the pieces of pre-contract information that must be provided by a trader under s.12. In any event, if the price has not been explicitly agreed in a consumer sale it is probably strong evidence that there has not been an agreement and that negotiations are still continuing.[8] It is possible that there might be misunderstanding about the price, perhaps in private sales. Where there is genuine misunderstanding about the price to be paid it may be that the contractual doctrine of error may operate to show that there has been no agreement.[9] However, it should be remembered that the courts are slow to allow resort to the doctrine of error.

3–14

It is not uncommon, where a consumer orders goods, for the seller to ask for a deposit. This serves two purposes: if the purchase goes ahead it is looked upon as an advance payment, but its principal purpose, to quote Lord Macnaghten in *Soper v Arnold*,[10] "is a guarantee that the purchaser means business". If the

3–15

---

[7] *Sneddon v Durant* and Erskine, *Institute*, III, 3, 13.
[8] Support for this may be seen in the judgment of Sellers LJ in *Ingram v Little* [1961] 1 Q.B. 31 at 49, where absence of agreement even about the method of payment was considered to indicate the lack of a concluded bargain.
[9] As in *Wilson v Marquis of Breadalbane* (1859) 21 D. 957.
[10] *Soper v Arnold* (1889) L.R. 14 App. Cas. 429.

purchaser fails to honour the contract the deposit is forfeited.[11] Should the trader, in breach of contract, fail to provide the goods ordered, the deposit is recovered using the restitutionary remedy *condictio causa data causa non secuta*.

BECOMING THE OWNER

3–16   When the consumer becomes the owner of goods has much less significance than once was the case. This is because becoming the owner is no longer linked to taking the risk of something going wrong with the goods such as their accidental destruction. However, it can be of critical importance where the seller becomes insolvent. There have been a number of insolvencies of retail companies recently, such as Land of Leather and Woolworths, where customers had placed orders—and sometimes paid—before the company became insolvent. If they had become the owners of the goods ordered they could require the liquidator to hand over what were legally their goods. If the goods still belonged to the company and they had already parted with the price they were in an unenviable position as unsecured creditors and usually very unlikely to get much, if any, of their money back.

3–17   For answers to the ownership issue the 2015 Act largely mainly refers back to the relevant provisions of the 1979 Act which deal only with sales contracts.[12] These are mainly ss.16–18. The starting point is to know what "specific goods" and "unascertained goods" are. Section 61 defines "specific goods" as "goods identified and agreed on at the time a contract of sale is made". In a consumer context an obvious example would be a product selected by the consumer in a shop. "Unascertained goods" are not defined in the 1979 Act but it is clear that the term is used in contradistinction to specific goods. It covers three situations. Where the goods are to be manufactured or grown by the seller they will be unascertained. While not so common in a consumer context this would include a product made to special order. It also includes generic goods such as a ton of coal or a consumer product referred to by its general description; and an unidentified part of a specific whole such as a case of Beaujolais Nouveau from the shipment in a particular wine merchant's warehouse. With the growth of internet sales purchases of unascertained goods have become much more common. When the order is placed, the consumer will not be contracting to buy a specific item but simply an item of the type in question which the seller has still to select from available stock. Traditional shop sales can also fall into this category as the consumer will not be contracting to buy a specific item such as a particular computer or type of television. The model of the TV or computer will be selected from the items displayed in the shop. It will only be later that a specific computer or TV will be selected for delivery.

---

[11] *Zemhunt (Holdings) Ltd v Control Securities Plc*, 1992 S.C.L.R. 151.
[12] See Consumer Rights Act 2015 s.4.

Specific goods

In the case of specific goods s.17 states that the ownership or property is transferred to the buyer at such time as the parties to the contract intend it to be transferred. This intention is to be ascertained from the terms of the contract, the conduct of the parties and the circumstances of the case. In consumer transactions it will be rare for explicit consideration to have been given to the passing of the property though conditional sale agreements are an exception. In such contracts it will be expressly stated that ownership remains with the seller until the final instalment has been paid.[13]

3–18

Where the parties have not indicated their intentions, the four rules in s.18 of the 1979 Act come into operation. It should be noted that any intention expressed by the parties must be manifested before the property has passed in accordance with these rules. A good example is *Dennant v Skinner and Collom*[14] where D had sold a car at an auction to a person who turned out to be a swindler. The swindler gave a false name and address and asked if he might take the car away in return for a cheque. This D permitted him to do so after getting the swindler to sign a document stating that the title to the car would not pass until the cheque was honoured. The cheque bounced and, meanwhile, the swindler sold the car that eventually came into the possession of the defendants. It was held that the document was too late to oust the statutory rules about the passing of the property because they had operated on the fall of the auctioneer's hammer.

3–19

Rule 1

"Where there is an unconditional contract for the sale of specific goods in a deliverable state the property in the goods passes to the buyer when the contract is made, and it is immaterial whether the time of payment or the time of delivery, or both, be postponed."

3–20

This rule will apply in the vast majority of sales in a shop. On the face of it, therefore, where a consumer agrees to buy a product but it is not to be removed from the store until some time later the consumer will have become the owner and should the trader become insolvent could demand delivery of their purchase.

For this rule to apply the goods must be in what the rule calls "a deliverable state". This is defined as being "in such a state that the buyer would under the contract be bound to take delivery of them". In *Philip Head & Sons v Showfronts Ltd*,[15] carpeting that had been sold to the defendants, and which the plaintiffs were required to lay, had been left at the defendant's premises. It was not regarded as in a deliverable state and thus ownership had not passed when it was stolen because it was in a heavy bundle and difficult to move.

---

[13] Romalpa clauses which state that goods are to remain the property of the seller until payment has been received are another example but are normally only found in. commercial contracts.

[14] *Dennant v Skinner and Collom* [1948] 2 K.B. 164.

[15] *Philip Head & Sons v Showfronts Ltd* (1969) 113 S.J. 978.

Rule 2

3–21   This rule provides that where the seller is bound to do something to the goods for the purpose of putting them into a deliverable state, the property does not pass until the thing is done and the buyer has notice that it has been done. If, for example, a consumer agrees to buy a car but it is part of the deal that the seller will add some accessories, the ownership would not pass until this has been done and the consumer has received notice that it has been done.

Rule 3

3–22   This rule is less likely to apply to consumer sales. Under it property does not pass where the seller has to do something by way of measuring or weighing to ascertain the price until it has been done and the buyer has notice.

Rule 4

3–23   Rule 4 deals with situations where goods have been supplied to the buyer either on sale or return terms or on approval. A common example in a consumer context of sale or return terms occurs where someone is holding a party. Off-licences commonly provide refreshments on this basis. In these situations ownership passes to the buyers if they intimate acceptance or otherwise adopt the transaction, or if they retain the goods beyond the stipulated time or, if no time has been stipulated, beyond a reasonable time. Selling the goods or pledging them as security would be evidence of the buyer adopting the transaction.[16]

How the above rules apply to some common situations is not altogether clear. It is well known that some retailers have sale policies that are more liberal than required by law. Marks and Spencer, for example, are prepared to give a refund to a customer without question. The catalogue trader, Argos, states that a full refund will be given without quibble where goods are returned within 16 days of purchase. In neither case, it may be argued, is the sale an unconditional one, and thus rule 1 is not applicable. The obvious rule is rule 4, but on further consideration it is by no means clear that these types of sale are properly to be classified as sale or return, or on approval. The ability to return the goods and obtain a refund has more to do with remedies than with the classification of the contract. Perhaps the answer to the question of when the ownership passes is to be found by remembering that the rules in s.18 are only guides and are subsidiary to s.17, which states that the intention of the parties is the primary guide. It is not difficult to suggest that in these cases a court would be likely to find that the circumstances pointed to the ownership passing when the goods were paid for in the shop.

---

[16] See *Liquidators of the Brechin Auction Co Ltd v Reid* (1895) 22 R. 711; *Bryce v Ehrmann* (1904) 7 F. 5.

UNASCERTAINED GOODS

In a consumer context, internet and mail order sales where the consumer orders a   **3–24**
product by a general description from the seller's stock are good examples of
sales of unascertained goods. It is even possible that at the time the order is
placed the trader does not have stocks. Unascertained goods might also be
involved where a consumer buys wine; and some difficult problems have resulted
where consumers have agreed to buy cases of wine from shippers and the
shippers have stored it in their cellars until the buyers wish to take delivery.

Section 16 makes clear that until goods have been ascertained no property in   **3–25**
them can be transferred. An example of this in operation comes from *Re
Goldcorp Exchange Ltd (in receivership).*[17] There, many New Zealanders had
been induced by a company dealing in gold and other precious metals to invest in
these metals. The investors then received a certificate of ownership stating that
they had the right, on giving seven days' notice, to take possession of the metal
purchased. In the meantime, the metal was stored by the company as part of their
overall stock of bullion. When the company became hopelessly insolvent there
was a dispute between the investors and various banks that had securities over the
stock of bullion. The Privy Council had no difficulty on these facts in holding that
the metal was unascertained and thus no property could have been transferred to
the investors.

More fortunate were some of the customers involved in the case of *Re   **3–26**
Stapylton Fletcher Ltd*[18] where the product concerned was wine. Various
customers had purchased stocks of wine from two companies who stored it for
them for a fee. Dispute arose between the receivers of these companies and the
customers over ownership of the stocks. On purchase, some cases of wine had
been moved from the part of the warehouse holding the company's stocks to
another part reserved for customers' stocks, though it was not allocated to a
specific customer by marking it. The amount owned by each customer was
clearly recorded in the company's record system. On these facts the English High
Court found that the wine had been ascertained for the purposes of s.16 and was
owned by the various customers as tenants in common, a form of joint ownership
in English law.

Section 17, which speaks of the intention of the parties determining when   **3–27**
property in the goods passes, must therefore, in this category of goods, be less
important and cannot operate until the goods have been ascertained. Here s.18,
rule 5 comes into play and provides that:

"(1)   Where there is a contract for the sale of unascertained or future goods by
        description, and goods of that description and in a deliverable state are
        unconditionally appropriated to the contract, either by the seller with the
        assent of the buyer or by the buyer with the assent of the seller, the property
        in the goods then passes to the buyer; and the assent may be express or
        implied, and may be given either before, or after the appropriation is made.

(2)   Where, in pursuance of the contract, the seller delivers the goods to the buyer
        or to a carrier or other bailee or custodier (whether named by the buyer or

---

[17] *Re Goldcorp Exchange Ltd (in receivership)* [1994] 2 All E.R. 806, P.C.
[18] *Re Stapylton Fletcher Ltd* [1994] 1 W.L.R. 1181.

not) for the purpose of transmission to the buyer, and does not reserve the right of disposal, he is to be taken to have unconditionally appropriated the goods to the contract."

The key to turning unascertained goods into specific goods in which ownership can pass seems to be appropriation. This seems to require more than just setting goods aside. According to an English judge:

"the parties must have had, or be reasonably supposed to have had an intention to attach the contract irrevocably to those goods so that those goods and no others are the subject of the sale and become the property of the buyer".[19]

However, this must be read in the light of the *Stapylton* case where moving the goods to a different warehouse and clearly indicating in the company's records who the owner sufficed to transfer the property.

Transfer of ownership of goods

3–28   Problems sometimes arise about the right of the seller to sell the goods. Difficult questions may arise involving the buyer, the person from whom the goods were acquired, and the true owner. In contracts to supply goods the starting point is s.17 of the 2015 Act. This states that all contracts to supply goods are to be treated as having a term about the seller's right to supply the goods. In previous legislation such as the 1979 Act and the Supply of Goods and Services Act 1982 this was referred to as an implied term. In the case of a contract of hire this is a term that at the beginning of the period of hire the trader must have the right to transfer possession of the goods by way of hire.[20] It is drafted in this way for two reasons. First, people hiring out goods need not be the owners: they themselves may have hired them from someone. Secondly, the hirer is not acquiring ownership only the more limited right to possess and use the goods for a limited time. In addition, in hire contracts there is a term that the consumer's possession will not be interrupted by someone entitled to a security or other right over the goods. In all other contracts to supply goods the trader must have the right to sell or transfer the goods at the time when ownership of the goods is to be transferred. The trader and consumer can agree that only such title as the trader or some third party has will be transferred.[21] In addition, the section also guarantees that no other person should have rights over the goods (e.g. a right to use the goods) unless the consumer is made aware of this before making the contract and that the consumer's possession of the goods should not be disturbed by anyone with rights over the goods except any rights of which the consumer has been made aware.[22]

3–29   These terms cannot be excluded. This is the effect of s.73(1)(a) of the 2015 Act which exempts from the fairness test (which the Act applies to exclusion clauses[23]) "mandatory statutory or regulatory provisions" of which s.17 is an

---

[19] Pearson J in *Carlos Federspiel & Co SA v Twigg (Charles) Ltd* [1957] 1 Lloyd's Rep. 240, at 255.
[20] Consumer Rights Act 2015 s.17(1)(a).
[21] Consumer Rights Act 2015 s.17(4).
[22] Consumer Rights Act 2015 s.17(2).
[23] See Ch.9.

example. Even if this exemption did not exist it is inconceivable that attempts to exclude such terms would succeed given the fact that the so-called "Grey List" in Pt 1 of Sch.2 creates a presumption that they are unfair.

McDonald v Provan (of Scotland Street) Ltd[24] provides a bizarre example of the operation of what is now s.17 of the 2015 Act. McDonald bought a car from Provan Ltd, who in turn had bought it in good faith. Three months after the sale the car was taken from McDonald by the police because at least part of it was stolen property. It appeared that the car consisted of parts of two separate cars, one of which had been stolen, that had been welded together. McDonald sued for damages for breach of what was then called the implied term about title and it was held that he was entitled to succeed if he could prove the assertions on which he relied.   **3–30**

The implied terms about title are useful provided that the seller can still be found and is worth suing. In many cases raising problems about ownership of goods this is not the case. The facts of *MacLeod v Kerr*[25] provide a typical example. Kerr had advertised his car for sale in a newspaper and sold it to a man who came to see it. He accepted a cheque in payment and permitted the man to take the car away together with the registration document. The man had given a false name and paid with a cheque from a stolen cheque book. On discovering that he had been tricked Kerr immediately informed the police. Meanwhile, the rogue sold the car to a Mr Gibson who knew nothing of these events. The rogue was not worth suing and the question in the case was which of two people who had been duped by him was the legal owner of the car. This unfortunate situation can also arise in other ways as the cases discussed below will demonstrate.   **3–31**

Prior to the passing of the original Sale of Goods Act 1893 (the 1893 Act), problems of this sort posed fewer problems at Scots common law. The approach of Scots law, contrasting sharply with that of England, was that, normally, someone could not become the owner of moveable property without *traditio*, which was the physical transfer of the article to the buyer. The 1893 Act changed this in relation to the contract of sale by imposing on Scots law the English idea that the transfer of ownership and possession could be separated. It is this approach that increases the number of situations in which problems akin to that mentioned in the previous paragraph can arise.   **3–32**

Contracts for the transfer of goods

In these contracts transfer of ownership will normally occur through the handing over of possession. As a result, in these contracts one can generally rely on the person in possession being the owner. As Erskine put it: **3–33**

> "Such is the natural connection between property and possession, that in moveables, even where they have had a former owner, the law presumes the property to be in the possessor; so that till positive evidence be brought that he is not the right owner, he will be accounted such by the bare effect of his possession."[26]

---

[24] *McDonald v Provan (of Scotland Street) Ltd*, 1960 S.L.T. 231.
[25] *MacLeod v Kerr*, 1965 S.C. 253.
[26] Erskine, *Institute*, II, 1, 24. See also Stair, II, 1, 42.

3–34   Lord Cockburn suggested in *Anderson v Buchanan*[27] that "[t]his is a presumption liable to be rebutted, and perhaps liable to be rebutted easily". In *Prangnell-O'Neill v Lady Skiffington*[28] Lord Hunter observed that how easy it might be to rebut the presumption depended on the circumstances. In his view, to overcome the presumption it was necessary to show that the goods had once belonged to the person claiming them and that their possession was terminated in such a way that the subsequent possessor could not have acquired a right to them. Theft will fulfil the second requirement but, as was observed in *Prangnell-O'Neill*, so would evidence of removal by force.

3–35   The presumption can be rebutted, but it seems that where the person in possession has acted in good faith and given value for the goods only proof of theft will be sufficient to permit the original owner to recover the property.

Sales contracts

3–36   There are a number of provisions in statutes which may be relevant to contracts to supply goods though they are not specifically mentioned in the 2015 Act. These are usually discussed under the heading of the *Nemo Dat* rule discussion of which follows as they may protect an innocent consumer purchaser.

NEMO DAT RULE AND ITS EXCEPTIONS

3–37   It is a general principle of the law relating to moveable property that someone who buys from a person who is not the owner can get no better title than that person has. This is sometimes referred to by the Latin tag *nemo dat quod non habet*: no one can give a better title than they themselves have. While logical, this can be an extremely inconvenient and unjust rule in some circumstances, and so there are a number of modifications of this principle. The first one protecting those who have innocently purchased motor vehicles subject to hire-purchase or conditional sale agreements applies to all contracts to supply goods except hire. The others apply specifically to sales contracts.

Dispositions of motor vehicles subject to hire-purchase or conditional sale

3–38   Section 27 of the Hire-Purchase Act 1964 was passed to alleviate the hardship that was caused where consumers bought cars and later discovered that they were subject to hire purchase agreements. The seller had no title and so could confer none on the buyer. The finance company financing the transaction was the owner and was entitled to recover the vehicle, leaving the buyer with an action against the seller. The seller would often be untraceable or not be worth suing. Section 27 applies where a motor vehicle has been hired under a hire-purchase agreement or has been agreed to be sold under a conditional sale agreement and, before the property in the vehicle has become vested in the debtor, they have disposed of it to another person. In this situation s.27(2) provides that:

---

[27] *Anderson v Buchanan* (1848) 11 D. 270 at 284.
[28] *Prangnell-O'Neill v Lady Skiffington*, 1984 S.L.T. 282.

"Where the disposition... is to a private purchaser, and he is a purchaser of the motor vehicle in good faith and without notice of the hire-purchase agreement or conditional sale agreement, ... that disposition shall have effect as if the creditor's title to the vehicle has been vested in the debtor immediately before that disposition."

Section 27(3) applies this also to the situation where the vehicle has been sold to a trade or finance purchaser who then hire-purchases or sells it to the private purchaser.

It is important to note that this protection only applies to hire-purchase and conditional sale agreements. It does not apply to simple hire agreements. Therefore, someone who buys a car from a person who has hired a car or leased it, as it is often termed, does not have the protection of this provision. With the increasing popularity of leasing as a method of acquiring motor vehicles there is evidence that more innocent purchasers are falling victims to this fraud. "Motor vehicle" is defined as "a mechanically propelled vehicle intended or adapted for use on roads to which the public has access".[29] It does not cover caravans or boats, both of which are commonly acquired by hire purchase.

3–39

There must also be a valid hire purchase agreement, as the House of Lords decision in *Shogun Finance Ltd v Hudson*[30] demonstrates. Mr Hudson had purchased a car in good faith from a rogue who had acquired it by impersonating a Mr Patel. The rogue had obtained Mr Patel's personal documents and used these and a forged signature to convince the finance company that he was Mr Patel and so to accept his offer to enter into a hire-purchase agreement. Mr Hudson sought to rely on s.27 to assert that he had a good title to the car. The House of Lords held that the hire purchase agreement was void for mistake and thus the rogue had not acquired title of any sort. There was thus no possibility of Mr Hudson taking advantage of s.27. This decision does turn on the rather obscure English law of contractual mistake but it seems likely that the same result would obtain in Scotland as the rogue would be regarded as having stolen the car and this taints the transaction with a *vitium reale* (fundamental flaw) and so it is void from its inception.

3–40

The term "private purchaser" is somewhat misleading as s.29(2) provides that it includes anyone who is not a trade or finance purchaser; that is, anyone who does not carry on a business involving trading in motor vehicles or providing finance for their hire-purchase or conditional sale. This means that many businesses will also obtain the protection of s.27.

3–41

To obtain the protection the buyer must be able to show that he did not have actual notice of the fact that there was an existing hire-purchase agreement.[31] It is also important to note that the buyer only gets the title of the person who was described as the creditor in the hire purchase or conditional sale agreement. Suppose that a stolen car is sold to a dealer who then lets it on hire-purchase to someone who sells it before the end of the hire-purchase agreement. Even if the buyer from that person takes in good faith and without notice of the hire-purchase agreement, s.27 does not come to their rescue. This is because the dealer did not have title to the car having bought from a thief who could not pass on a good title.

3–42

---

[29] Hire-Purchase Act 1964 s.29(1).

[30] *Shogun Finance Ltd v Hudson* [2003] UKHL 62; [2003] All E.R. (D) 258.

[31] *Barker v Bell* [1971] 1 WL.R. 983.

Personal bar exception

3–43   The first of these exceptions is to be found in s.21 of the 1979 Act, which first states the general principle. It reads as follows:

> "Subject to this Act, where goods are sold by a person who is not their owner, and who does not sell them under the authority or with the consent of the owner, the buyer acquires no better title to the goods than the seller had, unless the owner of the goods is by his conduct precluded from denying the seller's authority to sell."

3–44   There are no Scottish cases on this exception, though there are some examples of its operation in English case law. In *Eastern Distributors Ltd v Goldring*[32] it came into play through the owner of a van signing hire-purchase forms in blank, for completion by another person, thus allowing that person to appear to be the owner of the van. Generally, the English courts have construed the exception narrowly, as *Moorgate Mercantile Co Ltd v Twitchings*[33] demonstrates. The parties to this case were both finance companies and both were members of hire-purchase information (HPI). HPI is a trade association set up by finance companies to keep a register of hire purchase agreements relating to cars, and to give information to members, the police and motoring organisations in order to try to reduce hire purchase frauds. The plaintiffs let out a car on hire purchase and for some reason, contrary to their normal practice, failed to register the agreement with HPI. The hirer offered to sell the car to the defendant who, after checking with HPI and finding that no agreement had been registered, bought it. By a majority of three:two the House of Lords held that the plaintiff owed no duty of care to the defendant and was not precluded by its conduct from denying the authority of the hirer to sell the car.

3–45   This decision has been subjected to much criticism and it is not binding on the Scottish courts, which are free to come to a different decision in a similar case. It is suggested that it would be appropriate that this should be done. There would be no conflict with the approach of the Court of Session in *Mitchell v Z Heys & Sons*[34] where a claim that the owner was personally barred failed. There it was held that for such a claim to succeed it would have to be shown that a representation by words or conduct had been made to, and relied upon by, the person claiming now to be the owner.

Sale under a voidable title

3–46   Section 23 of the 1979 Act provides that when the seller of goods has a voidable title to them, but their title has not been avoided at the time of the sale, the buyer acquires a good title to the goods, provided they buy them in good faith and without notice of the seller's defect of title. The facts of *MacLeod v Kerr*[35] are a good example of the sort of situation in which this provision might be relied upon by the buyer. The language of the section is based on English law concepts and it may be misleading to rely on some of the English cases which make subtle

---

[32] *Eastern Distributors Ltd v Goldring* [1957] 2 Q.B. 600.
[33] *Moorgate Mercantile Co Ltd v Twitchings* [1977] A.C. 890 HL.
[34] *Mitchell v Z Heys & Sons* (1894) 21 R. 600.
[35] *MacLeod v Kerr*, 1965 S.C. 253. See para.3–31.

distinctions between situations where a contract is void, and therefore of no effect, and those where it is voidable, which means that it has effect until the seller has taken some action to rescind it.[36] Informing the police will not be sufficient to effect rescission. It seems that informing the person to whom one was persuaded to transfer the goods will be necessary as would informing a potential purchaser from that person.[37]

The approach of Scots law, as Professor Gow has cogently argued,[38] is that a buyer taking in good faith and for value acquires a title which is unimpeachable unless the seller acquired the goods by theft. The fact that the seller's title was tainted by error or fraud is not relevant. While this reasoning may not have been explicitly adopted in *MacLeod v Kerr*,[39] the decision in the case is consistent with it. It is an approach that has much to commend it on policy grounds. As Professor Gow points out, why should an innocent buyer be

3–47

> "penalised and enmeshed in expensive litigation simply because [the true owner] was so naive, or so credulous, or so gullible as to trust the seller, or so reckless as to take a long chance on his creditworthiness".[40]

Indeed, one might argue that the law should be amended to protect the buyer even where the goods have been stolen from the true owner. The true owner will probably be insured against this possibility, to which he may to some degree have contributed, whereas the buyer will not.

Sale by a buyer or seller in possession

Sections 24 and 25 of the Sale of Goods Act 1979 may protect someone who has purchased goods from a person who appears to be their owner. Section 23 deals with the situation where goods have been sold but, for some reason, they are left in the possession of the seller. Depending on the circumstances, the buyer may well have become the owner by this time. What if the seller purports to sell the goods to someone else? The answer given by s.23 is that that person becomes the owner provided that they acted in good faith and did not know of the previous sale.

3–48

Similarly, goods that the buyer has bought may come into their possession before they become the legal owner. If they sell or otherwise dispose of those goods the sale has the same effect as if the person making the delivery or transfer were a mercantile agent in possession of the goods or documents of title with the consent of the owner. This is conditional on the person to whom they sell having acted in good faith and having no knowledge of the original seller's rights. The significance of the reference to the sale having the same effect as if made by a mercantile agent is that sales by such persons give good title to the buyer. The English Court of Appeal in *Newtons of Wembley Ltd v Williams*[41] has gone so far

3–49

---

[36] This view is supported by para.21, Scottish Law Commission, *Corporeal Moveables: Protection of the Onerous Bona Fide Acquirer of Another's Property*, Scot Law Com No.27 (1976).

[37] *MacLeod v Kerr*, 1965 S.C. 253 and *Young v DS Dalgleish & Son (Hawick)*, 1994 S.C.L.R. 696.

[38] JJ Gow, *The Mercantile and Industrial Law of Scotland* (Edinburgh: W. Green, 1964) pp.118–122.

[39] *MacLeod v Kerr*, 1965 S.C. 253.

[40] JJ Gow, *Mercantile and Industrial Law of Scotland* (Edinburgh: W. Green, 1964) p.121.

[41] *Newtons of Wembley Ltd v Williams* [1965] 1 Q.B. 560.

as to say that this part of the section means that the sale does not simply have the same effect as if it had been made by such an agent but must actually have been made by such agent. This is an impossible situation and it must be open to doubt if a Scottish court would follow this case. There are dicta from Australian and New Zealand cases that take a contrary view and interpret this part of the section in a literal way.[42]

3–50   Before looking at some of the other points in relation to this provision it should be noted that a buyer under a conditional sale agreement[43] and someone who has acquired goods under a hire-purchase agreement are not "buyers" for the purpose of it.[44]

3–51   The protection of s.25 only applies if the buyer is in possession with the consent of the seller. However, the fact that the buyer obtained that consent by deception does not nullify consent for this purpose.[45]

3–52   A point of some uncertainty arises where the seller is not themselves the owner of the goods and was not authorised to sell them. This arose in the English case of *National Employers Mutual General Insurance Association Ltd v Jones*,[46] where Mr Jones had acquired a car that had originally been stolen from the plaintiff's insured and then passed through the hands of several parties who had dealt with it in ignorance of this fact. It was held that Mr Jones could not have the protection of s.25 because the person who sold to him did not have title to the car on the *nemo dat* principle. Strictly speaking, he was not a "seller" so Mr Jones could not be a "buyer". In effect, seller was being interpreted to mean "owner". It could, and it is submitted should, be argued that those in the position of Mr Jones are buyers for the purposes of s.25.

DELIVERY AND RISK

3–53   When goods are to be delivered can be a cause of friction between sellers and consumers. The common law rules were not altogether helpful so the creation of a framework of rules in s.28 of the 2015 Act is a welcome innovation. Unless a separate agreement is reached between the consumer and trader, the trader must deliver the goods to the consumer and must do so without undue delay and, in any event, within 30 days after the contract is made.[47] This is clearer than the common law rule about a reasonable time set out in *Charles Rickard Ltd v Oppenhaim*.[48]

3–54   Where the goods are to be delivered immediately at the time the contract is made, this counts as an agreement between the parties as to the time for delivery.[49] Therefore, if goods are not delivered immediately, the consumer is able to terminate the contract if immediate delivery was essential; otherwise, the

---

[42] See *Langmead v Thyer Rubber Co Ltd* (1947) S.A.S.R. 29 at 39; *Jeffcott v Andrew Motors Ltd* [1960] N.Z.L.R. 721 at 729.

[43] Sale of Goods Act 1993 s.25(2).

[44] *Helby v Matthews* [1895] A.C. 471.

[45] *Du Jardin v Beadman Brothers* [1952] 2 Q.B. 712.

[46] *National Employers Mutual General Insurance Association Ltd v Jones* [1987] 3 All E.R. 385.

[47] Consumer Rights Act 2015 s.28(3).

[48] *Charles Rickard Ltd v Oppenhaim* [1950] 1 K.B. 616.

[49] Consumer Rights Act 2015 s.28(4).

trader may deliver again within a period specified by the consumer.[50] It is expected that in most cases where a consumer purchases goods expecting to receive them immediately, that immediate delivery will be essential in the circumstances.

Where the trader refuses to deliver the goods delivery of which within the initial timeframe was essential (either because the consumer told the trader that it was essential or this was implicit from the circumstances) then the consumer may treat the contract as at an end if the trader fails to meet the initial delivery period. The consumer does not have to give the trader a further opportunity to deliver in these circumstances.[51] Examples of goods for which delivery within the initial delivery period might be taken to be essential would include a wedding dress or birthday cake.

In cases other than those above, if the trader fails to deliver the goods on an agreed date or within the 30 days, under subs.(7), the consumer may state a further reasonable time frame, as the buyer did in the *Charles Rickard Ltd v Oppenhaim* case, within which the trader is required to deliver the goods. If the trader again fails to deliver the goods in this time frame the consumer may treat the contract as at an end.

3–55

The consumer may choose to reject some of the goods rather than treating the contract as at an end, or, where the goods have not been delivered, the consumer may cancel the order for some or all of those goods. For example, if goods are delivered after the periods required by this section, the consumer may wish to reject some of the goods but keep others, as some may no longer be of use to the consumer. If some goods are delivered on time but others are outstanding, the consumer may wish to cancel the order for some or all of the outstanding goods. This will not be possible where the goods form part of what is called, in subs.(12), a "commercial unit". An example might be a three piece suite. If say, the settee only is delivered on time the consumer cannot choose to keep it and reject the two matching chairs that should have accompanied it.[52]

3–56

As subs.(14) makes clear, the delivery rules in s.28 apply to a contract for sale of second hand goods that are sold at a public auction, if individuals can attend the auction sale in person. It will be recalled that most of the other provisions of this chapter of the 2015 Act do not apply to such auctions.

3–57

In some cases it may be appropriate to deliver the goods in instalments. This may only be done with the agreement of the consumer.[53] The rules in s.28 already discussed apply to delivery by instalment.

Digital content

Digital technologies have changed the way people go about their daily lives. In Great Britain, 22 million households (84 per cent) had internet access in 2014 and over three quarters of adults in Great Britain used the internet every day (76 per cent) in 2014, with almost seven out of every 10 adults (68 per cent) using a mobile phone, portable computer and/or handheld device to access the internet

3–58

---

[50] Consumer Rights Act 2015 s.28(6) and (7).
[51] Consumer Rights Act 2015 s.28(6)(b) and (c).
[52] Consumer Rights Act 2015 s.28(11).
[53] Consumer Rights Act 2015 s.26(1).

"on the go".[54] Access was used for various purposes such as buying goods and services, playing games and downloading software or music and films. Other appliances depend on digital technology such as mobile phones, DVD players, washing machines and car engines. Behind these devices are data or information products supplied in digital format as a stream of zeroes and ones readable by computers and other devices. These "digital products" comprise computer software, videos, films, music, games, ebooks and apps amongst others. They can be supplied by means of a physical device such as music on a CD, films on a DVD or software on a disc. In addition, software is frequently downloaded over the internet and it is common to stream music or films over the same medium.

3–59   As Professor Bradgate observed,

> "notwithstanding the growing importance of the digital economy and the products which comprise it, it is not clear what, if any, legal rights the purchaser of a digital product has if the product proves defective or fails to live up to expectations".[55]

He concluded that:

> "The lack of any clear rule governing digital products is itself a serious weakness in the law. That weakness is compounded by the fact that the different interpretations are to be found scattered through reported cases and articles in academic and practitioner journals. The law is therefore not clear, not accessible; not easily comprehensible; and, insofar as the different analyses involve the drawing of arbitrary distinctions, not rational."[56]

The 2015 Act goes a long way to rectify these deficiencies by largely implementing the recommendations of the Bradgate Report. Some of the reforms are discussed below where what is meant by what the 2015 Act calls "digital content" is explained and issues about the rights of consumers in relation to its acquisition are examined. In Ch.4 the terms relating to quality and some other issues are dealt with.

What is digital content?

3–60   Section 2(9) states that "'digital content' means data which are produced and supplied in digital form", a definition that is taken from the consumer rights Directive. Recital 19 of that Directive shows that a wide meaning was intended as it states that the definition covers

> "data which are produced and supplied in digital form, such as computer programs, applications, games, music, videos or texts, irrespective of whether they are accessed through downloading or streaming, from a tangible medium or through any other means".

---

[54] Office of National Statistics, Statistical Bulletin, *Internet Access—Households and Individuals 2014* available at: *http://www.ons.gov.uk/ons/dcp171778_373584.pdf* [Accessed 15 June 2015].
[55] R Bradgate, *Consumer Rights in Digital Products: A research report prepared for the UK Department for Business, Innovation and Skills* (2010) para.5.
[56] R Bradgate, *Consumer Rights in Digital Products: A research report prepared for the UK Department for Business, Innovation and Skills* (2010) para.173.

Chapter 3 of Pt 1 of the 2015 Act deals specifically with digital content. Like other parts of Pt 1 it applies to contracts between traders and consumers in three situations. The first is where there is agreement to pay for the content with money. The second is where digital content (which is not otherwise available free) is supplied free with goods, digital content or services for which the consumer has paid a price. This would cover free software given away with a paid-for magazine. In relation to both these forms of supply price includes payment by means of facilities for which money has been paid. This is intended to cover payment with virtual currency such as Bitcoins, tokens or vouchers. It does not apply merely because the trader supplies a service by which digital content reaches the consumer. This would cover facilities such as such as the film downloading site Netflix or the music streaming site Spotify.

Trader's right to supply digital content

Section 41 is the equivalent of s.17 which applies to contracts to supply goods. It is significantly different because contracts for the supply of digital content do not usually transfer ownership of any intellectual property rights to the digital content to the consumer who does not become the owner in the sense that a consumer purchasing goods under a contract of sale does. More commonly, the trader passes on a limited right to use the digital content in certain defined circumstances as ownership of any rights to the content usually remains with the originator of the digital content. The section therefore provides that there is a term that the trader has a right to supply the content or will have by the time it is to be supplied. This term cannot be excluded or restricted.[57]   **3–61**

If the trader does not have the right to supply the digital content, the consumer will be entitled to a refund.[58] A refund means the return of all money paid for the content, though where only part of the content is involved it is only that part to which a refund will apply. A refund must be given without undue delay, and in any event, within 14 days of the trader agreeing that a refund is appropriate. No fee can be charged for the refund, which must be made using the same means of payment as the consumer used to pay for the content unless they expressly agree otherwise. This would mean, for example, that the trader cannot force a consumer to accept a credit note or vouchers.   **3–62**

Other pre-contract information included in contract

Section 37 establishes that information mentioned in Schs 1 or 2 of the Consumer Contracts (Information, Cancellation and Additional Charges) Regulations 2013[59] that does not relate to the main characteristics of the goods also forms part of the contract between the trader and the consumer. This is information such as the   **3–63**

---

[57] R Bradgate, *Consumer Rights in Digital Products: A research report prepared for the UK Department for Business, Innovation and Skills* (2010) p.48.
[58] Consumer Rights Act 2015 s.43(5).
[59] Consumer Contracts (Information, Cancellation and Additional Charges) Regulations 2013 (SI 2013/3134).

identity and address of the trader, the price and delivery charges. If this information is not accurate the consumer may recover compensation as set out in s.43.

CHAPTER 4

Product Quality

The vast majority of consumer complaints about goods are concerned with their quality. Consumers expect what they buy to be free from defects. Should their expectations be disappointed what can they do about it? This chapter explores the standards of quality that consumers are entitled to expect, concentrating on goods that are defective but have not caused physical injury. In the next chapter the way in which consumers are protected against unsafe goods is discussed. It is mainly the civil law that is relevant in determining what the legal standard of quality is, but it should not be forgotten that the criminal law has some role to play as well. The core of the chapter is devoted to the statutory rights about quality to which consumers are entitled under the Consumer Rights Act 2015 (the 2015 Act). The final section deals with the role of criminal law in setting standards for products. 4–01

The claims made for a product by the seller may also be relevant to the level of quality that can be expected. If these claims have become terms of the contract the buyer is entitled to expect that they will be fulfilled and if they are not the normal contractual remedies will be available. If the claims are not regarded as terms it may be that they will be misrepresentations. These issues are discussed in Ch.11. 4–02

STATUTORY TERMS IN CONTRACTS TO SUPPLY GOODS

The linchpin of consumer protection in relation to quality has for decades been the statutory terms found in the various Sales of Goods Act starting in 1893 and most recently in the 1979 Act as amended. The 2015 Act continues this policy but no longer refers to such terms as "implied terms" though the result is the same. The relevant sections state that "every contract to supply goods is to be treated as including a term ... ". With the enactment of the 2015 Act these statutory terms are now applied to all the various contracts to supply goods to which Ch.2 of Pt 1 of the 2015 Act applies. These are: a sales contract; a contract for the hire of goods; a hire-purchase contract; and a contract for the transfer of goods. Where, previously, one had to consult several different Acts to discover the relevant rights they are now in one statute. 4–03

The implied term about description found in s.11 is not discussed at this point but in Ch.11. This is because the modern tendency, as pointed out in that chapter, is to reserve that term for matters relating to the identity of the goods, leaving 4–04 issues of quality to be decided under what is now s.9. However, there is sometimes a fine line to be drawn between these two things as *Beale v Taylor*[1] demonstrates.

4–05   It hardly requires to be stated that as contractual liability is involved it is the supplier who is liable under the various contracts and that only the other party to the contract may invoke the implied terms. Whether this privity principle should be altered has been under consideration and was recommended in a discussion paper issued by the Department of Trade and Industry and the EC Green Paper which preceded the Directive on Sale of Consumer Goods and Associated Guarantees.[2] The Directive did not include a provision on this point.

4–06   As was the case under previous legislation, liability is strict: fault is not relevant. This was pointed out in *Randall v Newsom*[3]:

> "If there was a defect in fact, even though that defect was one which no reasonable skill or care could discover, the persons supplying the article, should nevertheless be responsible, the policy of the law being that in a case in which neither were to blame, he, and not the person to whom they were supplied, should be liable for the defect."

4–07   *Frost v Aylesbury Dairy Co Ltd*[4] provides a good example of this principle in operation. The dairy had supplied Mr Frost and his family with milk that contained typhoid germs which caused the death of his wife. The evidence showed that the dairy's processes were extremely careful and that typhoid germs could only be detected by prolonged investigation. Nevertheless, it was held that there was an implied term that the milk would be reasonably fit for consumption. It was irrelevant that the defect could not have been discovered at the time of sale.

4–08   As was the case with the Sale of Goods Acts, the various terms about quality and fitness found in ss.9, 10, 13 and 16 comprise the full extent of consumers' rights in this respect. Only an express term can add to the level of protection[5] though a term about quality may be treated as included as a matter of custom.[6] In consumer contracts this is unlikely to be common.

4–09   A welcome innovation in the 2015 Act is the separation of the main quality terms. In the Sale of Goods Act 1979 (the 1979 Act) and its predecessors the same section contained two terms, one requiring goods to be of satisfactory quality and another that they be fit for a particular purpose. This was confusing and there are now two separate sections dealing with these terms.

The satisfactory quality term

4–10   Section 9(1) of the 2015 Act provides that every contract to supply goods is to be treated as including a term that the quality of the goods is satisfactory.

---

[1] *Beale v Taylor* [1967] 1 W.L.R. 1193.
[2] See Department of Trade and Industry, *Consumer Guarantees: A Consultation Document* (Department of Trade and Industry, 1992). Commission of the European Communities, *Green Paper on Consumer Guarantees and After Sales Service*, COM (93) 409.
[3] *Randall v Newsome* (1876) 44 L.W.B. 364.
[4] *Frost v Aylesbury Dairy Co Ltd* [1904] 1 K.B. 608.
[5] Consumer Rights Act 2015 s.18.
[6] Consumer Rights Act 2015 s.9(8).

The term "satisfactory quality" was first introduced on the recommendation of **4–11**
the Scottish Law Commission in its report, *Sale and Supply of Goods*,[7] in 1994.
Section 1 of the Sale and Supply of Goods Act 1994 inserted a new version of
s.14(2) of the 1979 Act containing the implied term of "satisfactory quality".
Further changes were necessary to implement the Directive on Certain Aspects of
the Sale of Consumer Goods and Associated Guarantees[8] and the opportunity was
also taken to use language that is appropriate to Scots law. Section 9 reproduces
s.14 with some minor changes so the existing case law is relevant.

Satisfactory quality

As was the case in the latter days of its predecessor, satisfactory quality is **4–12**
defined. Section 9(2) provides that

> "goods are of satisfactory quality if they meet the standard that a reasonable person
> would regard as satisfactory, taking account of any description of the goods, the
> price (if relevant) and all the other relevant circumstances".

"Relevant circumstances" include "any public statement about the specific
characteristics of the goods made by the trader, the producer or any representative
of the trader or the producer"[9] and this explicitly includes advertising and
labelling.[10]

Section 9(3) goes on to expand on this by saying that the quality of goods: **4–13**

> "[I]ncludes their state and condition and the following (among others) are in
> appropriate cases aspects of the quality of goods—
> (a)   fitness for all the purposes for which goods of the kind in question are
>   commonly supplied,
> (b)   appearance and finish,
> (c)   freedom from minor defects,
> (d)   safety, and
> (e)   durability."

Exceptions

Before looking at this definition in detail two qualifications must be noted. First, **4–14**
the term does not extend to any matter "which is specifically drawn to the buyer's
attention before the contract is made".[11] It is important to note that the factor
must be specifically brought to the buyer's attention. In *Turnock v Fortune*[12] it
was held by the sheriff principal that a strong recommendation from a third party

---

[7] Law Commission and Scottish Law Commission, *Report on Sale and Supply of Goods* (HMSO,
1987) (Law Com. No.160; Scot Law Com. No.104) Cm.137.
[8] Directive 1999/44 of the European Parliament and of the Council of 25 May 1999 on certain aspects
of the sale of consumer goods and associated guarantees [1999] O.J. L171/12.
[9] Consumer Rights Act 2015 s.9(5), which is qualified where the trader was not and could not
reasonably have been aware of the statement, it has been corrected or it could not have influenced the
consumer's decision.
[10] Consumer Rights Act 2015 s.9(6).
[11] Consumer Rights Act 2015 s.9(4)(a).
[12] *Turnock v Fortune*, 1989 S.L.T. (Sh. Ct.) 32t

not to buy a car did not amount to specifically drawing attention to its unroadworthiness, and thus did not prevent the car from being regarded as unmerchantable.

4–15   Secondly, if a buyer has examined the goods before the contract was made nothing which "that examination ought to reveal" can be relied on to demonstrate that the goods are not of satisfactory quality.[13] There has been some doubt about the interpretation of this proviso as a result of *Thornett & Fehr v Beers & Son*[14] where the slightly different wording of the 1893 Act was interpreted as if it read "a reasonable examination". A commercial buyer who had made a cursory examination of some glue was held to have lost the protection of this qualification despite the fact that his examination was insufficient to have detected the defect. That case may have been wrongly decided, as it seems to be inconsistent with an earlier Court of Appeal decision, *Bristol Tramways Carriage Co Ltd v Fiat Motors Ltd,*[15] which was not cited. In any event, the present wording is slightly different and would seem to support the view that it is only defects which the type of examination actually carried out should have revealed that are relevant.

The definition

4–16   The definition of satisfactory quality retains several elements of the previous definition of merchantable quality, but what is novel about it is that new factors are to be taken into account.[16] It is based on the recommendations of the law commissions. They suggested "acceptable quality", but like the Consumer Guarantees Bill 1990, the Act refers to "satisfactory quality". Moving the second reading of the Bill, its sponsor explained that it was thought that:

> "A non-complaining buyer might decide reluctantly that goods he bought were of acceptable quality, even if by objective standards the quality was not satisfactory".[17]

In practice this change probably does not matter very much. What is important is that, as the law commissions recommended, there is an objective test of quality and one that is given content by the list of factors that are to be taken into account in assessing what is satisfactory in a given case. It remains a standard that can be applied to all kinds of goods whether new or second-hand.

4–17   The definition of "satisfactory quality" is in two parts. The basic test appears in s.9(2) and states the general principle. The test is that of the reasonable person, and in deciding if the standard has been met, any description applied to the goods must be taken into account as well as the price, if that is relevant, and all other relevant circumstances. As already pointed out, the reference to "a reasonable person" implies an objective standard and this appears to be how the judges confronted by the definition have applied it, though they have generally not thought it necessary to spell this out. The reasonable person is "not an expert"[18]

---

[13] Consumer Rights Act 2015 s.9(4)(b).

[14] *Thornett & Fehr v Beers & Son* [1919] 1 K.B. 486.

[15] *Bristol Tramways Carriage Co Ltd v Fiat Motors Ltd* [1910] 2 K.B. 831.

[16] See WCH Ervine, "Satisfactory quality: what does it mean?", 2004 J.B.L. 684.

[17] *Hansard*, HC, Vol.237, Col.633 (11 February 1994).

[18] *Clegg v Andersson* [2003] 1 All E.R. (Comm) 721 per Hale LJ, [73].

and Sedley LJ observed in *Jewson Ltd v Boyhan*[19] that the "reasonable person" is "a construct by whose standards the judge is required to evaluate the quality of the goods". Who this reasonable person is will depend in part on the description of the product and he gives the homely example of a soft toy where the test will have to be applied by reference to how a toddler might handle it. The reasonable person, he notes, is not one "equipped with the buyer's personal agenda"[20] even if this has been communicated to the seller. In *Jewson* the buyer had sought to argue that it was relevant to take into account under satisfactory quality that he did not simply want central heating boilers but that he wanted boilers that would not have a detrimental effect on his business of property development in selling the flats. If this could be relevant at all it could only be relevant to the other implied term of fitness for purpose. In *Lamarra v Capital Bank Plc*[21] it was pointed out that in applying the test "these statutory provisions are not concerned with the reasonableness or unreasonableness of any party to the transaction". That was not relevant to assessing whether the goods were satisfactory, so the sheriff in that case had clearly erred in taking into account what she considered the unreasonable behaviour of the pursuer in refusing offers of repair.[22]

In *Bramhill v Edwards*[23] the English Court of Appeal approved the approach to the reasonable person adopted in the leading English textbook on sale where it is stated that:

> "... [T]he reasonable person must be one who is in the position of the buyer, with his knowledge; for it would not be appropriate for the test to be that of a reasonable third party observer not acquainted with the background of the transaction."[24]

This led them to hold that an imported motor caravan that did not conform to UK regulations was not of unsatisfactory quality because it was widely known amongst those who used such vehicles that the authorities turned a blind eye to this breach.

The factors of price, description and other relevant circumstances were set out in the earlier definition of "merchantable quality". A description may affect the standard that can be expected. If goods are described as "second-hand" then it will usually not be reasonable to expect the quality of new goods. On the other hand, statements in advertising material suggesting that the article is at the top end of the range might increase the standard of quality that it would be reasonable to expect. In *Clegg v Andersson*, Hale LJ pointed out that the buyer of a very expensive, brand new, ocean-going yacht is entitled to expect it to be "perfect or nearly so".[25] Similarly, price may be important, though it is an ambiguous signal. The price may be reduced simply to encourage faster sale of the item without implying any diminution in quality. Taken with other factors, such as a statement that the goods are "seconds", or the mileage and general condition of a second-hand car, it might well indicate that a lower standard of quality can be

4–18

4–19

[19] *Jewson Ltd v Boyhan* [2003] EWCA Civ. 1030, [78].
[20] *Jewson Ltd v Boyhan* [2003] EWCA Civ. 1030, [78].
[21] *Lamarra v Capital Bank Plc* [2006] CSIH 49; 2007 S.C. 94.
[22] *Lamarra v Capital Bank Plc* [2006] CSIH 49; 2007 S.C. 94, [73].
[23] *Bramhill v Edwards* [2004] EWCA Civ. 403; [2004] 2 Lloyd's Rep. 643.
[24] *Benjamin's Sale of Goods*, edited by AG Guest, 6th edn (London: Sweet & Maxwell, 2002), para.11–049.
[25] *Clegg v Andersson* [2003] 1 All E.R. (Comm) 721, [73].

expected. In *Thain v Anniesland Trade Centre*,[26] for example, stress was put on the price together with the fact that the car was second-hand, not new, and had a high mileage as factors that lowered the level of quality that could be expected. At the other end of the scale payment of a high price, as the observation of Hale LJ in the previous paragraph demonstrates, will raise the standard of quality that can be expected.

4–20   *Jewson* raises generally the question of what might constitute "other relevant circumstances" that may be taken into account in addition to price and description. Clarke LJ's observation that "a circumstance would be relevant if a reasonable person would regard it as relevant"[27] does not take matters very far. As we have just noted, Sedley LJ considered that the personal agenda of the buyer will not usually be relevant. However, he did note that the place of sale could be a relevant circumstance. He gave the example of a soft toy whose safety and durability would normally have to be judged in relation to how a toddler might handle it. If a toddler were to choke on it there might be a breach of the implied term of satisfactory quality while, if the victim were a dog, the only claim would be under s.10 as not being fit for a particular purpose. However, he suggested that the fact that the object had been bought in a pet shop might be a relevant circumstance allowing the claim to be brought under s.9 in relation to harm to the dog.

4–21   In *Britvic Soft Drinks Ltd v Messer UK Ltd*[28] the other "relevant circumstance" appears to have been the commercial context of the problem and expected consumer reactions. The defendants sold carbon dioxide to the claimants who, as the defendants knew, intended to use it in the production of their alcoholic and soft drinks. The carbon dioxide was contaminated by benzene, a carcinogen, though not in quantities that posed any threat to health. The level of contamination was substantially higher than the maximum acceptable statutory limits subsequently agreed and at a level which led the seller, in consultation with the manufacturer from whom it had obtained the supplies, to issue immediate warnings to customers. Both the seller and the claimants were mindful of the catastrophic commercial repercussions on Perrier which had resulted from the poor handling of a contamination problem. As a result the claimants had recalled supplies of drinks thought to have been contaminated and their claim was for the losses flowing from this course of action.

4–22   The trial judge found:

> "[I]t impossible to conclude that a reasonable person would regard the CO_2 supplied as meeting a satisfactory standard. Consumers would not wish to drink products which had inadvertently been contaminated with a measurable quantity of a known carcinogen, notwithstanding the quantity was not harmful to their health... The affected products themselves were in a real sense unsaleable in the sense that no consumer would knowingly buy them and the manufacturers could not as responsible manufacturers be seen to attempt to sell them."[29]

---

[26] *Thain v Anniesland Trade Centre*, 1997 S.L.T. (Sh. Ct.) 102.

[27] *Clegg v Andersson* [2003] 1 All E.R. (Comm) 721, [67].

[28] *Britvic Soft Drinks Ltd v Messer UK Ltd* [2002] EWCA Civ. 448; [2002] 2 All E.R. (Comm) 321.

[29] *Britvic Soft Drinks Ltd v Messer UK Ltd* [2002] 1 Lloyd's Rep. 20, [92].

In coming to this conclusion Tomlinson J was applying the general definition and, in part, specifically referring to one of the factors, description, as the carbon dioxide had been described as suitable for food applications. However, this does also seem to be an example of taking into account "other relevant circumstances" in the form of consumer reactions.[30]

In *Lamarra v Capital Bank Plc*[31] an Extra Division of the Court of Session held that a manufacturer's warranty given with a new car could not be taken into account as a "relevant circumstance". Their Lordships pointed out that: 4–23

> "While the words 'all the other relevant circumstances' are potentially of wide scope, we consider that, in the context, they must be seen as referring only to circumstances actually bearing upon the quality of the goods in question. After all, [the relevant subsections] are concerned with that very matter. In our view, a warranty cannot be seen as a matter bearing upon the quality of the goods supplied. In its nature, a warranty can only be seen as an undertaking by the manufacturer of the goods concerned to remedy defects in the goods which emerge and are within the scope of the warranty and that within a specified period of time. Thus the warranty must be seen as a means whereby the defects in existence at the time of delivery, or emerging thereafter within the specified period, may later be remedied by the manufacturer at no cost to the customer. The fact that such defects may be so remedied appears to us not to bear upon the issue of the quality of the goods at the time of their delivery, which is the subject matter of the implied term... In its nature, a warranty is concerned with the provision of remedial action within a limited period after delivery. In short, it seems to us that, because the issue of whether the quality of the goods is satisfactory requires to be judged as at the time of delivery, the warranty can have no bearing upon that matter."[32]

They were fortified in this view by reference to the English Court of Appeal decision in *Rogers v Parish (Scarborough) Ltd*[33] and pointed out that the earlier Inner House decision in *Millars of Falkirk Ltd v Turpie* which might appear to support a different view was decided under different legislation and, in any event, the point was not the subject of argument in the case.

In addition to the basic principle, s.9(3) sets out a list of specific factors which, *in appropriate cases*, may be taken into account in assessing satisfactory quality. The words emphasised in the last sentence make it clear that not all the factors would be relevant in every case; and it is also stated that the list of factors is not exhaustive. 4–24

The first factor is that the goods are fit for all the purposes for which goods of the kind in question are usually supplied. The placing of this aspect of quality is significant. As the Law Commissions noted in their report, this is almost always a very important aspect of quality, but the drafting of the previous definition had over-stressed it. In several decisions usability had been the touchstone and the fact that there were defects affecting the appearance of the product were not 4–25

---

[30] The finding that the product was not of satisfactory quality was not challenged on appeal but comments in the judgments of the Court of Appeal suggest that it agreed with these observations: see *Britvic Soft Drinks Ltd v Messer UK Ltd* [2002] 2 Lloyd's Rep. 368, per Mance LJ at [11].

[31] *Lamarra v Capital Bank Plc* [2006] CSIH 49; 2007 S.C. 94. The case involved a hire-purchase transaction but it turned on the issue of satisfactory quality which is defined by the relevant legislation, the Supply of Goods (Implied Terms) Act 1973 in the same terms as in the Sale of Goods Act 1979.

[32] *Lamarra v Capital Bank Plc* [2006] CSIH 49; 2007 S.C. 94, [62].

[33] *Rogers v Parish (Scarborough) Ltd* [1987] Q.B. 933.

considered to be relevant.[34] In addition, the earlier definition had spoken of goods being fit for the purpose or purposes as "it is reasonable to expect". This, it can be argued, had lowered the standard of quality where the seller could establish that goods of the particular type, such as new cars, can reasonably be expected to possess a number of minor defects on delivery. *Millars of Falkirk Ltd v Turpie*[35] can be used in support of this argument.

4–26   The new definition diminishes the importance of fitness for purpose by including it in the list of factors which may be taken into account. As the law commissions' report pointed out,[36] a new car should not only be capable of being driven safely and effectively on the roads, but should also do so "with the appropriate degree of comfort, ease of handling and reliability and ... of pride in the vehicle's outward and interior appearance", to quote Mustill LJ in *Rogers v Parish (Scarborough) Ltd*.[37]

4–27   It goes further and reverses the previous law under which the test was satisfied if the goods were fit for any of the purposes for which goods of that type could be used.[38] The new version provides that goods must be suitable for "all the purposes for which goods of the kind in question are usually supplied". If goods have more than one purpose and the seller intends his product to fulfil only one of those purposes it will be necessary to make this clear. This may be done explicitly or, in some circumstances, other factors such as the price may indicate this fact.

4–28   This factor has only been explicitly discussed in *Jewson Ltd v Boyhan*.[39] This case raised the question, to quote Clarke LJ,

> "as to how far it is appropriate to have regard to the purposes for which goods are wanted by the purchaser in deciding what circumstances are relevant for the purposes of [what are now s.9(2) and (3)]",[40]

as opposed to what is now s.10. The buyer was a property developer who purchased a number of electric central heating boilers for installation in flats that he was constructing. He discovered that these boilers had poor energy ratings according to government approved tests and feared that the flats would be difficult or impossible to sell. This caused him to abandon the project and when Jewsons sued him for the price of the boilers he counterclaimed for several hundred thousand pounds based on his loss of profit and increased costs resulting from the installation of the boilers, as opposed to boilers with better energy ratings. He attempted to argue that among the purposes for which the boilers had to be fit was ensuring that they would not render the flats in which they were to be installed difficult or impossible to sell. In effect, the Court of Appeal did not accept that this was one of "the purposes for which goods of the kind in question are commonly supplied". Clarke LJ recognised that there is scope for debate about which purposes are relevant but went on to suggest the following test:

---

[34] More recent cases such as *Rogers v Parish (Scarborough) Ltd* [1987] Q.B. 933 have suggested a more realistic approach to fitness at least in relation to consumer goods.

[35] *Millars of Falkirk Ltd v Turpie*, 1976 S.L.T. (Notes) 66.

[36] Law Commission and Scottish Law Commission, *Report on Sale and Supply of Goods* (The Stationary Office, 1987) Cm.137, para.3–31.

[37] *Rogers v Parish (Scarborough) Ltd* [1987] Q.B. 933.

[38] *M/S Aswan Engineering Establishment Co v Lupdine Ltd* [1987] 1 W.L.R. 1.

[39] *Jewson Ltd v Boyhan* [2003] EWCA Civ. 1030.

[40] *Jewson Ltd v Boyhan* [2003] EWCA Civ. 1030, [69].

"There may be exceptions, but in general a particular purpose which is not one of the ordinary uses for which goods of the relevant type are generally supplied seems to me to be irrelevant. The question in most cases will be whether the goods are intrinsically satisfactory and fit for all purposes for which goods of the kind in question are supplied."[41]

He conceded that "some regard must be had to the use which is likely to be made of the goods"[42] but that would only extend in this case to saying that they had to be of satisfactory quality for use in flats, which they were. As Sedley LJ succinctly put it, "[the buyer] got exactly what he had bargained for: twelve boilers which worked perfectly well".[43]   **4–29**

Appearance and finish, and freedom from minor defects are also to be taken into account in determining whether goods are of satisfactory quality. These characteristics are more likely to apply to new rather than second-hand goods. A major uncertainty of the old law is thus removed.[44] The result is, to quote the law commissions' report, that: **4–30**

"Dents, scratches, minor blemishes and discolorations, and small malfunctions will in appropriate cases be breaches of the implied term as to quality, provided they are not so trifling as to fall within the principle that matters which are quite negligible are not breaches of contract at all."[45]

The importance of this aspect of the definition was highlighted in *Lamarra v Capital Bank Plc* by an Extra Division of the Court of Session in agreeing with the decision of the sheriff principal to allow an appeal against a decision of a sheriff who appears to have regarded minor defects and defects in the paintwork of a car as of no real significance.[46]

The regrettable decision in *Millars of Falkirk Ltd v Turpie*[47] is thus reversed and, if similar facts were to recur, it seems certain that the car would be regarded as of unsatisfactory quality. The application of this test will, of course, depend on the facts. Second-hand goods may be expected to have some minor marks or defects while, usually, new goods should not. Hale LJ pointed out obiter in *Clegg v Andersson*, a consumer case, that: **4–31**

"In some cases, such as a high priced quality product, the customer may be entitled to expect that it is free from even minor defects, in other words perfect or nearly so."[48]

However, certain kinds of product such as earthenware, pottery or natural products may be expected to have minor inconsistencies and blemishes and these

---

[41] *Jewson Ltd v Boyhan* [2003] EWCA Civ. 1030, [69].
[42] *Jewson Ltd v Boyhan* [2003] EWCA Civ. 1030, [70].
[43] *Jewson Ltd v Boyhan* [2003] EWCA Civ. 1030, [79].
[44] In *Bernstein v Pamson Motors (Golders Green) Ltd* [1987] 2 All E.R. 220 certain obiter remarks suggested that minor defects were not relevant to merchantability, while *Rogers v Parish (Scarborough) Ltd* [1987] Q.B. 933 considered that they were.
[45] *Report on Sale and Supply of Goods* (1987) Cm.137, para.3–40.
[46] *Lamarra v Capital Bank Plc* [2006] CSIH 49; 2007 S.C. 94, [69].
[47] *Millars of Falkirk Ltd v Turpie*, 1976 S.L.T. (Notes) 66.
[48] *Clegg v Andersson* [2003] 1 All E.R. (Comm) 721; [2003] EWCA Civ. 320; [2003] 2 Lloyd's Rep. 32, [72].

may well not render them of unsatisfactory quality. In some cases this test will have no application at all. The Law Commissions gave as examples cars sold as scrap and loads of manure.

4–32   There has never been any doubt that unsafe goods were not of the quality demanded by law[49] and this is explicitly recognised in the definition. The law commissions argued that this was necessary, despite the clarity of the existing law, for several reasons. It might make clear that hazardous products which can be used safely only if unusual precautions are taken or warnings given will not meet the standard of satisfactory quality unless those warnings are given; it would rebut the argument that safety was not relevant because it has not been included in the statute; and to omit a reference would be odd since safety is such an important part of the quality of modern consumer goods.[50] Safety was the central factor in *Clegg v Andersson*.[51] A new ocean-going yacht costing £250,000 was delivered to the buyer with a keel that was substantially heavier than the manufacturer's specification. Technical evidence showed that this would render the rigging unsafe and, in the circumstances, the Court of Appeal had no difficulty in finding that the yacht did not meet the standard of satisfactory quality.[52]

4–33   Somewhat less clear was whether goods had to be durable, though this does appear to have been the law.[53] The matter is now put beyond doubt by the new definition. It is important to realise that this term is to be satisfied at the time of delivery and not at some later date. Later events may be relevant in determining whether, at the time of sale, the goods were durable.[54] The criterion is durability not duration. The law commissions rejected any suggestion that normal lifespan for classes of goods should in some way be required. They emphasised, and this is reflected in the new definition, that durability is to be a flexible concept requiring that goods should last a reasonable time taking into account whether they have been well or badly treated.

4–34   The first case to discuss the new satisfactory quality term was *Thain v Anniesland Trade Centre*[55] a decision of the Sheriff Principal of Glasgow and Strathkelvin. Ms Thain had paid £2,995 for a second-hand Renault 19 car that had travelled about 80,000 miles and was about six years old. Two weeks after she purchased it an intermittent droning noise was noticed and this proved to be a failing differential bearing in the automatic gear box. The sellers refused to replace the gear box. Eventually, after about nine to 10 weeks, the car was unusable and Ms Thain rejected it. The sheriff principal upheld the sheriff's decision that the car was of satisfactory quality observing:

> "The sheriff's conclusion can only be described as that of the reasonable person. Even a negligible degree of durability may not represent unsatisfactory quality where the secondhand car supplied is as old and as heavily used as the Renault had been. The plain fact is that, given the Renault's age and mileage when supplied, its

[49] *Godley v Perry* [1960] 1 W.L.R. 9 CA; *Lambert v Lewis* [1982] A.C. 224.
[50] *Report on Sale and Supply of Goods* (1987) Cm.137, para.3–44.
[51] *Clegg v Andersson* [2003] 1 All E.R. (Comm) 721; [2003] EWCA Civ. 320; [2003] 2 Lloyd's Rep. 32.
[52] *Clegg v Andersson* [2003] 1 All E.R. (Comm) 721, [49] and [73].
[53] For a survey, see WCH Ervine, "Durability, Consumers and the Sale of Goods Act", 1984 J.R. 147.
[54] *Crowther v Shannon Motor Co Ltd* [1974] 1 W.L.R. 30.
[55] *Thain v Anniesland Trade Centre*, 1997 S.L.T. (Sh. Ct.) 102; 1997 S.C.L.R. 991.

durability was a matter of luck. Durability, in all the circumstances, was simply not a quality that a reasonable person would demand of it."[56]

One can only marvel at this view of reasonableness and ask how many car buyers would think it reasonable that they should take all the risk of a catastrophic breakdown almost immediately after purchase. The decision appears to make a mockery of the express inclusion of durability as one of the factors to be taken into account in assessing satisfactory quality. Perhaps emphasis should be placed on the fact that this case turns on its own somewhat special facts. There was evidence from Ms Thain's own expert witness that there was no sign of a problem during the first two weeks that she drove the car and that the part which failed could work well and suddenly deteriorate. Given that nine to 10 weeks was regarded as reasonable durability the problem of when the test has to be satisfied never arose. It is sometimes said that this is the date of the contract, at which point in this case there was no evidence of a defect. That could have been circumvented, as was done by Lord Denning in *Crowther v Shannon Motor Co*,[57] by using the fact of a short lifespan as evidence that the car did not meet the statutory standard at the date of the contract.[58]

4-35

Where it is possible to show that the goods were unsatisfactory because they were not durable the benefits of including durability in the definition of satisfactory quality will not be as great as one might expect. This stems from the fact that while a lack of durability will render goods unsatisfactory, the remedies open to the consumer may be limited. By the time a consumer realises that the goods are not durable it is very likely that the short term right to reject will have been lost and damages will, therefore, be the only remedy in most of the cases where goods prove not to be durable.[59] As we will see below there is a final right to reject that is not lost in the way that the short term right is. However, it is not the consumer's primary right and any reimbursement can be subject to a reduction to take account of the use that the consumer has enjoyed.

4-36

Fitness for purpose term

As well as being of satisfactory quality, s.10 of the 2015 Act adds a term that goods are reasonably fit for any particular purpose for which the consumer is buying the goods and which they have made known to the trader or a credit-broker either expressly or by implication. It does not matter that the purpose is one for which goods of that kind are usually supplied. The term does not apply if the circumstances show that the consumer did not rely, or was unreasonable for the consumer to rely, on the skill or judgment of the trader or credit-broker.

4-37

The reference to a credit-broker is necessary to take account of certain kinds of sales financed by a third party. The credit-broker will often be a retailer in whose shop the goods have been displayed and in which negotiations for their purchase

4-38

---

[56] *Thain v Anniesland Trade Centre*, 1997 S.L.T. (Sh. Ct.) 102 at 106.
[57] *Crowther v Shannon Motor Co* [1974] 1 W.L.R. 30.
[58] See WCH Ervine, "Satisfactory Quality, Thain v Anniesland Trade Centre", 1998 J.R. 379.
[59] In *Thain v Anniesland Trade Centre* the possibility that the right to reject had been lost was not discussed.

have taken place. If the retailer does not provide their own credit facilities what next happens is that the goods are sold to a finance company who then sells to the consumer. Examples of transactions that would be covered would be credit sale and conditional sale.

4–39   There is considerable overlap between this term and the satisfactory quality term, as satisfactory quality is partially defined in terms of fitness for purpose. There will be many situations where a product will fail to satisfy either term. The weed-killer in *Wormell v RHM Agricultural (East) Ltd*,[60] which had inadequate instructions, and the defective car in *Rogers v Parish (Scarborough) Ltd*[61] are examples. However, there are circumstances where a product might be of satisfactory quality but not pass the test of fitness for purpose. Suppose that someone has a metal gate that is to be painted. She goes to a DIY store and explains to an assistant that paint suitable for the job is required. The paint which the assistant sells her turns out to be unsuitable, being intended only for application to wood. In this case the customer will succeed in a claim under s.10 for breach of the implied term about fitness for purpose. She would not succeed with a claim for unsatisfactory quality because there is nothing wrong with the paint which would be perfectly satisfactory for painting wood.

4–40   The relationship between the two implied terms has been explored in two cases. In *Clegg v Andersson* Hale LJ observed:

> "The amendments made to s.14 [now the 2015 Act s.9] by the Sale and Supply of Goods Act 1994 also make it clear that fitness for purpose and satisfactory quality are two quite different concepts."[62]

It is true that there will be circumstances in which both implied terms are broken but there is a tendency to mark out more clearly the scope of each and this is explored in *Jewson Ltd v Boyham*.[63] There, Sedley LJ pointed out:

> "Section 14(2) [now s.9] is directed principally to the sale of substandard goods. This means that the court's principal concern is to look at their intrinsic quality, using the tests indicated in subsection (2A), (2B) and (2C) [now 9(2) and (3)]."[64]

He went on to point out that where it was sought to introduce "factors peculiar to the purposes of the particular buyer", that had to be done under s.14(3) [now s.10].[65] In the same case Clarke LJ stated,

> "it seems to me that under the statutory scheme set out in section 14 [now ss.9 and 10] it is the function of section 14(3) [now s.10] , not section 14(2) [now s.9], to impose a particular obligation tailored to the particular circumstances of the case".[66]

---

[60] *Wormell v RHM Agricultural (East) Ltd* [1986] 1 All E.R. 769.
[61] *Rogers v Parish (Scarbrough) Ltd* [1987] Q.B. 933.
[62] *Clegg v Andersson* [2003] 1 All E.R. (Comm) 721 at [72]; [2003] EWCA Civ. 320; [2003] 2 Lloyd's Rep. 32.
[63] *Jewson Ltd v Boyhan* [2003] EWCA Civ. 1030.
[64] *Jewson Ltd v Boyhan* [2003] EWCA Civ. 1030, [77].
[65] *Jewson Ltd v Boyhan* [2003] EWCA Civ. 1030, [77].
[66] *Jewson Ltd v Boyhan* [2003] EWCA Civ. 1030, [47].

To avail oneself of the protection of this term it is necessary to show that one **4-41** has, either expressly or by implication, indicated the particular purpose for which the goods are required. As Lord Wilberforce observed of both the implied terms, they are

> "readily and untechnically applied to all sorts of informal situations—such as retail sales over the counter of articles whose purpose is well known—and are applied rather more strictly to large scale transactions carried through by written contracts".[67]

In many cases it will not be necessary for the customer to have referred expressly to the particular purpose. The burden of proof is on the seller to show that reliance was unreasonable, as was pointed out in *Grant v Australian Knitting Mills Ltd*.[68]

> "The reliance will seldom be express: it will usually arise by implication from the circumstances. Thus to take a case like that in question, of a purchase from a retailer, the reliance will be in general inferred from the fact that a buyer goes to the shop in the confidence that the tradesman has selected his stock with skill and judgement: ... the main inducement to deal with a good retail shop is the expectation that the tradesman will have bought the right goods of a good make."

This quotation is redolent of an earlier age before the rise of modern retail **4-42** methods. Nevertheless, if the customer relies on the staff of a store it will be difficult for it to assert that this was unreasonable, unless it had been made quite plain that they had no specialised knowledge.[69] As this case makes clear, it is not necessary to specify a particular purpose where the goods, such as underpants or hot water bottles,[70] have only one purpose.

If the customer does have a particular purpose in mind that is not the usual **4-43** purpose or has some susceptibility, this must be communicated to the seller. *Baldry v Marshall*,[71] where the customer required a car which would be comfortable and suitable for touring, is an example of the first issue; and *Griffiths v Peter Conway Ltd*[72] an example of the second. In the latter case the plaintiff had developed a very severe attack of dermatitis as a result of wearing a tweed coat purchased from the defendants. Mrs Griffiths' skin was unusually sensitive and the evidence showed that there was nothing in the cloth that would have affected a normal person's skin. As Mrs Griffiths had not informed the sellers of her sensitivity they were not liable.

Flynn v Scott[73] makes clear that the particular purpose must be clearly **4-44** specified. There, the subject of the sale was a lorry which could have been used for a number of different functions, though the buyer intended to use it to

---

[67] *Henry Kendall & Sons v William Lillico & Sons* [1969] 2 A.C. 31 at 123.
[68] *Grant v Australian Knitting Mills Ltd* [1936] A.C. 84 at 99.
[69] A parallel might be drawn with the cases on services where the tradesman having done a poor job tried to assert that he did not have the specialised skill for the particular job. See cases discussed at para.6–11 onwards.
[70] See *Priest v Last* [1903] 2 K.B. 148.
[71] *Baldry v Marshall* [1924] K.B. 260.
[72] *Griffiths v Peter Conway Ltd* [1939] 1 All E.R. 684, approved in *Slater v Finning Ltd*, 1996 S.L.T. 912; [1996] 3 All E.R. 398 HL.
[73] *Flynn v Scott*, 1949 S.C. 442; 1949 S.L.T. 399.

transport furniture and livestock. A claim for breach of the implied term of fitness for purpose failed because it was not shown that the buyer had communicated his particular purpose.

Sale by sample

4–45 There are certain products that are commonly sold by reference to a sample. When buying carpets or curtains one usually looks at swatches of material to make a choice. Section 13 of the 2015 Act states that in such circumstances there is a term that the goods ultimately supplied will match the sample except to the extent that any differences between the sample and the goods are brought to the consumer's attention before the contract is made. In addition, there is a term that the goods will be free from any defect that makes their quality unsatisfactory and that would not be apparent on a reasonable examination of the sample.

Sale by model

4–46 It is quite common to view goods on display in a shop and decide on a product to buy after examining the displayed item but to receive a boxed version brought from a store room. As noted in *Atiyah's Sale of Goods*[74] this is not a sale by sample and ought to be covered by a separate term.[75] What one has inspected is the whole product not a part of it, so the terminology of sample is inappropriate. This gap has been filled by s.14 of the 2015 Act which provides that where goods have been supplied by reference to a model there is a

> "term that the goods will match the model except to the extent that any differences between the model and the goods are brought to the consumer's attention before the consumer enters into the contract".

REMEDIES

4–47 A major achievement of the 2015 Act is the clarification of the remedies available to consumers when goods do not meet the standards that they are entitled to expect under the legislation. In setting out the scheme of remedies it was necessary to implement the requirements of the EC Directive on Certain Aspects of the Sale of Consumer Goods and Associated Guarantees[76] but also preserve rejection of goods as the primary remedy. Under the Directive the primary remedies are repair or replacement whereas under UK Sale of Goods Acts rejection, that is the right to return the goods to the seller and obtain a refund of the price, was the primary remedy. There were problems with the implementation of this remedy that were particularly relevant to consumer transactions and these

---

[74] PS Atiyah, Prof J Adams, Prof H MacQueen, *Atiyah's Sale of Goods*, 12th edn (London: Longman, 2010).

[75] PS Atiyah, Prof J Adams, Prof H MacQueen, *Atiyah's Sale of Goods*, 12th edn (London: Longman, 2010) p.207.

[76] Directive 1999/44 of the European Parliament and of the Council of 25 May 1999 on certain aspects of the sale of consumer goods and associated guarantees [1999] O.J. L171/12.

too are addressed in the new legislation. There is now one set of remedies that apply to the various types of contracts dealing with the supply of goods covered by Chs 1 and 2 of Pt 1 of the 2015 Act.

The structure of this part of the 2015 Act is to state that where goods "do not conform to the contract" certain remedies are available. "Conforming to a contract" means meeting the various terms that the Act includes in contracts such as the terms about satisfactory quality and fitness for purpose. In addition, it also includes failure by the trader to install goods properly; and, if the goods include digital content, the failure of the digital content to meet its quality standards. In the limited range of situations where the consumer supplies some of the goods for the final product it will not fail to conform if the failure has its origin in the materials supplied by the consumer.[77]

4–48

The point at which goods must conform is the date of delivery and this has sometimes proved to be a problem for consumers. Section 19(14) is of assistance in that it provides that

4–49

> "goods which do not conform to the contract at any time within the period of six months starting with the date on which the goods were delivered to the buyer must be taken not to have so conformed at that date".

The next subsection disapplies this rule if the seller can show that the goods did in fact conform during that period, or the rule is incompatible with the nature of the goods or the nature of the lack of conformity. To take an extreme example of the application of the new regime, a consumer will get nowhere by arguing that fresh fruit is defective because they can show that a month after purchase it has gone mouldy. On the other hand, this provision could be very useful where the product in question is a consumer durable such as a car, a freezer or a computer. It is debatable how great an innovation this is when one recalls the approach of Lord Denning in *Crowther v Shannon Motor Co*,[78] where he found that the emergence of a defect some weeks after purchase indicated that the product had not conformed to the contract at the time of sale.

The remedies set out comprise the full set of remedies available to consumers. This is clear from s.19(12) which states that it is "not open to the consumer to treat the contract as at an end for breach" of the various terms set out in this part of the Act. This overrides any common law right to terminate the contract for breach of the terms that the 2015 Act requires to be treated as included in the contract. The main remedies available are:

4–50

- the short term right to reject;
- the right to repair or replacement; and
- the right to a price reduction or the final right to reject.[79]

Where a consumer seeks one of these remedies s.59 enables a court to order a different one. Section 19 recognises that in addition to, or in place of, these

---

[77] Consumer Rights Act 2015 s.19(2).
[78] *Crowther v Shannon Motor Co* [1974] 1 W.L.R. 30.
[79] Consumer Rights Act 2015 s.19(3).

remedies a consumer may wish to invoke certain other remedies such as damages[80] and these are discussed below.

The short term right to reject

4–51   The 2015 Act preserves, under the title of the short term right to reject, the long-standing primary remedy of consumers who find themselves with substandard goods. Rejection is a right, as s.20(4) puts it, which "entitles the consumer to reject the goods and treat the contract as at an end". In its nature it is a powerful remedy in the armoury of consumers. However, before the 2015 Act, its operation was surrounded by a number of difficulties one of the most conspicuous of which was that it was lost after the "lapse of a reasonable time". The 2015 Act gets round this by providing that the right can only be exercised for 30 days, a period which cannot be shortened even by agreement.[81] The 30 day period is a compromise. It gives consumers (and traders) a clear rule that is easy to apply. On the other hand it is, arguably, a reduction in the level of consumer protection as, under the old law, longer periods were considered reasonable. It also makes no allowance for special situations where there is no realistic chance of detecting a fault in the goods. For example, if a consumer buys a lawnmower in an end of season sale it is obvious that the machine will not be used for three or four months. The Law Commissions recommended that provision should be made for such situations but this was rejected by the Government.[82]

4–52   While the 30 day period cannot be shortened by agreement, there are two situations where it can be varied. If the goods are of a kind, such as fresh food, that can reasonably be expected to perish after a shorter period, the time limit for exercising the short-term right to reject in relation to those goods is the end of that shorter period.[83] On the other hand the 30 day limit will be extended if the consumer requests or agrees to a repair or replacement.[84] In many cases what the consumer wants is not money back but a fault-free product and will be prepared to accept such a solution. To encourage this approach the 2015 Act provides that the 30 day period is extended to the later of seven days after "the waiting period" or the original end of the 30 day period plus the waiting period.[85] The "waiting period" starts with the day on which the consumer requests or agrees to the repair or replacement of the goods and ends with the day on which they receive the repaired or replacement goods.[86]

The short term right to reject is not available where the non-conformity is caused by faulty installation. In this case the remedies are repair or replacement or price reduction or the final right to reject.[87]

4–53   A helpful aspect of the 2015 Act is the detailed regime for dealing with the rejection of goods. Prior to s.20 of the 2015 Act there were a number of aspects of

---

[80]   Consumer Rights Act 2015 s.19(9)–(11).
[81]   Consumer Rights Act 2015 s.22(2).
[82]   Law Commission and Scottish Law *Consumer Remedies for Faulty Goods* Commission (Law Com. No.317; Scot Law Com. No.216, November 2009) Cm.7725 para.3.88.
[83]   Consumer Rights Act 2015 s.22(4).
[84]   Consumer Rights Act 2015 s.22(6).
[85]   Consumer Rights Act 2015 s.22(7).
[86]   Consumer Rights Act 2015 s.22(9).
[87]   Consumer Rights Act 2015 s.19(4).

rejection which were not at all clear. Section 20 provides that to reject goods all that a consumer has to do is to indicate to the trader that they are rejecting the goods and treating the contract as at an end. This indication can be something that the consumer says or does and, as long as it is clear enough to be understood by the trader it will be effective.[88] Few consumers are likely to formally say that they are rejecting the goods but they might well say that they are not satisfied with the product and want their money back and this will be enough.

Once the consumer has indicated that the goods are being rejected the trader has a duty to give the consumer a refund where money or something else has been given in exchange for the goods.[89] With cash sales this is straightforward and the consumer should be given the same amount of money. Money will not always have been used to pay for the goods. For example, one item may have been exchanged for another or the goods may have been obtained using tokens which the consumer collected as part of a promotion. In these situations the consumer is not entitled to money back but the "refund" would be a return of whatever the consumer gave in exchange for the goods.[90] If this cannot be returned to the consumer due to the nature of the exchange, then the consumer may not demand a refund but may pursue a damages claim.[91] In the case of hire the refund extends only to the anything paid or transferred for a period of hire that the consumer did not get because the contract was terminated by rejection. Hire-purchase and conditional sales agreements also require slightly different treatment. Here, rejection will take place at some stage before all the instalments have been paid so the refund is only of the payments made. **4–54**

The refund must be given without undue delay and, in any event, within 14 days starting with the day on which the trader agrees that the consumer is entitled to the refund. Where it involves money it must be given using the same means of payment as the consumer used unless the consumer expressly agrees. For example, if the consumer paid cash they must receive cash not a credit note or vouchers; if they paid by credit card it would be appropriate to arrange the repayment through the credit card system. It is impermissible for the trader to impose any fee on the consumer for making the refund.[92] **4–55**

The consumer does not have to return goods that they have rejected unless there is an agreement to do so. However, consumers must make the goods available for collection by the trader. Whether or not the consumer has a duty to return the rejected goods, the trader must bear any reasonable costs of returning them, other than any costs incurred in returning the goods in person to the place where the consumer took physical possession of them.[93] **4–56**

In some cases only some of the goods may be faulty, or as the 2015 Act puts it, do not conform to the contract. Suppose a consumer buys several bags of potatoes and finds that those in one bag are rotten but those in the other bags are in good condition. They could reject all the goods but s.21 provides another option. The **4–57**

---

[88] Consumer Rights Act 2015 s.20(5) and (6).
[89] Consumer Rights Act 2015 s.20(18).
[90] Consumer Rights Act 2015 s.20(11) and (12).
[91] Consumer Rights Act 2015 s.20(19).
[92] Consumer Rights Act 2015 s.20(17). This reflects the decision of the ECJ in *Quelle AG v Bundesverband der Verbraucherzentralen und Verbraucherverbande* (C-404/06) [2008] E.C.R. I-2685.
[93] Consumer Rights Act 2015 s.20(8).

consumer may reject some or all of the goods that do not conform but may not reject any that do. Similarly, if the goods are being sold in instalments and some of the goods in one instalment are defective they may choose to reject some or all of the non-conforming goods though all the goods that do conform must be retained. However, this does not apply where the goods form what is called a "commercial unit". This is where division of the unit would materially impair the value of the goods or the character of the unit. For example, a set of golf clubs would probably constitute a commercial unit. If one of the irons was damaged the consumer could reject the whole set but could not choose to reject the defective iron and keep the rest of the set. The same provisions about the exercise of the right to reject partially as apply to rejection under s.20 are set out in s.21.

Repair or replacement

4–58   The remedy of repair or replacement is dealt with in detail in s.23. Subsection (2) provides that if the buyer requires the seller to repair or replace the goods, the seller must carry out the buyer's preferred option "within a reasonable time but without causing significant inconvenience to the consumer". What amounts to a reasonable time or significant inconvenience is, subs.(5) says, to be determined by reference to the nature of the goods and the purpose for which they were acquired. If the problem is a defective light bulb in a new car, instant repair might reasonably be expected whereas if the problem was the failure of some more complex mechanical part that might have to be ordered from the manufacturer, a longer time would be reasonable. If the defective product was, say, a wedding dress or video camera intended to film the wedding, the reference to the purpose for which the product was required might indicate that replacement should take priority over repair if repair could not be effected in time for the event. In addition, the seller must "bear any necessary costs incurred in [repair or replacement] (including in particular the cost of any labour, materials or postage)".[94]

4–59   However, the buyer cannot require the seller to carry out one of these remedies if it is not possible to do so or if the cost of doing so would be "disproportionate" either to carrying out the other remedy, offering a price reduction or rescinding the contract. Subsection (4) offers guidance on when one remedy is disproportionate to another. This will be the case where the cost of a remedy is unreasonable taking into account the value of the goods if they conformed to the contract, the significance of the defect and whether the alternative remedy could be effected without significant inconvenience to the buyer. For example, this will probably mean that if there is a cosmetic defect in a domestic appliance on a part that will not be visible when it is installed, it will be difficult to insist on a repair that might be quite expensive, taking into account labour charges, in comparison to giving a reduction in price. Similarly, where the value of the product is low and the cost of repair would exceed that value it is unlikely that repair could be insisted upon when replacement would be a cheaper option.

---

[94] Consumer Rights Act 2015 s.23(2)(b).

Price reduction or final right of rejection

The remedies of price reduction or final right of rejection only come into play if   **4–60**
the first two cannot be, or have not been, carried out. They apply in three
situations. These are: that one repair or replacement of the original goods has
resulted in goods that still do not meet the relevant standards; neither repair nor
replacement can work because it is impossible or disproportionate to other
remedies; or the trader has failed to carry out the consumer's request for a repair
or replacement within a reasonable time and without significant inconvenience to
the consumer.[95] For the purposes of determining when one repair has been carried
out subs.(7) states that, where the repair is carried out on the consumer's
premises, the repair is not complete until the trader indicates to the consumer that
the repairs are finished. This means that a single repair may be carried out over
more than one visit, without triggering the right to a price reduction or the final
right to reject until the trader notifies the consumer that it is complete.

Price reduction will not be available if anything transferred in return for the   **4–61**
goods cannot be given back in its original state or cannot be divided up to provide
the appropriate reduction.[96] There is little guidance on how to calculate the price
reduction. Section 24(1) refers to a reduction "by an appropriate amount" that can
be the full price or whatever the consumer is required to transfer in return for the
goods.[97] The explanatory notes on the Bill state that:

> "It is intended that the reduction in price should reflect the difference in value
> between what the consumer paid for and the value of what they actually receive,
> and could be as much as a full refund or the full amount already paid."[98]

Where the consumer's remedy is the final right to reject the mechanisms that   **4–62**
apply to the exercise of the short term right to reject discussed above apply.[99]
Controversially, in some circumstances, when the final right to reject is exercised
the consumer will not get a full refund. This is the case where the right is
exercised more than six months after ownership or possession of the goods has
been transferred, they have been delivered and, where appropriate, been
installed.[100] However, the six month rule does not apply to motor vehicles.[101] In
all cases no deduction may be made to take account of use in any period when the
consumer had the goods only because the trader failed to collect them at an
agreed time.[102] This rule looks superficially fair but can be criticised on several
grounds. Where consumers eventually feel compelled to resort to the final right
of rejection it is likely that they will have had a good deal of hassle over the
purchase. Although it might look like rough justice, not making any allowance
for such use as has been possible would provide an element of compensation.

---

[95] Consumer Rights Act 2015 s.24(5).
[96] Consumer Rights Act 2015 s.24(4).
[97] Consumer Rights Act 2015 s.24(2).
[98] These are available on the Parliament website at *http://www.parliament.uk/business/bills-and-legislation/* [Accessed 15 June 2015].
[99] See Consumer Rights Act 2015 s.20.
[100] Consumer Rights Act 2015 s.20(8), (10) and (11).
[101] Consumer Rights Act 2015 s.20(10). Consumer Rights Act 2015 s.20(14) gives the Secretary of State power to extend the goods to which this exemption can apply.
[102] Consumer Rights Act 2015 s.20(9).

There is no guidance on how to calculate the deduction and this will lead to difficulties for consumers. Here the 2015 Act is getting away from one of its basic principles of providing remedies that are as simple as possible to apply.

Delivery of the wrong quantity

4–63   If the wrong quantity of goods is delivered s.25 provides that the consumer may reject the whole delivery. Should they choose to accept the goods then they must pay the contract rate for what they receive. If more is delivered than was contracted for, the consumer has the additional option to reject the excess and keep the contracted amount. This section only entitles the consumer to reject goods: rules of contract law will determine whether or not the contract can be treated as at an end.

Other remedies

4–64   In some cases, as s.19(9) recognises, a consumer may wish to pursue remedies other than those discussed above. If the goods are faulty and the consumer has not paid for them they might face a claim from the trader for the price and in this case it would be appropriate to rely on breach of one of the statutory terms as a defence.[103] Where the term that that the trader has breached is an express one rather than one of those created by the 2015 Act the consumer might choose to exercise the common law contractual right to treat the contract as at an end or, to use the technical term, to repudiate the contract.[104]

4–65   The most common addition to the statutory remedies is likely to be damages which may sometimes be claimed as an alternative to one of them or in addition. An example is *Godley v Perry*[105] where a defective catapult resulted in the purchaser losing an eye, and the claim for breach of contract was mainly for damages for this injury. Similarly, in *Wilson v Rickett, Cockerell & Co Ltd*[106] the breach of contract consisted in the delivery of defective Coalite and resulted in damage to the buyer's living room, for which compensation was awarded. One can apply the principles of these cases to other situations such as one where a washing machine proves to be faulty. The nature of the fault may have been such that clothes placed in it were damaged. In addition to exercising one of the remedies, such as the short term right to reject, the consumer would also wish to receive compensation for the damaged clothes. In some circumstances damages may be recovered for inconvenience or distress flowing from a breach of a supply of goods contract. This will only be possible where the seller is aware that breach is likely to have this result as in *Bernstein v Pamsons Motors (Golders Green) Ltd*[107] where the buyer recovered damages for inconvenience caused when his car proved not to be of satisfactory quality by breaking down on a busy motorway some distance from his destination or *Jackson v Chrysler Acceptances Ltd*[108]

---

[103] Consumer Rights Act 2015 s.19(11)(d).
[104] Consumer Rights Act 2015 s.19(11)(e).
[105] *Godley v Perry* [1960] 1 W.L.R. 9.
[106] *Wilson v Rickett, Cockerell & Co Ltd* [1944] 1 Q.B. 498.
[107] *Bernstein v Pamsons Motors (Golders Green) Ltd* [1987] 2 E.R. 220.
[108] *Jackson v Chrysler Acceptances Ltd* [1978] R.T.R. 474.

where the sellers of a new car knew that the buyer wanted it for a foreign holiday and thus were liable for damages for the distress caused through a holiday ruined by the car breaking down frequently.

Another possibility is specific implement, which is an order of a court to perform a contract. In theory in Scots law this is the primary remedy for breach of contract but in practice this is rarely the case. Courts will only make an order of specific implement where damages would not be an adequate remedy. In consumer purchases this will rarely be the case as the disappointed consumer can always obtain a substitute elsewhere claiming damages if this is more expensive than that which was not delivered. It is only in the case of a unique item such as an heirloom or a painting that an order might be appropriate. **4–66**

MANUFACTURERS' LIABILITY

Delictual liability

So far the discussion has concentrated on the liability of the supplier. In addition, it is possible for the manufacturer, or someone else in the chain of production and distribution, to be liable as well. This may be delictual liability or it may be the result of the manufacturer having offered a guarantee. **4–67**

Where goods are defective the consumer will normally find it much easier to attempt to make the supplier liable for breach of one of terms included in the contract by the 2015 Act. As we have seen, liability is strict. However, there are circumstances where the consumer will not be able to sue the supplier. The seller may have become insolvent or the person who suffered the harm may, like Mrs Donoghue, in *Donoghue v Stevenson*,[109] not be the purchaser. This may result in a delictual action and will often arise from goods being dangerous and not merely shoddy. The possible types of action in these circumstances are discussed in Ch.5. **4–68**

One avenue discussed in that chapter is the delictual action for breach of duty which stems from *Donoghue v Stevenson*. That line of authority appears to have been extended in another Scottish appeal to the House of Lords, *Junior Books Ltd v Veitchi Co Ltd*.[110] It was held that the owner of a factory had a claim in delict against a subcontractor who had laid a floor negligently, thus causing economic loss. There was no allegation that the floor was dangerous or had caused any physical injury. Liability was said to depend on the degree of proximity of the parties and in this case it was very close. It was expressly said, however, that the decision would not apply to consumer situations where the complaint was that the goods were of poor quality. This, it was said, was because there would not be the requisite degree of proximity between a manufacturer and the ultimate consumer. In view of the influence of mass advertising carried out mainly by manufacturers, and occasional cases where the retailer is little more than a conduit between the consumer and the manufacturer, this seems open to doubt. There may be situations where a consumer wants something made to special order and goes to a retailer who puts him in touch with the manufacturer. The ultimate sale may be routed through the retailer, but discussion about the product will have been **4–69**

---

[109] *Donoghue v Stevenson*, 1932 S.C. (H.L.) 31.
[110] *Junior Books Ltd v Veitchi Co Ltd*, 1982 S.C. (H.L.) 244; 1982 S.L.T. 492; [1983] A.C. 420.

directly between the customer and the manufacturer. There would seem to be little difference in principle between such a situation and *Junior Books*.

Manufacturers' guarantees

4–70   A useful supplement to the legal protection regarding quality is often given by manufacturers' guarantees, usually called warranties in the case of cars. These may consist of a written undertaking to the purchaser to replace or repair a faulty product, or to give a refund, should problems develop within a stated period. This is usually one year in the case of domestic appliances and, in the case of cars, it can be longer. Such guarantees can be a very useful addition to the consumer's statutory rights. It avoids the problems surrounding the standard of quality that the consumer is entitled to expect under the 2015 Act and, in particular, can overcome the deficiencies in the legal remedies where goods do not prove to be durable.

4–71   Despite their widespread use, the legal status of guarantees was not altogether clear,[111] though it was probably the case that they were contracts. This issue is now put beyond doubt so far as consumer guarantees are concerned by s.30(3) of the 2015 Act which implements art.6 of the EC Directive on Certain Aspects of the Sale of Consumer Goods and Associated Guarantees.[112] This it does by providing that

> "the consumer guarantee takes effect at the time the goods are delivered as a contractual obligation owed by the guarantor under the conditions set out in the guarantee statement and any associated advertising".

4–72   There is no obligation on a manufacturer, or anyone else in the supply chain, to offer a guarantee but if one is offered the section goes on to impose certain requirements on such a guarantee. It must be set out in plain and intelligible language (which must be English if the goods are offered within the UK) and must include the particulars for making claims. Those who offer guarantees, be they manufacturers, retailers or others, must make them available to potential customers on demand. The definition regulation makes clear that what is controlled is a guarantee given without extra charge whether by the manufacturer or anyone else in the course of a business. It includes the typical manufacturer's guarantee but not extended warranties for which the consumer has to pay separately.

4–73   The obligations relating to guarantees are enforceable by the Competition and Markets Authority (CMA) and local weights and measures authorities, which in practice means the trading standards departments of local councils. If a guarantor fails to comply with the provisions of the regulation the CMA or a local authority may seek an order for specific performance from the sheriff court or the Court of Session.[113]

---

[111] For a discussion of this issue, see D Cusine, "Manufacturers' Guarantees and the Unfair Contract Terms Act", 1980 J.R. 184.

[112] Directive 1999/44 of the European Parliament and of the Council of 25 May 1999 on certain aspects of the sale of consumer goods and associated guarantees [1999] O.J. L171/12.

[113] Consumer Rights Act s.30(8) and (10)(c).

In this case s.66 of the 2015 Act prevents a guarantee being used to exclude or restrict liability for loss or damage, including death or personal injury, arising from the goods proving to be defective as a result of a breach of duty by a manufacturer or distributor.

4–74

CRIMINAL LAW

From the consumer's point of view the civil law relating to the quality of goods is the most important aspect of this topic. In addition, there is a good deal of legislation sanctioned by criminal penalties which plays an important part in ensuring that the quality of goods is satisfactory. Under the Food Safety Act 1990 (the 1990 Act) the quality and composition of food is controlled. The detailed control is to be found in a mass of subordinate legislation made principally under powers conferred by the 1990 Act. Similar powers in relation to drugs are given by the Medicines Act 1968. The Hallmarking Act 1973 updated one of the oldest forms of consumer protection and governs the quality of gold, silver and platinum.

4–75

CHAPTER 5

Product Safety

While it is irritating and can have serious financial consequences to find that a product that one has bought is shoddy, this is as nothing to the dangers posed by unsafe goods. This chapter considers the legal response to the problem of unsafe goods. Broadly speaking, this falls into two categories: attempts to provide compensation for the consequences of unsafe goods; and legislation to prevent unsafe goods reaching the market in the first place. The two categories are not exclusive, as the threat of having to compensate a victim of unsafe goods must act as an incentive to a trader to ensure that unsafe goods do not reach the market place.

5–01

We have already seen that goods which are dangerous will not be regarded as meeting the standard of satisfactory quality, and that damages for personal injury may be an element in the damages for breach of that term of the contract of supply. This is of limited utility as it will only benefit the purchaser. What happens if the injured person is someone other than the purchaser? Until recently the answer to that question was that the injured person could only succeed by bringing an action for breach of duty as Mrs Donoghue did in the famous case. As Lord Atkin put it in that case:

5–02

> "A manufacturer of products, which he sells in such a form as to show that he intends them to reach the ultimate consumer in the form in which they left him, with no reasonable possibility of intermediate examination, and with the knowledge that the absence of reasonable care in the preparation or putting up of the products will result in an injury to the consumer's life or property, owes a duty to the consumer to take that reasonable care."[1]

That principle has been applied in a wide range of situations, many of them outwith the realm of consumer protection. Within the category of consumer examples is *Grant v Australian Knitting Mills Ltd*,[2] where a consumer contracted dermatitis from negligently manufactured underpants; and *Malfroot v Noxal Ltd*,[3] where a motorcycle manufacturer was held liable to a passenger in a side car which, as a result of the negligence of the manufacturer, parted company with the motorcycle and caused injury to her. A more recent example of a manufacturer's design defect founding this kind of liability is to be found in *Lambert v Lewis*,[4]

5–03

---

[1] *Donoghue v Stevenson* [1932] A.C. 562 at 599.
[2] *Grant v Australian Knitting Mills Ltd* [1936] A.C. 85.
[3] *Malfoot v Noxal Ltd* (1935) 51 T.L.R. 551.
[4] *Lambert v Lewis* [1982] A.C. 225.

'where a passenger in a car was killed and others injured when a trailer being towed behind a Land Rover became unhitched and collided with the car in which they were travelling.

5–04   It is not only manufacturers who can be liable, as *Fisher v Harrods Ltd*[5] demonstrates. In that case the well-known London store was held liable for the injuries suffered by a lady who had been injured when defective packaging of jewellery cleaning fluid purchased by someone else damaged her eye. It was shown that the store had obtained the product from a small company with whom it had never dealt before and of which it knew nothing. Despite this, it had failed to have the product tested before putting it on sale. Repairers can also be liable to their customers, as *Stennett v Hancock & Peters*[6] shows, as can those who sell reconditioned products[7] or those who hire out products.[8]

5–05   The difficulty with the *Donoghue v Stevenson*[9] principle of liability is that it depends on showing that the defender has failed to display reasonable care for the safety of the pursuer. Despite the assistance of the maxim res ipsa loquitur (the facts speak for themselves), this is not always easy or possible to prove, as the thalidomide tragedy[10] graphically demonstrated. This led to demands to introduce legislation imposing strict liability on manufacturers of defective products which have resulted in the enactment of Pt 1 of the Consumer Protection Act 1987 (the 1987 Act).

5–06   Before looking at that Act it is important to point out that, despite its enactment, *Donoghue v Stevenson*[11] liability will, in some circumstances, still be relevant. This is because the 1987 Act has a limitation period that may rule out claims that could still be made at common law; and there are some forms of loss which it does not cover, such as pure financial loss.

STRICT LIABILITY OF MANUFACTURERS IN DELICT

5–07   Part 1 of the 1987 Act introduces what is often—though somewhat misleadingly—referred to as strict liability for manufacturers. Incidents such as the thalidomide tragedy had led consumer organisations to campaign for the introduction of such legislation paralleling judicial developments in the United States.[12] This was supported in a joint report by the Law Commission and the Scottish Law Commission,[13] and the report of the Pearson Commission.[14] Both the Council of Europe and the EC took up the issue at European level. The

---

[5] *Fisher v Harrods Ltd* [1966] 1 Lloyd's Rep. 500.
[6] *Stennett v Hancock & Peters* [1939] 2 All E.R. 578.
[7] *Herschtal v Stewart & Ardern Ltd* [1940] 1 K.B. 155.
[8] *Griffith v Arch Engineering (Newport) Ltd* [1968] 3 All E.R. 217.
[9] *Donoghue v Stevenson*, 1932 S.C. (H.L.) 31.
[10] Thalidomide was a drug widely prescribed to combat morning sickness in pregnant women. In a large number of cases it caused their children to be born with serious abnormalities.
[11] *Donoghue v Stevenson*, 1932 S.C. (H.L.) 31.
[12] The landmark decision in the US was that of the California Supreme Court in *Greenman v Yuba Power Products Inc*, 377 P. 2nd 897 (1963).
[13] Law Commission and Scottish Law Commission, *Liability for Defective Products* (HMSO, 1977) (Law Com. No.82, Scot Law Com. No.45) Cmnd.6831.
[14] The Pearson Commission, *Royal Commission on Civil Liability and Compensation for Personal Injury* (HMSO, 1978) Cmnd.7054, Ch.22.

immediate spur to legislative action in the UK was the Directive on Product Liability,[15] which Pt 1 of the 1987 Act implements in the UK. The original Directive has been amended.[16] The effect of this is to remove the exemption from the Directive for unprocessed agricultural products, fish and game.

Part 1 of the 1987 Act introduces a regime of strict liability on manufacturers **5–08** of products which prove to cause harm by reason of a defect. For several years almost no use seems to have been made of it but more recently there have been several reported cases.[17] It should be noted that s.1(1) refers to the origin of this part of the Act:

> "This Part shall have effect for the purpose of making such provision as is necessary in order to comply with the product liability Directive and shall be construed accordingly."

In view of the fact that there are several obscure provisions in the Act, which **5–09** in some cases do not appear to conform to the Directive, this provision may be of considerable importance. This was recognised by the European Court of Justice (ECJ) when the Commission challenged the implementation by the UK of the Directive.[18] In *A v National Blood Authority (No.1)*[19] the judge referred almost exclusively to the wording of the relevant parts of the Directive rather than the statute.

The key provision of the 1987 Act is s.2(1): **5–10**

> "Subject to the following provisions of this Part, where any damage is caused wholly or partly by a defect in a product, every person to whom subsection (2) . . . applies shall be liable for the damage."

As pointed out above, the liability under Pt 1 is strict but it is not absolute. The pursuer must prove that he has been injured; that the defendant manufacturer was the producer of the product; and that it was the manufacturer's product that caused the injury. Two recent cases underline this point. In both *Hufford v Samsung Electronics (UK) Ltd*[20] and *Love v Halfords Ltd*[21] the claimants were unable to show that the product was defective when supplied to them.

As many negligence cases have shown, it is the issue of causation which **5–11** frequently proves a stumbling block to claimants. An example is *Kay's Tutor v*

---

[15] Directive 85/374/EEC of 25 July 1985 on the approximation of laws, regulations and administrative provisions of the Member States concerning liability for defective products [1985] O.J. L210/29.

[16] Directive 1999/34 amending Council Directive 85/374/EEC on the approximation of laws, regulations and administrative provisions of the Member States concerning liability for defective products [1999] O.J. L141/20.

[17] It appears to be have been one of the grounds on which those harmed by a polluted water supply in the Camelford area of Cornwall were successful: see *AB v South West Water Services Ltd* [1993] Q.B. 507 CA. For discussion of possible reasons for the paucity of cases, see National Consumer Council, *Unsafe Products* (London: National Consumer Council, 1995).

[18] *Commission of the European Communities v United Kingdom* (C-300/95) [1997] All E.R. (EC) 481.

[19] *A v National Blood Authority (No.1)* [2001] 3 All E.R. 289.

[20] *Hufford v Samsung Electronics (UK) Ltd* [2014] EWHC 2956 (TCC).

[21] *Love v Halfords Ltd* [2014] EWHC 1057 (QB).

Ayrshire and Arran Health Board.[22] The causation issue can also defeat a claim where the manufacturer is able to show some other convincing reason for the pursuer's loss, as in *Evans v Triplex Safety Glass Co Ltd.*[23] Such cases may turn on complex scientific evidence and, like negligence actions raising similar issues, can be extremely expensive.[24]

Products

5–12   "Product" is given a very wide meaning for the purpose of Pt 1 of the 1987 Act. The starting point is the definition in s.1(2) which defines a product as

> "any good or electricity and ... includes a product which is comprised in another product, whether by virtue of being a component part or raw material or otherwise".

The term "goods" is then amplified in s.45, the definition section of the Act, to include "substances, growing crops and things comprised in land by virtue of being attached to it and any ship, aircraft or vehicle". "Substance", in turn, is defined as

> "any natural or artificial substance, whether in solid, liquid or gaseous form or in the form of a vapour, and includes substances that are comprised in or mixed with other goods".

5–13   The effect of s.46(4) is that buildings are not products for the purposes of Pt 1. However, while buildings are not within the 1987 Act, s.46(3) makes clear that products incorporated in a building are subject to it. The result seems to be that if a building collapses because of design faults the builder is not liable under the 1987 Act. However, if injury is caused by a defective central heating boiler blowing up there will be liability.

5–14   The original Directive provided in art.2 for the exclusion of what it called "primary agricultural products" from the new product liability regime. However, art.15(a) permitted Member States to derogate from this provision and impose liability on producers of primary agricultural products. This the UK did not choose to do. The Directive has now been amended to apply the product liability regime to agricultural products, fish and game, and the Act was amended to take account of this.[25]

5–15   For convenience it is usual to speak of product liability as the liability of the manufacturer, but it should be remembered that the range of people liable is rather wider than this. The following are potentially liable by virtue of s.2(2)–(4):

(a)   producers;
(b)   own-branders;

---

[22] *Kay's Tutor v Ayrshire and Arran Health Board*, 1987 S.C. (H.L.) 145.

[23] *Evans v Triplex Safety Glass Co Ltd* [1936] 1 All E.R. 283.

[24] See also *Love v Halfords Ltd* [2014] EWHC 1057 (QB); *McGlinchey v General Motors UK Ltd* [2012] CSIH 91. *Loveday v Renton* [1990] 1 Med. L.R. 117 and Pamela R. Ferguson, *Drug Injuries and the Pursuit of Compensation* (London: Sweet & Maxwell, 1996) Ch.9.

[25] Consumer Protection Act 1987 (Product Liability) (Modification) (Scotland) Order 2001 (SSI 2001/265).

(c)   importers; and

(d)   suppliers.

Producers (s.2(2)(a))

The "producer" of a product is defined in s.1(2) to mean: **5–16**

> "(a)   the person who manufactured it;
> (b)   in the case of a substance which has not been manufactured but has been won or abstracted, the person who won or abstracted it;
> (c)   in the case of a product which has not been manufactured, won or abstracted but essential characteristics of which are attributable to an industrial or other process having been carried out (for example, in relation to agricultural produce), the person who carried out that process."

The expression "the person who manufactured it" is not defined in the 1987 **5–17** Act. The Directive can be helpful as in art.3 "producer" is said to mean "the manufacturer of a finished product, the producer of any raw material or the manufacturer of a component part". The manufacturer of the finished product and the producer of a component or raw material are both liable where the finished product is defective by virtue of a defect in the raw material or the component. In this context it is worth noting s.1(3), which states:

> "For the purposes of this Part a person who supplies any product in which products are comprised, whether by virtue of being component parts or raw materials, or otherwise, shall not be treated by reason only of his supply of that product as supplying any of the products so comprised."

The provision is not intended to contradict the assertion that the manufacturer **5–18** of the finished product and the raw material or component producer are both liable. The significant word is "only". It appears that the manufacturer cannot be liable for defects in raw material or components if, for some reason, they are not liable for defects in the finished product.

For the most part it is not difficult to appreciate who is a manufacturer. The **5–19** term "producer" also includes those who have "won or abstracted" a substance. This is the appropriate terminology for substances, such as ores, which are mined. The third category of producers comprises those who do not manufacture, win or abstract, but who produce products, the "essential characteristics of which are attributable to an industrial or other process". This would cover producers of petroleum products who produce their products by refining raw materials. This is uncontroversial. However this phrase is also relevant to the production of foodstuffs.

Own-branders (s.2(2)(b))

This clumsy heading is used to sum up the group of persons who are liable by **5–20** s.2(2)(b):

"Any person who, by putting his name on the product or using a trade mark or other distinguishing mark in relation to the product, has held himself out to be the producer of the product."

It is quite common for supermarkets to arrange for the manufacturer of a product to supply them with that product labelled or wrapped with the supermarket's own well-known brand name or logo. It is to both these situations that s.2(2)(b) applies, and the supermarket will be liable under the Act.[26] This will only increase their liability to a limited extent as they have liability without fault to purchasers under the Sale of Goods Act 1979. However, it does mean that in a case such as *Fisher v Harrods Ltd*[27] the pursuer would be able to sue under the 1987 Act rather than having to raise an action for negligence.

Importers (s.2(2)(c))

5–21   To avoid the possibility of injured consumers having to bring actions in far off jurisdictions, s.2(2)(c) provides that the term producer includes

"any person who has imported the product into a Member State [of the EU] from a place outside the Member States in order, in the course of any business of his, to supply it to another".

A simple example of the effect of this provision would be the situation where a car is manufactured in Japan and imported into Italy. The Italian importer then sells it to an English dealer who sells it to a customer. The car proves to be defective, the brakes fail, and injury is sustained by the customer. The injured person does not have to sue the Japanese manufacturer; as a result of s.2(2)(c) they can sue the Italian importer as the person who imported the product into the EU.

Suppliers (s.2(3))

5–22   The first three categories of persons liable for defective products can be seen as primarily liable to the injured person. The final category comprised in s.2(3) is different: persons in this category become liable only where the person primarily liable cannot be identified. Liability arises if three conditions are fulfilled. The injured person must request the supplier to identify one or more of the persons listed in categories (a)–(c) above; that request must be made within a reasonable time after the damage has occurred and at a time when it is not reasonably practicable for the person making the request to identify those persons; and the supplier must fail to supply the information requested within a reasonable time. An example of a situation where a supplier's liability might be extended occurs where a retailer's goods have injured someone other than the purchaser. If the retailer cannot identify their supplier then under this provision they find

---

[26] An example is *Tesco Stores Ltd v Pollard* [2006] EWCA Civ. 393.
[27] *Fisher v Harrods Ltd* [1966] 1 Lloyd's Rep. 500.

themselves strictly liable.[28] *O'Byrne v Aventis Pasteur MSD Ltd*,[29] on the other hand, demonstrates the importance of correctly identifying the supplier.

Defect

A key concept in the 1987 Act is that of "defect" and this is defined in s.3. The principal part of the definition is contained in s.3(1):   **5–23**

> "Subject to the following provisions of this section, there is a defect in a product for the purposes of this Part if the safety of the product is not such as persons generally are entitled to expect; and for those purposes 'safety', in relation to a product, shall include safety with respect to products comprised in that product and safety in the context of risks of damage to property, as well as in the context of risks of death or personal injury."

It is clear from this definition that the strict liability regime is concerned only with safety, not with shoddiness. It provides no remedy where the product is defective in the sense that it does not work or has some other flaw (other than a safety defect) that might render it of unsatisfactory quality. In this situation the purchaser is thrown back on the existing remedies under the Consumer Rights Act 2015 (the 2015 Act), or other legislation setting standards of quality in relation to the supply of goods.   **5–24**

Safety is relative

It is clear that s.3 of the 1987 Act is concerned with relative safety. There is probably no such thing as a completely safe product. Even such innocuous substances as cotton wool might, in the hands of an infant, prove dangerous, if the infant put large quantities into its mouth. On the other hand there are other products which are inherently dangerous: sharp knives, cars and matches are examples. The question is, to quote s.3(1), when is the degree of safety "not such as persons generally are entitled to expect"? To answer this question s.3(2) gives some further guidance. After stating that "all the circumstances shall be taken into account", it goes on to set out a number of specific circumstances which are to be taken into account.   **5–25**

Before looking at these it is important to point out that the role of the court is to act as what Burton J in *A v National Blood Authority (No.1)*[30] referred to (quoting one expert) as "the appointed representative of the public at large".[31] The factors set out in s.3(2) are: **5–26**

> "(a)   the manner in which, and purposes for which, the product has been marketed, its get-up, the use of any mark in relation to the product, and any instructions for, or warnings with respect to doing or refraining from doing anything with or in relation to the product;

---

[28] That traders sometimes cannot identify who their suppliers were is demonstrated in *Lambert v Lewis* [1982] A.C. 225.
[29] *O'Byrne v Aventis Pasteur MSD Ltd* [2010] UKSC 23.
[30] *A v National Blood Authority (No.1)* [2001] 3 All E.R. 289.
[31] *A v National Blood Authority (No.1)* [2001] 3 All E.R. 289 at [31].

(b)   what might reasonably be expected to be done with or in relation to the product;

and

(c)   the time when the product was supplied by its producer to another."

5–27   The subsection concludes by stating that the fact that products produced after an injury has occurred have a greater level of safety may not be used to infer that earlier products were defective. These factors will be discussed in turn. It should be noted that while, for the purposes of exposition, it is necessary to discuss them in isolation, in real life they will tend to interact with each other and overlap with such issues as the defences considered below and the question of causation.

Marketing, warnings and instructions

5–28   It is probably the case that these factors only come into play when it is not feasible to make the product safe through better design. It was said in the American case of *Schell v AMF Inc*[32] that

> "as a matter of policy, it is questionable whether a manufacturer which produces a machine without minimal available safeguards is entitled to escape liability by warning of dangerous condition which could reasonably have been avoided by a better design".

5–29   The importance of warnings is not a novelty: it has been pointed out in negligence cases such as *Clarke v Army and Navy Co-operative Society Ltd*.[33] Mrs Clarke had purchased a bottle of disinfectant, at the defendant's shop. There was no warning on the bottle, despite the fact that the defendant's shop manager had been informed by customers of incidents causing injury. When the plaintiff opened the bottle some of the contents flew out injuring her eyes. She sued, inter alia, alleging negligence in failing to issue a warning about this danger. The defendants were held to be in breach of their duty to the plaintiff in failing to attach a warning to the bottle. Collins M.R. said that there was:

> "A duty, if there is some dangerous quality in the goods sold, of which he knows, but of which the purchaser cannot be expected to be aware, of taking reasonable precautions in the way of warning the purchaser that special care will be requisite."[34]

5–30   Where the danger is a matter of common knowledge a warning will not be necessary,[35] but where warnings should be given they must be adequate, precise and appropriately placed. In this context the distinction between instructions and

---

[32] *Schell v AMF Inc*, 567 F. 2d. 1259 (1977) (3rd Cir).

[33] *Clarke v Army and Navy Co-operative Society Ltd* [1903] 1 K.B. 155.

[34] The same point was made in *Vacwell Engineering Co Ltd v BDH Chemicals Ltd* [1971] 1 Q.B. 88, where liability in negligence was found on the breach of a duty adequately to warn of the explosive properties of boron tribromide on contact with water. The importance of accurate instructions was demonstrated in relation to the merchantability and fitness for purpose of products in *Wormell v RHM Agriculture (East) Ltd* [1987] 1 W.L.R. 1091 where the problem was the ineffectiveness of herbicide, not personal injury.

[35] See *Yachetti v John Duff & Son Ltd* [1943] 1 D.L.R. 194 where the Ontario High Court found that there was no need to warn of the danger of trichinosis from uncooked pork.

warnings is sometimes relevant. The function of a warning is to inform the user of the dangers of a product: directions or instructions for use are intended to indicate how the best results may be obtained when using the product. When dangers from failing to follow directions for use are not obvious such directions by themselves may not be sufficient to absolve the manufacturer from liability.

A good example of a warning that was not adequate comes from the Californian case of *Boyl v California Chemical Co*.[36] The plaintiff used a liquid weed-killer frequently sold to ordinary consumers for garden use. The warnings given on the label by the defendant included the avoidance of breathing the spray mist, of contact with eyes, skin or clothing, and the necessity of washing after use. It also warned that livestock and poultry would be poisoned if allowed to feed on treated areas, which indicated that the defendant manufacturers knew of the weed-killer's propensity to contaminate the earth. The label also warned that the container should be washed after use and carefully disposed of. After using the weed-killer on her driveway the plaintiff rinsed the container, disposing of the rinsing water on some grass in her garden. Five days later she sunbathed in this area and absorbed some of the weed-killer into her skin causing serious injury. It was held that the defendants were negligent in failing to give an adequate warning of the danger of contact with contaminated earth. **5–31**

Warnings about the possible of danger of toxic shock syndrome were central to the decision in *Worsley v Tambrands*[37] that the tampons were not defective. Mrs Worsley had used the defendant's tampons for many years and had read and acted on the instructions and warnings supplied with them. On the outside of the packet was a warning of the possibility of toxic shock syndrome (TSS) and a reference to the leaflet inside. The leaflet contained detailed information about the risk of TSS and its symptoms and advised that urgent medical advice be sought if certain symptoms were experienced while using tampons. While using them, in 1994, Mrs Worsley did experience such symptoms but, at first, thought that she was suffering from food poisoning. When she went to her doctor she did not tell him that she was using tampons and he did not diagnose TSS. When her condition did not improve she looked for the leaflet but it had been discarded a few days earlier and she did not have access to the information that would probably have alerted her to the fact that she had the symptoms of TSS. Her condition deteriorated and she was eventually admitted to hospital in a serious condition. **5–32**

When she recovered she sued the manufacturers both in negligence and under Pt 1 of the 1987 Act. Her claim under the 1987 Act was based on the argument that the product was defective because it contained inadequate warnings. The claimant was able to prove that she was using the product at the relevant time although the defendant denied that it had caused the illness. In the event the causation issue did not have to be resolved as the judge found that the product was not defective. She observed: **5–33**

"As a matter of common sense, I conclude the duty of the manufacturer, and that to which persons generally are entitled to expect in relation to the product, is that the box contains an unambiguous and clear warning that there is an association between TSS and tampon use and directs the menstruating woman to the internal leaflet for

---

[36] *Boyl v California Chemical Co*, 221 F. Supp. 669 (1963).
[37] *Worsley v Tambrands* [2000] P.I.Q.R. 95 QBD.

full details. TSS is a rare but potentially very serious condition which may be life threatening, but it is necessary to balance the rarity and the gravity. That balance is reasonably, properly and safely struck by the dual system of a risk warning on the box and a full explanation in the leaflet if the former is clearly visible and the latter is both legible and full."

5–34   The product, thus, provided the requisite degree of safety and was not defective.

5–35   Burton J in *A v National Blood Authority (No.1)*[38] also referred to the fact that no warnings had been given about the danger of infection from blood transfusions in deciding that the product was defective. The importance of warnings was also referred to by Pill LJ in *Abouzaid v Mothercare Plc*.[39] He observed that the product was defective "because it was supplied with a design which permitted the risk to arise and without giving a warning that the user should not so position himself that the risk arose".

5–36   *McLauglin v Mine Safety Appliances*[40] illustrates that the location of the warning can be important. The warning was on the cardboard container in which the defective appliance was boxed, rather than on the appliance itself. It was held that this was not sufficient and the warning should have been on the appliance.

5–37   In addition to warnings, the way in which the product is promoted is relevant. A good example is to be found in the negligence case of *Watson v Buckley, Osborne, Garrett & Co Ltd*[41] where the fact that a hair dye had been advertised as needing no preliminary tests contributed to a finding that the distributor had been negligent. In *Richardson v LRC Products*[42] this seems to have been important. In that case Mrs Richardson had become pregnant after a condom used by her husband had failed. In essence, following the rejection of evidence that the condom had been damaged during production, her case was that the fact of the fracture in use demonstrated a defect. The judge drew attention to the fact that it was well known that a proportion of condoms fail for no known reason and that the manufacturers do not claim absolute reliability.

Reasonable expectations about use

5–38   This criterion raises the difficult question of how far abnormal use, or use not intended by the manufacturer, should be taken into consideration in determining whether a product is defective. Cases such as *Yachetti v John Duff & Son Ltd*[43] where the purchaser had not carried out an obvious process will be relevant. There the Ontario High Court found that there was no need to warn of the necessity to cook pork to avoid the danger of trichinosis. The American case of *Reid v Spadone Machine Co*[44] may also be helpful. There it was held to be foreseeable that, if a dangerous machine for cutting up plastic could be used by two persons, it would be so used, because used in that way the job could be done

---

[38] *A v National Blood Authority (No.1)* [2001] 3 All E.R. 289.
[39] *Abouzaid v Mothercare Plc*, The Times, December 21, 2000 CA.
[40] *McLaughlin v Mine Safety Applicances*, 181 Ne. 2d. 430 (1960).
[41] *Watson v Buckley, Osborne, Garrett & Co Ltd* [1940] 1 All E.R. 74.
[42] *Richardson v LRC Products* [2000] Lloyd's Rep. Med. 280 QBD.
[43] *Yachetti v John Duff & Son Ltd* [1943] 1 D.L.R. 194.
[44] *Reid v Spadone Machine Co*, 404 A. 2d. 1094 (1979).

faster. As designed, the machine, though not intended for use by two persons, was dangerous when so used. It was shown that it would have been fairly easy to have designed the machine so that one person could not have set the machine in motion while the other was in a position of danger and so the manufacturer was liable. *Palmer v Palmer*,[45] which involved a seat belt device seems to be an example from an English case.

Time of supply

This factor requires a court to take into account standards applicable when the product was put into circulation, not those developed since the product was supplied. Another American case, *Bruce v Martin Marietta Corp*,[46] illustrates this point. This action arose out of the crash in 1970 of a plane, which had been manufactured by the defendants in 1952. When the plane crashed, seats in the passenger cabin broke loose from their floor attachments and were thrown forward against a bulkhead, blocking the exit. A fire broke out and it was alleged that the escape of passengers was impeded by the seats. Evidence was produced by the plaintiffs to show that seats could now be produced that would withstand a crash. The defendants showed that when the plane was built by them it met or exceeded all relevant design requirements, safety requirements, and other criteria prescribed by the regulatory body. It was held that the plaintiffs had not shown that the ordinary consumer would expect a plane made in 1952 to have the safety features of one made in 1970:

5–39

> "A consumer would not expect a Model T to have the safety features which are incorporated in automobiles made today. The same expectation applies to airplanes."

Other factors

As s.3 makes clear, the factors listed are not the only ones that may be taken into account in determining whether a product is defective. What other factors might a court consider? This issue was extensively canvassed in *A v National Blood Authority (No.1)*.[47] The claimants had been infected with hepatitis C through blood transfusions which had used blood from infected donors. During the period when most of the claimants had been infected the risk of such infection in this way was known to exist but was impossible to avoid, either because the virus itself had not yet been discovered or because there was no way of testing for its presence in blood. It was for that reason that the claims were brought under Pt I of the 1987 Act rather than in negligence. There was much discussion of the meaning of art.6 of the Directive which states that:

5–40

---

[45] *Palmer v Palmer* [2006] EWHC 1284 (QB).
[46] *Bruce v Martin Marietta Corp*, 544 F. 2d. 442 (1976) (10th Cir.).
[47] *A v National Blood Authority (No.1)* [2001] 3 All E.R. 289.

"A product is defective when it does not provide the safety which a person is entitled to expect, taking all circumstances into account."[48]

5–41   In a very detailed judgment following lengthy argument by counsel Burton J considered this provision. He emphasised in his judgment the context of the enactment of the Directive pointing out that it was a consumer protection measure designed to provide strict liability and overcome the difficulties for consumers of obtaining reparation through fault-based remedies. "All circumstances", he held, meant all *relevant* circumstances. The defendants argued that among such circumstances in a case like this would be: whether there were tests that could ensure that infection could be avoided; were such tests unreasonably expensive; and the benefit to society or the utility of the product. Burton J considered that none of these factors could be regarded as relevant circumstances. The first two, in particular, would subvert the purpose of a Directive as a measure introducing strict liability by reintroducing ideas more relevant to fault-based liability. They are irrelevant to the issue of consumers' expectations about safety that in this case were that blood was free from infection. It should be remembered that though the risk of infection was known to the medical profession they did not pass on that knowledge to patients, unless they asked, which they rarely did.

5–42   In this case Burton J appears to have adopted a different approach to that of Ian Kennedy J in *Richardson v LRC Products*.[49] The approach to defectiveness was not clearly articulated in that judgment, but there are comments that suggest an approach more appropriate to negligence than to strict liability. The judgment in *Richardson* appears to have considerably influenced the decision in *Foster v Biosil*,[50] a decision of Ms Booth QC sitting as a recorder. The claimant had received silicone gel breast implants in 1994. Five months later the left implant was removed and was found to have ruptured. The claimant brought an action under Pt 1 of the 1987 Act alleging that it was defective and had caused her loss. The court found that the implant by reason of the rupture was unsafe and accepted that this had caused her loss. On a literal reading of s.3 it might be thought that this would have been enough for the claim to succeed. The court, however, accepted the defendant's argument that the claimant bore the onus of proving "not merely the fact of the defect but also the cause of the defect". There seems to be no warrant for this in the 1987 Act much less the Directive and the decision in this case must be open to doubt.

5–43   In *B (A Child) v McDonald's Restaurants Ltd*[51] the approach in *A v National Blood Authority (No.1)*[52] was followed in a case where a number of children had been scalded by hot tea and coffee in a McDonalds restaurant. It was argued that tea and coffee provided in containers at such high temperatures were not safe products. It was held that this was not so. The judge pointed out that McDonalds had trained its staff about the dangers and had provided the beverages in cups with lids. Furthermore, he did not consider that customers would have been

---

[48] Directive 85/374/EEC of 25 July 1985 on the approximation of laws, regulations and administrative provisions of the Member States concerning liability for defective products [1985] O.J. L210/29.

[49] *Richardson v LRC Products* [2000] P.I.Q.R. 164.

[50] *Foster v Biosil* (2001) 59 B.M.L.R. 178.

[51] *B (A Child) v McDonald's Restaurants* [2002] EWHC 490.

[52] *A v National Blood Authority (No.1)* [2001] 3 All E.R. 289.

prepared to accept the beverages at temperatures that would have avoided scalding. In his view the beverages did achieve the "safety which a person is entitled to expect", to quote art.6 of the Directive.

Defences

Section 4 of the 1987 Act sets out a number of defences open to the producer. The burden of proof is on the producer to establish the defence.

    5–44

    The manufacturer has a defence if they can show "that the defect is attributable to compliance with any requirement imposed by or under any enactment or with any Community obligation".[53] An example of a situation where this defence might apply is where safety regulations have been made in relation to a specific product under Pt 2 of the 1987 Act. The producer also has a defence if they can show that they did not supply the product to another. This could apply when stocks of a product are stolen from a manufacturer and reach the market through illicit channels. In a Danish case a public hospital argued that a kidney and the fluid used to prepare it for donation to a patient should not be considered as put into circulation, the phrase used in art.7(a) of the Directive on which this provision in the 1987 Act is based. The ECJ held that a defective product was put into circulation when it was used during the provision of a specific medical service, such as preparing an organ for transplantation, and where the damage caused to that organ had resulted from the preparatory treatment.[54]

    5–45

    Not unreasonably, s.4(1)(d) provides that it is a defence to show that there was no defect in the product at the time that the product was supplied. For this purpose it is important to note that the 1987 Act in s.4(2) states what is the "relevant time" for this purpose. The basic idea is that a supplier should only be liable for defects present when they put it into circulation. In the case of manufacturers, own-branders and importers this is the time at which they supplied the product to another. In the case of other persons it is the time when the product was last supplied by one of the producers just referred to. This defence will absolve a manufacturer from liability if they can show that some defect has arisen through damage caused to the product after it left their hands. This may take the form of deterioration through ordinary wear or tear; or the product may have become defective through unskilled servicing or mainte-nance.[55]

    5–46

    The final defence in s.4(1)(c) is intended to protect those involved in non-commercial activities such as those who provide homemade goods for a charity sale. They will have a defence where they can show that the only supply of the product to another by the person proceeded against was otherwise than in the course of a business, and that that person is not a producer, own-brander or

    5–47

---

[53] Interpretation Act 1978 Sch.1 applies to all legislation the definition contained in of European Communities Act 1972 Sch.1.

[54] *Veedfald v Arhus Amtskommune* (C-203/99) [2001] E.C.R. I-3569; [2003] 1 C.M.L.R. 41 ECJ (Fifth Chamber).

[55] For an example from a negligence case, see *Evans v Triplex Safety Glass Co Ltd* [1936] 1 All E.R. 283. In *McGlinchey v General Motors UK Ltd* [2011] CSOH 206 the trial judge, as an alternative ground for finding in favour of the defenders, relied on this defence though he referred to the wrong subsection of the Consumer Protection Act 1987.

importer as defined in s.2(2) or, if they are, that they are not acting in that capacity with a view to profit. This did not extend to the case of a defective product that had been manufactured and used in the course of a specific medical service which was financed entirely from public funds.[56]

State of the art defence

5–48   The most controversial defence is that which is popularly known as the state of the art defence, or sometimes the development risk defence. The Directive permits such a defence but also provides that Member States may choose not to include it in their national legislation. The UK has chosen to include the defence although its inclusion was not recommended by the law commissions or the Pearson Committee in their reports.[57] Its inclusion is a weakness of our products liability law, though the way that it has been interpreted by the courts suggests that its inclusion may not be as deleterious as had been thought.

5–49   The defence is set out in s.4(1)(e) and applies where it can be shown:

> "That the state of scientific and technical knowledge at the relevant time was not such that a producer of products of the same description as the product in question might be expected to have discovered the defect if it had existed in his products while they were under his control."

5–50   The Commission sued the UK in the ECJ alleging that this formulation did not properly implement art.7(e) which provides that a manufacturer shall not be liable if he proves "that the state of scientific and technical knowledge at the time when he put the product into circulation was not such as to enable the existence of the defect to be discovered". The Commission argued that the Directive sets out an objective test where the Act, with its reference to the possibility of another producer discovering the defect, suggests a subjective test. It is even possible that this formulation of the defence would allow the courts to give the defence the meaning that it has been given in some American states. As was observed in one case, "'state of the art' . . . is sometimes confused with 'standards of the industry'".[58] The ECJ rejected the challenge by the Commission. It agreed that the test was an objective one and observed:

> "Article 7(e) is not specifically directed at the practices and safety standards in use in the industrial sector in which the producer is operating, but, unreservedly, at the state of scientific and technical knowledge, including the most advanced level of such knowledge, at the time when the product in question was put into circulation."[59]

5–51   It went on to add that in order to have a defence:

---

[56] *Veedfald v Arhus Amtskommune* (C-203/99) [2001] E.C.R. I-3569.
[57] Law Commission and Scottish Law Commission, *Liability for Defective Products* (HMSO, 1977) (Law Com. No.82, Scot Law Com. No.45) Cmnd.6831. See Pearson Commission, *Royal Commission on Civil Liability and Compensation for Personal Injury* (HMSO, 1978) Cmnd.7054–I, Ch.22.
[58] Supreme Court of the state of Washington, *Cantu v John Deere Co*, 603 P. 2d. 839 at 840.
[59] *Commission v UK* [1997] All E.R. (EC) 481; [1997] 3 C.M.L.R. 923 at [26].

"[T]he producer of a defective product must prove that the objective state of scientific and technical knowledge, including the most advanced level of such knowledge, at the time when the product in question was put into circulation was not such as to enable the existence of the defect to be discovered. Further, in order for the relevant scientific knowledge to be successfully pleaded against the producer, that knowledge must have been accessible at the time when the product in question was put into circulation. On this last point ... the Directive raises difficulties of interpretation which, in the event of litigation, the national courts will have to resolve."[60]

It concluded that there was no evidence that UK courts would fail to interpret s.4(1)(e) in this way.   **5–52**

This has been borne out in a passing reference to the state of the art defence by Ian Kennedy J in *Richardson v LRC Products*[61] who confirmed this view. He observed that: **5–53**

"The test provided by the statute is not what the defendants knew, but what they could have known if they had consulted those who might be expected to know the state of research and all available literature sources."[62]

In *Abouzaid v Mothercare Plc*[63] the Court of Appeal in England also clearly accepted this approach. It rejected the defence based on expert evidence that engineers had not encountered such accidents and that the Department of Trade and Industry's accident database contained no reports of such accidents. Indeed, Pill J observed that he was

"very doubtful whether, in the present context, a record of accidents, comes within the category of scientific and technical knowledge. The defence contemplates scientific and technical advances which throw additional light, for example, on the propensities of materials and allow defects to be discovered."

A v National Blood Authority (No.1)[64] also applied the approach of the ECJ and rejected the defendant's state of the art defence. Burton J held that the defence did not apply where the existence of a generic defect was known or should have been known in the context of accessible information. Once the existence of a defect was known, there was the risk of that defect materialising in any particular product, and it was immaterial that the known risk was unavoidable in the particular specimen of the product.   **5–54**

Concerns that the formulation of the state of the art defence in the Act might result in UK courts interpreting it less favourably than intended by the Directive have proved groundless. Other fears about the state of the art defence also need to be seen in perspective. As was pointed out in the parliamentary debates, the true undiscoverable development risk is likely to be very rare. It is only to the category of design defects that it is likely to have any relevance. Where the defect is a manufacturing defect it is unlikely to have any relevance; and can have no application where the product is defective through a failure to warn.   **5–55**

---

[60] *Commission v UK* [1997] 3 C.M.L.R. 923 at [29].
[61] *Richardson v LRC Products* [2000] P.I.Q.R. 164.
[62] *Richardson v LRC Products* [2000] P.I.Q.R. 164 at 172.
[63] *Abouzaid v Mothercare Plc, The Times*, December 21, 2000 CA.
[64] *A v National Blood Authority (No.1)* [2001] 3 All E.R. 289.

Components

5–56 Many products contain component parts made by various manufacturers. An excellent example is the motorcar where the manufacturer of the finished product may actually fabricate only the bodywork, the seats and the interior trim, but purchase many other parts such as brakes, gear boxes, tyres and electrical accessories from independent suppliers. As was pointed out above, a component manufacturer is liable as a producer for any defects in products of his which are incorporated in a finished product. In certain circumstances the component manufacturer will have a defence under s.4(1)(f). This is the case where the component supplier can show that the defect in the finished product which resulted from the article supplied by them was wholly attributable to the design of the finished product or to compliance with instructions given by the producer of the finished product.

5–57 This defence will be particularly important to manufacturers of components that are widely used in industry without the component manufacturer having any control over their use, such as nuts and bolts. Provided the component manufacturer has produced articles without a flaw and has correctly described their product, they will have no further responsibility for problems resulting from the use to which an assembler puts their product.

Contributory negligence

5–58 As we have seen already, s.2(1) states that various persons are liable "where any damage is caused wholly or partly by a defect in a product". Thus where the damage is caused partly by the defect and partly by some third party the producer is liable to the victim, though they will be able by virtue of s.2(5) to obtain a contribution from the third party. When the damage is caused partly by a defect in the product and partly by the fault of the victim the normal rules of apportionment for contributory negligence apply. These are to be found in the Law Reform (Contributory Negligence) Act 1945.

Causation

5–59 The new product liability regime introduced by the 1987 Act does not require proof that the loss suffered by the victim was foreseeable. This does not rule out consideration of causation. It is not enough to show that the product was defective and that the plaintiff was injured by it. It must be shown that there was a causal connection between these two facts. The 1987 Act states in s.21(1) that the damage must be "caused wholly or partly by a defect in a product". If the defendant can show some break in the chain of causation they will be able to avoid liability. Questions of causation will undoubtedly overlap with issues of improper use and contributory negligence.[65]

---

[65] See *Ide v ATB Sales* [2008] EWCA 424.

Damage

For the purposes of liability for defective products damage is defined in s.5 of the **5–60** 1987 Act to mean death or personal injury or any loss of or damage to any property including land. There is no mention of economic loss and it is generally assumed by the textbook writers that this is not recoverable under the 1987 Act. Although the 1987 Act does not state the basis on which damages are to be calculated, it is reasonable to assume that it will be on the normal delictual principles. Damages for personal injury will include damages for pain and suffering. Article 9 of the Directive[66] states that such damages are to be awarded if, as is the case in Scotland, they are awardable under domestic law. Where the victim has died as the result of their injuries s.6(1)(c) preserves the rights of dependants and relatives to bring actions under the Damages (Scotland) Act 1976. Section 6(3) aligns the Congenital Disabilities (Civil Liability) Act 1976 with the new product liability regime.

Liability for damage to property is limited in various ways. Damages are not **5–61** available for any loss of, or damage to, the defective product itself. Compensation for other property is available only where the property is, to quote s.5(3), "of a description of property ordinarily intended for private use, occupation or consumption" and "intended by the person suffering the loss or damage mainly for his own private use, occupation or consumption". Where compensation for property loss is sought s.5(4) provides that there is to be no award unless the amount awarded exceeds £275.

For the purpose of deciding who has the right to sue for loss to property, and **5–62** when such loss occurred, s.5(5) provides that it

> "shall be regarded as having occurred at the earliest time at which a person with an interest in the property had knowledge of the material facts about the loss or damage".

Section 5(6) goes on to state that material facts

> "are such facts about the loss or damage as would lead a reasonable person with an interest in the property to consider the loss or damage sufficiently serious to justify his instituting proceedings for damages against a defendant who did not dispute liability and was able to satisfy a judgement".

The Directive permits Member States to limit a producer's liability for damage **5–63** resulting from death or personal injury and caused by identical items with the same defect to be limited to an amount that is not less than €70 million (approximately £55 million). The UK has chosen not to take advantage of this facility.

---

[66] Directive 85/374/EEC of 25 July 1985 on the approximation of laws, regulations and administrative provisions of the Member States concerning liability for defective products [1985] O.J. L210/29.

Time-limits

5–64 The Prescription and Limitation (Scotland) Act 1973 is amended by Sch.1 of the 1987 Act and provides that product liability actions are extinguished 10 years after the product was supplied by its manufacturer, importer or the person who put their own name on it. In addition, the same action shall be brought three years after the later of the date on which the cause of action accrued and the date of knowledge of the injured person. It is important to note that the 10-year limit can have the effect of abbreviating the three-year limit. Where someone is injured say, nine years after the product was supplied, that person has only one year in which to raise an action. This seems to have been accepted in *Re MMR and MR Vaccine Litigation*[67] although it should be noted that these changes to the normal rules required to be made separately for each jurisdiction.

5–65 The litigation in *O'Byrne v Aventis Pasteur MSD Ltd* deals with a different aspect of limitation of actions. In this case the claimant had mistakenly raised an action against X, the wholly owned subsidiary of the Aventis Pasteur MSD Ltd (APMSD), within the 10 year period. By the time that it was realised that APMSD was the proper defendant this period had expired. An application was made to substitute APMSD for the subsidiary in the original proceedings. After a series of cases involving two references to the ECJ the Supreme Court held, applying a decision of the ECJ, that it was clear that once 10 years had expired after the product had been put into circulation a producer could not be sued unless proceedings had been commenced against the producer (in this case APMSD) within the 10-year period. Further, the situation did not fall under a qualification to the normal rule where the circulation of the product had been determined by the producer allowing the producer to be substituted for the supplier.[68]

EXCLUSION OF LIABILITY

5–66 It will not be possible to contract out of liability under Pt 1 of the 1987 Act. Section 7 makes this clear stating that liability

> "to a person who has suffered damage caused wholly or partly by a defect in a product, or to a dependent or relative of such a person, shall not be limited or excluded by any contract term, by any notice or by any other provision".

CIVIL LIABILITY UNDER THE CONSUMER PROTECTION ACT 1987 PT 2

5–67 The criminal law is used, as is discussed below,[69] to try to ensure that only safe goods reach the market place. In addition to incurring criminal liability, breach of the safety regulations can lead to civil liability. Section 41 of the 1987 Act is one

---

[67] *Re MMR and MR Vaccine Litigation* [2001] EWCA Civ. 2006; [2002] 1 W.L.R. 1662; [2002] C.P. Rep. 20; (2002) 65 B.M.L.R. 79.

[68] *O'Byrne v Aventis Pasteur MSD Ltd* [2010] UKSC 23; [2010] 1 W.L.R applying the judgment of the European Court of Justice in *Aventis Pasteur SA v OB* (C-358/08) [2010] 1 W.L.R. 1375.

[69] See para.5–68 onwards.

of those rare provisions in legislation imposing criminal penalties which explicitly states that this is the case. It provides that breach of safety regulations gives a right of action for breach of statutory duty to anyone affected. It is to be noted that while this applies to breach of the safety regulations it does not apply to breach of the general safety requirement. In practice little use seems to be made of this provision and there are no reported cases on it from any part of the UK.

ROLE OF THE CRIMINAL LAW

The civil law controls on product standards discussed above apply after the harm has occurred. Where the failure of a product to meet the required legal standard may cause personal injury or death it is important to attempt to prevent such a product being put into circulation at all. The Consumer Protection Act 1961[70] was the legislative response to the need identified by the *Molony Report*[71] for legislation governing dangerous products. Its central feature was the creation of a power to make regulations specifying safety criteria for products. The 1978 Act followed a review of product safety controls in a government consultative document[72] that revealed inadequacies in the earlier legislation. Among these were: criticisms of slowness in establishing and revising safety standards; the lengthy consultations involved when hazards came to light; and the absence of powers to deal promptly with new products which proved to be hazardous but which were not subject to existing regulations.

5–68

The 1978 Act met these criticisms by introducing three new techniques. Where the Secretary of State considered that a product or a component part of a product was not safe they were empowered to issue a "prohibition order" prohibiting the supply of goods which were considered to be unsafe, or permitting their supply only on such conditions as were specified in the notice.[73] Finally, a "notice to warn" could be served on any person, requiring that person to publish, at their own expense, a warning about unsafe goods that they had supplied. Further improvements to the legislation were made by the Consumer Safety (Amendment) Act 1986, which implemented many of the proposals in the 1984 White Paper.[74] This was concerned mainly with improving the enforcement of the legislation.

5–69

All this legislation was repealed by the 1987 Act,[75] which is primarily a consolidating measure, although it did include some new provisions, most notably the creation of a general safety requirement.[76] While there were other

5–70

---

[70] Consumer Protection Act 1961 was repealed by Consumer Safety Act 1978 s.10(1) Sch.3 on 1 October 1987; Consumer Safety Act 1978 (Commencement No.3) Order 1987 (SI 1987/1681).

[71] The Molony Report, *Final Report of the Committee on Consumer Protection* (HSMO, 1962) Cmnd.1781.

[72] Department of Prices and Consumer Protection, *Consumer Safety: A Consultative Document* (HMSO, 1976) Cmnd.6398.

[73] See Consumer Safety Act 1978 s.3 Sch.1 (repealed).

[74] Department of Trade and Industry, *The Safety of Goods* (HMSO, 1984) Cmnd.9302.

[75] Consumer Protection Act 1987 s.48 Sch.5. The repeals came into force on 1 October 1987; Consumer Protection Act 1987 (Commencement No.1) Order 1987 (SI 1987/1680) art.3(k) Sch.1 Pt 1.

[76] Repealed by General Product Safety Regulations 2005 (SI 2005/1803) reg.46(1)–(2).

pieces of safety legislation, the law was reasonably clearly set out. That can no longer be said with the enactment of the General Product Safety Regulations 2005.[77] These regulations implement the EC's General Product Safety Directive 2001[78] and replace the similarly named 1994 Regulations.[79] In order to try to make sense of the present law it will be necessary to discuss Pt 2 of the 1987 Act and then the new regulations. This is because both are relevant and complement each other. As we shall see, the new regulations refer to the enforcement techniques of Pt 2.

Safety regulations

5–71   The 1987 Act, like earlier safety legislation, gives the Secretary of State for Trade and Industry extensive powers to make regulations relating to the safety of goods.[80] Regulations may be made to ensure that goods are safe; that unsafe goods are not made available generally, or to persons in whose hands they would be unsafe; and that appropriate information is provided. Section 11(2) goes on to specify a wide range of matters with which the regulations may deal such as their composition, testing and inspection.[81] Before making such regulations the Secretary of State has a duty to consult organisations that appear to them to be representative of interests substantially affected by their proposal and any other persons they consider appropriate.[82]

5–72   The power to make safety regulations is exercisable by statutory instruments subject to annulment by resolution of either House of Parliament.[83] Under previous legislation regulations were subject to affirmative resolution of both Houses of Parliament. Breach of safety regulations is not itself a criminal offence. It is an offence to supply (as widely defined in s.46)[84] where the regulations prohibit such supply. Offences are punishable on summary conviction by imprisonment for a term not exceeding six months or by a fine not exceeding level 5 on the standard scale or by both.[85]

---

[77] General Product Safety Regulations 2005 (SI 2005/1803).

[78] Directive 2001/95/EC of the European Parliament and of the Council of 3 December 2001 on general product safety [2002] O.J. L11/4, which repealed Directive 1992/59 on general product safety [1992] O.J. L228/24.

[79] General Product Safety Regulations 1994 (SI 1994/2328).

[80] See Consumer Protection Act 1987 s.11. For the goods to which s.11 does not apply, see s.11(7).

[81] A large number of regulations have been made covering such goods as toys, see Toys (Safety) (Amendment) Regulations 1993 (SI 1993/1547); cosmetics, see Cosmetic Products (Safety) (Amendment) Regulations 1992 (SI 1992/1525); and see Low Voltage Electrical Equipment (Safety) Regulations 1989 (SI 1989/728).

[82] See s.11(5). This function has been discussed in *R. v Secretary of State for Health, Ex p. United States Tobacco International Inc* [1992] 1 Q.B. 353; [1992] 1 All E.R. 212.

[83] See Consumer Protection Act 1987 s.11(6).

[84] See *Drummond-Rees v Dorset County Council* (1998) 162 J.P. 651 DC.

[85] See, generally, s.12. Level 5 is £5,000: Increase of Criminal Penalties etc. (Scotland) Order 1984 (SI 1984/526) art.4.

Prohibition notices and notices to warn

The prohibition notices introduced by the Consumer Safety Act 1978 are re-enacted in the 1987 Act, as are notices to warn,[86] and the 1987 Act sets out in detail the procedure to be used when it is proposed to issue such notices.[87] In *R v Liverpool City Council, Ex p. Baby Products*[88] it was held that the council was acting outside its powers in issuing a press release alleging that a product was dangerous. The statutory procedure under the safety legislation was the appropriate way to prevent the sale of goods suspected to be dangerous. The court conceded that this was cumbersome and slow and the Lord Chief Justice commented:

5–73

> "I can imagine circumstances in which an emergency procedure to supplement the s.13 procedure would be desirable. The remedy for a defective statutory procedure is not, however, to ignore or circumvent it but to amend it."[89]

Suspension notices

The Consumer Safety (Amendment) Act 1986 gave enforcement authorities, in practice trading standards officers, an important new power to deal with dangerous goods when it introduced the suspension notice. This is re-enacted in the Consumer Protection Act 1987. A trading standards officer may serve a suspension notice prohibiting the supply of specified goods if they have reasonable cause to believe that any safety provision has been, or may be, contravened.[90] Such a notice applies beyond the area of the local authority that issued it but may only be enforced in other areas by the local authorities for them.[91] A suspension notice may not extend beyond six months and a further notice may only be served in respect of the same goods if proceedings have first been instituted for breach of a safety provision or for the forfeiture of the goods.[92] The owner of suspended goods may appeal against the suspension notice.[93]

5–74

In *R v Birmingham City Council, Ex p. Ferrero Ltd*[94] the English Court of Appeal held that the proper method of challenging a suspension notice was by means of the appeal procedure set out in s.15 of the 1987 Act, not by judicial review. Taylor LJ (as he then was) said:

5–75

---

[86] See Consumer Protection Act 1987 s.13.

[87] See Consumer Protection Act 1987 s.13(2) Sch.2.

[88] *R v Liverpool City Council, Ex p Baby Products* (2000) 2 L.G.L.R. 689; [2000] B.L.G.R. 171; [2000] C.O.D. 91, DC.

[89] *R v Liverpool City Council, Ex p Baby Products* (2000) 2 L.G.L.R. 689 at 694.

[90] See Consumer Protection Act 1987 s.14(1), (5). A suspension notice may also require that the authority be informed of the whereabouts throughout the suspension period of suspended goods: Consumer Protection Act 1987 s.14(3). As to the contents of a suspension notice, see Consumer Protection Act 1987 s.14(2).

[91] *Brighton and Hove City Council v Woolworths Plc* [2002] EWHC 2565; (2003) 167 J.P. 21; (2003) 167 J.P.N. 52, QBD.

[92] See Consumer Protection Act 1987 s.14(1), (4). As to forfeiture of goods, see Consumer Protection Act 1987 s.17.

[93] See Consumer Protection Act 1987 s.15(1), (2), (4).

[94] *R v Birmingham City Council, Ex p. Ferrero Ltd* [1993] 1 All E.R. 530; (1991) 155 J.P. 721; 89 L.G.R. 977; (1991) 3 Admin. L.R. 613; (1991) 10 Tr. L.R. 129.

"The real issue was whether the goods contravened a safety provision and the section 15 appeal was geared exactly to deciding that issue. If the goods did contravene the safety provision and were dangerous to children then, surely, procedural impropriety or unfairness in the decision-making process should not persuade a court to quash the order. The determining factors are the paramount need to safeguard consumers and the emergency nature of the section 14 powers."[95]

5–76   Where the power to suspend a supply has been exercised, an enforcement authority is liable to pay compensation to any person having an interest in the goods, in respect of any loss or damage caused by reason of the exercise of the power, if there has been no contravention in relation to the goods of any safety provision and the exercise of the power is not attributable to any neglect or default by that person.[96]

Defence of due diligence

5–77   There is a due diligence defence in the 1987 Act,[97] but reliance on information supplied by someone else will not establish this defence unless it can be shown that it was reasonable in all the circumstances to have relied on the information having regard in particular to: (1) the steps which were taken, and which might reasonably have been taken, to verify the information; and (2) whether they had any reason to disbelieve the information.[98]

5–78   It has not been easy to take advantage of this defence. In *Riley v Webb*,[99] a case under the Consumer Protection Act 1961, the defendant, who was a wholesaler, showed that it had a condition on its order forms that orders were placed in the understanding that the goods met any relevant statutory requirements. It also argued that it was a small company and had dealt with the supplier of the unsafe goods for many years. Random sampling, it claimed, would have been unreasonable. The English divisional court held that the defendants could have taken a simple step to avoid breaching the Act. It could either have asked for specific assurances about the goods; or it could have imposed contract terms under which its suppliers would have had to ensure that the regulations had been complied with. By using only the general term in its order form it had not exercised due diligence.

5–79   In *Rotherham Metropolitan Borough Council v Rayson (UK) Ltd*[100] a request to overseas suppliers to report any failures to meet UK standards had been sent to them, and the defendants had tested one packet out of an annual purchase of several thousand. The divisional court did not regard this as meeting the due diligence standard. In *P & M Supplies (Essex) Ltd v Devon County Council*[101] the

---

[95] *R v Birmingham City Council, Ex p. Ferrero Ltd* [1993] 1 All E.R. 530 at 539.
[96] See Consumer Protection Act 1987 s.14(7). Any dispute as to the right to or the amount of any compensation is to be determined by a single arbiter appointed, failing agreement between the parties, by the sheriff: Consumer Protection Act 1987 s.14(8).
[97] Consumer Protection Act 1987 s.39. The offences in Consumer Protection Act 1987 Pt 2, to which the defence relates, are offences under ss.10 and 12(1)–(3), offences against safety regulations, and s.14(6) offences in respect of suspension notices: Consumer Protection Act 1987 s.39(5).
[98] See Consumer Protection Act 1987 s.39(4).
[99] *Riley v Webb* (1987) 151 J.P. 372.
[100] *Rotheram Metropolitan Borough Council v Rayson (UK) Ltd* [1988] B.T.L.C. 292.
[101] *P & M Supplies (Essex) Ltd v Devon County Council* (1992) 11 Tr. L.R. 52.

appellants had been convicted of an offence against the Toys (Safety) Regulations 1974[102] relating to a soft toy. Evidence showed that 0.49 per cent of stock was tested randomly, and some samples were sent to the public analyst. Dismissing the appeal, the English divisional court said that it was for the company to produce evidence, preferably independent statistical evidence, to show the soundness of their sampling methods.

It is generally believed that a high proportion of dangerous goods are imported. For this reason the provision giving powers to the Commissioners of Customs and Excise to disclose information to those who enforce safety legislation, which was introduced by the Consumer Safety (Amendment) Act 1986, is re-enacted in the 1987 Act.[103] A customs officer may also, for the purpose of facilitating the enforcement of the safety provisions, seize any imported goods and detain them for not more than two working days.[104] 　　5–80

Where there has been a contravention of the safety provisions the procurator fiscal may apply to a sheriff for an order for the forfeiture of any unsafe goods. The owner, or anyone having an interest in the goods, must be given notice of the application and may appear at the hearing to oppose the making of such an order.[105] 　　5–81

General Product Safety Regulations 2005

The General Product Safety Regulations,[106] which implement the General Product Safety Directive,[107] follow the deplorable recent tendency of implementing Directives in areas where there is already important domestic primary legislation by means of regulations instead of legislating afresh in the area. New primary legislation would have produced a more coherent and clearer legislative regime than the confusion with which industry, consumers and enforcement agencies have been saddled. 　　5–82

The central provision of the regulations is found in reg.5(1) which states "[n]o producer shall place a product on the market unless the product is a safe product". The succeeding subparagraphs apply this to other forms of supply. The heading in the regulations calls this "the general safety requirement". This is supported by reg.7, which imposes various obligations on producers to give information to consumers and obtain information about the performance of their products; reg.8, which requires a distributor to "act with due care in order to help ensure compliance with the applicable safety"; and reg.9, which places obligations on both producers and distributors. In all these situations failure to observe the requirements of the regulations is a criminal offence.[108] 　　5–83

Before considering these provisions in more detail it will first be useful to discover what products are covered and who are producers and distributors. 　　5–84

For the purpose of the regulations "product" means: 　　5–85

---

[102] Toys (Safety) Regulations 1974 (SI 1974/1367).
[103] See Consumer Protection Act 1987 s.37.
[104] See Consumer Protection Act 1987 s.31.
[105] See Consumer Protection Act 1987 s.17.
[106] General Product Safety Regulations 2005 (SI 2005/1803).
[107] Directive 2001/95/EC of the European Parliament and of the Council of 3 December 2001 on general product safety [2002] O.J. L11/4.
[108] See General Product Safety Regulations 2005 (SI 2005/1803) reg.20.

"[A] product which is intended for consumers or likely, under reasonably foreseeable conditions, to be used by consumers even if not intended for them and which is supplied or made available, whether for consideration or not, in the course of a commercial activity and whether it is new, used or reconditioned and includes a product that is supplied or made available to consumers for their own use in the context of providing a service. 'Product' does not include equipment used by service providers themselves to supply a service to consumers, in particular equipment on which consumers ride or travel which is operated by a service provider."[109]

5–86   While not explicitly stated, it is clear from looking at the regulations as a whole that "product" does not include services and reg.30 provides that antiques are not covered. Second-hand goods are covered by the regulations but reg.4 excludes second-hand goods supplied as a product to be repaired or reconditioned provided that the supplier clearly informs the person to whom they supply the product. The definition also makes clear that goods transferred in private transactions are not covered. Some other aspects of the definition require comment. It refers to products, "likely, under reasonably foreseeable conditions, to be used by consumers even if not intended for them", sometimes referred to as "migrating" products. Various kinds of building equipment such as cement mixers and scaffolding are available from hire shops. The producer may have intended that they would be used by professional builders but they are also used by individuals for DIY jobs and so would come within the definition. The final part of the definition excludes "equipment used by service providers themselves to supply a service to consumers". Reference is made to equipment on which consumers ride or travel so buses or taxis would be examples. However, gym equipment or supermarket trolleys which are supplied for the use of consumers would be included within the definition of product.

5–87   Another important category of products exempt from the regulations is those where there are specific provisions in rules of EU law governing all aspects of the safety of the product. This means that there will be no overlap between these regulations and other EU product safety rules. For example, various community directives contain a wide range of specific provisions governing the safety of medicinal products, medicated feeding stuffs and medicinal feed additives. Products that are licensed in the UK in accordance with these EU rules will not be subject to the regulations. But it is important to note that this exemption applies only where the EU law relates to all aspects of the safety of the product. Regulation 3(1) makes clear that it does not apply where the product is subject to some other EU law that does not make provision about its safety.

Producers

5–88   The regulations place the primary duty of ensuring that only safe products are marketed on "producers" a term which is defined in reg.2. It covers manufacturers established in the EU which, for the purposes of these regulations, means not just the Member States of the EU but the European Economic Area (EEA), a very much larger group of countries. The term "producer" also includes those who pass themselves off as manufacturers, such as own-branders and those

---

[109] See General Product Safety Regulations 2005 (SI 2005/1803) reg.2.

who recondition products. Where the manufacturer is not established in the EEA the producer, their representative or, if there is none, the importer is liable. "Producer" also includes other professionals in the supply chain, insofar as their activities may affect the safety properties of a product. This might bring transport or storage companies within the ambit of the definition.

Distributors

As we shall see, certain duties are placed upon distributors. They are defined as "any professional in the supply chain whose activity does not affect the safety properties of a product".

5–89

Safety

The definition of safety in reg.2 bears some resemblance to that in Pt 1 of the 1987 Act and is a pragmatic one. A safe product is one:

5–90

> "[W]hich, under normal or reasonably foreseeable conditions of use including duration and, where applicable, putting into service, installation and maintenance requirements, does not present any risk or only the minimum risks compatible with the product's use, considered to be acceptable and consistent with a high level of protection for the safety and health of persons."

In assessing whether this standard has been met a number factors related to the product are to be taken into account. These are:

5–91

(a) the characteristics of the product, including its composition, packaging, instructions for assembly and, where applicable, instructions for installation and maintenance;
(b) the effect of the product on other products, where it is reasonably foreseeable that it will be used with other products;
(c) the presentation of the product, the labelling, any warnings and instructions for its use and disposal and any other indication or information regarding the product; and
(d) the categories of consumers at risk when using the product, in particular children and the elderly.

However, the fact that higher levels of safety can be obtained, or that there are other products presenting a lesser degree of risk does not of itself mean that a product is unsafe. An example of this in practice might be provided by cars. Some, usually the more expensive, models of cars have anti-lock braking systems. This provision probably means that cars that do not have such systems will not be regarded as unsafe because they do not have such a system.

5–92

Duties of producers

As pointed out above, the principal obligation of a producer is to ensure that no unsafe products are placed on the market. There are several ways in which it can be shown that a product conforms to this safety obligation. If it complies with

5–93

specific provisions in rules of EU law governing safety it will do so.[110] If there are no such provisions there are a number of other ways in which conformity may be demonstrated. If there are specific rules of the law of part of the UK laying down the health and safety requirements which the product must satisfy in order to be marketed in the UK, the product is to be deemed safe so far as concerns the aspects covered by such rules.[111] An example would be a product which meets the requirement of safety regulations made under Pt II of the 1987 Act. For the first time there is a presumption of conformity to the general safety requirement if a product conforms to the UK transposition of a voluntary European standard that has had its references published in the *Official Journal of the European Union*, but only as far as the risks are covered by that standard.[112] Where neither a specific regulation nor national safety law applies, safety will be assessed taking into account voluntary European standards, EU technical specifications, national standards (that is British standards that are not UK versions of European standards), industry codes of good practice, the state of the art and technology, and the safety which consumers may reasonably expect.[113]

5–94 It is highly likely that a product that meets one or more of the above standards will provide an acceptable level of safety. However, as reg.6(4) points out, conformity to such a standard does not prevent an enforcement authority from taking action if there is evidence that it is dangerous. *Balding v Lew-Ways Ltd*[114] is an example of a case where the court found that a toy conformed to British Standard EN71 but it was still found to be unsafe for the purposes of the Toys (Safety) Regulations 1995.

5–95 In addition to supplying products that are safe, producers must provide consumers with information to enable them to assess the risks inherent in a product throughout its normal or reasonably foreseeable life where these are not immediately obvious without adequate warnings and to enable them to take precautions against such risks.[115] They must also take measures commensurate with the characteristics of the product to keep themselves informed of any risks which a product might pose and to enable them to take appropriate action such as withdrawal of the product, effective warnings and, as a last resort, recall of the product.[116] Such measures might consist of marking the products, their packaging or other materials supplied with the product, such as an instruction booklet, with the name and address of the producer, product reference and batch number. Other possibilities are sample testing of products on the market, investigation of complaints relating to safety, keeping a register of such complaints, and informing distributors of the monitoring work and its results.

Duties of distributors

5–96 Distributors as defined in the regulations are required by reg.8 to act with due care in order to help ensure compliance with the general safety duty. In particular,

---

[110] See General Product Safety Regulations 2005 (SI 2005/1803) reg.6(1).
[111] See General Product Safety Regulations 2005 (SI 2005/1803) reg.6(1).
[112] See General Product Safety Regulations 2005 (SI 2005/1803) reg.6(2).
[113] See General Product Safety Regulations 2005 (SI 2005/1803) reg.6(3).
[114] *Balding v Lew-Ways Ltd* [1995] Crim. L.R. 878.
[115] See General Product Safety Regulations 2005 (SI 2005/1803) reg.7(1).
[116] See General Product Safety Regulations 2005 (SI 2005/1803) reg.7(3).

they must not supply products which they know, or should have presumed, on the basis of the information available to them, were dangerous. They must, within the limits of their activities, participate in monitoring the safety of products, pass on information about their safety, and co-operate in action to avoid those risks.

Enforcement

Day to day enforcement of the regulations is in the hands of the trading standards departments of district and island councils. In addition, the Secretary of State, any other minister of the Crown in charge of a government department and any such department also have such powers. There are a number of techniques that can be used to enforce the regulations. Regulation 11 permits a suspension notice to be served to prohibit temporarily the placing of a product on the market while safety checks are arranged. Regulation 12 allows an enforcer to serve a "requirement to mark" notice requiring warnings about the dangers of the product to be put on it or referred to in its marketing. A "requirement to warn" notice involves providing warnings about the dangers of the product to those who could be endangered by it.[117] Regulations 14 and 15 contain more drastic powers. The former allows an enforcer to serve a "withdrawal notice" requiring the person to whom it is addressed not to place the product on the market. The latter contains a most important power which has been missing from previous safety legislation, the power to order the recall of a product that is considered to be dangerous. Such a notice can order a trader to "use his reasonable endeavours to organise the return of the product from consumers". As this will be an expensive process it is subject to various qualifications and is intended as a last resort where no other action would suffice. Another enforcement power is that of the procurator fiscal to apply to the sheriff court for an order for the forfeiture and destruction of unsafe products. An alternative permits a court to permit the products to be supplied to someone for repair, reconditioning or scrap.[118]

5–97

Products found to be unsafe in one Member State may well be circulating in other states so the Directive contains provisions designed not only to ensure that each state monitors product safety within its own borders but informs other Member States of potential dangers. Part 4 of the Regulations implement these provisions. Emergency procedures are in place where there is what the Directive calls a "serious and immediate risk" and these not only require that there are domestic arrangements for rapid exchange of information but also that the EC Commission is informed. The Commission system is known as RAPEX and Department for Business, Innovation and Skills is the UK contact point.

5–98

The EU has been considering the revision of the product safety regime for some time and the European Commission published the Product Safety and Market Surveillance Package in February 2013.[119] The package includes a proposal for a Regulation of the European Parliament and of the Council on consumer product safety, repealing the General Product Safety Directive and the Directive on dangerous imitations. In addition, a regulation creating stronger

5–99

---

[117] See General Product Safety Regulations 2005 (SI 2005/1803) reg.13.
[118] See General Product Safety Regulations 2005 (SI 2005/1803) reg.19.
[119] European Commission, *Product Safety and Market Surveillance Package* (February 2013) COM 74 final.

market surveillance is proposed together with various other actions to ensure safer products. It was intended that this package would be implemented in 2015 but at the time of writing this seems unlikely.

Services

5–100   As noted above, safety legislation relates to goods not services. Having updated the Directive on safety of goods the European Commission turned its attention to services. In 2002 it published a consultation document, *Safety of Services for Consumers*, and the following year a report to the Council and Parliament on the subject.[120] This conceded that lack of evidence of internal market problems would seem to preclude action at Community level. In 2013 the Commission announced that it had plans to launch in that year a wide consultation on the safety of certain consumer services.[121] Nothing happened until 29 July 2014 when a Green Paper on the *Safety of Tourism Accommodation Services* was published.[122]

---

[120] Commission of the European Communities, Report from the Commission to the European Parliament and the Council on the safety of services for consumers (2003) COM 313 final.

[121] See *http://ec.europa.eu/consumers/archive/safety/serv_background/index_en.htm* [Accessed 16 June 2015].

[122] See *http://ec.europa.eu/consumers/consumers_safety/safety_of_services/index_en.htm* [Accessed 16 June 2015].

CHAPTER 6

Services

Services encompass a very wide range of activities. These are as diverse as laundry and dry cleaning, furniture removal, home improvements, educational services, car maintenance and servicing and professional services. Even this latter category, which one might have supposed would include a relatively narrow range of services, displays astonishing diversity. The Monopolies Commission, when it was asked to investigate the professions, received evidence from 161 professional bodies, although some of those bodies were concerned with the same, or a closely related, profession. The commission found it impossible to define the distinguishing characteristics of professions or to establish a definitive list, a feat that has taxed others.[1]

    6–01

The service sector of the economy expanded enormously during the twentieth century and the range of services offered to the public is extremely varied. It is sometimes said that in the UK we have become a service economy. This is based on the fact that, like other developed economies, more than half of output is generated by the service sector.

    6–02

While the service sector has expanded in economic terms, legally it has been somewhat neglected. The preliminary problem encountered in the range of services is the difficulty in determining into which legal category some kinds of services fall. In the case of most professional services this problem does not arise, the service clearly being *locatio operis faciendi*. As Professor McBryde observes, "[t]his contract is very common in practice but has been somewhat neglected by our textbook writers".[2] Many non-professional services will fall into the same category where the essence of the service is the bringing about of a result as, for example, where a repair is to be effected or a thing is to be cleaned. In other cases classification is much less easy and is not aided by a paucity of authority, both institutional and judicial. The situation in England until recently was not dissimilar.

    6–03

In England and Wales this was ameliorated by the passing of the Supply of Goods and Services Act 1982 (the 1982 Act), Pt 2 of which put into statutory form some of the main terms to be implied in contracts for services. Part II did not apply to Scotland and it was observed in previous editions of this book that it would be a useful service to Scottish consumers if similar legislation were introduced in this jurisdiction. That has now been done with the enactment of the Consumer Rights Act 2015 (the 2015 Act). Part 1 Ch.4 of that 2015 Act deals

    6–04

---

[1] See the Monopolies Commission, *A report on the general effect on the public interest of certain restrictive practices so far as they prevail in relation to the supply of professional services* (HMSO, 1970) Cmnd.4463, pp.1 and 3.

[2] WW McBryde, *The Law of Contract in Scotland* (Edinburgh: W. Green, 2007) para.9.23.

with services provided to consumers by traders and applies to the whole of the UK. It largely follows the structure of Pt II of the 1982 Act. Having defined which services it applies to, it then sets out the duties imposed on traders who provide services. There are some services where stricter duties are placed on traders or quite separate regimes have been created by Parliament for a particular service. Financial services which are governed by the Financial Services and Markets Act 2000 are a good example. Section 53 of the 2015 Act makes clear that it does not affect such legislation.

SERVICES COVERED

6–05   The 2015 Act applies only to a contract for a trader to supply a service to a consumer. The scope of the terms "consumer" and "trader" have already been discussed in Ch.3. It is worth emphasising that the definition of "trader" covers situations where someone is acting in the trader's name or on their behalf.[3] This underlines the important point that where a trader chooses to subcontract some of the work they are contractually responsible for the work. For example, in building contracts it is common for the main contractor to arrange for specialist tradesmen such as glaziers or electricians to do some of the work. There is little further guidance in the 2015 Act on what a service is. Section 48(2) states that it does not include a contract of employment or apprenticeship and the following subsection says that it does not apply to gratuitous contracts. There is power for the Secretary of State to add to these exclusions, as was the case with the 1982 Act provisions applying to England and Wales, where a similar power was used to disapply an implied term to take reasonable care and skill to the services provided by an advocate in a court or tribunal, by a company director, by a director of a building society and the management of a provident society to that building or provident society and to services rendered by arbitrators in their capacity as such.

6–06   Broadly speaking, services can be divided into what are sometimes called pure services and contracts for work and materials though that term is a term of art from English law that has not been clearly recognised in Scots law. Most professional services such as those of lawyers, accountants and doctors would fall into this category as would the services of a hairdresser or travel services none of which results in any tangible output. Contracts for work and materials involve both the supply of goods and the provision of services. Examples of such situations are contracts for the construction of a building, the repair of a car, the installation of a central heating system and the provision of a meal in a restaurant. Contracts for work and materials would be what the 2015 Act in s.1(4) calls "mixed contracts" being partly concerned with services and partly with the provision of goods. As a result the appropriate parts of the Act would be applied to the component parts.

6–07   Before examining the various terms inserted in contracts for services it is first necessary to note that it will often be important to establish exactly what it was that the consumer and the provider of the service agreed should be done. Section 50 of the 2015 Act appears to be helpful here in that it provides that anything that

---

[3] Consumer Rights Act 2015 s.2(2).

is said or written to consumers by or on behalf of traders about the themselves or their services is a term of the contract if consumers take it into account when deciding to enter into contracts or when making a decision about services after entering into them. However, this begs the question as it is necessary to prove what was said which may prove difficult. Written statements are less of a problem. For this reason it is worth looking at existing case law dealing with the issue of just what the consumer and trader agreed.

Brown v J Nisbet & Co Ltd[4] is a good example of this issue. The defenders had acquired a van that was not in a very good state of repair. They took it to the pursuer who ran a motor repair business and various repairs were carried out. When some problems later developed with the van the pursuers refused to pay for the repairs, alleging that the work had not been carried out properly. They claimed that it had been agreed that a complete overhaul of the van would be carried out. The repairer stated that he had not agreed to this but merely to put the van into good running order. There was evidence that the defenders had first obtained a quotation for the cost of a complete overhaul from another garage and, finding this to be too expensive, had then approached the pursuer who had offered to do work at a much lower cost. Looking at the evidence the sheriff came to the conclusion that "[t]he defenders tried to get along with something much less expensive". He found that the garage's evidence of the nature of the job agreed upon was to be preferred and, having agreed only to carry out limited work on the van, they were not liable for breakdowns which were unrelated to the repair work which they had been asked to do.

6–08

Walter Wright & Co Ltd v Cowdray[5] is another example of the objective approach that the courts take to this problem of assessing what the parties had agreed should be done. Electric motors on an estate had been damaged by floodwater and the pursuers, who were electrical engineers, were asked to dry out and test them. The engineers carried out this work. The defender refused to pay part of the charge for the work on the ground that it involved expensive repairs to one of the motors which had not been instructed. The sheriff considered the evidence and concluded from it that, looked at objectively, there was no justification for assuming that these repairs had been authorised.[6]

6–09

SERVICE TO BE PERFORMED WITH REASONABLE SKILL AND CARE

A central issue in the provision of a service is the standard of quality which the client is entitled to expect. In contracts for services this is summed up in one of those Latin maxims with which lawyers seek to dazzle the uninitiated, *spondet peritiam artis et imperitia culpae enumeratur*. In English this means that a person is responsible for exercising skill in their trade or profession, and lack of such skill will be regarded as a fault. Section 49 of the 2015 Act puts that rule developed in case law into statutory form by saying that contracts for the supply of services are "to be treated as including a term that the trader must perform the

6–10

---

[4] *Brown v J Nisbet & Co Ltd* (1941) 57 Sh. Ct. Reps. 202.
[5] *Walter Wright & Co Ltd v Cowdray*, 1973 S.L.T. (Sh. Ct.) 56.
[6] See also *Dalblair Motors Ltd v J Forrest & Son (Ayr) Ltd* (1954) 70 Sh. Ct. Reps. 107.

service with reasonable skill and care". The standard is that of the reasonable practitioner of the particular trade or profession and there are a number of examples in the law reports.

6–11   *McIntyre v Gallacher*[7] is a good example of the application of the principle. Mr Gallacher was a Glasgow plumber who had been employed to carry out plumbing work in a row of tenements. This included sealing off some pipes. One of the pipes was not properly sealed off and some time later leaked causing damage to property on lower floors for which the landlord, Mr McIntyre, was liable. Evidence proved that the proper and workmanlike method of sealing a pipe was to solder it. In this case Mr Gallacher, or one of his workmen, had only hammered the end of the lead pipe together and it eventually leaked. He was thus liable for failing to carry out the job with the requisite level of skill.

6–12   In *Brett v Williamson*[8] the sheriff principal referred to the fact that in building contracts arranged on either a fixed-price basis or, as in that case, on a "time and lime" basis, the problems resulting from unsatisfactory workmanship are particularly difficult to resolve. In that case the pursuer had undertaken to lay terazzo tiles and having done so in a manner which the defender regarded as unsatisfactory was obliged to bring an action for payment. It was argued for the pursuer that since such tile-laying was a specialist job but had been entrusted by the defender to him (who did not claim to be a specialist) he could not complain that the work was not up to the standard of a specialist. This argument was inspired by *Dickson v Hygienic Institute*[9] where it was said that a contractor need attain only "the skill which he professes or announces". As the sheriff principal pointed out, that did not go far enough for the pursuer's purposes because on examining *Dickson* it will be seen that Lord Dundas held that the standard of care is that of the type of practitioner which the client believed he or she was dealing with. Applying this approach to the case before him the sheriff principal stated:

> "In my view, when a tradesman undertakes to carry out a particular job in his trade, his obligation is to carry it out properly, unless he either makes known to his customer when contracting that the job requires more special skill than he commands, or can show that the customer was aware of that when contracting with him. I consider that a tradesman who accepts instructions professes to be able to carry them out, and it is he not the customer who will normally know whether he has or lacks the special skill which the job requires."[10]

6–13   This approach has much to commend it especially, as is frequently the case with small building jobs, where the client commissions the work directly from the tradesman and does not engage the services of an architect or surveyor.

6–14   *Brett v Williamson*[11] was applied to slightly different circumstances by the same sheriff principal in *Macintosh v Nelson*[12] where the pursuer claimed damages for loss sustained when seriously defective building work was carried out at her house. The defender had been an art teacher for several years before going into business on his own account as an industrial cleaning contractor who

---

[7] *McIntyre v Gallacher* (1883) 11 R. 64.
[8] *Brett v Williamson*, 1980 S.L.T. (Sh. Ct.) 56.
[9] *Dickson v Hygenic Institute*, 1910 S.C. 352; 1910 1 S.L.T. 111.
[10] *Brett v Williamson*, 1980 S.L.T. (Sh. Ct.) 56.
[11] *Brett v Williamson*, 1980 S.L.T. (Sh. Ct.) 56.
[12] *Macintosh v Nelson*, 1984 S.L.T. (Sh. Ct.) 82.

also undertook window cleaning, car valeting, external paintwork and landscape gardening. The pursuer had admired a sun lounge that the defender had built at his own home and had inquired whether he could do similar work at her house. While the pursuer understood that the defender was in business as a window-cleaning contractor, it was clear from the evidence that he held himself out as being capable both of drawing up the necessary plans and carrying out the building work in a workmanlike manner. He argued that in the circumstances he should only be held to the standards of an amateur builder. The sheriff principal referred to his decision in *Brett v Williamson* and was:

> "Prepared to hold that the same considerations apply where one who is not a tradesman contracts to do work for another. In other words, he must be held to have professed the requisite skill to do the job which he undertakes. Plainly, if he says that the job may be more than he can promise to do well or if the customer is shown to have known that, it would be open to the court to hold that his customer had taken the risk of unsatisfactory work on himself."[13]

A different aspect of the problem of the standard of the work arises where the issue is not the competence which the tradesman professes but the advice or warnings that they gave to their customer before carrying out the job. *Terret v Murphy*[14] is a good example. The owner of a furniture shop engaged the pursuer to paint an extension to his shop. He was eager to have the work completed and when the painter reported that supplies of the primer that he wished to use would not be available for several days he persuaded the painter to carry on with the job. This was done despite warnings from the painter that the absence of primer could result in problems later on. Problems did, indeed, arise and the owner of the shop withheld payment. Finding in favour of the painter the sheriff, to whom an appeal had been taken, pointed out that if a householder merely asked for a job to be done then the contractor would be liable if he did not draw attention to a particular risk. He went on: **6–15**

> "But if, in spite of a clear warning from the painter that the work should be executed in a particular manner, the householder instructs him to proceed in a different way or without some recommended precaution, I cannot see why he should be entitled later on to say that the warning was not loud enough or that it was not repeated often enough or that he did not appreciate the full measure of the risk."[15]

The result to be expected from the service performed is also related to the agreement between the parties. *Brown v J Nisbet & Co Ltd*[16] was referred to above in relation to this issue. It is to be noted that it also had implications for the liability of the repairer and the kind of result that the customer was entitled to expect. Had it been proved that he had agreed to a complete overhaul of the van the repairer might well have been liable for a failure to display the requisite level of competence when the van broke down if these were faults which had existed **6–16**

---

[13] *Macintosh v Nelson*, 1984 S.L.T. (Sh. Ct.) 82.
[14] *Terret v Murphy*, 1952 S.L.T. (Sh. Ct.) 51.
[15] *Terret v Murphy*, 1952 S.L.T. (Sh. Ct.) 51 at 55.
[16] *Brown v J Nisbet & Co Ltd* (1941) 57 Sh. Ct. Reps. 202.

when he had been asked to work on it. As he had only been asked to carry out specific tasks, which it was proved that he had carried out in a workmanlike manner, he was not liable.

6–17   The principle has also been applied to professional services. One of the best known explanations of reasonable skill and care in relation to professional services is that of Lord President Clyde in *Hunter v Hanley*[17] where he said:

> "[W]here the conduct of a doctor, or indeed of any professional man, is concerned the circumstances are not so precise and clear cut as in the normal case. In the realm of diagnosis and treatment there is ample scope for genuine difference of opinion and one man clearly is not negligent merely because his conclusions differ from that of other professional men, nor because he has displayed less skill or knowledge than others would have shown. The true test for establishing negligence in diagnosis or treatment on the part of a doctor is whether he has been proved to be guilty of such failure as no doctor of ordinary skill would be guilty of if acting with ordinary care."

6–18   This has been interpreted to mean that if any other professional can be found to agree with the actions of the doctor or other professional sued there is no negligence.[18] A close reading of the case suggests that this is going too far and that McNair J in *Bolam v Friern Hospital Management Committee*[19] correctly paraphrased the test when he said of the standard required of a doctor that "it is sufficient if he exercises the ordinary skill of an ordinary competent man exercising that particular art".

6–19   This view certainly seems to be consistent with other professional negligence cases. It is the test laid down in *Jameson v Simon*,[20] which involved the supervision of a building contract by an architect. There are numerous cases involving solicitors to similar effect of which *Hart v Frame & Co*[21] is an early example.

6–20   A professional person does not give an absolute undertaking to achieve a particular result: that would be inappropriate in most cases of professional services. A doctor, in the nature of things, cannot undertake to cure their patients, and a lawyer can give no guarantee to a client that they will win their case.

6–21   This latter point was emphasised in a medical negligence case, *Eyre v Measday*.[22] Mr and Mrs Eyre decided that they did not wish to have any more children and consulted the defendant, a gynaecologist, to discuss the sterilisation of Mrs Eyre. The defendant explained the nature of the operation and emphasised that it was irreversible and must be regarded as a permanent procedure. He did not explain that there was a small risk of failure. The Eyres believed that the result of the operation would be to render Mrs Eyre incapable of having further children. However, after the operation Mrs Eyre did become pregnant and had

---

[17] *Hunter v Hanley*, 1955 S.L.T. 213 at 217.
[18] See K. Norrie, "Common Practice and the Standard of Care in Medical Negligence", 1985 J.R. 145. For a different view, see RBM Howie, "The Standard of Care in Medical Negligence", 1983 J.R. 193.
[19] *Bolam v Friern Hospital Management Committee* [1957] 2 All E.R. 118.
[20] *Jameson v Simon* (1899) 1 F. 1211.
[21] *Hart v Frame & Co* (1839) McL. & Rob. 595.
[22] *Eyre v Measday* [1986] 1 All E.R. 488

another child. She sued the gynaecologist alleging, among other things, that there was an implied term that she would be rendered sterile by the operation.

It was held that the defendant had undertaken to carry out a particular type of operation rather than to render Mrs Eyre absolutely sterile and that his statement that the operation was irreversible was not an express guarantee that the operation was bound to achieve its objective. As the judge put it: **6–22**

> "I think there is no doubt that the plaintiff would have been entitled reasonably to assume that the defendant was warranting that the operation would be performed with reasonable care and skill. That, I think, would have been the inevitable inference to be drawn, from an objective standpoint, from the relevant discussion between the parties... However, that inference on its own does not enable the plaintiff to succeed in the present case. She has to go further. She has to suggest... that the defendant, by necessary implication, committed himself to an unqualified guarantee as to the success of the particular operation proposed, in achieving its purpose of sterilising her, even though he were to exercise all due care and skill in performing it. The suggestion is that the guarantee went beyond due care and skill and extended an unqualified warranty that the plaintiff would be absolutely sterile.
>
> On the facts of the present case, I do not think that any intelligent lay bystander (let alone another medical man), on hearing the discussion which took place between the defendant and the other two parties, could have reasonably drawn the inference that the defendant was intending to give any warranty of this nature... But, in my opinion, in the absence of any express warranty, the court should be slow to imply against a medical man an unqualified warranty as to the results of an intended operation, for the very simple reason that, objectively speaking, it is most unlikely that he would intend to give a warranty of this nature."[23]

A case involving professional services which does show that a standard higher than that of due skill and care can be expected in certain circumstances is *Greaves & Co (Contractors) Ltd v Baynham Meikle & Partners*.[24] The plaintiffs, who were building contractors, had agreed to design and build a warehouse for a customer. They employed the defendants, who were structural engineers to design the warehouse and advised them that it was essential that it should be capable of permitting materials to be moved around on forklift trucks. Shortly after the warehouse was handed over to the customer the floor began to crack as a result of vibration caused by the forklift trucks. The plaintiffs accepted that they were liable to their customer and brought this action to recover, by way of indemnity, from the structural engineers the cost of repairs to the building. It was held that on the facts as proved in this case there was a term to be implied into the contract that the engineers would design a building that would be fit for the purpose which the plaintiffs had stipulated. **6–23**

---

[23] *Eyre v Measday* [1986] 1 All E.R. 488 at 495. It was held in this case that the plaintiff had been adequately informed of the possibility that the operation might not be successful. For a case where the plaintiff succeeded because an adequate warning of the possibility of failure was not given, see *Thake v Maurice* [1986] Q.B. 644.

[24] *Greaves & Co (Contractors) Ltd v Baynham Meikle & Partners* [1975] 1 W.L.R. 1095.

SERVICES TO BE PERFORMED WITHIN A REASONABLE TIME

6–24   A perennial source of complaint from consumers is failure of a contractor to complete a job in good time, or sometimes to complete it at all. The National Consumer Council's report *Service Please*[25] found that this was a very frequent source of annoyance to consumers. Problems in this area tend to fall into two categories. There are those cases where the date for the commencement or completion of the work has been agreed between the parties and subsequently ignored by the contractor. The other is where no time has been agreed for the completion of the work but the consumer thinks that the contractor has taken an unreasonably long time to complete the work.

6–25   The contract may specify the time by which the service is to be completed. This is subject to the proviso that the contractor will not be liable for failure to comply with a time limit if his failure to do so is the fault of the client. This point was made in *T & R Duncanson v Scottish County Investment Co Ltd*[26] where a plasterer was unable to complete his agreed tasks because the client had failed to ensure that other tradesmen, completion of whose work was necessary to allow him to start, had kept to their schedules.

6–26   If the contract does not expressly fix the time for the service to be performed and does not say how it is to be fixed, and the information included in the contract by virtue of s.50(3) of the 2015 Act does not help, the gap is filled by s.52(2). This provides that the contract must be performed within a reasonable time, which is a question of fact.[27] This reflects the case law such as the English case of *Charnock v Liverpool Corporation*.[28] Mr Charnock's car had been damaged in an accident and he took it to the defendant's for repair. An estimate for the work required was agreed but the job was not completed for eight weeks. Mr Charnock sued the repairers for the cost of hiring a car for three weeks, the period by which, in his opinion, the time taken for the repair exceeded what was reasonable. It was held that there was an implied term that the repairers would carry out the repair with reasonable expedition and on the facts eight weeks was not a reasonable time. Evidence had shown that the job should have taken not longer than five weeks.

REASONABLE PRICE TO BE PAID FOR A SERVICE

6–27   Ideally, the cost of a service will be agreed beforehand and in that event it is the price agreed that must be paid even if it is not in accordance with the normal practice in the trade or profession.[29] Where it has not and the contract is silent about the matter, s.51 now fills the gap by saying that the contract is to be treated as including a term that a reasonable price must be paid. There are cases which

---

[25] B Lantin and G Woodroffe, *Service Please: Services and the Law—A Consumer View* (London: National Consumer Council, 1981).

[26] *T & R Duncanson v Scottish County Investment Co Ltd*, 1915 S.C. 1106.

[27] Consumer Rights Act 2015 s.52(3).

[28] *Charnock v Liverpool Corporation* [1968] 1 W.L.R. 1498.

[29] *Wilkie v Scottish Aviation Ltd*, 1956 S.C. 198.

illustrate this problem. On occasions a professional man is instructed to carry through some piece of work but no discussion of the fee or payment takes place. The general rule is

> "that tradesmen and professional men who provide services of the kind by which they earn their livings are presumed not to do so gratuitously and are entitled to reasonable remuneration".[30]

Robert Allan and Partners v McKinstray[31] is a good example. A firm of architects after a meeting with a client prepared preliminary drawings for a house which he proposed to build. Thereafter the client requested and was supplied with more detailed information to enable a builder to provide an estimate of the cost of construction. When the project was abandoned by the client he refused to pay the architect's fees arguing that the work had been in the nature of an estimate and, the project having been abandoned, no fee was payable. The sheriff principal held that there was no evidence to displace the general rule quoted above and that the architects were entitled quantum meruit to a fee for the project.

There is a distinction to be made between cases such as *Robert Allan and Partners v McKinstray*[32] and cases where no more has been done than the submission of an estimate or tender. This was pointed out in *Sinclair v Logan*[33] where a builder had drawn up plans for alterations to licensed premises, negotiated with the police and obtained approval from the licensing court before it became clear that the client was not going to go ahead with the project. In finding that the builder was entitled to a fee for the preliminary work that he had done the sheriff pointed out that:

6–28

> "The position of the pursuer is clearly distinguishable from that of a tradesman or contractor who submits a tender or estimate. The tender or estimate is in general submitted without any intention to benefit the person or authority requiring work to be done but purely to benefit the tradesman or contractor. It is generally submitted, in competition with others, so that the employment of the particular person submitting it is not a precondition to its submission."[34]

From this it is clear that the common practice of asking for an estimate for a proposed piece of work does not imply that the tradesman is entitled to charge a fee for this work. This was also held in *Murray v Fairlie Yacht Slip Ltd*[35] where the company, having been asked to prepare an estimate for the cost of repairs, attempted to charge for bringing a yacht ashore and storing it for three months.

6–29

To establish a right to a fee more needs to be done than this and, as the quotation from *Sinclair v Logan*[36] makes clear, one element that will be relevant will be whether the client has derived any benefit from the services rendered.

6–30

---

[30] *Robert Allan and Partners v McKinstray*, 1975 S.L.T. (Sh. Ct.) 63 at 64, echoing WM Gloag, *Contract*, 2nd edn (Edinburgh: W. Green, 1929) p.291. See also *Bell v Ogilvie* (1863) 2 M. 336; *Landless v Wilson* (1880) 8 R. 289; *Sinclair v Logan*, 1961 S.L.T. (Sh. Ct.) 10.

[31] *Robert Allan and Partners v McKinstray*, 1975 S.L.T. (Sh. Ct.) 63.

[32] *Robert Allan and Partners v McKinstray*, 1975 S.L.T. (Sh. Ct.) 63.

[33] *Sinclair v Logan*, 1961 S.L.T. (Sh. Ct.) 10.

[34] *Sinclair v Logan*, 1961 S.L.T. (Sh. Ct.) 10 at 12.

[35] *Murray v Fairlie Yacht Slip Ltd*, 1975 S.L.T. (Sh. Ct.) 62.

[36] *Sinclair v Logan*, 1961 S.L.T. (Sh. Ct.) 10.

This seems to have been decisive in *Landless v Wilson*,[37] where an architect submitted detailed plans for the development of a site in Glasgow that, in the end, the client did not proceed with. There was evidence that the client showed the plans to prospective purchasers of the site, and this and the general presumption referred to above resulted in a finding that the architect was entitled to a fee.

6–31   Where there is a contract for services but the amount to be paid has not been stated, how is that amount to be calculated? The tradesman or professional is entitled to payment quantum meruit. This can be calculated by referring to a customary rate if there is one. To establish this it must be shown that the custom is reasonable, certain and notorious.[38] Failing this the court will fix reasonable remuneration which will be ascertained from such evidence as has been adduced. Evidence which might be adduced would include the level of charges of other tradesmen or professionals in the area or reference to scale charges of a profession.

DUTY TO TAKE CARE OF GOODS DEPOSITED

6–32   Some services will involve the contractor in taking possession of the customer's goods in order, for example, to effect a repair. There is one aspect of this that may not be covered by the 2015 Act and that is a duty to take care of goods deposited with a trader. It might be argued that this is part of the term about exercising reasonable care and skill but it is not entirely clear. If it does not come within that term one can look at the common law. In this situation the type of contract, a *locatio operis faciendi,* is normally presumed to include, as an inherent ingredient, an element of *locatio custodiae* or contract of custody. The standard of care which the trader must observe is to take such care as a prudent man would take of his own property in the circumstances.[39] It has sometimes been described as an obligation to take reasonable care.

6–33   The onus of proving that reasonable care has been taken is on the trader. In *Sinclair v Juner*[40] the garage that had undertaken to repair the pursuer's car failed to discharge this onus when it failed to produce any evidence about the cause of the fire which destroyed the customer's car. In *Forbes v Aberdeen Motors Ltd*[41] the defenders were held not to have displayed the requisite degree of care when they left the pursuer's Bentley car in an unsupervised hotel car park in the middle of Aberdeen with the keys in the ignition. It was stolen by an inebriated naval rating whose motoring skills resulted in it suffering serious damage in an accident. Likewise, a garage was held liable for damage caused to a car in its custody when left in the street outside the garage overnight[42]; and, in an example from an earlier age, someone who undertook for reward to break in a horse was liable when it was injured when it bolted on being startled by an explosion under

---

[37] *Landless v Wilson* (1880) 8 R. 289.
[38] *Strathlorne Steamship Co Ltd v Hugh Baird & Sons Ltd*, 1916 S.C. (H.L.) 134.
[39] *Sinclair v Juner*, 1952 S.C. 35; *Verrico v George Hughes & Son*, 1980 S.C. 179.
[40] *Sinclair v Juner*, 1952 S.C. 35.
[41] *Forbes v Aberdeen Motors Ltd*, 1965 S.C. 193.
[42] See *Vericco v George Hughes & Son*, 1980 S.C. 179.

the stables. It was relevant that the explosion was not unexpected as the defender knew that a railway company was constructing a tunnel underneath his premises.[43]

One might have thought that the liability of a company operating a car park to someone leaving their motorcycle in it might have been the same as in these cases. *Drynan v Scottish Ice Rink Co Ltd*[44] casts doubt on this. In the sheriff court it was held that leaving the scooter in the park and purchasing a ticket created a relationship of licensor and licensee, not that of custody. The correctness of this view must be in doubt but, as has been observed, "what suffices to create a contract of custody remains to be decided in Scots law".[45]

6–34

It is not clear whether the standard of care in cases of custody for reward is the same as in cases of gratuitous deposit. In *Copland v Brogan*[46] a case of gratuitous deposit, the Court of Session spoke of the standard in the same terms as have been used in cases of custody for reward.

6–35

LIABILITY IN DELICT FOR NEGLIGENCE

So far, the standard of care and skill required of those who offer services has been discussed solely in terms of contractual liability. It is important to stress that there is also the possibility of liability for the delict of negligence. Indeed, in some situations there may be no other avenue open to the customer or client. An example of this is the situation of patients who allege that the treatment that they have received under the National Health Service has not been up to the required standard and that they have been harmed as a result. It appears from judicial decisions that such patients have no contractual relationship with the health service and can sue only in delict.[47] Such patients could not avail themselves of the implied terms. Negligence may also be the appropriate type of legal action because, in other circumstances, someone who has not contracted with the provider of the service has suffered loss as a result of his activities.

6–36

Lawyers will usually have a contractual duty to their clients so delictual liability may not be so important. However, *White v Jones*,[48] an English case, demonstrates where it might be important. After a family quarrel a father disinherited his two daughters. A few years later he relented and decided to change his will by giving them legacies of £9,000 each. Despite the attempts of family members to get the father's solicitors to carry out his instructions nothing had been done by the time he died. The daughters sued the solicitors and the House of Lords held that they owed the daughters a duty of care as disappointed legatees. It now seems to be settled that this case will be followed in Scotland.[49]

6–37

An advocate does not have a contractual relationship with the lay client and so any action will have to be in delict. Whether an advocate is still immune from

6–38

---

[43] *Laing v Darling* (1850) 12 D. 1279.

[44] *Drynan v Scottish Ice Rink Co Ltd*, 1971 S.L.T. (Sh. Ct.) 59.

[45] WW McBryde, *The Law of Contract in Scotland*, 3rd edn (Edinburgh: W.Green, 2007) para.9.59.

[46] *Copland v Brogan*, 1916 S.C. 277.

[47] *Pfizer Corp v Ministry of Health* [1965] 1 All E.R. 450, per Lord Reid at 455.

[48] *White v Jones* [1995] 2 A.C. 207.

[49] See *Robertson v Watt & Co* unreported 4 July 1995 and *Holmes v Bank of Scotland*, 2002 S.L.T. 544.

action for breach of duty is not clear. There is no direct authority on this point in Scots law, but the House of Lords in an English appeal where, most unusually, 10 law lords sat, abolished the advocate's immunity from legal action even for things done in the course of litigation both civil and criminal.[50] There are extensive obiter dicta on this issue in the Inner House decision in *Wright v Paton Farrell*.[51] The First Division took the view that the immunity of the advocate (including a solicitor conducting litigation) should be preserved in criminal trials. The Lord President and Lord Johnston took the view that, as in England, it should not apply in civil litigation though Lord Osborne disagreed.

6–39   Surveyors may also incur liability to those, such as prospective mortgagors, if they are in breach of their duty to take reasonable care. This was established in *Smith v Eric S Bush & Co*[52] which was followed in *Robbie v Graham & Sibbald*.[53]

REMEDIES

6–40   The 2015 Act sets out the remedies that are available to a consumer where the contract is breached. Which remedies are available depends on which terms have not been carried out. If the service is not provided with reasonable care and skill and so breaches s.49 or the service is not performed in line with information given about it in s.50, the service will not conform to the contract. This entitles a consumer to require that the service is properly performed by being done again. Where repeat performance is requested it must be done within a reasonable time and without causing significant inconvenience to the consumer. However, repeat performance cannot be required if it is impossible. This would be the case where the contract was for taking photographs at an event such as a wedding and the photographer either failed to turn up or did appear but did a very poor job. If, for these reasons, repeat performance is not appropriate a consumer is entitled to a reduction in price. The reduction is to be of an appropriate amount and this will depend on the circumstances of each individual case and can amount to a refund of the whole price. It will normally mean that the price is reduced by the difference in value between the service the consumer paid for and the value of the service as provided. In practice, this will mean that the reduction in price from the full amount takes into account the benefit the consumer has derived from the service. In the example of the absent photographer this would be the whole amount if it had been paid in advance. Where a substandard job has been done less than a total refund might be appropriate. For example, if a hairdresser does not carry out hair treatment as agreed but does complete the job the only realistic remedy may be price reduction. The hair has been restyled and until it grows again it may not be possible to style as originally intended. The customer will have got some benefit and price reduction may be the solution.

---

[50] *Arthur JS Hall & Co (A Firm) v Simons* [2002] 1 A.C. 615.

[51] *Wright v Paton Farrell*, 2006 S.C. 404 Inner House. For a comment on this case see G Gordon, "Not yet dead: *Wright v Paton Farrell* and Advocates' Immunity in Scotland", (2007) 70 M.L.R. 471.

[52] *Smith v Eric S Bush & Co* [1990] 1 A.C. 831.

[53] *Robbie v Graham & Sibbald*, 1989 S.C.L.R. 578. The defenders escaped liability because they were protected by an exclusion clause to which, at the time, the Unfair Contract Terms Act 1977 had no application in Scotland.

There may be some cases where a consumer is able to ask for a reduction in price even where it may be argued that the value of the service as provided has not been reduced by the breach of the consumer's rights. Suppose that the trader has not complied with information they gave about themselves. For example, if the trader tells the consumer that they will pay their workers the living wage and this is important to the consumer and a reason why they decided to employ this particular trader. This probably does not affect the value of the service but the consumer would still have the right to request a reduction of an "appropriate amount" to account for the breach.

6–41

Where a consumer has the right to ask the trader for repeat performance the trader must redo all or part of the service as needed to bring it into conformity with the contract. Where the consumer has the right to a reduction in price, the refund must be made without undue delay and in any event within 14 calendar days of the date when the trader agreed that a refund was appropriate. The refund must be made using the same means as the consumer used to pay for the service unless they expressly agree to a different method and no fee may be imposed for making it.

6–42

When the term about performing a service within a reasonable time is broken the statutory remedy is price reduction. This subject to the same qualifications discussed in the previous paragraphs.

The 2015 Act does not prevent other remedies being sought instead of, or in addition to, the remedies discussed above. These might be damages, recovery of money paid where the consumer has got nothing in return for a payment, specific implement or using the trader's breach as a defence.

6–43

Damages may well be an appropriate remedy and, if they are sought, the normal rules about damages will apply. The general rule is that damages are intended to put the consumer in the same position as if there had not been a breach. The level of damages awarded will depend on the specific circumstances and the term that the trader has breached. Typically, damages would cover the estimated loss directly resulting from the breach, in the ordinary course of events. There is also an obligation on the consumer to take reasonable steps to mitigate the scale of loss.

6–44

There is a principle that damages are not normally recoverable for injury to feelings occasioned by a breach of contract.[54] It is recognised that there are exceptions to this principle that may be summed up by saying that it does not apply when the purpose of the contract is to provide pleasure. Such contracts are particularly likely to be contracts for the provision of services. In *Diesen v Samson*[55] a photographer failed to turn up to take photographs of the pursuer's wedding and damages were awarded for the disappointment that this caused. In England damages have been awarded on this basis where package holidays have failed to live up to the claims made in the brochure,[56] and the principle was also applied where a firm of solicitors failed to take appropriate legal action to prevent

6–45

---

[54] *Addis v Gramophone Co Ltd* [1909] A.C. 488.
[55] *Diesen v Samson*, 1971 S.L.T. (Sh. Ct.) 49.
[56] *Jarvis v Swans Tours Ltd* [1973] 1 Q.B. 233; *Jackson v Horizon Holidays Ltd* [1975] 1 W.L.R. 1468.

the plaintiff's husband harassing her in breach of an injunction.[57] In *Farley v Skinner*[58] the House of Lords confirmed that damages could be awarded on this basis but that amounts should not normally exceed £10,000.

EXCLUSION CLAUSES

6–46   It is not possible for a trader to exclude liability for breach of the terms about reasonable care and the information required to be included by the 2015 Act s.50 as well as those on price and time. This extends beyond straightforward attempts to exclude liability to subtler ways of reducing a consumer's rights. Terms are not binding that exclude restrict consumers' rights or remedies. For example, a clause that seeks to limit the remedies to repeat performance would be caught. Similarly making a right or remedy subject to restrictive conditions is not binding nor is one that allows a trader to put a person at a disadvantage as a result of pursuing a remedy or restricts rules of evidence or procedure. An agreement to submit disputes to arbitration is not covered by this bar on excluding or restricting liability. However, para.20 of Sch.2 makes clear that a term requiring the consumer to take disputes exclusively to arbitration may be regarded as unfair. Furthermore, the Arbitration Act 1996 provides that a term which constitutes an arbitration agreement is automatically unfair (under Pt 2 of the 1996 Act) if the claim is for less than an amount specified in an Order made under s.91 of the 1996 Act. This amount is currently set at £5,000 in the Unfair Arbitration Agreements (Specified Amount) Order 1999.[59]

CRIMINAL LAW

6–47   Criminal law has a role to play in protecting consumers of services. The main provisions are to be found in the provisions of the Consumer Protection from Unfair Trading Regulations 2008[60] that provide criminal sanctions for breach of their obligations not to indulge in various unfair commercial practices. These are discussed in Ch.10.

SELF-REGULATION

6–48   In addition to the legal rules that have been discussed above it is important to note that codes of conduct drawn up by members of some trade associations may offer assistance to consumers. The Association of British Travel Agents, the electricity companies, the motor trade and funeral directors are examples of providers of services who subscribe to such codes. Their chief benefit is that codes can attempt to cope with matters which it would be difficult, if not impossible, to deal

---

[57] See *Heywood v Wellers* [1976] Q.B. 44, and Andrew Phang, "The crumbling edifice? The award of contractual damages for mental distress", 2003 J.B.L. 341, for a review of some of the cases in his area.

[58] *Farley v Skinner* [2001] UKHL 49; [2002] 2 A.C. 732.

[59] Unfair Arbitration Agreements (Specified Amount) Order 1999 (SI 1999/2167).

[60] Consumer Protection from Unfair Trading Regulations 2008 (SI 2008/1277).

with statutorily. For example, the code governing electrical repairers provides that where a home visit is needed, "the first visit should (wherever possible) be made within three working days from receipt of the request". The Scottish Motor Trade Association code states that members will ensure "sensitive treatment of vulnerable consumers".[61]

CASE STUDY: PACKAGE HOLIDAYS

The package holiday is an important part of the lifestyle of many consumers and accounts for a significant part of their spending. From a consumer protection perspective it is particularly interesting because it provides an example of various techniques being used to protect the consumer. The criminal and civil law are brought into play as well as self-regulation.

6–49

While it is not the only relevant source of law in this area it will be convenient to structure this discussion around the Package Travel, Package Holidays and Package Tours Regulations 1992 (the 1992 Regulations).[62] These regulations were enacted to implement the EC Package Travel Directive.[63] The regulations came into effect on 3 December 1992. They use both the civil and criminal law to improve the protection afforded to consumers.

6–50

Before looking at the 1992 Regulations in detail it is first necessary to look at the definition of a package. Regulation 2 defines it as the pre-arranged combination of at least two of the following elements when offered for sale at an inclusive price, and when the service covers a period of at least 24 hours or includes overnight accommodation. The three elements are: transport; accommodation; and, other tourist services not ancillary to transport or accommodation and accounting for a significant proportion of the package. The European Court of Justice (ECJ) has ruled that "package" could include a holiday organised by a travel agent at the request of, and in accordance with the specifications of, a consumer or a limited group of consumers.[64]

6–51

The regulations set out various civil obligations of the package organiser or retailers. Regulation 4 of the 1992 Regulations provides that tour organisers or retailers must not provide consumers with information that is misleading. If they do they are liable to compensate consumers for any loss which is suffered.[65] Particulars in brochures constitute implied terms of the contract unless the brochure states that the information in it may change and the changes are clearly

6–52

---

[61] Available on the website of the Scottish Motor Trade Association: *http://www.smta.co.uk* [Accessed 16 June 2015].

[62] Package Travel, Package Holidays and Package Tours Regulations 1992 (SI 1992/3288), as amended by Package Travel, Package Holidays and Package Tours (Amendment) Regulations 1995 (SI 1995/1648); Package Travel, Package Holidays and Package Tours (Amendment) Regulations 1998 (SI 1998/1208); Enterprise Act 2002 (Part 8 Notice to OFT of Intended Prosecution Specified Enactments, Revocation and Transitional Provision) Order 2003 (SI 2003/1376) art.3; and Enterprise Act 2002 (Part 9 Restrictions on Disclosure of Information) (Amendment and Specification) Order 2003 (SI 2003/1400) art.7 and Sch.5.

[63] Directive 90/314 of 13 June 1990 on package travel, package holidays and package tours [1990] O.J. L158/59.

[64] *Club-Tour, Viagens e Turismo SA v Garrido and Club Med Viagens Ld* (C-400/00) [2002] O.J. C144/10.

[65] *Mawdsley v Cosmoair Ltd* [2002] EWCA Civ. 587.

communicated before the contract is concluded.[66] It is an implied term of the contract that the other party to the contract will ensure that the contract contains at least the information specified in Sch.2.[67] This is basic information about price, means of transport, destination, type of accommodation, meals and payment schedule. The contract terms must be set out in writing or such other form as is accessible to the consumer who must be given a written copy of them.

6–53 In addition, the regulations imply various terms into contracts. Where the consumer is prevented from proceeding with the package there is an implied term that they may transfer the booking to any person who satisfies all the package conditions.[68] Surcharges have been a source of considerable friction in package tours and controls are placed on them. Price revision clauses are void unless they provide for the possibility of upward and downward revision. They must also state precisely how the revised price is to be calculated and that revisions are to be made solely to allow for variations in transport costs, service charges and currency fluctuations. In any event, they cannot be made less than 30 days before departure and the tour operator must absorb the first 2 per cent of any increase.[69] Further terms are implied by the 1992 Regulations regs 13 and 14. These deal with compensation for cancellation of the holiday and failure to provide a significant proportion of the services contracted for.

6–54 In many ways the central feature of the civil law provisions of the regulations is to be found in reg.15. This imposes strict liability on the package organiser or retailer for the proper performance of the contract, whether its obligations are to be performed by them or another supplier. Failure to do so renders them liable for any damage caused, unless the failure is attributable to the consumer or due to unusual and unforeseeable circumstances beyond the control of the other party.[70] In *Simone Leitner v TUI Deutschland GmbH & Co KG*,[71] the ECJ held that the Directive on which the Regulations are based conferred on consumers a right of compensation for non-material damage, including disappointment and distress. This liability cannot be excluded but it may be limited in accordance with international conventions; and, in the case of damage other than personal injury, may be limited, provided that the limitation is reasonable.

6–55 One of the greatest problems that can beset a holidaymaker is the insolvency of the tour operator or the financial failure of the travel agent. For some years there have been various methods of ensuring that holidaymakers will not suffer financial loss in these events. The Civil Aviation Authority licenses travel organisers who must have an Air Traffic Organiser's Licence (ATOL) which requires them to provide a bond. This amounts to 15 per cent of licensable turnover, or 10 per cent if the licence holder is a member of the Association of British Travel Agents (ABTA) which has arrangements to cope with these

---

[66] See Package Travel, Package Holidays and Package Tours Regulations 1992 (SI 1992/3288) reg.6.
[67] See Package Travel, Package Holidays and Package Tours Regulations 1992 (SI 1992/3288) reg.9.
[68] See Package Travel, Package Holidays and Package Tours Regulations 1992 (SI 1992/3288) reg.10.
[69] See Package Travel, Package Holidays and Package Tours Regulations 1992 (SI 1992/3288) reg.11.
[70] The meaning of "improper performance" was discussed in *Hone v Going Places Leisure Travel Ltd* [2001] EWCA Civ. 947.
[71] *Simone Leitner v TUI Deutschland GmbH & Co KG* [2002] E.C.R. I-2631.

problems. For more serious failures the Air Travel Trust, which succeeded to the assets of the reserve fund set up under the Air Travel Reserve Fund Act 1975, provides protection.[72]

One of the most important aspects of the regulations is contained in reg.16, which places an obligation on tour operators and travel agents to provide evidence of security for the refund of money paid by customers and for their repatriation in the event of insolvency. This obligation is sanctioned by criminal penalties. Regulations 17–20 of the 1992 Regulations provide a choice of methods through which this obligation can be met. These include taking out a bond, having an ATOL, being a member of a scheme which operates a reserve fund, or having insurance or placing money in a trust fund.

6–56

The scope of reg.16 which implements art.7 of the Directive was demonstrated in a decision of the ECJ.[73] There it was said that:

6–57

"Article 7 of Directive 90/314 was to be interpreted as covering, as security for the refund of money paid over, a situation in which the purchaser of a package holiday who had paid the travel organiser for the costs of his accommodation before travelling on his holiday was compelled, following the travel organiser's insolvency, to pay the hotelier for his accommodation again in order to be able to leave the hotel and return home."

Criminal law is also used to ensure compliance with other requirements of the regulations. Regulation 5 makes it an offence for a holiday organiser to make brochures available to potential customers which do not indicate the price and adequate information about specified matters in a "legible comprehensible and adequate manner". A retailer who makes such a brochure available knowing that it does not comply also commits an offence. Regulation 7 requires tour operators or travel agents to make available before the contract is concluded general information about visa requirements applying to British citizens, information about health formalities, and arrangements for security of money paid over and repatriation arrangements. Failure to comply is also a criminal offence as is failure to provide "in good time before the start of the journey" certain information about what to do in the event of some problem arising during the holiday!

6–58

The use of the criminal law is, of course, not new in the package holiday world. The Trade Descriptions Act 1968 had considerable effect in ensuring high standards of accuracy in brochures and the law on price indications contained in Pt 3 of the Consumer Protection Act 1987 also applied to package holidays. These have been repealed and replaced by the Consumer Protection from Unfair Trading Regulations 2008[74] discussed in Ch.10.

6–59

Not only has the law been used to protect holidaymakers, but also the industry itself has taken steps to improve matters. One of the more successful codes of practice has been that of ABTA. This covers many of the matters now required by law under the regulations. Two particularly important features are the

6–60

---

[72] The Civil Aviation Authority is currently considering responses to its consultation paper *Rebalancing ATOL* with a view to adjusting the scheme.

[73] *Verein für Konsumenteninformation v Österreichische Kreditversicherrungs AG* (C-364/96) [1999] 1 C.M.L.R. 1430 at [23].

[74] Consumer Protection from Unfair Trading Regulations 2008 (SI 2008/1277).

compensation arrangements in the event of a travel agent or tour operator facing financial difficulties, and the low cost arbitration provisions. The latter are discussed in Ch.12.

CHAPTER 7

The Public Sector

A number of important goods and services are supplied by nationalised or recently privatised companies. In addition, the state, through local and central government, provides services and facilities for its citizens. Health, education and the courts are examples. In the latter case there has been an increasing tendency to apply consumer principles to the provision of these services. In this chapter we look at the implications for consumers of the provision of services by these providers.   **7–01**

In the case of the nationalised and the privatised industries where the consumer complains of defective goods or services the remedy will usually be no different from that pursued against any other supplier. The legislation and common law rules discussed in earlier chapters will be relevant. To this there are some exceptions. The liability of the Post Office (and any other universal service provider) is restricted in relation to the provision of a "universal postal service" by Pt I of the Postal Services Act 2000.   **7–02**

REGULATED INDUSTRIES

A major feature of the last two decades of the twentieth century was the privatisation policy pursued by the Conservative administration under which many nationalised industries have been returned to private ownership. The major examples have been British Gas, British Telecom, British Airways, the English and Welsh water companies, the electricity and bus industries, the railways and the coal industry. As a result, few major industries are in state ownership, the Post Office being the most notable example.   **7–03**

While, in theory, these state monopolies have been broken, in practice, in many cases, the privatised companies have near monopoly power. British Telecom does face increasing competition but is the dominant enterprise in telecommunications in the UK. While there is increasing competition in the gas and electricity industries this has been slow to develop. The privatisation legislation recognised that, in most cases, there might not be a high level of competition in the markets supplied by the new corporations.   **7–04**

To provide a proxy for the protection afforded to the consumer by competition in the market place the solution adopted in the privatisation legislation was the creation of independent statutory regulators who in the original privatisation statutes was usually given the title of director general. These regulators had extensive powers to control the industries concerned. More recently as these   **7–05** arrangements have been revised the model of an office with a corporate identity has been adopted, as we shall see in the cases of communications and energy.

Communications

7–06   The Communications Act 2003 completely reorganised the regulation of the communications industries in the UK. It covers not only telecommunications but also the internet and broadcasting. The Office of Communications Act 2002 set up Ofcom which has taken over the functions of five regulators in this field. These were the Broadcasting Standards Commission, the Director General of Telecommunications (OFTEL), the Independent Television Commission, the Radio Authority, and the Secretary of State, who had a regulatory role through the Radiocommunications Agency. It is believed that this will give a more coherent form of regulation through a body that has both competition and consumer protection functions. Ofcom is a corporate body with a chairman, chief executive and a number of board members. In addition to its general role as a regulator of communications, s.3(1) of the Communications Act 2003 (the 2003 Act) provides that:

> "It shall be the principal duty of Ofcom, in carrying out their functions: (a) to further the interests of citizens in relation to communications matters; and (b) to further the interests of consumers in relevant markets, where appropriate by promoting competition."

7–07   Section 16(2) of the 2003 Act requires Ofcom to establish an independent consumer panel to advise on the consumer interest in the markets it regulates. The panel is independent of Ofcom and operates at arm's length from it, setting its own agenda and making its views known publicly. It has a responsibility to understand consumer issues and concerns related to the communications sector (other than those related to content of advertising and programming) and will help inform Ofcom's decision-making by raising specific issues of consumer interest. These will include issues affecting rural consumers, older people, people with disabilities and those who are on low incomes or otherwise disadvantaged. To ensure that its recommendations to Ofcom are based on sound evidence, the panel has an appropriate budget to commission its own research, and will be developing new means of communicating with consumers.

7–08   Ofcom has also established Ofcom "Advisory Committees for the Nations" on the whole breadth of its communications responsibilities in Scotland, Wales, Northern Ireland and for the English regions. These have been set up under s.20(1) of the 2003 Act. The advisory committee for each nation has been chosen by open public process and is composed of people who have special knowledge and interests in each nation. The remit of the advisory committee for Scotland states that it is to seek to identify issues affecting the communications sector in Scotland, both collectively as a committee and individually for members, with particular reference to the sectors where they have particular knowledge or expertise and to provide advice to Ofcom.[1]

---

[1] See *http://www.ofcom.org.uk* [Accessed 16 June 2015].

Energy

The Utilities Act 2000 reorganised the regulation of the UK energy sector. The **7–09** Offices of the Directors General of Electricity and Gas (OFFER and OFGAS) were abolished and their functions transferred to the Gas and Electricity Markets Authority, the public face of which is the Office of Gas and Electricity Markets (OFGEM). This body has the same structure as Ofcom with a chairman and board which make all major decisions and set policy priorities for OFGEM which is the public face of the new regulator. OFGEM's powers are provided for under the Gas Act 1986 and the Electricity Act 1989, as amended by the Utilities Act 2000. It also has enforcement powers under the Competition Act 1998. One of its principal objectives is to protect the interests of consumers, wherever appropriate, by promoting effective competition. In performing its functions it must also have regard to the interests of low-income consumers, the chronically sick, the disabled, pensioners and consumers in rural areas.[2] The legislation also gives it powers to impose financial penalties on utility companies for breaches of licence conditions and other specified statutory requirements.[3]

Part 3 of the Utilities Act 2000 replaced the separate Gas and Electricity **7–10** Consumers' Councils with one Gas and Electricity Consumers' Council which has adopted the name Energywatch for its activities. The main functions of Energywatch were to keep itself informed of consumer matters and the views of consumers and to provide advice and information to regulatory authorities, government, utility companies and anyone else whose activities may affect the interests of consumers. It also provided information and advice to consumers and published information in the interests of consumers. Like OFGEM it had a specific duty to have regard to the interests of the disabled or chronically sick, individuals of pensionable age, those with low incomes and people living in rural areas.

In April 2012, the government decided that a new regulated industries unit **7–11** (RIU) should be established to represent consumers in essential markets subject to economic regulation. Operational by April 2013 and working with a new name (Consumer Futures) and identity—but within the legal framework of Consumer Focus—the new unit took on the responsibilities of the statutory consumer body in energy and postal services, as well as water services in Scotland. It also had a wider role in learning and applying lessons and insight across other markets. In April 2014 Consumer Futures, including the extra help unit (EHU), moved out of the public sector to become part of the Citizens Advice Scotland (CAS).

---

[2] For the gas industry, see Gas Act 1986 s.4AA; for electricity, see Electricity Act 1989 s.3A.

[3] For the gas industry, see Gas Act 1986 s.30A; for electricity, see Electricity Act 1989 s.27A. For an example of the exercise of these powers affecting two energy companies, see OFGEM press release, 20 February 2004, reporting that npower and Scottish Power had each been fined £200,000 for unfairly stopping customers from switching to a new gas or electricity supplier in breach of licence conditions.

Transport

7–12   Section 4(1)(b) of the Civil Aviation Act 1982 gives the Civil Aviation Authority (CAA) a duty to "further the reasonable interests of users of air transport services" and this has led to the creation of the CAA consumer panel in place of the air transport users council.

Water

7–13   The restructuring of local government effected by the Local Government (Scotland) Act 1994 has had implications for water and sewerage services which were previously services provided by the regional authorities. In response to public opinion in Scotland these services have not been privatised. Instead, these were provided originally by three new regional water authorities. With effect from April 2002 these authorities were merged to form Scottish Water as a result of Pt 3 of the Water Industry (Scotland) Act 2002. Scottish Water has a duty to promote conservation and effective use of water resources, ensure that there are adequate supplies, and have regard to the interests of customers especially those with special needs occasioned by a persistent medical condition or family circumstances.

7–14   When the regional water authorities were set up it was the Government's view that it would not be appropriate for a service that was still in the public sector to have a regulator based on the model of the privatised public utility regulators. That view changed and the office of the Water Industry Commissioner for Scotland was created by Pt 2 of the Water Industry Act 1999, and came into operation on 1 November 1999.[4] Part 1 of the Water Services etc. (Scotland) Act 2005[5] replaced the commissioner by the Water Industry Commission for Scotland. The primary role of the commission is to promote the interests of customers of Scottish Water who include both business and domestic users. It also is the economic regulator of the industry.

7–15   Consumer advocacy functions in relation to the water industry are now the responsibility of CAS as a result of the changes to the consumer landscape which transferred Consumer Futures to it. Section 2A of the Water Industry (Scotland) Act 2002 provides that Scottish ministers, Scottish Water, the Water Industry Commission, the Scottish Environmental Protection Agency and the Drinking Water Quality Regulator "must have regard to any advice, information, proposal or representation made to them by Citizens Advice Scotland . . . ". The complaints handling function of Consumer Futures Scotland was transferred in August 2011 to the Scottish Public Services Ombudsman. An interesting innovation in the water industry has involved the creation of the Customer Forum. This body set up at the instigation of the Scottish Government, the Water Industry Commission, Scottish Water and Consumer Futures (as it then was) to ensure that customers' opinions are heard and taken into account in determining charges and spending priorities in the Strategic Review of Charges. The purpose of this review, which takes place every six years, is to ensure that Scottish Water is adequately funded to meet the demands of providing Scotland's water and wastewater services. The

---

[4] The office was continued by Water Industry (Scotland) Act 2002 s.1.
[5] Water Services etc. (Scotland) Act 2005 (asp 3).

forum, after working with Scottish Water in scrutinising its customer research programme and analysing and interpreting the results was asked by the Water Industry Commission to seek to agree with Scottish Water the priorities for future investments to bring about service improvements, and the price household and business customers should pay. This negotiated settlement that has no parallel in the UK, but which has been used in utility industries in North America, seems to have worked well.[6]

CITIZEN'S CHARTER

Another approach to improving service in the public sector was launched in 1991 through the citizen's charter initiative. In a glossy White Paper, *The Citizen's Charter*,[7] the Government announced a programme to improve the quality of public services. This applied to a wide range of central and local government services as well as the privatised utilities. It recognised that in many of these areas competition has a limited role to play in ensuring high quality services. It stated that there were four main themes in the programme: quality, choice; setting of standards; and value for money. In promoting these themes a number of mechanisms were to be used. In some cases further privatisation was to be the preferred method, in others the possibility of contracting out services was to be explored along with other ways of using competition. An important mechanism was the setting of targets such as the targets for train punctuality. Other important mechanisms were the creation of inspectorates to ensure that standards were being met, more effective complaints systems, and better redress for citizens when things go wrong.   **7–16**

The original *Citizen's Charter* set out the basic principles of the initiative but it also envisaged that there would be further charters dealing with specific areas. By the time that the new Labour Government came to review the operation of the charter programme in 1997 there were about 200 national charters. This figure includes 40 that were termed "national charters" by the previous administration and the "Charter Standard Statements" drawn up by executive agencies and non-departmental public bodies.[8] In addition, there are thought to be about 10,000 local charters. Charters cover a diverse range of services including health, education, public utilities and the courts. Of particular interest in Scotland are the *Parents' Charter in Scotland* and the *Justice Charter*. The former deals mainly with what parents can expect of the schools which their children attend; the latter with the court and procurator fiscal system, prisons and related aspects of social work services.   **7–17**

In June 1998 the new Labour administration, under the title of *Service First*, relaunched the charter initiative. A year later the main elements of *Service First* were incorporated into the Government's White Paper.[9] This foreshadowed the use of "People's Panels" to carry out regular consumer surveys across a range of public services and this initiative ran from 1998–2002. The Office of Public   **7–18**

---

[6] For a detailed account of the forum see, S Littlechild, *The Customer Forum: Customer engagement in the Scottish water sector*, Vol.31 (2014) Utilities Policy 216.

[7] Citizen's Charter, *Raising the Standard* (HMSO, 1991) Cm.1599.

[8] Cabinet Office, *Service First: The New Charter Programme* (1998).

[9] Cabinet Office, *Modernising Government* (The Stationery Office, 1999) Cm.4310.

Service Reform was set up in 2001 to carry forward the drive to improve public services by improving current structures, systems, incentives and skills to deliver better, more customer-focused public services. The strategy to achieve this was set out in more detail in March 2002[10] and in February 2004 the Chartermark scheme was relaunched. In 2005 Cabinet Office ministers commissioned an independent review of the scheme that appeared as "The Customer Voice in Transforming Services" in June 2006.

7–19   The Coalition Government that took office in 2010 did not continue these policies having a different approach. Nevertheless, they observed in a White Paper:

> "However, we also believe that the state has a key role in defining outcomes, and in setting standards for public services and ensuring that they continue to rise. In its capacity as guarantor of standards the state will play an important part in setting the bar for existing and new providers who want to compete to provide public services. This will send a clear message that 'unless you can match or better our minimum standards, you have no place delivering public services'."[11]

How effective the charter initiative has been is difficult to say. However, the 1997 Labour Government observed that "[t]here is little doubt among those people who commented on the original Charter programme that it made a major contribution to the improvement in public services during the 1990s".[12] One commentator has observed:

> "[T]he spirit of the original Citizens' Charter lives on—albeit with new nomenclature and as part of a wider agenda of 'modernisation' and consumer focus ... The Charter principles have become absorbed into the bloodstream of the public service and are taken largely for granted by both the producers and the users of those services."[13]

In Scotland charters still exist in certain areas such as the NHS's *The Charter of Patient Rights* and the *Responsibilities and Scottish Social Housing Charter* required by the Housing (Scotland) Act 2010.

LOCAL GOVERNMENT

7–20   Related to the *Service First* programme is the Best Value initiative. This was a manifesto commitment of the Government and it seeks to improve local government performance in the delivery of services to local communities throughout Scotland. It has also been extended to police forces and fire brigades. It aims to ensure that the cost and quality of these services are at a level acceptable to local people. This is to be achieved by increasing the role of local people in deciding the priorities for local government services; improving the

---

[10] Office of Public Services Reform, *Reforming our Public Services: Principles into Practice* pamphlet (HMSO, March 2002).
[11] White Paper, *Open Public Services* (July 2011) Cm.8145.
[12] See Government press release CAB/075-06 of 14 December 2006, para.2.1.
[13] G Drewry, "Whatever Happened to the Citizens' Charter?" [2002] P.L. 9 at 12.

way authorities manage and review their business; and building on the experience and expertise of staff. In Scotland, unlike England and Wales:

> "Best Value has developed on a partnership basis . . . although backed by the threat of the re-imposition of [compulsory competitive tendering] in case of failure".[14]

In July 1997, the Secretary of State and the Convention of Scottish Local Authorities (COSLA) set up a joint Task Force on Best Value, comprising the Scottish Office, COSLA and Accounts Commission, to develop and implement best value across local government. In its final report the task force concluded:

> "[A]ll Scottish local authorities have shown a commitment to Best Value and have attempted to incorporate the essential principles of Best Value in the way they serve their communities. They have achieved varying levels of understanding and success in doing so, and we doubt that any would claim the process to be complete."[15]

7–21

The task force concluded that it would be desirable to provide a legislative basis for best value but that this should not be highly prescriptive to allow for flexibility in developing the programme. Section 1 of the Local Government in Scotland 2003 places a duty on all Scottish local authorities to secure best value and describes best value in terms of the continuous improvement of performance of functions. The Accounts Commission for Scotland in its March 2014 report, *An overview of local government in Scotland 2014*, noted the importance of Best Value in times of austerity.

7–22

---

[14] Best Value Task Force, *Final Report: Best Value in Local Government* (HMSO, December 1999) para.2.5.
[15] Best Value Task Force, *Final Report: Best Value in Local Government* (HMSO, December 1999) para.1.10.

CHAPTER 8

Buying on Credit

INTRODUCTION

There can be no doubt about the importance of credit in our society. Even a **8–01** casual walk down any high street or a glance at newspaper advertising indicates the prevalence of credit; and the statistics on consumer credit confirm its immense importance in the economy.[1] Outstanding consumer credit lending was £168.8 billion at the end of December 2014. This works out at an average debt of £6,322 per household. Of this credit card debt was £61.1bn or £2,287 per household. In addition, mortgage lending stood at £1.298 trillion at the same date.[2]

The provision of credit has a long and chequered history, becoming especially **8–02** important in this country following the industrial revolution. This made credit granting both possible and necessary. If it was to become feasible for a much-increased volume of goods to be acquired it would be necessary for much of this increased consumption to be financed by the extension of credit. To depend on consumption being paid for out of short-term savings would not have worked. In the latter half of the nineteenth century with increasing production of mass-produced consumer goods such as sewing machines and pianos, the credit market developed. Reliance on personal security alone would have been commercially imprudent and would have restricted the development of credit selling. The result was the development of hire-purchase. The advantage of this was that it provided the lender with security in the event that the purchaser defaulted. From the consumers' point of view it enabled them, in the words of the credit card slogan, "to take the waiting out of wanting". The *Crowther Report* noted that hire-purchase "has been one of the chief contributory causes of the great rise in the material standard of living of the British people in the last generation".[3]

Hire-purchase could be provided by the seller or manufacturer, though **8–03** retailers would often not have the resources to finance hire-purchase transactions. There soon grew up finance companies, often companies expanding their activities from commercial financing into the developing area of consumer

---

[1] See Department of Trade and Industry, *Fair, Clear and Competitive: The Consumer Credit Market in the 21st Century* (The Stationery Office, 2003) Cm.6040, para.1.8. Chapter 1 has a very useful overview of the way in which consumers use credit. The White Paper is accompanied by a consultation document, Department of Trade and Industry, *Establishing a Transparent Market*.
[2] See the Money Charity website *http://themoneycharity.org.uk* [Accessed 16 June 2015].
[3] See Committee on Consumer Credit, *Report of the Committee on Consumer Credit* (HMSO, 1971) Cmnd.4596, Vol.1, para.2.3.17. Hereinafter "the *Crowther Report*".

finance. The consumer credit market developed markedly during the twentieth century, not only in terms of the volume of credit extended, but also in the sophistication and range of methods used. The so-called credit boom of the late 1980s gave considerable impetus to these trends. As the White Paper on consumer credit issued in December 2003 observed, "[t]he consumer credit market has changed fundamentally since the introduction of the Consumer Credit Act 1974".[4] This is because:

> "Specialist lenders are targeting specific sections of the market, and the widespread introduction of new and innovative products means consumers now have an ever-increasing number of credit options available to them."[5]

Before considering the legal background to consumer credit it is necessary to summarise the main methods of obtaining credit and then to consider why special attention is paid to the protection of the consumer obtaining credit.

METHODS OF OBTAINING CREDIT

8–04   There is a wide variety of methods of obtaining credit. One way of categorising these methods is, using a classification adopted by the *Crowther Report*, to divide them into lender credit and vendor credit. Lender credit involves transactions whose legal form is that of a loan of money, whether or not the loan is associated with a particular purchase. Vendor credit relates to transactions that, legally, are not loans but contracts for the sale or hire of goods. As there are some methods of obtaining credit that do not easily fit into either category, a third category of hybrid transactions is added.

Lender credit

8–05   There are many ways of obtaining loans. Banks offer loans by way of overdraft where the customer is permitted to overdraw on a current account and the rate of interest is liable to fluctuate during the lifetime of the overdraft. There may be no fixed rate at which the customer is to pay off the loan. More common are bank loans, often marketed as "personal loans". In this case the customer borrows a fixed sum at a specified rate of interest and agrees to pay it off by regular instalments. Since the expansion of the facilities which building societies may offer, they, too, provide personal loans. The building societies are best known for offering loans for the purchase of property which are secured by way of mortgage.

8–06   Other institutions, such as finance houses, also provide loans. Recently considerable attention has been focussed on the subprime or high cost short term credit (HCSTC) market where "payday loans" have been causing particular concern. Loans are also a number of other sources such as insurance companies that may make loans against the cash-in value of a life assurance policy,

---

[4] See Department of Trade and Industry, *Fair, Clear and Competitive: The Consumer Credit Market in the 21st Century* (2003) Cm.6040, para.1.8.
[5] See Department of Trade and Industry, *Fair, Clear and Competitive: The Consumer Credit Market in the 21st Century* (2003) Cm.6040, para.1.11.

pawnbrokers who will do so in return for the pledge of some item of property, and credit unions will lend to their members.

Vendor credit

The most common form of vendor credit is hire-purchase. This is an arrangement that combines the hire of goods with an option to purchase. Typically, the retailer sells the goods to a finance company which enters into the hire-purchase agreement with the consumer. The consumer agrees to make a series of weekly or monthly payments that are, technically, rental payments, so the consumer is not at this point the owner of the goods and may not dispose of them without the consent of the finance company. The agreement gives the consumer an option to purchase the goods on making a small final payment, an option which, in practice, is normally exercised. The arrangement need not, but usually does, involve a finance company as the retailer may enter into the hire-purchase agreement directly with the consumer.   **8–07**

A very similar transaction is conditional sale. This is an agreement for the sale of goods under which the property remains in the seller until payment of the price. The main difference between this and hire-purchase is that in conditional sale the consumer automatically becomes the owner on making the final payment, whereas in hire-purchase the consumer is not obliged to do so.   **8–08**

Hire-purchase and conditional sale both give the person providing credit a security over the goods. A third type of transaction, credit sale, is very similar to conditional sale. The difference is that the property in the goods passes immediately to the consumer, so the seller has no security.   **8–09**

Another form of vendor credit is the leasing or rental agreement. These have been common for many years in the commercial sphere but have become more common in consumer transactions, especially those relating to cars. The legal form is that of a simple hire agreement similar to that entered into when a car is hired for a short time from a car rental firm. The same legal form can be used to finance a transaction where the lease is for a fixed period at a rent equivalent to the sale price of the goods and the cost of credit. The consumer does not have title to the goods and so cannot pass a good title to anyone else. The provisions of Pt 3 of the Hire-Purchase Act 1964, which protect those who acquire cars subject to a hire-purchase agreement, do not apply. As a result, there have been instances recently of innocent purchasers of cars sold by persons who had been leasing them being without a practical remedy when the true owners reclaimed their property.[6]   **8–10**

Hybrid transactions

Check trading

The following description is taken from the *Crowther Report*[7]:   **8–11**

---

[6] The defrauded purchaser would have a claim against the seller for breach of the implied term about title in Sale of Goods Act 1979 s.12. Often, in these cases, the person sued does not have the means to meet a decree.

[7] *Crowther Report* (2003) para.2.4.1.

"Check trading is an outgrowth from the spontaneous development of mutual clubs in the industrial centres of the North of England. A check is a document, issued by the check trader and purchased by the customer, which entitles him to buy goods, of a wide variety, at any of a long list of shops. The customer buys a check for, say £10 or £20 or £30, paying [5p] in the pound at the start, and undertaking to pay a further [5p] in the pound weekly for 20 weeks—that is, a total of [£1.05] of face value. When he uses the check to buy goods, he is charged the cash price, and the amount of his purchase is noted on the back of the check. The check trader then reimburses the retailer, but after deduction of a discount which may range from 12 per cent to 15 per cent. Moreover, settlements are usually made monthly, which means that the average period during which the retailer is out of his money is probably from six to seven weeks."

8–12 In recent years there has been a growth in the issue of high unit vouchers payable over longer periods by monthly instalments, payment being made by the customer to the check trader direct or through the customer's bank by standing order or direct debit.[8] Check trading is largely confined to the north of England and Scotland and the dominant company is Provident Clothing and Supply. The exact legal nature of check trading has never been authoritatively decided.[9]

Credit cards

8–13 Over the last 40 years credit cards have become increasingly popular in this country. The card is issued by a company specialising in the issue of cards which arranges that the card can be used to purchase goods and services from various traders.[10] The cardholder receives a monthly statement from the credit card company. In one type of card, sometimes referred to as a "t and e" card (travel and entertainment), of which the best known is American Express, the customer is expected to pay off the full amount each month. Apart from the period between paying for the goods or service with the card and the date by which payment must be made to the credit card company, there is no credit element. The other type of card, such as Mastercard or Visa, gives the customer a choice. The full amount may be paid up and no interest charge incurred; or, subject to the payment of a minimum amount, the customer may choose to pay off the account in succeeding months. For this facility there is a charge which varies between 1.5 to 2 per cent per month. In addition, it is becoming more common for card companies to charge an annual fee. Traders submit their accounts to the credit card company which pays them the amount of the account minus a commission charge.

---

[8] See R Goode (ed), *Consumer Credit Law and Practice* (London: Butterworths, 1999), Division 1A, para.2.35.

[9] There is an English county court decision, *Premier Clothing Co Ltd v Hillcoat* unreported 13 February 1969, in which it was held that it was money lending. It is referred to in the *Crowther Report*, para.4.1.64.

[10] For a recent illuminating examination of the credit card and related store card industry, see House of Commons Treasury Committee, *Transparency of Credit Card Charges* (2003) HC Paper No.125–I (Session 2003/2004) Vol.1.

There has been very little litigation concerning credit cards in any part of the UK. In *Re Charge Card Services Ltd*[11] the English Court of Appeal held that payment by credit card discharged the consumer's liability for the price to the trader. The cardholder was liable to pay the credit card company, whether or not the company paid the trader. If, as occurred in this case, the credit card company had failed to pay traders they could not recover from the cardholder. **8–14**

Budget accounts

Budget accounts have become common, especially in retail stores. They are a form of revolving credit where the consumer agrees to make a regular monthly payment, say £20, and may then purchase goods of up to a certain multiple of this figure, perhaps 10 times or £200. As each payment is made new purchases are permitted provided that the balance outstanding on the account does not exceed £200. A charge that covers interest is made at a specified rate on the amount outstanding at the end of the month. **8–15**

The precise legal nature of these accounts has never been clear. They are not hire-purchase agreements but were thought by some to be money lending transactions. The *Crowther Report* noted that in the trade they "are usually treated as giving rise to a series of credit sale agreements" and this view derives support from certain Scottish decisions.[12] **8–16**

LEGAL REGULATION OF CREDIT GRANTING

The law on consumer credit was reshaped by the Consumer Credit Act 1974 (the 1974 Act), which adopted many of the recommendations of the *Crowther Report* on consumer credit. The committee carried out the most comprehensive review of the topic ever undertaken in this country. The report found the state of the law to be gravely defective, one of their most serious criticisms being that legislation regulated transactions on the basis of their form rather than their substance. Hire-purchase, some forms of money lending and pawnbrokers were subject to strict regulation, whereas loans made by high street banks and the large finance houses were virtually unregulated. **8–17**

The Crowther Committee considered that tinkering with the law would not be appropriate and recommended a complete revision. They suggested that two new Acts should be drafted: a Lending and Security Act which would rationalise the treatment of security interests and set up a security register, and a Consumer Sale and Loan Act which would govern the treatment of all forms of consumer credit, the linchpin of which would be a Consumer Credit Commissioner. The Consumer Credit Act is essentially the proposed Consumer Sale and Loan Act, the Government having decided that the Lending and Security Act was unnecessary. **8–18**

---

[11] *Charge Card Services Ltd, Re* [1988] 3 W.L.R. 764; [1988] 3 All E.R. 702; (1988) 4 B.C.C. 524. See also the important case of *Office of Fair Trading v Lloyds TSB Bank Plc* [2007] UKHL 48 and in the Court of Appeal at [2006] EWCA Civ. 268 discussed later in relation to the Consumer Credit Act 1974 s.75.
[12] *Crowther Report* (2003), para.4.1.64.

8–19   The Consumer Credit Act 2006 implemented reforms advocated in a 2003 White Paper.[13] They included: improvements in advertising and other information made available to consumers; facilities to enable credit agreements to be concluded online; reform of the law relating to early settlement; strengthening of the licensing regime; removal of the £25,000 limit on the protections afforded by the 1974 Act; and the replacement of the limited test for reopening extortionate credit bargains with a wider unfairness test. A more fundamental overhaul of the regulation of consumer credit came into operation on 1 April 2014. A National Audit Office report[14] had concluded that the current regulatory regime lacked the capacity and powers to tackle the bulk of detriment in the consumer credit market and estimated that the unaddressed detriment cost consumers £450 million in 2011–2012. Much of the regulation has been transferred to the newly created Financial Conduct Authority from the former OFT and firms in the credit industry will be subject to a regime operated under the Financial Services and Markets Act 2000 (the 2000 Act). While many provisions of the 1974 Act have been repealed a good deal of the Act will still remain. The result, particularly in the short term, is to turn an already complex area of law into one that is at times near to impenetrable.

8–20   As we shall see there is detailed regulation of the credit industry to a degree that is greater than that which normally obtains for protecting the consumer. Why should this be? The *Crowther Report*[15] summarised the factors that prevent the ideal of a fair balance between consumers and credit granters being attained in all cases. An important constraint is consumers' lack of knowledge both of the forms of credit available and their legal rights. In some cases inertia prevents appropriate action being taken. Some consumers are either reckless or improvident in their use of credit; and in other cases, through no fault of their own, families find themselves requiring to borrow because their income is inadequate. As the Crowther Committee added,

> "There is little point in talking of thrift to one who needs money to keep warm or to buy the minimum of food and clothing necessary for subsistence."

Such people are particularly vulnerable to harsh and oppressive terms. Inequality of bargaining power and the existence of a small minority of sellers who indulge in trading malpractice causing great hardship were also noted. It should be added that the committee did not delude themselves that all these problems could be solved by legislation.

The Consumer Credit Act 1974 and the Financial Services and Markets Act 2000

8–21   The regulation of consumer credit is now governed not only by the 1974 Act but also by the Financial Services and Markets Act 2000. The original 1974 Act, with its 193 sections and five Schedules, has been described by a judge as "an Act of

---

[13] See Department of Trade and Industry, *Fair, Clear and Competitive: The Consumer Credit Market in the 21st Century* (2003) Cm.6040, p.3.
[14] National Audit Office, *Regulating Consumer Credit*, (December 2012) *http://www.nao.org.uk/publications/1213/oft_regulating_consumer_credit.aspx* [Accessed 22 June 2015].
[15] For a discussion, see *Crowther Report* (2003), Ch.6.1.

extraordinary length and complexity".[16] And even at this the 1974 Act is only a framework on which much flesh has been put by numerous statutory instruments. Such was its complexity that it was not until 1985 that it came fully into force. To that has now been added much of the 2000 Act, another Act of some complexity and, like the 1974 Act, supplemented by many statutory instruments and rules made by the Financial Conduct Authority (FCA).[17] The FCA was created by amendment of the 2000 Act by the Financial Services Act 2012. The most important of the regulations made under the 2000 Act are the much amended Financial Services and Markets Act 2000 (Regulated Activities) Order 2001[18] (hereafter the RAO). Also of great significance is the FCA Handbook, especially the Consumer Credit Source Book (CONC3 as it is known), one of its specialist parts, which has detailed rules[19] many of which have been transferred from Consumer Credit Act statutory instruments or guidance on consumer credit issued by the OFT. In addition, it must be remembered that it is not comprehensive. Aspects of the ordinary law of contract, such as the law on formation and misrepresentation still apply, and the 1974 Act does not apply to all credit contracts, as we shall see below.[20]

Definitions

Before looking at the various techniques which the legislation uses to protect credit consumers it is vital to consider the scope of the 1974 Act. The central concept is the "regulated agreement" as, with some exceptions, it is only such agreements that are controlled by the Act. Before the term "regulated agreement" can be understood it is essential to look at various definitions which the legislation uses. It will also be convenient at this point to consider some other definitions which will crop up later. The draftsman of the 1974 Act invented new terminology to distinguish various types of credit. In a novel departure from the methods normally adopted by parliamentary draftsmen examples of the terminology were also provided in Sch.2 to the 1974 Act.

8–22

Fixed and running account credit

Section 10(1)(a) provides:

8–23

> "Running-account credit is a facility under a consumer credit agreement whereby the debtor is enabled to receive from time to time (whether in his own person, or by another person) from the creditor or a third party cash, goods and services (or any of them) to an amount or value such that, taking into account payments made by or to the credit of the debtor, the credit limit (if any) is not at any time exceeded."

---

[16] Goff LJ (as he then was) in *Jenkins v Lombard North Central Plc* [1984] 1 W.L.R. 307 at 308.

[17] The Financial Services Authority was renamed the Financial Conduct Authority by s.1A of the Financial Services and Markets Act 2000, which was inserted by s.6 of the Financial Services Act 2012.

[18] Financial Services and Markets Act 2000 (Regulated Activities) Order 2001 (SI 2001/544).

[19] The power to make rules is conferred by Financial Services and Markets Act 2000 (the 2000 Act) s.137A and they have the force of law. Breach may give a private right of action but does not amount to a criminal offence or render a contract unenforceable see ss.137D and 137E of the 2000 Act.

[20] See paras 8–37–8–41.

The most common examples of running account credit are an overdraft or a shop revolving credit account. Fixed-sum credit is any other facility under which credit can be obtained. An obvious example would be a personal loan from a bank or a building society for a specific amount.

Debtor-creditor-supplier agreements

8–24 A debtor-creditor-supplier agreement can arise in three ways.[21] It occurs where a restricted use credit agreement is made to finance a transaction between a debtor and a creditor. An example would be a hire-purchase or credit sale agreement where the supplier provides the finance. Where, as is probably more common, a third party provides restricted use finance this, too, is a debtor-creditor-supplier agreement if made under pre-existing arrangements, or in contemplation of future arrangements between the creditor and the supplier. The typical hire-purchase arrangement, where the finance is provided by a finance company, is a good example, but credit card and check trading transactions provide further examples. The third situation deals with the case where a third party provides unrestricted use credit under pre-existing arrangements with the supplier in the knowledge that the credit is to be used to finance a transaction between the debtor and the supplier. This brings within the ambit of debtor-creditor-supplier agreements situations where a supplier, such as a retailer, has agreed to refer customers to a finance company that will provide them with loans that, though technically not limited to the purchase of a specific product, all parties know will be so used.

Debtor-creditor agreements

8–25 Restricted use credit agreements that would be debtor-creditor-supplier agreements but for the fact that there are no pre-existing arrangements between the creditor and the supplier are known as debtor-creditor agreements. Restricted use credit arrangements to refinance any existing indebtedness of the debtor are in the same category. So are unrestricted use credit agreements which are not made by the creditor under pre-existing arrangements with a supplier.[22] Examples are bank overdrafts, moneylenders' advances and loans from pawnbrokers.

Linked transactions

8–26 Certain transactions are said to be linked to a regulated agreement. This is important, particularly in relation to withdrawal from, and cancellation of, agreements, as well as the provisions about unfair credit relationships. A linked transaction is dealt with in s.19 of the 1974 Act and does not include a transaction for the provision of a security. Subject to this, it covers transactions entered into in compliance with a term in the principal agreement such as the taking out of a policy of life insurance by the debtor under a loan agreement. In a debtor-creditor-supplier agreement the sale and loan contract are linked; and there is a link where the debtor entered into a transaction in order to induce the creditor to enter into the principal credit agreement.

---

[21] See Consumer Credit Act 1974 s.12.
[22] See Consumer Credit Act 1974 s.13.

Total charge for credit and annual percentage rate

A central feature of the recommendations of the *Crowther Report* was the **8–27** necessity for consumers to have better information about credit deals. This, it was hoped, would allow consumers to make rational decisions about credit transactions. It was also expected to benefit them by stimulating competition between lenders who would be exposed to a market where there was greater transparency.

Section 20 of the 1974 Act required regulations to be made for working out the **8–28** true cost of credit to the borrower and they still apply to agreements made before 1 April 2014. From that date art.20 of the RAO authorises the FCA to make such rules.

The true cost of credit is referred to in the Act and regulations as the "total charge for credit" and is to be contrasted with the credit advanced. This is a most important concept for a number of reasons. For example, in relation to computing some of the monetary limits the total charge for credit is not included, only the amount of credit advanced. As we shall see, it is also relevant to the formalities which must be complied with in drafting a credit agreement, the liability of a debtor after a debtor-creditor agreement has been cancelled and the control of extortionate credit bargains. However, its most important function is probably as the first step in arriving at the annual percentage rate (APR), an important piece of information which must be given to consumers and prospective consumers of credit.

The detailed working out of the total charge for credit and the related APR are **8–29** set out in the Consumer Credit (Total Charge for Credit) Regulations 2010[23] for agreements entered into before 1 April 2014 and the Consumer Credit Handbook section of the FCA's Rule Book.[24] These are necessarily somewhat complex. This is because a credit transaction may not merely include interest. There may well be other charges such as arrangement fees, maintenance charges, or insurance premiums. In giving a true picture of the cost of credit some or all of these charges may have to be taken into account. The main provisions of the 2010 Regulations are regs 4 and 5. Regulation 4 provides that, in calculating the total charge for credit, the total interest charge and any other charges at any time payable under the transaction by or on behalf of the debtor must be taken into account. Regulation 5 then provides that certain charges are to be excluded. Examples are premiums for insurance not taken out as a condition of the loan, or life insurance premiums where the proceeds of the policy will be used to repay the loan.[25] The equivalent provisions of the FCA Rule Book are in CONC Appendix 1.2.5.

Having worked out the total charge for credit it is then possible to calculate the **8–30** APR. This is now done by applying a complex equation set out in reg.7.[26] The function of the APR is to provide a means of comparison between the cost of

---

[23] Consumer Credit (Total Charge for Credit) Regulations 2010 (SI 2010/1010).

[24] This specialist part of the handbook is commonly referred to as CONC and can be found on the FCA website *http://www.fshandbook.info/FS/html/FCA/CONC* [Accessed 22 June 2015], see Appendix 1.

[25] For a case demonstrating the complexity of this task see *London North Securities v Meadows* [2005] EWCA Civ. 956.

[26] For the FCA equivalent see CONC App.1.2.6.

various kinds of credit and different credit offers of the same type. It has been argued that consumers have little understanding of APRs and tend to place more reliance on the size and frequency of repayments.[27] However, research by the OFT suggests that understanding of APRs is increasing. It was found that 64 per cent of those surveyed would generally draw the right conclusion from using APRs, even though they might not fully appreciate precisely what they represented.[28]

Regulated credit agreements[29]

8–31   The meaning of this phrase requires a lengthy trawl through various sections of the 1974 Act starting with s.189(1), the definition section, which says

> "'regulated agreement' means a consumer credit agreement, or consumer hire agreement, other than an exempt agreement, and 'regulated' and 'unregulated' shall be construed accordingly".

8–32   This raises a number of questions such as "what is meant by 'credit'?"; "what are consumer credit and hire agreements?"; and "which agreements are exempt?" "Credit" is very widely defined to include "a cash loan, and any other form of financial accommodation",[30] and s.189 goes on specifically to say that a purchaser on hire-purchase obtains credit.

Consumer credit agreement

8–33   The definition of a consumer credit agreement is to be found in s.8. Section 8(1) states that:

> "A consumer credit agreement is an agreement between an individual ('the debtor') and any other person ('the creditor') by which the creditor provides the debtor with credit of any amount."

Subsection (3) goes on to state that a consumer credit agreement is regulated by the 1974 Act if it is "if it is a regulated credit agreement for the purposes of Chapter 14A of Part 2 of the Regulated Activities Order"[31]. This leads to RAO art.60B which, using slightly different terminology, defines a "regulated credit agreement" as any credit agreement that is not an exempt agreement. Exempt agreements are exhaustively defined in arts 60C–60H. The net result of the definition is that the 1974 Act applies to the common forms of instalment credit such as hire-purchase, conditional and credit sale as well as budget accounts, credit cards, loans and overdrafts.

---

[27] National Consumer Council, *Consumers and Credit* (London: National Consumer Council, 1980) Ch.4.

[28] OFT, *Consumer Credit Deregulation* (London: OFT, 1994) para.7.14.

[29] The current position i.e. that relating to agreements entered into since 1 April 2014 is dealt with here.

[30] See Consumer Credit Act 1974 s.9(1).

[31] The Financial Services and Markets Act 2000 (Regulated Activities) Order 2001 SI 2001/544 (RAO).

Consumer hire agreements

A consumer hire agreement is defined in s.15 of the 1974 Act as one that is made   **8–34**
by an individual (the "hirer") for the hiring of goods to the hirer and which is not
a hire-purchase agreement and is capable of lasting for more than three months. It
is regulated if it is not exempt under arts 60O–60Q of the RAO which apply to
hiring to "high net worth" individuals, hiring for business purposes if the
payments exceed £25,000 and hiring of water meters.

Who is protected?

The definition of "individual" in the 1974 Act means that both consumer credit   **8–35**
and consumer hire agreements may involve debtors who are not what might
usually be thought of as private consumers. This is because "individual" in the
Act includes not only humans but also a partnership or other unincorporated body
of persons (not consisting entirely of bodies corporate).[32] Originally, this meant
that the 1974 Act drew a clear line between corporations, e.g. limited liability
companies, who did not get its protection, and others who did. This had the merit
of being easy to operate but the disadvantage that some large businesses run as
partnerships came within the protection of the Act. Amendments made by the
Consumer Credit Act 2006 mean that corporations are still outside the Act but
that only small partnerships and some other unincorporated bodies are protected
by it. This is achieved by defining "individual" as including "a partnership
consisting of two or three persons not all of whom are bodies corporate" and
unincorporated bodies provided that they do not consist entirely of bodies
corporate and are not partnerships.[33]

Exempt agreements

Having discovered what a consumer credit agreement is, we next must note that   **8–36**
some of these agreements will be exempt from the Act. These were originally
contained in the 1974 Act but are now to be found in the RAO. The first is related
to the changes in the meaning of "individual" just discussed. What art.72J of the
RAO calls "high net worth debtors" can choose to waive its protections if they
make a declaration to this effect and an accountant has certified that they have the
required level of assets. The second exemption in the 1974 Act relates to
businesses. Article 60C provides that consumer credit agreements for credit not
exceeding £25,000 and consumer hire agreements involving payments not
exceeding £25,000 are not regulated if entered into "wholly or predominantly for
the purposes of a business". Where the debtor or hirer has made a declaration in
an agreement that it relates to a business there will be a presumption that it does.
That may rebutted where the creditor or owner of someone acting on their behalf
knows or has reasonable cause to suspect that this is not so.[34]

Other exemptions apply to agreements where the creditor is a local authority,   **8–37**
building society, or one of a number of other organisations listed in the section

---

[32] See Consumer Credit Act 1974 s.189(1).
[33] Consumer Credit Act 1974 s.189(1) as amended by s.1 of the Consumer Credit Act 2006.
[34] See RAO art.60C(5) and (6).

such as insurance companies, friendly societies, and organisations of workers or employers. The effect of these is to exempt many loans secured on land.[35]

8–38   Other parts of the same order based on other powers in s.16 create the following further exemptions:

(1)   Debtor-creditor-supplier agreements financing purchases of land that do not gain exemption under the previous exemptions will be exempt if the number of payments to be made does not exceed four.[36]

(2)   A debtor-creditor-supplier agreement for fixed sum credit which is not hire-purchase or conditional sale where the number of payments to be made by the debtor in respect of the credit does not exceed four and must be made within 12 months of the date of the agreement. A straightforward example of this would be trade credit on terms such as payment within 30 days of invoice.[37]

(3)   A debtor-creditor-supplier agreement which is not for hire-purchase or conditional sale and provides running account credit where the whole of the credit is repayable in one instalment.[38]

(4)   A low interest exemption for debtor-creditor agreements, low being defined as an annual percentage rate which does not exceed 1 per cent above the highest base rate of an English or Scottish clearing bank in the 28 days prior to the making of the agreement.[39]

Partially regulated agreements

Small agreements

8–39   Small agreements as defined by s.17 of the 1974 Act are only partially subject to the controls in the Act. A small agreement is a regulated consumer credit agreement for credit not exceeding £50 which is not a hire-purchase or conditional sale agreement; or a regulated consumer hire agreement which does not require the hirer to make payments exceeding £50.

Non-commercial agreements

8–40   Non-commercial agreements are also freed from many of the controls of the 1974 Act such as those on the formalities about agreements and connected lender liability. Such an agreement is a consumer credit or consumer hire agreement not made by the creditor or owner in the course of a business carried on by them.[40]

---

[35] RAO arts 60D and 60E.
[36] RAO art.60F.
[37] See RAO art.60F(2). See *Zoan v Rouamba* [2000] All E.R. 620, CA.
[38] RAO art.60F(3).
[39] RAO art.60G.
[40] See Consumer Credit Act 1974 s.189(1).

Controlling business activities

The legislation regulates the way in which those in the credit industry can carry on their businesses and most of this is now found in the 2000 Act and its supplementary regulations and rules. There are controls on advertising, canvassing for business, the marketing of credit cards and the operation of credit reference agencies. In addition, there is an over-riding requirement that those involved in the credit industry observe the FCA's Principles for Business. These as they apply to consumer credit are[41]:

8–41

- a firm must conduct its business with integrity;
- a firm must conduct its business with due skill, care and diligence);
- a firm must take reasonable care to organise and control its affairs responsibly and effectively, with adequate risk management systems);
- a firm must pay due regard to the interests of its customers and treat them fairly);
- a firm must pay due regard to the information needs of its clients, and communicate information to them in a way which is clear, fair and not misleading);
- a firm must take reasonable care to ensure the suitability of its advice and discretionary decisions for any customer who is entitled to rely upon its judgment);
- a firm must arrange adequate protection for clients' assets when it is responsible for them); and
- a firm must deal with its regulators in an open and co-operative way, and must disclose to the appropriate regulator appropriately anything relating to the firm of which that regulator would reasonably expect notice.

Under the 1974 Act one of the most important controls on the credit industry took the form of the licensing system. With the transfer the responsibility for consumer credit regulation from the Office of Fair Trading (OFT) to the FCA firms no longer need licences but must become "authorised".

Authorisation

The creation of an effective and comprehensive licensing system was one of the central recommendations of the *Crowther Report*. It pointed out that protective measures focusing on individual transactions, important as they are, have limited efficacy.[42] One of the members of the Crowther Committee has explained in more detail the necessity for having a licensing system:

8–42

"No consumer legislation, however sophisticated, is likely to have more than a marginal impact if it is not underpinned by effective enforcement machinery. The Hire-Purchase Acts provided no mechanism whatever for systematic enforcement. The onus was placed on the individual consumer to take the initiative in invoking the Acts. In many cases he was not equipped to do so, through ignorance of his rights, timidity or inability to incur the legal costs that might be involved. The

[41] See FCA, *Handbook Specialist Sourcebook*, CONC3 1.1.4.
[42] *Crowther Report* (2003), para.6.3.3.

reputable trader or finance house would endeavour to comply with the law. The less scrupulous creditor, against whose activities the legislation was primarily aimed, could afford to cock a Snook—provided he stood clear of the small number of criminal' offences provided by the statutes—since at worst he would lose the occasional case, and this loss was far outweighed by the benefits to be derived from diligent and persistent flouting of the statutory requirements and the recovery from uninformed debtors of sums which they could not legally have been compelled to pay."[43]

8–43 The licensing system operated under the OFT has been abolished and firms in the credit industry must comply with the requirements of the 2000 Act which requires those in the financial services industry to be "authorised". There is a "general prohibition" on carrying on regulated activities unless a business is authorised or exempt in s.19 of the 2000 Act. Various activities are specified and those relating to consumer credit are to be found in the RAO.[44] The list is very similar to that under the 1974 Act licensing system. They are:

- lending;
- hiring;
- credit broking;
- operating an electronic system in relation to lending;
- debt-adjusting;
- debt-counselling;
- debt-collecting;
- debt administration;
- credit information services; and
- credit reference agency.

8–44 It should be remembered that credit is defined very widely for the purposes of both the 1974 Act and the 2000 Act to include "a cash loan and any other form of financial accommodation"[45] so the heading of "lending" will include personal loans, credit card lending, overdrafts, pawnbroking, hire-purchase and conditional sales. Some of the other categories require more comment. Credit brokerage covers those introducing consumers seeking credit or goods on rental to those whose businesses involve the grant of consumer credit or consumer hire facilities. It is for this reason that retailers, for example, even though they themselves do not provide credit may need authorisation because they introduce customers to sources of finance such as hire-purchase companies. Debt administration covers businesses that provide portfolio administration services to creditors or owners of hired goods. Credit information services sometimes referred to as "credit repair agencies" are another type of business that has emerged since the 1974 Act was passed. These businesses offer their services to those individuals who find it difficult to obtain credit or hire facilities because of their credit history.

8–45 For those already operating credit business there is an interim permission regime running until the end of March 2016 during which those with existing

---

[43] RM Goode, *Introduction to the Consumer Credit Act 1974* (Butterworths: London, 1974) p.103.
[44] See RAO arts 36A–36G, 36H–36IA, 39D–39L, 60B–60K, 60N–60R and 89A–89D.
[45] RAO art.60L and Consumer Credit Act 1974 s.9(1).

OFT licences can continue to conduct business subject to ensuring that the information that they provided to the OFT is updated. New entrants and, by 1 April 2016, existing businesses will have to gain authorisation, a more rigorous process than obtaining a licence under the OFT system. The starting point is to meet the "threshold conditions", which are minimum standards set out in the 2000 Act. These involve examination of the legal status of the business, its resources, the location of its offices, the suitability of its controllers, and its business model. These requirements will be applied less rigorously in the case of firms applying for limited permission than for those seeking full permission. Limited permission activities are those where lending, credit-broking or hiring is a secondary activity or debt related activities are not for profit. An example would be a high-street retailer whose main business is selling goods. Such a retailer will often have arrangements with a finance company to provide customers with credit and will put them in touch with the finance company from whom credit will be obtained. Under the legislation the retailer is a credit-broker and needs to be authorised. As selling goods is the main business and broking is a secondary activity to help finance the purchase only a limited permission authorisation is necessary. Other examples are not-for-profit debt counselling and debt adjusting, not-for-profit credit information services and some local authority lending.

Once authorised, a firm will also have to meet requirements on approved persons, controllers, regulatory reporting and complaints reporting, though again these are less onerous for limited permission businesses.[46] Under the old regime, the OFT monitored a licence holder's fitness to hold the licence, which included taking account of the conduct of the firm's employees, agents and controllers. Under the new regime, the FCA will apply the "approved persons" regime that already applies to financial services firms. The FCA will require individuals in consumer credit firms who will be carrying out significant or management functions (known as "controlled functions") to be approved by the FCA before they do so. This will mean that chief executives, directors and other senior management will need to be individually approved by the FCA by 2016. The approved persons regime is well-established under the 2000 Act and means that approved persons will be personally liable for the actions of an FCA-authorised firm. The FCA's powers include the ability to fine an approved person or to ban them from working within the financial services industry for any length of time.

8–46

The FCA has a wide range of disciplinary and enforcement tools in its armoury, deriving significant statutory powers from the 2000 Act. Formal regulatory sanctions vary from a relatively low-key public censure without a fine, at one end of the spectrum, to the cancellation of an authorised firm's permission or withdrawal of an approved person's approval at the other end. The latter sanction would often have the effect of putting a firm out of business. The imposition of financial penalties is the most frequent sanction. There are significant powers under FSMA to prosecute a number of criminal offences relating to consumer credit authorisation. The "credible deterrence" strategy of the former regulator, the Financial Services Authority (FSA), has been carried forward by the FCA, and underpins its overall approach to enforcement. The aim

8–47

---

[46] The consumer credit section of the FCA website has a great deal of information on the authorisation process, see *http://www.fca.org.uk/firms/firm-types/consumer-credit/authorisation* [Accessed 22 June 2015].

is to deter the firm or individual being disciplined from "reoffending" and to deter others from making the same mistakes through the publication of enforcement actions. These are intended to send clear messages as to what is considered to be unacceptable behaviour and confirm that the FCA will not hesitate to make examples of those firms and individuals who are guilty of misconduct.

8–48   There are a number of alternatives to becoming authorised that allow firms carrying on certain consumer credit activities, or meeting certain criteria, to carry on regulated activities, without breaching the 2000 Act. One method is to become an appointed representative of an authorised firm[47] which means that the firm will be subject to the supervision of an authorised firm. It does not apply to lenders, unless they lend interest-free, or credit reference agencies. Another alternative is open to self-employed agents of authorised home collected credit firms and mail order firms. The third possibility is being an exempt professional firm. This applies where credit activities are incidental to the main business of the firm. It is available to Scottish solicitors through the Law Society of Scotland rules though some firms, especially those with large debt-collecting work, will need authorisation.

Seeking business

8–49   In any context accurate information is of importance to a consumer in coming to a rational decision about the purchase of goods and services. Where a purchase is to be made on credit this is particularly important as consumers contemplating taking on credit commitments are especially vulnerable. There is much pressure through the media to acquire goods and services, and the availability of credit can beguile people into taking on commitments that they cannot afford. In addition, it is not easy to make comparisons between various offers of credit in the absence of common methods of setting major terms such as the rate of interest.

8–50   For these reasons the legislation has placed considerable importance on pre-contractual information. There are controls on advertising, controls on quotations given to those considering credit arrangements, and restrictions on canvassing credit agreements and distributing credit cards.

Controls on advertising and other promotions

8–51   Regulation of consumer credit advertising is now the responsibility of the FCA and as a result Pt IV of the 1974 Act, which dealt with it has been repealed. Advertising is one aspect of what the FCA terms financial promotion. Section 21 of the 2000 Act is the source of its jurisdiction but the details are in the FCA's CONC, s.3. The overarching rule of CONC3 is that all financial promotions that are made in respect of a credit-related regulated activity are clear, fair and not misleading. This is expanded on in CONC s.3.3.2, which provides that to comply with the general rule, firms should: use plain and intelligible language; ensure that the financial promotion is easily legible; ensure the name of the person making the communication or communicating the financial promotion is specified on the financial promotion; ensure that, where the financial promotion

---

[47] RAO art.15.

is made on behalf of another person, the name of the person of whose behalf the financial promotion is made is included in the financial promotion; and ensure that where the financial promotion is made in relation to credit broking, the identity of the lender (where known) is specified on the financial promotion.

To assist firms, CONC s.3.3 sets out some examples of practices that are likely to contravene the clear, fair and not misleading rule. An example is stating or implying that the firm is a lender where this is not the case, misleading a consumer as to the availability of a particular credit product, concealing or misrepresenting the identity or the name of the firm and using false testimonials, endorsements, or case studies.[48]

8–52

Certain types of promotion have more specific rules. A topical example is HCSTC of which payday loans would be an example. High risk short term credit means, in summary, an unsecured borrower-lender agreement in relation to which the APR is equal to or exceeds 100 per cent, where it is either indicated or required that the credit is to be repaid within 12 months or is otherwise short term. A financial promotion must contain in a practical way the following warning:

> "Warning: Late repayment can cause you serious money problems. For help, go to *http://moneyadviceservice.org.uk*."

There are specific rules for financial promotions for credit not secured on land that apply to firms who make a financial promotion or communication in respect of lending relating to regulated credit agreements and related credit broking agreements.[49] If the promotion is a regulated restricted-use consumer credit agreement (as defined in RAO art.60(L)), in relation to goods or services to be supplied by any person, the firm must hold itself out as prepared to sell the goods or provide the services for cash.[50] If a rate of interest or an amount relating to the cost of credit is included (whether expressed as a sum of money or a proportion of a specified amount), a representative example stating various matters such as the interest rate, other charges, a representative sample and the APR must be set out.[51]

Credit agreements that are secured on land have additional requirements in terms of warnings that must be included in the communication or financial promotion. One of the key statements that must be included in the advertisement where the security or a charge is taken over the borrower's home is the so-called "wealth warning":

8–53

> "Your home may be repossessed if you do not keep up repayments on a mortgage or any other debt secured on it."[52]

CONC 3.8 has examples of practices, that, if carried out by a firm in relation to a financial promotion or communication about a regulated credit agreement with a customer, are considered to be unfair business practices. These include providing

---

[48] FCA, *Handbook Specialist Sourcebook*, CONC3 3.3.10.
[49] FCA, *Handbook Specialist Sourcebook*, CONC3 3.5.
[50] FCA, *Handbook Specialist Sourcebook*, CONC3 3.5.2.
[51] FCA, *Handbook Specialist Sourcebook*, CONC3 3.5.5R(1).
[52] FCA, *Handbook Specialist Sourcebook*, CONC3 3.6.5(2)(a).

unfair trading examples?

an application for credit with a pre-completed amount of credit that is not based on having carried out an assessment of the borrower's creditworthiness or, if the credit is to be secured on land, stating expressly or implying that providing the credit is dependent solely on the value of equity in the property on which the agreement is to be secured. A further example is to promote credit where the firm knows (or has reason to believe) that the agreement would be unsuitable for that customer in the light of the customer's financial circumstances.

8–54   Some of the rules are specific to advertisements. For example, where an advertisement must display a representative example the content of that example is set out in the rules and must be set out in a clear and concise way accompanied by the words "representative example".[53] In some circumstances a postal address must be included. Certain credit advertisements must display a representative APR. However, this does not in itself trigger the requirement for the rest of the standard information though in certain situations this is the case. This occurs where credit is available to persons who might otherwise consider their access to credit restricted, or any of the terms on which credit is available is more favourable than corresponding terms applied in any other case or by any other lender.[54] An advertisement will also trigger the representative APR requirement if it includes any incentive to apply for credit or to enter into an agreement under which credit is provided. The representative APR must be displayed with greater prominence than the relevant indication or incentive, and must be accompanied by the word "representative example".[55]

8–55   Credit and hire advertising is also regulated by the Consumer Protection from Unfair Trading Regulations 2008 discussed in Ch.10 and by the self-regulatory system operated by Advertising Standards Authority (ASA) through the British Code of Advertising Practice. The FCA's system of controls has affected how the ASA deals with complaints about credit. As we have seen technical aspects of non-broadcast advertising, such as APRs and representative examples, are subject to statutory control by the FCA and complaints received about these issues are forwarded by the ASA to them. However, the ASA considers all complaints about "non-technical" aspects of advertisements in all media, such as those relating to offence, social responsibility, fear and distress and competitor denigration. The ASA also assesses all complaints about broadcast advertisements and liaises with the FCA on technical matters covered by their rules. There have recently been many complaints about advertisements for payday lenders. The ASA recently ruled on an advertisement by a Glasgow based company that references to "a weekend away" and "a slap up meal" were problematic.[56]

Quotations

8–56   While traders do not have to provide quotations to prospective customers they may choose to do so and the FCA rules regulate how such quotations are to be drafted. This is dealt with in CONC 4.1.

---

[53] FCA, *Handbook Specialist Sourcebook*, CONC3 3.5.5(5).
[54] FCA, *Handbook Specialist Sourcebook*, CONC3 3.5.7.
[55] FCA, *Handbook Specialist Sourcebook*, CONC3 3.5.5(5)(b).
[56] For details see the ASA website *http://www.asa.org.uk/* [Accessed 22 June 2015].

Canvassing

The Moneylenders Acts banned the peddling of loans from door to door. Similar but more wide-ranging controls are included in the 1974 Act. Canvassing debtor-creditor agreements (of which the most common type will be personal loans) off trade premises is a criminal offence. So is soliciting the entry of an individual into such an agreement during a visit carried out in response to a request made on a previous occasion, if the request was not in writing and signed by the person making it. "Canvassing" means making oral representations off trade premises. Premises are still trade premises if a business is carried on there by the creditor, a supplier, the canvasser or, even the consumer. It does not matter that the place is only a temporary place of business such as a stand at a trade show.[57]

8–57

Circulars to minors

In line with the policy of protecting vulnerable consumers, the 1974 Act makes it a criminal offence to send to a person under 18 years old, with a view to financial gain, any document inviting them to borrow money, obtain goods or services on credit, hire goods, or even apply for information about doing any of these things. It is a defence for the accused to show that they did not know and had no reasonable cause to suspect that the person to whom the document was sent was a minor. However, where the address to which the document is sent is a school, or other educational establishment for minors, reasonable cause to suspect that the recipient is under 18 years of age will be assumed.[58]

8–58

Credit reference agencies

Those who lend will wish to have as much assurance as possible that borrowers will pay back what they have been lent. In the past lenders may have tended to do this through personal knowledge of clients. With the scale of credit today that is not possible and attempts to interview all borrowers would be prohibitively expensive. Many lenders have streamlined the process by using credit scoring techniques to determine whether credit should be granted. Credit scoring is a method of assessing applications for credit using statistical techniques and is widespread among stores and financial institutions throughout the UK. Specialist consultants design individual scorecards for lenders using information about previous credit accounts that have been analysed to show which personal details are associated with good payment records and which with bad. When an individual applies for credit from that company, information on the application form will be combined with information from other sources to obtain a credit score.[59] Usually the other information is obtained from credit reference agencies which are organisations specialising in storing information about people's credit history.

8–59

---

[57] See Consumer Credit Act 1974 ss.48 and 49.
[58] See Consumer Credit Act 1974 s.50.
[59] For further detail on how credit scoring works, see *Which?*, July 1989, p.316.

8–60   Given the importance of credit scoring and access to credit, the accuracy of the information held by credit reference agencies is vital. Their existence also raises other issues related to privacy. For this reason the legislation contains protections for consumers. Such agencies must be authorised under the 2000 Act and there are also important safeguards in the 1974 Act. Section 157 of the 1974 Act imposes a duty on a creditor, owner or negotiator to respond within seven working[60] days to a written request for the name and address of any credit reference agency from which information has been sought about the customer's financial standing. The application must be made within 28 days after the end of antecedent negotiations as defined in s.56.[61]

8–61   This obligation is complemented by s.7 of the Data Protection Act 1998 (DPA 1998), which casts a duty on a credit reference agency to give consumers a copy of any file relating to them which they have, putting it into plain English if necessary. This duty only arises where the consumer has made a written request (accompanied by a fee of £3) and given sufficient details to enable the agency to identify the file. As well as providing the information an agency must also send consumers a statement of their right to have mistakes corrected.

8–62   This statement refers to the right set out in s.159 of the 1974 Act to have wrong and prejudicial information removed from a file or amended. Where the agency complies it must give the consumer a notice stating that it has done so and send a copy of the amended entry. Where the agency and the consumer cannot reach agreement on the issue either side may apply to the Information Commissioner or, in the case of a partnership or other incorporated body, to the FCA which will resolve the matter.

8–63   Part II of the DPA 1998 is also relevant and gives individuals whose personal data is held by a data user an action for damages if loss is occasioned to them through unauthorised destruction, disclosure or access. There is also a right to compensation where loss is caused as a result of the information being inaccurate. Where damage is caused compensation for the distress flowing from the breach can also be claimed.[62] In *Grace v Blackhorse Ltd*[63] it was held that it was not accurate to describe Mr Grace as a "defaulter" under his credit agreement where this was irremediably unenforceable without, at least, the unenforceable nature of the debt also being recorded in the same entry. This was therefore found to be a breach of a statutory duty under the DPA 1998 (namely a breach of the fourth principle, accuracy) and actionable under s.13 of the DPA 1998.

---

[60] See Consumer Credit (Credit Reference Agency) Regulations 2000 (SI 2000/290) reg.3.
[61] See para.8–65 onwards.
[62] Data Protection Act 1998 s.13.
[63] *Grace v Blackhorse Ltd* [2014] EWCA Civ. 1413.

FORMATION AND CANCELLATION OF THE AGREEMENT

Making an agreement

Antecedent negotiations

In practice there will frequently be situations where an important role in a credit transaction will be played by a person who does not provide the credit or with whom the consumer has no legal relationship because the goods are transferred to the financier before being transferred to the consumer. A typical example would be a hire-purchase transaction where the consumer selects the goods in a shop which does not provide hire-purchase finance itself, but has arrangements with a financier. As we have seen, the consumer's contract is with the hire-purchase company and the shop drops out of the picture. However, what if, in the course of discussions in the shop, false or misleading statements were made to the consumer? Under common law the hire-purchase company would not have any responsibility for the activities of the shop as the courts have not been prepared to find that an independent retailer is the agent of the credit granter.[64] The consumer would have no contractual link with the shop and thus might not be able to obtain redress.   **8–64**

Section 56 of the 1974 Act seeks to deal with this situation. The central provision is s.56(2) which provides that,   **8–65**

> "negotiations with the debtor . . . shall be deemed to be conducted by the negotiator in the capacity of agent of the creditor as well as in his actual capacity".

The "antecedent negotiations" that are covered by s.56, in addition to those carried out by the owner or hirer, are set out in s.56(1). The first are those

> "conducted by a credit-broker in relation to goods sold or proposed to be sold by the credit-broker to the creditor before forming the subject-matter of a debtor-creditor-supplier agreement within section 12(a)".

Section 12(a) of the 1974 Act refers to restricted-use credit. The typical situation would be a hire-purchase transaction where the credit-broker is the shop which sells the goods to the hire-purchase company which then hire-purchases them to the consumer.   **8–66**

The second situation is where negotiations have been "conducted by the supplier in relation to a transaction financed or proposed to be financed by a debtor-creditor-supplier agreement within section 12(b) or (c)".   **8–67**

This covers negotiations such as those conducted by a supplier before putting consumers into contact with a finance house which, under pre-existing arrangements, provides them with loans enabling them to purchase goods or services from the supplier.   **8–68**

The creditor will be liable under s.56(4) for contractual statements and misrepresentations made by the negotiator during the antecedent negotiations.   **8–69**

---

[64] *Branwhite v Worcester Works Finance Ltd* [1969] 1 A.C. 552; [1968] 3 All E.R. 104; [1999] G.C.C.R. 397.

These begin when the negotiator and the consumer first enter into communication, and for this purpose an advertisement can constitute communication. It is important to note that s.56(3) prevents attempts to exclude liability under the section.

8–70   Section 56 does not apply to implied terms or to hire contracts, as opposed to hire-purchase contracts.[65] It will sometimes overlap with s.75.[66] Indeed, the two Scottish decisions on s.75 should really have been decided under s.56.[67]

8–71   Creditors or owners can be liable for a very wide range of representations. It must be noted that the liability is for antecedent negotiations "in relation to goods sold or proposed to be sold" in the case of s.56(1)(b), and "in relation to a transaction financed or proposed to be financed" in the case of subs.(1)(c). However, in *Powell v Lloyds Bowmaker Ltd*[68] a narrow and unrealistic view of s.56(1)(b) was taken. Mr Powell had traded his Vauxhall in part exchange against a Toyota that he wished to purchase. The vendors negotiated finance on the deal and agreed that it would settle an existing hire-purchase commitment (with a finance company called AM) on the vehicle being traded in. The vendors did not settle the commitment and Mr Powell raised an action for damages basing his claim on the proposition that by virtue of s.56(1)(b) the vendors were the deemed agents of Lloyds Bowmaker, who were thus liable for the failure to pay off the earlier hire-purchase commitment. The sheriff disagreed with a decision of an English county court judge in *UDT v Whitfield*[69] where, on very similar facts, the finance company was held liable. He accepted that "the legislation is intended to benefit consumers and that the *Crowther Report* laid some stress on the need to base the law on commercial reality as opposed to legal abstractions". While agreeing that it could have applied to a representation about the price of the car he did not consider that it applied to the promise to pay off the existing hire-purchase debt.

8–72   The English Court of Appeal decided *Forthright Finance Ltd v Ingate*,[70] shortly after *Powell*. Staughton LJ examined the decisions of *UDT v Whitfield* and *Powell v Lloyds Bowmaker Ltd* and the legislative origins of s.56. He stated:

> "In my judgement what s.56(1)(b) means is that there must be goods sold or proposed to be sold by the credit-broker to the creditor, which will form the subject matter of a debtor-creditor-supplier agreement. If that condition is fulfilled, one next inquires whether there were negotiations in relation to those goods. If there were, then all that was said by the credit-broker in those negotiations is deemed to have been said on behalf of the creditor. On the other hand, what is said in any other negotiations which do not relate to those goods is not deemed to be said on behalf of

[65] See *Lloyds Bowmaker Leasing Ltd v MacDonald* [1993] C.C.L.R. 65; [1999] G.C.C.R. 3443 Sh. Ct.; and the English Court of Appeal decision, *Woodchester (Equipment Leasing) Ltd v British Association of Canned and Preserved Food Importers and Distributors Ltd* [1995] C.C.L.R. 51; [1999] G.C.C.R. 1923.

[66] See para.8–106 onwards.

[67] See *United Dominions Trust Ltd v Taylor*, 1980 S.L.T. (Sh. Ct.) 28 and *Forward Trust Ltd v Hornsby and Windermere Aquatic Ltd* [1996] C.C.L.R. 18, discussed at paras 8–114 to 8–117. The same error occurred in the English case of *Porter v General Guarantee Corp Ltd* [1982] R.T.R. 384.

[68] *Powell v Lloyds Bowmaker Ltd*, 1996 S.L.T. (Sh. Ct.) 117; [1999] G.C.C.R. 3523.

[69] *UDT v Whitfield* [1987] C.C.L.R. 60.

[70] *Forthright Finance Ltd v Ingate* [1997] 4 All E.R. 99.

the creditor. The question is then a simple one of fact, were the negotiations in this case all relating to the goods to be sold?"[71]

On the facts he found that only one transaction was involved and that *UDT* was rightly decided. Henry LJ, in agreeing, indicated that s.56 should be construed widely, stating:

> "A narrow construction of the words would not only be artificial but would fly in the face of the clear purpose of this Act to protect consumers. While I would favour a wide construction of the words on that ground alone, subs.(4) of s.56 seems to be to put the matter beyond doubt in favouring a wide construction."[72]

8–73

Black Horse Ltd v Langford[73] demonstrates a loophole in the operation of s.56. The facts were the same as in the *Forthright Finance Ltd v Ingate* with an important variation. The car dealer, X, who arranged the sale of the new car to Mr Langford and who promised, but failed, to pay off the balance of the purchase price on his trade-in did not, in the end, arrange finance for the new car. Instead X contacted a credit-broker who arranged finance and the new car was sold by X to this credit dealer who in turn sold it to the finance company who hire-purchased it to Mr Langford. When he was sued by Black Horse for the balance due under the hire-purchase agreement on his trade-in Mr Langford relied on s.56. This argument failed and the judge observed:

8–74

> "I cannot accept that the inclusion of the phrase 'or proposed to be sold' can be construed as having the consequence that [X] is deemed to have conducted the negotiations as agent for Black Horse. On its proper construction s 56(1)(b) applies only to the credit-broker who actually sells or proposes to sell the goods to the finance company. At no stage did [X] sell or propose to sell the Lotus to Black Horse."

It is quite common for car dealers to operate in this way so consumers can unwittingly lose the valuable protection of s.56. The law commissions have suggested that it is unlikely that the *Langford* decision will be endorsed by the appeal courts but recommended that that the law should be clarified to the effect that the supplier acts as agent of the creditor even if the sale from supplier to creditor takes place through an intermediary.[74]

Section 55 of the 1974 Act permits regulations to be made requiring information to be given to consumers before they enter into credit or hire agreements. This is part of a policy of encouraging consumers to become aware of what they are taking and to compare what is on offer. The Consumer Credit (Disclosure of Information) Regulations 2010[75] have been made and require lenders or owners to disclose certain information before an agreement is made. This pre-contract information is the same as that which must be in the agreement itself and which is discussed below.

8–75

---

[71] *Forthright Finance Ltd v Ingate* [1997] 4 All E.R. 99 at 105.
[72] *Forthright Finance Ltd v Ingate* [1997] 4 All E.R. 99 at 105.
[73] *Black Horse Ltd v Langford* [2007] EWHC 907 QBD.
[74] The Law Commission and the Scottish Law Commission, Consumer Redress for Misleading and Aggressive Practices (Law Com No.332 and Scot Law Com No.226) paras 10.9 and 10.16.
[75] Consumer Credit (Disclosure of Information) Regulations 2010 (SI 2010/1013).

Form and content of agreements

8–76 In a further attempt to ensure that consumers know exactly what they are doing, the 1974 Act requires the Treasury to make regulations as to the form and content of regulated agreements.[76] These must have provisions to ensure that a debtor or hirer is made aware of:

    (a)   the rights and duties conferred or imposed on them by the agreement;

    (b)   the cost of credit;

    (c)   the protection and remedies available under the 1974 Act; and

    (d)   any other matters which it is desirable that creditors should know.

8–77 Since the implementation of the Consumer Credit Directive exactly what secondary legislation is applicable to the documentation of regulated agreements is not always a straightforward matter to determine. For regulated consumer credit agreements that either are not secured on land, the amount of credit provided exceeds £60,260 or the agreement is not entered into wholly or predominantly for the purposes of a business carried on, or intended to be carried on, by the debtor the Consumer Credit (Agreements) Regulations 2010 (the 2010 Regulations)[77] apply. For other consumer credit and consumer hire agreements the relevant secondary legislation remains the Consumer Credit (Agreements) Regulations 1983 (the 1983 Regulations).[78]

8–78 The 2010 Regulations set out in great detail the form, content, legibility and signature of documents containing regulated consumer credit and hire agreements. Different types of agreement require different types of information to be given and the regulations set out the requirements for each type in Schedules. These have in common the fact that the kind of information which must be given falls into five main categories:

    (1)   heading on the first page of the document prominently stating the legal nature of the agreement;

    (2)   name and address of each party;

    (3)   financial information, such as the subject matter of the agreement, the timing and amount of payments, and the cost of credit, including the APR;

    (4)   other information about the agreement, such as details of any security provided and charges payable on default; and

    (5)   protection and remedies available under the 1974 Act.

8–79 The 2010 Regulations also require that there should be a signature box in an agreement and go into detail on exactly how this is to be set out. In the case of credit token agreements the name, address and telephone number of the person to whom notice is to be given of loss or misuse must be included.

8–80 Failure to comply with the 2010 Regulations can have serious consequences for the creditor or hirer. Before dealing with that issue it is better to consider first

---

[76] See Consumer Credit Act 1974 s.60.
[77] Consumer Credit (Agreements) Regulations 2010 (SI 2010/1014).
[78] Consumer Credit (Agreements) Regulations 1983 (SI 1983/1553).

the related rules in the 1974 Act dealing with the signing of agreements, the provision of copies to the debtor, and rights to cancel or withdraw.

Proper execution of an agreement

Execution of an agreement is the technical term for the signing of it by both parties. The 1974 Act has stringent requirements about proper execution of an agreement which go well beyond simply ensuring that both parties put their names to it. To be properly executed, as the Act calls it, the following requirements must be complied with:

8–81

(1) the document must be in the prescribed form containing all the prescribed terms and conform to the agreement regulations;
(2) it must contain all the terms of the agreement apart from the implied terms;
(3) it must be legible;
(4) the requirements of ss.62 and 63 about supplying copies[79];
(5) the cancellation provisions of s.64 or the special provisions of s.58 for a consideration period where there is a heritable security[80]; and
(6) it must be signed in the prescribed manner by the debtor and the creditor or owner.[81]

The 2010 Regulations require the debtor or hirer to sign within the signature box in the agreement. Where the debtor or creditor is a partnership or unincorporated association the signature may be that of someone signing on its behalf.

8–82

Copies of the agreement

The implementation of the Consumer Credit Directive made radical changes to the rules relating to copies in relation to those agreements to which it applies. Although the original 1974 Act rules were retained after the changes came into effect on 1 February 2011, they were restricted to agreements outside the scope of the Directive. Such excluded agreements are still governed by 1974 Act ss.62 and 63. They are consumer hire agreements, cancellable agreements, agreements secured on land, agreements for credit exceeding £60,260, and regulated business agreements. The debtor or hirer must get at least one copy of an agreement and ss.62 and 63 of the 1974 Act have detailed rules about this. If the debtor signs an agreement at the same time as the creditor, a copy of the executed agreement must be given to the debtor then and there. Where an unexecuted agreement is presented to the debtor and they sign it but the creditor does not sign at that time, the debtor must then and there be given a copy of the unexecuted agreement. In addition, within seven days of the agreement being signed by the creditor a further copy must be sent. Where an agreement is sent to the debtor a copy must also accompany it. If the agreement has already been signed by the creditor and so becomes an executed agreement on the debtor signing it, no further copy need

8–83

---

[79] See para.8–83.
[80] See para.8–85.
[81] Requirements 1, 2, 3 and 6 are found in Consumer Credit Act 1974 s.61.

be sent. If, however, the creditor has not signed it at that stage a copy of the executed agreement must be sent within seven days of being signed by the creditor. Copies of credit token agreements need not be given within seven days of being made as long as they are given before, or at the same time as, the credit token is given to the debtor.[82]

8–84   The new law in ss.61A and 61B applies to all consumer credit agreements not in the lists above and all consumer credit agreements in those lists where the creditor has contracted into the new law. New s.61A provides that the creditor must give a copy of the executed agreement (and any other document referred to in it) to the borrower once the agreement has been made. If this is not done, the agreement is not properly executed and cannot be enforced against the borrower without a court order. Section 61A does not apply where the creditor has already given the borrower a copy of the unexecuted agreement and this is identical to the executed agreement. In this event, the creditor must inform the borrower in writing that the agreement has become executed (including the date of execution), that it is in identical terms to the copy of the unexecuted agreement already provided and that the borrower is entitled to a copy of the executed agreement if they ask for it before the end of the 14 day right of withdrawal period. If the borrower asks for a copy of the executed agreement during this period, this must be provided without delay. If the creditor delays sending a copy of the executed agreement, this may have the effect of extending the right of withdrawal period.

The provisions set out in s.61A replace those set out in ss.62 and 63 (concerning the duty to supply copies of the unexecuted and executed agreement) for all types of regulated agreement other than "excluded agreements". For the purposes of s.61A, an excluded agreement is a cancellable agreement, an overdraft agreement to which s.61B applies, an agreement secured on land, an agreement for credit exceeding £60,260, or an agreement entered into by the borrower wholly or predominantly for business purposes.

Special rules for cancellable agreements

8–85   In the case of cancellable agreements[83] these rules are modified. A copy of a cancellable agreement must contain a notice in the form prescribed by the 1983 Regulations,[84] drawing attention to the right to cancel and saying how and when it may be exercised as well as the name and address of a person to whom notice may be given. As we have seen, in some cases a second copy of an agreement must be sent. In the case of a cancellable agreement it must be sent by post.[85] Where a second copy of an agreement is not required a notice containing the information about cancellation must be sent by post.

---

[82] See Consumer Credit Act 1974 s.63(4). Because of the practical difficulties in some cases of complying with the requirements about copies Consumer Credit (Cancellation Notices and Copies of Documents) Regulations 1983 (SI 1983/1557) derogate from the full rigour of the copies rules. They also prescribe the form and content of documents to be issued as executed copies.

[83] For discussion of cancellable agreements, see para.8–95 onwards.

[84] See Consumer Credit Act 1974 s.64(1)(a) and Consumer Credit (Cancellation Notices and Copies of Documents) Regulations 1983 (SI 1983/1557).

[85] See Consumer Credit Act 1974 s.63(3).

Consequences of improper execution

Where an agreement has not been properly executed it can only be enforced against a creditor or hirer by an order of the sheriff court.[86] The more draconian consequences of some forms of improper execution which made enforcement impossible, as dramatically illustrated by *Wilson v First County Trust Ltd*,[87] were removed by the Consumer Credit Act 2006, which repealed s.127(3)–(5).

8–86

Withdrawal and cancellation

Withdrawal from prospective agreement

It is a general principle of contract law that an offer may be revoked prior to acceptance. There is such an opportunity in the context of a consumer credit agreement where the debtor signs the agreement before the creditor or owner signs it. At this point there is an offer by the prospective debtor which has yet to be accepted by the creditor. The consumer, therefore, has an opportunity to withdraw from the agreement.

8–87

The 1974 Act clarifies how this may be done. Section 57 provides that no special form of wording is required; all that is required is that it "indicates the intention of the [consumer] to withdraw from a prospective regulated agreement".[88] The notice of withdrawal can be written or oral. The same section also sets out the list of persons to whom such a notice can be given. Notice can, of course, be given to the creditor or hirer, but, in addition, it can be given to others who are deemed to be agents of the creditor or hirer. A credit-broker or supplier who is the negotiator in antecedent negotiations is deemed to be such an agent. Surprisingly, perhaps, so is any person who, in the course of a business carried on by them, acts on behalf of the debtor or hirer in any negotiations for the agreement. This means that if, for example, a solicitor was carrying on negotiations on behalf of a client it would be sufficient for the client to give notice of withdrawal to their own solicitor.[89]

8–88

Withdrawal has the same effect as cancellation and is discussed below.[90]

8–89

Withdraw from credit agreement under the Consumer Credit Act 1974 s.66A

In the case of many regulated credit agreements entered into after 1 February 2011, s.66A of the 1974 Act enables debtors to withdraw from regulated agreements without giving any reason. However, this right of withdrawal does not extend to what it terms "excluded agreements". These are agreements for credit exceeding £60,260, agreements secured on land, restricted-use credit agreements to finance the purchase of land, and agreements for bridging loans in

8–90

---

[86] See Consumer Credit Act 1974 s.65(1).
[87] *Wilson v First County Trust Ltd* [2003] UKHL 40; [2003] 4 All E.R. 97.
[88] See Consumer Credit Act 1974 s.57(2).
[89] Consumer Credit Act 1974 s.175 provides that the deemed agent is under a contractual duty to the creditor or owner to transmit the notice to them forthwith.
[90] See paras 8–100—8–102.

connection with the purchase of land. In these cases, and in the case of hire agreements, the borrowers or hirers will have to rely on rights provided under other sections of the 1974 Act, notably s.67. It must be stressed that the right of withdrawal is from the credit agreement: the underlying contract for the purchase of goods or services is not affected. The purpose of s.66A is to allow a consumer who, on reflection, decides that the credit arrangements are not appropriate to get out of them.

8–91   To withdraw from agreements, the debtor must give oral or written notice of the withdrawal before the end of 14 days beginning with the day after the latest of the following: the day on which the agreement is made; the day on which the creditor first advises the debtor of their credit limit under the agreement (where required to so advise the debtor under the agreement); the day on which the debtor receives a copy of the executed consumer credit agreement required by the 1974 Act s.61A; or the day on which the debtor receives a copy of the agreement as required by s.63.[91] Oral notice of withdrawal must be in the manner specified in the agreement[92] and notice given in writing, by post or electronic transmission must be sent to the address or electronic address specified for the purpose in the agreement. The section gives no further guidance on the form of written notice so, presumably, any communication that indicates that the consumer is withdrawing will be acceptable. A written notice is regarded as having been received by the creditor at the time the notice was sent/posted.[93]

Upon withdrawal under the 1974 Act s.66A, the agreement and any ancillary service contract relating to it are treated as if they had never been entered into.[94] If the ancillary service is to be provided by a third party, the creditor is under a duty, without undue delay, to notify the third party that the debtor has withdrawn from the credit agreement.[95]

8–92   When a debtor withdraws from an agreement under the 1974 Act s.66A, they must repay to the creditor any credit provided and the interest accrued upon it[96] without undue delay and, in any event, no later than the end of the period of 30 days beginning with the day after the day on which the notice of withdrawal was given.[97] Where the regulated agreement from which the consumer withdraws is a conditional sale, hire-purchase or credit-sale agreement and the debtor and repays all the sums due under s.66A(9), the title in the goods purchased or supplied under the agreement is to pass to the them on the same terms as would have applied had they not withdrawn from the agreement.[98] Accordingly, if a debtor withdraws from a hire-purchase agreement under s.66A, they remain liable to pay the price of the vehicle and accrued interest: this is very different to the position of a debtor who cancels a hire-purchase agreement under the 1974 Act s.67.

---

[91] Consumer Credit Act 1974 s.66A(2) and (3).
[92] Consumer Credit Act 1974 s.66A(4).
[93] Consumer Credit Act 1974 s.66A(5) and (6).
[94] Consumer Credit Act 1974 s.66(7).
[95] Consumer Credit Act 1974 s.66A(8).
[96] Consumer Credit Act 1974 s.66A(9).
[97] Consumer Credit Act 1974 s.66A(10).
[98] Consumer Credit Act 1974 s.66A(11).

Cancellation

As a result of the creation of the right of withdrawal in s.66A just discussed the original right of withdrawal in ss.67–73 of the 1974 Act has a much narrower scope and applies to relatively few agreements. **8–93**

A regulated consumer credit or hire agreement may be cancelled if two conditions are met. First, oral representations by an individual acting as, or on behalf of, the negotiator must have been made in the presence of the debtor or hirer during the course of antecedent negotiations. In addition, the subsequent agreement must not have been signed by the debtor or hirer at trade premises of either the creditor or owner, or the negotiator, or any party to a linked transaction (other than the debtor or hirer or a relative of theirs). While it is often said that the cancellation provisions apply to doorstep sales it should be noted that they can apply in other circumstances. If, for example, the consumer discusses the proposed transaction at a shop or in the offices of a finance company but takes the agreement away and signs it at home it will be cancellable. **8–94**

The "cooling-off" period begins when the debtor or hirer signs the unexecuted agreement. It ends five days after the second statutory notice or copy is received by the debtor or hirer. To exercise the right to cancel a notice must be served within the cancellation period on one of a number of people. This notice, unlike a notice that one is withdrawing from a prospective agreement, must be in writing. However, it need not be in any particular form. It is sufficient if it "indicates the intention of the debtor or hirer to withdraw from the agreement".[99] If it is posted it is deemed to be served on the recipient at the time of posting, whether or not it ever arrives.[100] **8–95**

The notice can be given to any one of several people. These are the same people to whom an intention to withdraw from a prospective agreement may be sent,[101] as well as anyone specified in the statutory cancellation notice.[102] **8–96**

The effect of a notice of cancellation is to cancel the agreement and any linked transaction; and to withdraw any offer by the debtor or hirer, or a relative, to enter into a linked transaction.[103] To this there are some exceptions. Where the agreement is a debtor-creditor-supplier agreement for restricted-use credit to finance the doing of work or the supply of goods to meet an emergency it cannot be cancelled. If the same sort of agreement is used to finance the supply of goods which have been incorporated in land or something else before service of the notice of cancellation it cannot be cancelled.[104] **8–97**

Section 71 of the 1974 Act makes clear that where an agreement other than a debtor-creditor-supplier agreement for restricted-use credit is cancelled it still remains alive for the purposes of repayment of credit and the payment of interest. This provision would be important where the credit under a personal loan had been advanced before the end of the cooling-off period. It would be inequitable if the consumer could simply keep the loan. While s.71 prevents this, its other **8–98**

---

[99] See Consumer Credit Act 1974 s.69(1).
[100] See Consumer Credit Act 1974 s.69(7).
[101] See para.8–88.
[102] See Consumer Credit Act 1974 s.69(1).
[103] See para.8–26.
[104] See Consumer Credit Act 1974 s.70(2).

provisions are likely to discourage lenders from advancing loans early as there are considerable disadvantages from their point of view.

8–99 Some linked transactions also survive the cancellation of an agreement. These are insurance contracts, guarantees, and deposit and current accounts.[105]

Consequences of cancellation

8–100 The debtor or hirer can recover any sum paid under the agreement or linked transaction except for the first £5 of any fee or commission charged by a credit-broker. Any sum payable by the debtor or hirer or their relative under the agreement ceases to be payable. For any sum repayable the consumer has a lien on any goods in their possession under the cancelled agreement.[106]

8–101 Should the consumer have acquired goods under a restricted use debtor-creditor-supplier agreement that is subsequently cancelled, they must be restored to the person from whom they were obtained. All that is required of consumers is that they should, if they receive a written request, hand them over at their own premises. While the goods are in their possession they must take reasonable care of them. This obligation does not apply to perishable or consumable goods which are consumed prior to cancellation. In this case the consumer will receive a windfall.[107]

8–102 Should goods have been given in part exchange, the debtor or hirer is entitled to their return in substantially the same condition as when they were given. This must be done within 10 days of cancellation by the consumer, otherwise the debtor or hirer is entitled to a sum equal to the part-exchange allowance.[108]

Certain conveyancing transactions

8–103 Because of the conveyancing difficulties that would arise, the cancellation provisions do not apply to agreements secured on heritable property. Instead there is a "consideration period" during which the consumer can reflect on the wisdom of the proposed transaction and, if they have second thoughts, withdraw from it. The way that this works is that the creditor or hirer must, at least seven days before sending an agreement for signature, send a copy. With this copy must be sent a notice in the prescribed form indicating the consumer's right to withdraw and saying how and when the right may be exercised. During the period for consideration the creditor must not approach the consumer in any way except in response to a specific request from the consumer.[109]

8–104 This consideration period does not apply in two situations.[110] The first is where the agreement is a restricted-use credit agreement to finance the purchase of the heritable property which is the subject of the security. The other is where the agreement is for a bridging loan in connection with the purchase of the land

---

[105] Consumer Credit (Linked Transactions) (Exemptions) Regulations 1983 (SI 1983/1560). Insurance contracts might be cancellable under the Insurance Companies Act 1982.
[106] See Consumer Credit Act 1974 s.70.
[107] See Consumer Credit Act 1974 s.72.
[108] See Consumer Credit Act 1974 s.73.
[109] See Consumer Credit Act 1974 ss.58 and 61(2).
[110] See Consumer Credit Act 1974 s.58(2).

subject to the security, or other land. The reason for this is that in both these situations speed may be of the essence if the deal is not to fall through.

During the agreement

Implied terms

In a credit transaction there will be terms relating to the credit and others relating to the goods or services supplied. We will first look at the latter. This leads to discussion of terms relating to the quality of the goods or services, the title of the supplier and the date of delivery. In all credit transactions there will be terms relating to such matters that supply of goods legislation requires to be included. These terms hire-purchase are now to be found in ss.9–18 of the Consumer Rights Act 2015. The content of these terms was discussed in Ch.4. The ability of a trader to exclude these terms is restricted and this is discussed in Ch.9.

8–105

Connected lender liability

While the use of implied terms in credit transactions is nothing new, there is a novel provision relating to the liability of those involved in such transactions. In certain circumstances, the consumer has a claim not only against the supplier of the goods or service but also the provider of the credit. There are two versions of this liability applying in different circumstances and they are found in ss.75 and 75A of the 1974 Act.

8–106

Section 75

Section 75(1) of the 1974 Act provides:

8–107

> "If the debtor under a debtor-creditor-supplier agreement falling within section 12(b) or (c) has, in relation to a transaction financed by the agreement, any claim against the supplier in respect of a misrepresentation or breach of contract, he shall have a like claim against the creditor, who, with the supplier, shall accordingly be jointly and severally liable to the debtor."

This is what is commonly known as "connected lender liability" and it has considerable advantages for consumers where it applies. For the 1974 Act s.75 to apply four conditions must be met:

8–108

(1) the cash price of the goods or service being supplied must exceed £100 but not be more than £30,000 (including VAT);
(2) there must be a debtor-creditor-supplier agreement regulated by the Act, i.e. an agreement where credit is advanced to an individual and which is not exempt under the Act;
(3) the provider of the credit is in the business of giving credit and the credit agreement is made in the course of that business; and
(4) the credit is advanced under pre-existing arrangements, or in contemplation of future arrangements, between the provider of credit and the supplier.

8–109   One of the most common situations where connected lender liability applies is a credit card transaction such as Mastercard or Visa. It would also apply where a consumer wished to buy a car from a motor dealer and the dealer arranged finance with a finance company with whom they had pre-existing arrangements. It would not apply where the consumer wished to buy the car and went to his bank and arranged a personal loan, even where the bank was aware that the loan was specifically for the purchase of the car. In this case the credit is not advanced under pre-existing arrangements between the supplier and the bank and there is not a debtor-creditor-supplier agreement. It should also be noted that debit cards provided with current accounts are not within this protection, nor are payment cards like Diners Club or American Express where credit must be paid off at the end of each month.

8–110   Section 75 has no relevance to hire-purchase, conditional sale or credit sale agreements, despite the comments of the judge in *Porter v General Guarantee Corp*[111] in relation to a hire-purchase agreement. This is because of the way in which such agreements are structured. The dealer sells the goods to the finance company which then supplies them to the consumer. Any claim for breach of the supply contract must be against the finance company which is both creditor and supplier as far as the consumer is concerned.

8–111   The consumer has "a like claim" against the creditor and this has proved controversial. In *United Dominions Trust v Taylor*[112] it was held that this extended beyond claims for damages arising from breaches of contract and misrepresentation to a claim to rescind both the supply and the credit contracts. This decision has been considered by most commentators to be wrong[113] though it was followed in *Forward Trust Ltd v Hornby*.[114] It was overruled by the Inner House of the Court of Session in *Durkin v DSG Retail*.[115] On further appeal to the Supreme Court[116] that Court agreed that s.75 gave no right to rescind the credit agreement but they found another route by which the credit agreement could be rescinded.

8–112   In *Durkin* the facts were that Mr Durkin bought a laptop computer from DSG Retail on 28 December 1998 but rejected it and returned it the following day on discovering that it did not have the promised inbuilt modem. There was no doubt that the supply contract had been validly rescinded. However, the transaction was to be financed by what all parties agreed was a debtor-creditor-supplier agreement with the second defendants, HFC Bank Plc, to which s.75 could apply. The bank continued to demand repayment of the loan, which Mr Durkin refused to make. The bank reported his failure to repay to two credit reference agencies with the result that Mr Durkin found it difficult to obtain credit. They did this although Mr Durkin had orally informed their agent, an employee of the supplier, in December 1998 that he was rescinding the credit agreement and had confirmed

---

[111] *Porter v General Guarantee Corp* [1982] R.T.R. 384.

[112] *United Dominions Trust v Taylor*, 1980 S.L.T. (Sh. Ct.) 28.

[113] See Davidson, *The Missing Link Transaction*, (1980) 96 L.Q.R. 343; Lowe, *Missing Link Transactions—Further Observations* (1981) 97 L.Q.R. 532; P Dobson, *Consumer Credit: A Connected Lender Conundrum*, 1981 J.B.L. 179; R Goode, *Consumer Credit Law and Practice*, para.33.165.

[114] *Forward Trust Ltd v Hornby*, 1995 S.C.L.R. 574.

[115] *Durkin v DSG Retail* [2010] CSIH 49.

[116] *Durkin v DSG Retail* [2014] UKSC 21.

that in a letter in March 1999 to the supplier's managing director. In addition, he had told the creditor during telephone calls in February and March 1999 that he was rescinding the credit agreement.

Mr Durkin raised an action in Aberdeen sheriff court in early 2004 against both DSG and HFC. He sought a declarator that he had validly rescinded both the contract of sale and the credit agreement and claimed damages of £250,000 from HFC for its negligence in representing to the credit reference agencies that he had defaulted on the credit agreement. He claimed damages from HFC under three heads of loss: damage to his financial credit; loss from interest charges caused by his inability to exploit offers of 0 per cent credit; and loss caused by his inability to put down a 30 per cent deposit on a house in Spain in October 2003, measured essentially by the difference between the price available in 2003 and the enhanced value of that property three years later.

8–113

The sheriff awarded Mr Durkin £8,000 for injury to his credit, £6,880 for the extra interest that he had had to pay and £101,794 for the loss of a capital gain arising from his inability to purchase the Spanish property in 2003. On appeal to the Inner House of the Court of Session it was held that s.75 did not allow him to rescind the credit agreement. It was also held that Mr Durkin had not shown that HFC had failed in its duty of care. Significantly in the light of the appeal to the Supreme Court, counsel for HFC analysed the evidence in the transcripts of evidence and the documents and persuaded the court that the evidence did not permit the sheriff to hold that a breach of duty by HFC had caused Mr Durkin loss under the second and third heads of claim. The court therefore amended the sheriff's findings of fact to exclude his claims for loss of interest and the loss arising from his inability to purchase the property in Spain. HFC conceded that if they had been in breach of duty they would have been liable for the first head of damages.

8–114

The Supreme Court agreed that s.75 gave no right to rescind the credit agreement giving five reasons for so holding. These were that[117]:

8–115

- it is consistent with the ordinary meaning of the words of s.75(1);
- it is consistent with that concurrent primary liability that the debtor and supplier should be jointly and severally liable to the debtor;
- the creditor's entitlement to indemnity from the supplier under s.75(2) is consistent with his incurring of concurrent liability for matters which he cannot control;
- it reflects the relevant recommendation of the Crowther Report, which led to the Consumer Credit Act 1974; and
- s.75 also applies to an unrestricted-use credit agreement under s.12(c). In such a case, if the supply contract were rescinded and the purchase price repaid, the debtor could use the money for other purposes. In such case there is no obvious need for a right to rescind the credit agreement.

However, the Supreme Court still found that Mr Durkin was entitled to, and had on the facts, rescinded the credit agreement. Lord Hodge observed ([26]) that:

8–116

---

[117] *Durkin v DSG Retail* [2014] UKSC 21, [19]–[21].

"In my view, the law implies a term into such a credit agreement that it is conditional upon the survival of the supply agreement. The debtor on rejecting the goods and thereby rescinding the supply agreement for breach of contract may also rescind the credit agreement by invoking this condition."[118]

8–117   Lord Hodge noted that the creditor can also rescind the agreement by invoking the implied term. Given the course that Mr Durkin's case had taken the detailed consequences of reliance on the implied term by either party are not spelt out. If the purchase price is repaid to the debtor they would be bound to repay it to the creditor. The debtor might well have incurred other losses as a result of entering into the credit transaction such as administrative fees and interests payments. It would seem that these could be recovered from the supplier as losses flowing directly from entering into the supply contract. Section 75 could thus be invoked and such losses could be claimed from the creditor.

8–118   Mr Durkin's tenacity has clarified an important point in credit law. However, it did not end entirely happily for him. The Supreme Court disagreed with the Inner House on the delictual claim and held that in failing to make any enquiries before intimating the alleged default to the credit agencies HFC were in breach of duty. Damages of £8,000 for injury to Mr Durkin's credit were restored. However, the other two heads of damage could not be considered by the Supreme Court in the light of the amendment of the sheriff's findings of fact by the Inner House. Under s.32 of the Court of Session Act 1988 an appeal to the Supreme Court may deal only with matters of law not the findings of fact and, in this case, the Inner House had found that there was no evidence to found the claims for loss of extra interest that had to paid and the potential capital gain on the abortive Spanish property transaction.

8–119   In *Dalgleish v National Westminster Bank Plc*[119] the claimant sought to bring a claim under s.75 against the card issuer for the repayment of an overpayment to builders who had charged him more than they were entitled to under a contract. The sheriff held that where a claim could be made both as *a condictio indebiti* (i.e. an unjust enrichment claim) or a contractual action it was permissible to frame it as a contractual action for the purpose of bringing a claim under s.75.

8–120   While creditors are liable under s.75 it should be noted that they are entitled to be indemnified by suppliers for any liability incurred. They can, and this is the policy of s.75, protect themselves by ensuring that dealers with whom they enter into arrangements are reputable.

8–121   Credit card companies have long argued that they were not liable for transactions entered into overseas by cardholders resident in the UK. This point was finally resolved by the House of Lords in *Office of Fair Trading v Lloyds TSB Bank Plc*[120] where it was held that the credit card companies are liable.

---

[118] *Durkin v DSG Retail* [2014] UKSC 21, [26].
[119] *Dalgleish v National Westminster Bank Plc* [2001] G.W.D. 3-112 D.
[120] *Office of Fair Trading v Lloyds TSB Plc* [2007] UKHL 48.

Section 75A

Section 75A of the 1974 Act was enacted to implement part of the EU Consumer **8–122**
Credit Directive 2008.[121] It has a similar function to s.75 but is narrower in scope.
It gives the debtor a claim only in contract whereas s.75 also applies to
misrepresentations. It applies only if s.75 does not apply, and only if all of the
following conditions are satisfied:

- the cash price of the goods or services is more than £30,000;
- the amount of the credit agreement used to purchase the goods or services
  is £60,260 or less;
- the goods or services are purchased under a "linked credit agreement";
- there has been a breach of contract; and
- the borrower is unable to obtain satisfaction from the supplier.

A "linked transaction" is defined in s.75A(5), as:

> "a regulated consumer credit agreement which serves exclusively to finance an
> agreement for the supply of specific goods or the provision of a specific service and
> where—
> (a)   the creditor uses the services of the supplier in connection with the
>   preparation or making of the credit agreement, or
> (b)   the specific goods or provision of a specific service are explicitly specified in
>   the credit agreement".

The fact that this definition makes clear that it does not apply where credit has
been provided for general purposes as opposed to specific purchases of goods or
services means that it will not usually apply to credit cards. The effect of
subss.(7) and (8) is that agreements for business purposes and those relating to
land are not covered.

Section 75A is narrower than s.75 in that the debtor must show that the
supplier of the goods or service has not responded satisfactorily to a claim. This
may be because of insolvency, the inability to trace the supplier or its failure to
respond. In addition, debtors must show that they have taken reasonable steps to
pursue their claims against suppliers though this need not include litigation. The
Government guidance[122] suggests that reasonable steps might, for example,
include using a supplier's complaints system. Section 75A(4) provides that the
borrower is considered to have obtained satisfaction where they have accepted a
replacement product or service or other compensation from the supplier in
settlement of their claim.

---

[121] Directive 2008/48/EC of the European Parliament and of the Council of 23 April 2008 on credit
agreements for consumers and repealing Council Directive 87/102/EEC.
[122] *Consumer Credit Regulation: Guidance on the regulations implementing the Consumer Credit
Directive*, BIS 10/1053 (August 2010) Ch.13.9.

Information remedies

8–123   As part of the policy of ensuring that consumers have appropriate information, the 1974 Act provides in ss.77[123] and 78 that they have the right to obtain information from the creditor about such matters as the amount already paid and the amount owing. In the case of fixed sum agreements the new s.77A(1) requires the creditor to give the debtor a statement within one year from the date of the agreement and thereafter at intervals of not more than one year. A new s.78A imposes a duty to give information of changes in the rate of interest. To supplement the early repayment provisions in ss.94 and 95, s.97 obliges the creditor to inform consumers of the amount required to settle their accounts. Those hiring goods have similar rights under s.79. Those who have agreed to act as sureties are entitled, on payment of a fee, to similar information.[124]

Notice about certain actions

8–124   Agreements will often allow creditors to demand early repayment, recover possession of goods or land, or treat any right under the agreement as terminated. Such action cannot be taken without giving the consumer at least seven days' notice in an approved form.[125] Debtors must be given at least seven days' notice of variations of agreements before they can become effective.[126]

Appropriations of payments

8–125   A debtor who has more than one agreement with a creditor may not be able to make a payment that discharges the total sum due under the agreements. Section 81 provides that each agreement should be credited with that proportion of the payment which each sum due bears to the whole sum due under the various agreements. For example, suppose that there are two agreements under which £100 and £50 are due and the debtor can only afford to pay a total of £90. £60 will be appropriated to the agreement under which £100 was due and £30 to that under which £50 was due.

Liability of credit card holders

8–126   Unless the card has been used with the consent of the cardholder, the maximum liability of the cardholder is £50. However, if someone has acquired the card with the consent of the cardholder there is no limit on liability. Once the cardholder has given notice of loss or misuse there is no further liability. Notice is effective

---

[123] Discussed in *McGuffick v Royal Bank of Scotland Plc* [2009] EWHC 2386 (Comm); [2010] 1 All E.R. 634.

[124] See Consumer Credit Act 1974 ss.107–109.

[125] See Consumer Credit Act 1974 s.76 and Consumer Credit (Enforcement, Default and Termination Notices) Regulations 1983 (SI 1983/1561), amended by Consumer Credit (Enforcement, Default and Termination Notices) (Amendment) Regulations 1984 (SI 1984/1109).

[126] See Consumer Credit Act 1974 s.82 and Consumer Credit (Notice of Variation of Agreements) Regulations 1977 (SI 1977/328), amended by Consumer Credit (Notice of Variation of Agreements) (Amendment) Regulations 1979 (SI 1979/661) and Consumer Credit (Notice of Variation of Agreements) (Amendment No.2) Regulations 1979 (SI 1979/667).

when received. If given orally the credit token agreement can stipulate that it is not effective unless confirmed in writing within seven days.[127]

Termination and default

In this section we are, with the possible exception of the early settlement rules, dealing with cases where consumers have run into financial difficulties. In such a situation they are particularly vulnerable and the policy of the law is to provide a measure of protection against the worst excesses of some elements of the credit industry. As a practical point, it may be said in passing that consumers encountering difficulties are well advised to seek help sooner rather than later. Generally speaking, creditors are willing to be accommodating where, as is usually the case, the difficulties stem from some unexpected cause such as domestic problems, unemployment or illness.

8–127

Termination

At this point termination is being considered in the sense of the statutory right of the debtor or hirer voluntarily to bring the agreement to an end. Later, we shall be discussing the circumstances surrounding termination by the creditor or hirer.[128]

8–128

As a response to financial difficulties, termination, using the rights given in ss.99–101 of the 1974 Act will rarely be in the consumer's interests. However, the facility is available.

8–129

Regulated hire-purchase and conditional sale agreements may be terminated by the debtor at any time before the final payment falls due by giving notice to anyone who is entitled to receive payments under the agreement. To this right there are two exceptions, both relating to conditional sale agreements. Such an agreement relating to land, title to which has passed to the buyer, or one relating to goods where the property has vested in the debtor who has transferred the goods to someone else, cannot be terminated. A new s.98A extends the right of termination to open-ended credit agreements. The best examples are credit cards.

8–130

Termination only operates for the future. Section 99(2) of the 1974 Act makes clear that liability that has accrued prior to termination is not affected. On termination the debtor must pay the difference between what has been paid and half the total price of the goods. In making this calculation any installation charge is deducted first and the whole of that charge added as it is clearly reasonable that such a charge should be payable. It is possible that the amount due could be less if it can be shown that the creditor's loss is less.

8–131

In the case of a consumer hire agreement there is also a right to terminate, but the earliest time at which this can occur is 18 months after the making of the agreement. Notice of not less than the shorter of the shortest payment interval or three months must be given. Because early termination can cause hardship to the owner there are three circumstances in which the right is not available. These are: where the total payments, ignoring sums payable on breach, exceed £1,000 in any year; where the goods are let out for the hirer's business and were selected by

8–132

---

[127] See Consumer Credit Act 1974 s.84(5).
[128] See para.8–134.

them and acquired by the owner at their request from a third party; and, finally, where the hirer requires the goods to re-let them in the course of business.

Early settlement

8–133   At any time during a regulated consumer credit agreement the debtor may give notice to the creditor of an intention to complete payments either in full or in part early.[129] This is only economic if there is a rebate on the total charge for credit and regulations prescribe how this is to be calculated. The regulations introduced in 2004 use a new actuarial method to calculate the early resettlement figure as well as measures to ensure that consumers are aware of the costs associated with early repayment.[130]

DEFAULT

8–134   The plight of consumers who fail to comply with their obligations under credit and hire agreements is often very difficult. As a result the legislation has for some time provided them with special protection and this has been strengthened by amendments made by the Consumer Credit Act 2006. To try to ensure that consumers are aware that they are getting into difficulties, 1974 Act s.86B, which applies to fixed sum and hire agreements, and s.86C, which applies to running-account credit, require the creditor to send notices informing consumers of their arrears. This must be done 14 days after the debtor or hirer has failed to make four instalments (if instalments are paid weekly) and in other cases after two instalments are overdue. This is subject to the total that has already been paid being less than is due up to that time and that the shortfall exceeds the equivalent of either two or four instalments depending on the frequency of payments. In addition, if the debtor continues to be in arrears the creditor must provide a notice of arrears at intervals of six months until they are paid off. When this notice is given to debtors it must be accompanied by an information sheet prepared by the FCA. The information sheet encourages consumers to take action about their problem and lists agencies to which they can turn for help.[131] Failure to serve notices of arrears results in creditors being unable to enforce an agreement until they do so and the debtor is not liable for any interest relating to that period.[132]

8–135   There is further relief for those experiencing financial difficulties. Where they are in breach of their agreement it is usual for certain charges to be payable. For example, there may be a charge for late payment of an instalment or for exceeding a credit limit on a credit card. These "default sums"[133] as they are termed in the 1974 Act must be notified to the debtor and interest on them may

---

[129] See Consumer Credit Act 1974 s.94.

[130] The new regulations, the Consumer Credit (Early Settlement) Regulations 2004 (SI 2004/1483) came into force on 31 May 2005.

[131] Information sheets can be found on the FCA website: *http://www.fca.org.uk/firms/firm-types/ consumer-credit/information-sheets* [Accessed 22 June 2015].

[132] See Consumer Credit Act 1974 s.86D.

[133] For a definition see Consumer Credit Act 1974 s.189(1).

only be charged 28 days after that notice is given.[134] In addition, s.86F provides that only simple interest may be charged on a default sum.

Where a debtor has breached an agreement the creditor cannot automatically take steps to enforce the agreement as would normally be the case with a contractual arrangement. Section 87 of the 1974 Act provides that before various forms of enforcement action can be taken against a debtor a "default notice" must be served. Such a notice is required where the creditor or owner intends: **8–136**

(a) to terminate the agreement;
(b) to demand earlier payment of any sum;
(c) to recover possession of any goods or land;
(d) to treat any right conferred on the debtor or hirer by the agreement as terminated, restricted or deferred; and
(e) to enforce any security.

This notice must specify what the breach is, what action needs to be taken to remedy it and, if it is not capable of remedy, the amount of compensation required and the date by which this must be paid has to be stated. Any action to enforce the agreement cannot be taken earlier than 14 days after the default notice has been served. *Eshun v Moorgate Mercantile Co Ltd*[135] is an example of the result of failure to comply with the similar provisions of the Hire-Purchase Act 1965. The defendant finance company was ordered to pay compensation to the debtor for the loss caused by terminating his agreement. **8–137**

A remedy which is open at common law to creditors in the case of hire-purchase and conditional sale is repossession of the goods. Under these agreements the consumer does not acquire title to the goods initially and it is usual for agreements to provide that there shall be this right in case of default. This can operate very harshly where the consumer has paid a substantial proportion of the price, and in the past some creditors abused their rights. As a result, "snatch back" provisions were enacted in the Hire-Purchase Act 1938. Similar provisions are now found in ss.90 and 91 of the 1974 Act. **8–138**

Under these provisions, if the debtor has paid one third or more of the total price of the goods, and the property in the goods remains in the creditor, the goods are known as "protected goods". This means that the creditor is not entitled to recover possession from the debtor except on an order of the sheriff court. Where an installation charge is part of the total price the amount relevant for deciding whether the goods are protected is calculated by adding the installation charge to one third of the remainder of the total price. It is not possible for a creditor to circumvent this protection by making a fresh agreement that includes goods additional to those that were protected under an earlier agreement, or by modifying an agreement.[136] **8–139**

This protection also applies where the debtor has died. In this case the person in possession of the goods benefits initially from the protection and, after confirmation has been granted, the executor.[137] **8–140**

---

[134] See Consumer Credit Act 1974 s.86E.
[135] *Eshun v Moorgate Mercantile Co Ltd* [1971] 1 W.L.R. 722; [1971] 2 All E.R. 402.
[136] See Consumer Credit Act 1974 s.90(3) and (4).
[137] See Consumer Credit Act 1974 s.90(6).

8–141   The protected goods provision only applies where the goods have to be recovered "from the debtor". This includes anyone to whom the debtor has entrusted the goods, such as a garage in which a car has been left for repair, or someone to whom the goods have been lent. However, if the goods have been abandoned the restrictions on repossession do not apply. This is illustrated by *Bentinck Ltd v Cromwell Engineering*[138] where the debtor had obtained a car on hire-purchase. After the car had become protected goods he defaulted on the repayments and the car was seriously damaged in an accident. Following the accident the debtor took the car to a garage and then disappeared and could not be traced. The hire-purchase company did manage to trace the car, which by then had been at the garage for some months, and repossessed it. In this action against the defendants, who had agreed to act as sureties, it was held that there was such clear evidence of an intention to renounce all rights to the goods that the equivalent of s.90 did not apply.

8–142   Protected goods may be repossessed without a court order if the debtor consents. The cases show that the courts will wish to be satisfied that the consent is a genuine and informed consent. In *Chartered Trust v Pitcher*[139] the debtor, having lost his job, telephoned the hire-purchase company to say that he could not keep up the payments on his car and was advised to write to them asking them to repossess the car. The letter that he wrote clearly showed that he did not want to do this and that he was hoping that some other solution might be possible. Without telling him that the car was protected goods, and that on an application to repossess the court might reschedule the payments, the car was repossessed. It was held that this was in breach of what is now s.90.[140]

8–143   Where the debtor does not choose to hand over the goods it is arguable that in Scotland it is always necessary to obtain a court order to recover them. This is certainly the case where the goods are on someone's premises whether or not they are protected goods. Section 92(1) of the 1974 Act provides:

> "Except under an order of the court, the creditor or owner shall not be entitled to enter any premises to take possession of goods subject to a regulated hire-purchase agreement, regulated conditional sale agreement or regulated consumer hire agreement."

8–144   Section 173 provides that this provision cannot be overridden by anything in the agreement between the debtor and the creditor.[141]

8–145   This leaves the question of the creditor's right to repossess goods which are not on "premises". In practice this means repossessing goods found in the street or a public road and will apply mainly to cars, motorcycles, caravans and the like. Before there can be any question of repossession the debtor must be in breach of an agreement that has a term allowing the creditor in those circumstances to

---

[138] *Bentinck Ltd v Cromwell Engineering* [1971] 1 Q.B. 324.
[139] *Chartered Trust v Pitcher* [1988] R.T.R. 72.
[140] The facts of this case are less likely to recur now as the statutory default notice must give more detailed information about a debtor's rights than was the case at the time of this case or the harsh and unrealistic decision in *Mercantile Credit Co Ltd v Cross* [1965] 2 Q.B. 205.
[141] If the goods are on someone else's premises, e.g. a garage, it would appear that the consent needed is that of the owner of those premises.

repossess the goods (which invariably agreements do have). The creditor must also have served a default notice (as required by s.87) which has expired.

The reason that it is suggested that it is never possible to repossess goods **8–146** under Scots law is that the policy of the law is against such a self help remedy as the nineteenth century institutional writer, Professor Bell, explained:

> "Possession attempted to be acquired by force may be resisted by force; but possession, being once obtained in this way, must be reclaimed by the true creditor judicially; the party who has ceased to possess being bound to trust to the protection of the law for restitution, and not to the strength of his own arm."[142]

If this is the case where possession has been obtained by force how much **8–147** more powerful where possession has initially been obtained perfectly legally under a hire-purchase or conditional sale agreement. Professor Walker expresses similar views,[143] though he would allow more latitude to those recovering property.[144] Nevertheless he points out that the repossession must be carried out without committing trespass, assault or any other wrong. This will often be quite difficult to achieve if, for example, the hirer is in the vicinity. In short, Professor Gow's observation,[145] that "it seems that the owner who resorts to self help acts at his peril", has still much to commend it. The parliamentary draftsman also thinks so to judge by the statement in the notice required by para.7 of Sch.2 to the Consumer Credit (Enforcement, Default and Termination Notices) Regulations 1983.[146] After pointing out that protected goods can only be recovered by the creditor against the wishes of the debtor by means of a court order it adds, "[i]n Scotland he may need to get a court order at any time".

Judicial control

As part of the policy of trying to provide adequate protection for those involved **8–148** in credit transactions, the 1974 Act gives wide powers to the sheriff court in relation to credit agreements. Such powers do, of course, suffer from the inherent disadvantage of private law remedies that consumers must take some action. It is well known that consumers rarely invoke these protections and as a result the White Paper announced the Government's intention to consult on the possibility of creating an alternative dispute resolution (ADR) procedure for dealing with consumer credit disputes and the Consumer Credit Act 2006 extended the jurisdiction of the Financial Ombudsman Scheme to include consumer credit disputes.[147]

---

[142] R Bell, *Dictionary and Digest of the Law of Scotland*, edited by George Watson, 7th edn (Edinburgh: Bell & Bradfute, 1890) p.826.

[143] DM Walker, *Civil Remedies* (Edinburgh: W. Green, 1974) p.39.

[144] DM Walker, *Civil Remedies* (1974) pp.263 and 264.

[145] JJ Gow, *The Law of Hire-Purchase in Scotland*, 2nd edn (Edinburgh: W. Green, 1968).

[146] Consumer Credit (Enforcement, Default and Termination Notices) Regulations 1983 (SI 1983/1561).

[147] See Department of Trade and Industry, *Fair, Clear and Competitive: The Consumer Credit Market in the 21st Century* (The Stationery Office, 2003) Cm.6040, para.3.46. See also consultation paper, Department of Trade and Industry, *The Provision of Alternative Dispute Resolution for Disputes arising under the Consumer Credit Act 1974* (2003).

8–149   Before considering the various ways in which the courts can regulate agreements it is worth noting the rules about jurisdiction. We have already seen that actions relating to consumer credit agreements must be brought in the sheriff court. This is an advantage for consumers in that expenses in that court are lower than in the Court of Session. In addition, the jurisdiction rules assist the consumer in that actions relating to the enforcement of such agreements, and most other actions relating to them, must be brought in the sheriff court of the place where the debtor is domiciled or carries on business.[148] However, if the purpose of the action is to determine proprietary or possessory rights or security rights over moveable property, the action may be brought in the sheriff court of the place where the property is located.[149]

Enforcement orders

8–150   We have already seen that in certain circumstances an agreement can only be enforced by means of a court order. Where an application has to be made to the sheriff, s.127(1) of the 1974 Act provides that it must be dismissed only if the sheriff considers that it is just to do so taking into account two sets of circumstances. First, account must be taken of the prejudice caused to any person by the contravention, and the degree of culpability for it. In addition, the powers which the court has under ss.135 and 136 must also be taken into account. These give wide powers to vary agreements; and the implication of referring to them in this context is that, by using them, it may be possible to remove any disadvantageous aspects of an agreement by their use.

Time orders

8–151   Section 129 of the 1974 Act gives wide powers to the sheriff to make time orders. These are orders that permit the sheriff to adjust the rate and time of payments of instalments by debtors, hirers or sureties. In addition, they can be used to specify the time within which a breach of an agreement, other than non-payment of money, should be rectified.

8–152   A time order may be made in a variety of circumstances. It is possible where there has been an application for an enforcement order or in any other action to enforce a regulated agreement or a security, or to recover possession of goods or heritable property to which an agreement relates. Debtors or hirers can apply for a time order where default notices have been served on them or where the new arrears notice referred to in ss.86B and 86C has been served on them.

8–153   In deciding on the making of a time order the sheriff must consider whether it is just to do so taking into account whether the sum suggested is reasonable, having regard to the means of the debtor, hirer or surety.[150] Section 130 of the 1974 Act deals with the situation where the debtor has made an offer to pay instalments which has been accepted by the creditor. In such a case a time order

---

[148] See Consumer Credit Act 1974 s.141(3A)(a) and (b), which were added by Civil Jurisdiction and Judgments Act 1982 Sch.12 Pt 2 para.4.

[149] See Consumer Credit Act 1974 s.141(3A)(c).

[150] The factors relevant in granting a time to pay direction under Consumer Credit Act 1974 s.1 were considered in *Capital Bank Plc v Paterson*, 2002 S.L.T. (Sh. Ct.) 100.

may be made without hearing evidence of means. In the case of hire-purchase and conditional sale agreements only, time orders dealing with instalments may deal with sums not yet due.[151] Sheriff Fitzsimmons has held that wide as these powers are they do not extend to varying the rate of interest.[152] In England, the Court of Appeal has held in *Southern and District Finance Plc v Barnes*[153] that this is possible under s.136 and approved of the decision of a county court judge who used this power.

Financial relief for hirers

Those who hire goods do not have the benefit of the protected goods rule which applies only to hire-purchase and conditional sale agreements. Prior to the 1974 Act they could find themselves in a particularly difficult and unfair position when they ran into financial difficulties.[154] They might have had use of the goods for only a short time yet, on failure to keep up payments, might become liable to pay substantial sums. Section 132 now provides a solution in this situation. It applies where an owner has recovered possession of goods otherwise than by court action. The hirer may ask the sheriff to order that the whole or part of any sum paid should be repaid, and that the obligation to pay any sums owed should cease.

8–154

The only reported case on s.132 appears to be *Automotive Financial Services Ltd v Henderson*.[155] The defenders had leased a car, the purchase price of which was £8,144, from the pursuers. After the agreement had run for six months they got into financial difficulties, stopped making the rental payments, and the pursuers repossessed the car. By this time the defenders had made payments of £2,150 under the lease. The car was sold by the pursuers for £6,000 and they then sued for £3,840 as an amount due under the terms of the agreement. The defenders asked the sheriff principal to exercise his discretion under s.132 but he refused to do so saying:

8–155

> "To suggest that somehow the payments made should entitle the defenders to relief seems to me an unlikely proposition unless the defenders can set out a good reason why the pursuers should be satisfied in the commercial sense with what they have received. The defenders have not attempted to do so. Looking at the matter another way they have not even started to suggest that the payment sought is by way of a penalty."[156]

The sheriff principal upheld the decision on appeal saying that this was an exercise of discretion based on a proper assessment of relevant materials. He did not think that it was appropriate to use either of the formulae which the defenders had put forward to justify invoking the section's protection. These were to base the operation of s.132 on the interest and administration costs incurred by the lessors during the period during which the defenders had the car; or the monetary value of the depreciation of the car during the same period.

8–156

---

[151] See Consumer Credit Act 1974 s.130(2).
[152] See *Murie McDougall Ltd v Sinclair*, 1994 S.L.T. (Sh. Ct.) 74; 1994 S.C.L.R. 805.
[153] *Southern and District Finance Plc v Barnes* [1996] 1 F.C.R. 679.
[154] See, e.g. *Galbraith v Mitchenhall Estates Ltd* [1965] 2 Q.B. 473.
[155] *Automotive Financial Services Ltd v Henderson*, 1992 S.L.T. (Sh. Ct.) 63.
[156] *Automotive Financial Services Ltd v Henderson*, 1992 S.L.T. (Sh. Ct.) 63 at 64.

8–157   On the facts this seems a suitable case for the exercise of s.132. For a car, the purchase price of which was £8,144, the pursuers were found to be entitled to recover just short of £12,000 from the defenders within six months of entering into the agreement. Even allowing for the fact that the pursuers will have incurred various costs this seems excessive. The problem may have been that the sheriff did not feel able to exercise his discretion on the basis of the financial information put before him by the defenders. The moral of this case may be that more sophisticated accounting information should be produced to support an application.

Special powers relating to hire-purchase and conditional sale agreements

8–158   In cases of hire-purchase or conditional sale agreements s.133 of the 1974 Act contains special provisions involving "return orders" and "transfer orders". Such orders may be made where an application for an enforcement order or time order has been made, or where the creditor has brought an action to recover possession of goods. These powers can be exercised together with the power to make a time order or vary an agreement. The return order is self explanatory, being an order for the return of goods to the creditor.

8–159   A transfer order can only apply where the agreement relates to more than one item of goods. In such a situation an order can be made transferring to the debtor the creditor's title to some of the goods and the return to the creditor of the remainder. Such an order can only be made where the debtor has already paid an amount at least equal to the part of the total price which relates to the goods transferred and one third of the unpaid balance of the total price. The goods transferred shall be "such of the goods to which the agreement relates as the court thinks just".[157]

UNFAIR CREDIT RELATIONSHIPS

8–160   As a number of reports[158] have stressed, the vast majority of credit transactions do not result in any difficulties and most traders act in a responsible manner. However, there is a minority of transactions that do give cause for concern. The Department of Trade and Industry's (DTI) consultation paper, *Tackling Loan Sharks—and more*, summed up the situation in this way:

> "Most credit, for most consumers, most of the time causes no problems. However there is an ongoing concern about some activities mainly on the margins of the market that can be described as socially harmful lending, i.e. transactions where the costs of credit (in terms of price and associated terms and conditions) substantially

---

[157] See Consumer Credit Act 1974 s.133(3).

[158] OFT, *Unjust Credit Transactions* (OFT 1991) OFTO46; E Kempson and C Whyley, *Extortionate Credit in the UK—A report to the DTI* (Department of Trade and Industry, 1999); N Lord, *Daylight Robbery—The CAB case for effective regulation of extortionate credit* (London: National Citizens' Advice Bureaux, 2000); Department of Trade and Industry, *Fair, Clear and Competitive: The Consumer Credit Market in the 21st Century* (The Stationery Office, 2003) Cm.6040.

exceed levels which would be generated by a fully competitive market and/or are so oppressive or exploitive that no sensible person, independently advised, would find them acceptable."[159]

The nature and scale of the problem is difficult to assess. The OFT when it came to review the controls on socially harmful lending introduced by the Consumer Credit Act 1974 noted that "there is indeed no documented evidence about the extent of extortionate credit in the United Kingdom".[160] The experience of the OFT and the views of both consumer and industry sources led it to conclude that:

8–161

> "... [C]redit transactions of the sort which so troubled the Crowther Committee, and at which the extortionate credit provisions of the Consumer Credit Act were targeted, continue to take place and, indeed, the concerns are now wider."[161]

Later research conducted on behalf of the DTI by Kempson and Whyley[162] confirmed this view. Those most likely to be affected are among the most vulnerable consumers who, as the OFT's 1991 report had put it, engaged in "necessitous borrowing for the management of poverty rather than the facilitation of affluence".

The lending factors that are associated with potentially extortionate lending relate both to the substance of the transaction and lending practices. Substantive factors involve high rates of interest and charges and onerous conditions. The onerous conditions include dual rates of interest which involve concessionary rates which can easily be lost, often for trivial defaults, and never regained.[163] Lending practices that have caused concern are the targeting of vulnerable people for whose problems credit may not be an appropriate solution, the use of high pressure sales tactics, failure to check the ability of borrowers to repay and even the falsification of income data on application forms.

8–162

Kempson and Whyley concluded that:

8–163

> "Only a relatively small number of people use lenders who offer credit agreements that would be considered extortionate in most people's eyes—possibly no more than a hundred thousand people at any one time."

However, they went on to point out that:

> "... [T]here are many more (indeed millions) who borrow in the alternative and non-status markets and are potentially at risk of extortionate terms on their loans. Consequently, the terms and conditions attached to credit from some lenders present a bigger problem in relation to extortionate credit than interest rates alone. This is exacerbated by the fact that terms and conditions are less transparent than the cost of a loan."[164]

---

[159] See Department of Trade and Industry, *Tackling Loan Shark—and more* (Department of Trade and Industry, 2003) para.2.1.

[160] See OFT, *Unjust Credit Transactions* (OFT 1991) para.4.5.

[161] See OFT, *Unjust Credit Transactions* (OFT 1991) para.4.14.

[162] See OFT, *Unjust Credit Transactions* (OFT 1991) fn.49.

[163] For a good example see *Falco Finance Ltd v Gough* [1999] C.C.L.R. 16.

[164] E Kempson and C Whyley, *Extortionate Credit in the UK—A report to the DTI* (Department of Trade and Industry, 1999) p.34.

This conclusion is corroborated by research carried out by the National Association of Credit Bureaux and its Scottish counterpart, Citizens' Advice Scotland.[165]

8–164 Until the enactment of the 1974 Act UK law made very limited attempts to deal with the problem. That Act gave potentially far-reaching powers to the courts in ss.137–140 of the Consumer Credit Act 1974 to reopen a credit bargain found to be extortionate so as to do justice between the parties. However, it is generally accepted that these powers were ineffective as very little use was made of them. Academic opinion has been critical for many years[166] and official reports have also noted the weaknesses of the legislation. As long ago as 1991 the OFT stated that it "does not believe that the extortionate credit provisions . . . have effectively addressed the problem . . . "[167]

8–165 The Consumer Credit Act 2006 added new ss.140A–140D to the 1974 Act in a new attempt to address this problem. The new provisions permit the courts to exercise a wide range of powers set out in s.140B of the 1974 Act in order to negate the unfairness in the relationship between the creditor and the debtor. These powers permit a court to order the repayment of any sum paid by a debtor or surety, require a creditor "to do or not to do (or to cease doing) anything specified in the order", "reduce or discharge any sum payable by a debtor or by a surety", "direct the return to a surety of property", "otherwise set aside . . . any duty imposed on the debtor or on a surety" or "alter the terms of the agreement or any related agreement".

8–166 Section 140A(1) provides that these powers can be exercised if a court determines:

"... [T]hat the relationship between the creditor and the debtor arising out of the agreement (or the agreement taken with any related agreement) is unfair to the debtor because one or more of the following—
(a)   any of the terms of the agreement or of any related agreement;
(b)   the way in which the creditor has exercised or enforced any of his rights under the agreement or any related agreement;
(c)   any other thing done (or to be done) by, or on behalf of, the creditor (either before or after the making of the agreement or any related agreement)."

The phrase "by, or on behalf of, the creditor" was central to the decision in *Plevin v Paragon Personal Finance Ltd*.[168] It was held that it restricted the things that could be taken into consideration to the acts or omissions of those for whom the creditor was responsible. These would be activities arising from agency, or deemed agency relationships. On the facts of that case, which involved the misselling of payment protection insurance, the lender was not regarded as acting

---

[165] N Lord, *Daylight Robbery—The CAB case for effective regulation of extortionate credit* (London: National Citizens' Advice Bureaux, 2000) Ch.3; and C Sharp, *On the cards: The debt crisis facing Scottish CAB Clients* (Edinburgh: Citizens Advice Scotland, 2004).
[166] GG Howells and L Bently, "Judicial Treatment of Extortionate Credit Bargains" (1989) 16. Conv. 164 and (1989) 16 Conv. 234; G Howells, I Crow and M Moroney (eds), *Aspects of Credit and Debt* (London: Sweet & Maxwell, 1993) pp.11–14, and in the same book Borrie, "Lending to Those in Need—The Responsibilities of Lenders, Borrowers and Regulators" at p.62.
[167] See OFT, *Unjust Credit Transactions* (OFT 1991) para.4.18.
[168] *Plevin v Paragon Personal Finance Ltd* [2014] UKSC 61; [2014] 1 W.L.R. 4222.

unfairly because a broker who was Mrs Plevin's agent had acted unfairly. She did succeed in demonstrating that the lender acted unfairly on other grounds.

The section goes on in subs.(2) to provide that in deciding whether a relationship is unfair a court "shall have regard to all matters it thinks relevant (including matters relating to the creditor and matters relating to the debtor)".

It is important to note that an unfair relationship may arise by virtue not only **8–167** of a credit agreement but also of a "related agreement". This is defined in s.140C as meaning:

- a credit agreement consolidated by the main credit agreement;
- a linked transaction in relation to the main agreement (or a consolidated agreement); or
- a security provided in relation to the main agreement (or a consolidated agreement or linked transaction).

This will bring within the ambit of the unfair relationship test several areas which have caused concern such as consolidated loans and "linked transactions". "Linked transactions" are defined in s.19 of the 1974 Act. They include transactions entered into in compliance with a term of the principal credit agreement. Also covered are transactions financed, or to be financed, by the principal agreement (where the latter is a debtor-creditor-supplier agreement), and the borrower (or a relative) enters into the transaction on the suggestion of the lender (or an associate or certain other persons) to induce the lender to enter into the principal agreement. Many contracts for payment protection insurance (PPI) which have been heavily criticised are likely to be linked transactions.

Even a cursory comparison of these provisions and those they replace is **8–168** enough to suggest that a substantial change has taken place in the control of inequitable credit agreements. It is significant that these provisions speak of "relationships" between creditors and debtors. The subheading to this part of the 1974 Act is "Unfair Relationships" and s.140A(1) provides that:

> "The court may make an order under section 140B in connection with a credit agreement if it determines that the *relationship* between the creditor and the debtor arising out of the agreement (or the agreement taken with any related agreement) is unfair to the debtor . . . " [emphasis added].

This contrasts sharply with the wording of the previous provisions on extortionate credit in the original 1974 Act. The subheading there was "extortionate credit bargains" and the court was given power in s.137 to reopen a credit agreement where it found the "credit bargain" extortionate.

The use of the word "relationship" indicates that wider considerations must be **8–169** taken into account than under the previous wording using the term "bargain". Bargain has connotations of contract whereas relationship imports a much wider field of activity that might be considered. The effect of this is to help ensure that all the circumstances surrounding the credit transaction are taken into account. Tomlinson LJ has endorsed this point in the English Court of Appeal when he said:

"It is the relationship between the parties which must be determined to be unfair, not their agreement, although it is envisaged that the terms of the agreement may themselves give rise to an unfair relationship."[169]

8–170 In addition to permitting a wider examination of the circumstances of the whole relationship the unduly high hurdle facing consumers under the old law has been considerably reduced. The test is no longer one of extortion but of fairness. This will be a much easier test for a debtor to satisfy and it is one with which lawyers in the UK are becoming less uncomfortable. For a generation they have been accustomed to a fairness test in the Unfair Contract Terms Act 1977 and, since 1994, in the legislation implementing the Unfair Contract Terms Directive.[170]

8–171 Section 140A provides that unfairness is to be judged in relation to three considerations. It is clear that these encompass both substantive and procedural unfairness. Section 140A(1)(a) refers to taking into account "any of the terms of the agreement or of any related agreement". In addition to this possible substantive unfairness the other two paragraphs of the subsection plainly direct attention to procedural unfairness as they refer to how the creditor has exercised his rights and things done both before and after the making of the agreement. This has been a broad approach of the UK courts to the interpretation of the Unfair Terms in Consumer Contracts Regulations 1999.[171] However, the wording of s.140A(1) arguably goes further for it enables a court to consider not only the substantive unfairness of the agreement and take into account the process by which it came into existence but also the way in which it has been operated. Under the Unfair Terms in Consumer Contracts Regulations 1994 it is only factors existing at the date of the agreement that are relevant: under this provision the courts can go much further.

8–172 Concern was expressed during the parliamentary debates on the new provisions that there was a lack of guidance on unfairness. This was deliberate as precise guidance might limit the freedom of action of the courts. However, it should be noted that s.140D requires the FCA to publish guidance indicating how it expects the unfair relationships provisions to interact with Pt 8 of the Enterprise Act 2002. Part 8 implements the Injunctions Directive and enables the FCA to obtain enforcement orders requiring traders to desist from conduct which injures the "collective interests of consumers".[172] While this information is not directly relevant to the decision in an individual case raising the issue of an unfair credit relationship it must have significance as part of the background to what is acceptable practice in the industry. The guidance which has been issued[173] demonstrates that it is likely that many of the practices of the credit industry that have exercised Members of Parliament are likely, in the view of the FCA, to be

---

[169] *Harrison v Black Horse Ltd* [2011] EWCA 1128. The decision in the case has been overruled by the Supreme Court but this point is still valid.

[170] Originally the Unfair Terms in Consumer Contracts Regulations 1994 (SI 1994/3159) but replaced with the 1999 Regulations of the same name. See Unfair Terms in Consumer Contracts Regulations 1999 (SI 1999/2083).

[171] *Director General of Fair Trading v First National Bank Plc* [2001] UKHL 52.

[172] Enterprise Act 2002 Pt 8 is discussed in Ch.10.

[173] See OFT, *Unfair relationships: Enforcement action under Pt 8 of the Enterprise Act 2002* (OFT, 2006) OFT 854.

considered unfair. Specifically mentioned in the guidance are excessive interest rates, high charges for breaches of the terms of the agreement, doubtful marketing practices and irresponsible lending.

Another important aspect of the new test relates to the burden of proof. As with the old extortion test, s.140B(10) gives consumers assistance by providing that where they allege that the relationship between the creditor and the debtor is unfair to the debtor, "it is for the creditor to prove to the contrary".[174] On the other hand a weakness in the powers is that in individual cases they can only be invoked by the consumer making an application to impugn the agreement, in court proceedings between the debtor and the creditor to enforce the agreement, or in any court proceedings where the amount paid or payable under the agreement is relevant.[175] Some, including the OFT, have argued that judges ought to have the power of their own motion to raise the issue.[176] However, in the face of strong opposition from the judiciary who considered that their impartiality could be jeopardised, this has not been pursued.

8–173

Section 140A of the 1974 Act appears to have been used fairly frequently in the English county courts. One case has reached the Supreme Court. This is *Plevin v Paragon Personal Finance Ltd*, which has clarified the law to some extent.[177] Mrs Plevin is a widowed college lecturer who was planning to borrow to pay off existing debts and carry out some home improvements. She received an unsolicited leaflet from L, a broker, authorised by the FSA (the FCA's predecessor) to be an insurance intermediary and so required to observe the FSA's rule book as was Paragon. Mrs Plevin contacted L and it conducted a "demands and needs assessment" over the phone. L recommended PPI and sent her a letter enclosing a policy summary and a "key facts" document. They suggested that Mrs Plevin should borrow £34,000 from Paragon repayable over 10 years and also take out PPI for five years with an insurance company, the premium being £5,780. After signing L's application form, and after Paragon had telephoned her to deal with anti-money laundering issues, she entered into a credit agreement with Paragon in March 2006 which was secured against her home by a second legal charge. Under the terms of the agreement, Paragon lent Mrs Plevin £34,000 and another £5,780 to pay for a single premium PPI policy. The commission which amounted to 71 per cent of the premium was split between Paragon, who received £2,280, and L who received £1,870. Mrs Plevin's claim against L was settled in 2010 for £3,000. She carried on with her claim against Paragon arguing that the arrangement was unfair under s.140A because of: (a) things done "on behalf of" Paragon by L; and/or (b) the non-disclosure by Paragon of the amount of commission paid for the PPI.

8–174

As noted earlier in this chapter the Supreme Court held that Paragon were not responsible for L's actions or omissions. Nevertheless, they still found that

---

[174] *Bevin v Datum Finance Ltd* [2011] EWHC 3542 (Ch).
[175] Consumer Credit Act s.140B(2).
[176] See OFT, *Unjust Credit Transactions* (OFT 1991) para.5.9. The National Association of Citizens' Advice Bureaux, while recognising the problems involved in the proposal, advocate it in para.4.26 of their report N Lord, *Daylight Robbery—The CAB case for effective regulation of extortionate credit* (London: National Citizens' Advice Bureaux, 2000).
[177] *Plevin v Paragon Personal Finance Ltd* [2014] UKSC 61; [2014] 1 W.L.R. 4222,

Paragon had acted unfairly. This was despite the fact that Paragon owed no legal duty to Mrs Plevin under the FSA rule book or the general law to disclose the commission.

8–175   Lord Sumption who gave the only reasoned judgment said that:

> "Bearing in mind the breadth of section 140A and the incidence of the burden of proof according to section 140B(9), the creditor must normally be regarded as responsible for an omission making his relationship with the debtor unfair if he fails to take such steps as (i) it would be reasonable to expect the creditor or someone acting on his behalf to take in the interests of fairness, and (ii) would have removed the source of that unfairness or mitigated its consequences so that the relationship as a whole can no longer be regarded as unfair."[178]

He went on to say that in the interests of fairness it would have been reasonable to expect Paragon to have revealed the size of the commissions. It was the only party who knew the size of both commissions and the significance of this for Mrs Plevin's decision to take the loan. Failure to do so, given Mrs Plevin's evidence that had she known of them she would have questioned them, meant that Paragon's relationship with her unfair.

8–176   This conclusion required the Court of Appeal's decision in *Harrison v Black Horse Ltd*[179] to be overruled. That case had held that compliance with the FSA's rules prevented a lender from being found to have acted unfairly. The Supreme Court disagreed:

> "The standard of conduct required of practitioners by the ICOB Rules is laid down in advance by the Financial Services Authority (now the Financial Conduct Authority), whereas the standard of fairness in a debtor-creditor relationship is a matter for the court, on which it must make its own assessment. Most of the ICOB Rules, including those relating to the disclosure of commission, impose hard-edged requirements, whereas the question of fairness involves a large element of forensic judgment. It follows that the question whether the debtor-creditor relationship is fair cannot be the same as the question whether the creditor has complied with the ICOB Rules, and the facts which may be relevant to answer it are manifestly different. An altogether wider range of considerations may be relevant to the fairness of the relationship, most of which would not be relevant to the application of the rules. They include the characteristics of the borrower, her sophistication or vulnerability, the facts which she could reasonably be expected to know or assume, the range of choices available to her, and the degree to which the creditor was or should have been aware of these matters."[180]

The *Paragon* case illustrates one case of unfairness. It also gives some limited general guidance while observing that it is not possible to state a precise or universal test for its application, which must depend on the court's judgment of all the relevant facts. Lord Sumption made some general points:

> "First, what must be unfair is the relationship between the debtor and the creditor. In a case like the present one, where the terms themselves are not intrinsically unfair, this will often be because the relationship is so one-sided as substantially to limit the debtor's ability to choose. Secondly, although the court is concerned with

---

[178] *Plevin v Paragon Personal Finance Ltd* [2014] UKSC 61; [2014] 1 W.L.R. 4222, [19].
[179] *Harrison v Black Horse Ltd* [2012] Lloyd's Rep. IR 521.
[180] *Plevin v Paragon Personal Finance Ltd* [2014] UKSC 61; [2014] 1 W.L.R. 4222, [17].

hardship to the debtor, subsection 140A(2) envisages that matters relating to the creditor or the debtor may also be relevant. There may be features of the transaction which operate harshly against the debtor but it does not necessarily follow that the relationship is unfair. These features may be required in order to protect what the court regards as a legitimate interest of the creditor. Thirdly, the alleged unfairness must arise from one of the three categories of cause listed at sub-paragraphs (a) to (c). Fourthly, the great majority of relationships between commercial lenders and private borrowers are probably characterised by large differences of financial knowledge and expertise. It is an inherently unequal relationship. But it cannot have been Parliament's intention that the generality of such relationships should be liable to be reopened for that reason alone."[181]

An example of the second point would appear to be *Shaw v Nine Regions Ltd*[182] where the claimant borrowed £3,000 in July at an APR of over 350 per cent and found himself liable to repay £10,500 later that year. This was one of the notorious logbook loan cases from England and it was shown that the borrower had been fully informed about the terms and realised their implications. He was a poor risk and this was taken to justify the huge interest charge that, when coupled with default provisions, produced the repayment figure. Another example is *Khodari v Al Tamini*,[183] which involved substantial loans to enable the defendant to gamble at London clubs. The claimant provided money as required and charged a fee of 10 per cent of the loan. The English Court of Appeal did not find the relationship unfair as the trial judge had found that the claimant, who was rich, did what the defendant told him to do. Furthermore, these were unsecured loans to a person resident outside England and a fee of 10 per cent or even more was fairly normal in these circumstances. Crucially, there was no evidence that prior to the litigation the defendant had questioned the 10 per cent fee or had sought to make less expensive arrangements for funding his gambling.

Carey v HSBC Bank Plc[184] decided that failure to comply with the 1983 Regulations or the 1974 Act provisions concerning copies of documents and statements does not of itself make the relationship unfair.

These provisions, as the White Paper acknowledged, are not a complete **8–177** answer to the problem of socially harmful lending. They need to be complemented by enforcement action against illegal money lending and those who regularly act oppressively against consumers. Better advice and information would also alleviate the problem for consumers. The development of other forms of lending would also be beneficial. Credit unions have not had the success in Scotland (or the UK as a whole) that they have had, for example, in Ireland or North America. Even the advent of all these measures would still not solve the problems of those most at risk and there is no escape from the conclusion that wider questions of social policy are involved in this issue.

---

[181] *Plevin v Paragon Personal Finance Ltd* [2014] UKSC 61; [2014] 1 W.L.R. 4222, [10].
[182] *Shaw v Nine Regions Ltd* [2009] EWHC 3417 (QB).
[183] *Khodari v Al Tamini* [2008] EWHC 3065.
[184] *Carey v HSBC Bank Plc* [2009] EWHC 3417.

CHAPTER 9

Unfair Contract Terms

INTRODUCTION

This chapter is concerned with the problem of the fairness of terms found in contracts. It will deal mainly, but not exclusively, with exclusion clauses. Such clauses are often unfair to consumers but other terms of a contract can also be unfair and, as we shall see, to some extent these too can be controlled.

9–01

The problem of exclusion clauses or exemption clauses, as they are also called, is one that has a long history. It is common to find one party to a contract limiting or excluding entirely the legal liability that would otherwise attach. Everyday examples are to be found in any package holiday brochure, car hire contract or a furniture remover's contract. The following are some examples:

9–02

(1) All cars parked at the owner's risk.
(2) All photographic materials are accepted on the basis that their value does not exceed the cost of the material itself. Responsibility is limited to the replacement of films. No liability will be accepted, consequential or otherwise, however caused.[1]
(3) In the case of loss or damage the liability of the company is limited to the value of the garment.
(4) All claims must be notified to the company within seven days.
(5) Our liability to you in contract law or in tort or delict or otherwise howsoever arising in relation to this contract is limited to £1,000,000 for any one incident or related series of incidents and £2,000,000 for any series of incidents related or unrelated in any period of 12 months.

Such clauses are frequently found in standard form contracts. These are contracts drawn up by one party setting out the terms on which it will do business. Such contracts are not necessarily objectionable. Indeed, they can be seen as the legal or administrative counterpart of mass production and marketing. Using such forms cuts out the necessity for detailed negotiation in every transaction and saves time and money. Standard forms and their exclusion clauses work best where both parties know and understand their significance and can take appropriate action to protect themselves against any potential hardship resulting from the other side limiting its liability.

9–03

These are conditions that generally do not exist in the typical consumer transaction. How many of us even realise that when we travel by rail, for

9–04

---

[1] See *Woodman v Photo Trade Processing Ltd* unreported 20 June 1981 Exeter County Court.

example, that we are travelling on the rail companies' conditions of carriage which contain exclusion clauses? Even where we do know that there are exclusion clauses in the small print of, say, a car hire contract, how often do we stop to read them. If we did read them would we understand them and would it make any difference? Lord Denning answered that question in his usual forthright way, "[t]he big concern said, 'Take it or leave it'. The little man had no option but to take it".[2]

9–05   The underlying approach of the law has been informed by the doctrine of freedom of contract. This fails to take account of the power imbalances in consumer situations, a fact which has been recognised both by the common law and by legislation. How the law has intervened to control the use of exclusion clauses is discussed below under three main headings. First, we consider the role of the common law and then the intervention of the legislature. Originally, this was mainly through the Unfair Contract Terms Act 1977 (the 1977 Act) and then the regulations implementing the Unfair Contract Terms Directive.[3] The legislation has now been consolidated as far as consumers are concerned in Pt 2 of the Consumer Rights Act 2015 (the 2015 Act).

COMMON LAW CONTROLS

9–06   In controlling exclusion clauses the common law applies two techniques. The first is to consider whether the clause is part of the contract, i.e. has it been incorporated into the contract? If so, the second question is: does it cover the situation that has arisen? These techniques are in addition to the various doctrines referred to below under which contracts may be struck down because of some other element of unfairness. The protection of those under the age of 18 whose contracts may be reopened if "prejudicial" is also relevant, as is the law on unfair credit relationships.[4]

Incorporation

9–07   The parties may have agreed that the exclusion clause is to be part of the contract. The easiest way to demonstrate this is to show that a document including that clause has been signed. There can then be no argument, in the absence of fraud or misrepresentation, that the consumer is bound by the agreement. Support for this proposition can be found in *Henderson v Stevenson* where, in a Scottish appeal to the House of Lords, the Lord Chancellor observed that, where a document had been signed:

---

[2]   *George Mitchell (Chesterhall) Ltd v Finney Lock Seeds Ltd* [1982] 3 W.L.R. 1036 at 1043.
[3]   Council Directive 93/13/EEC of 5 April 1993 on unfair terms in consumer contracts.
[4]   See Ch.8.

"There might, indeed, be a question what was the construction of the contract, or how far the contract was valid. But there could be no question whatever that the contract, such as it was, was assented to and entered into by the person who received the ticket."[5]

A case where this principle did not apply because the effect of the clause had been misrepresented to the consumer is *Curtis v Chemical Cleaning and Dyeing Co.*[6] Staff at a dry cleaners incorrectly assured a customer that a clause exempted the cleaners only for limited kinds of damage when it covered any kind of damage. Fraudulent conduct by the party seeking to rely on the clause would have the same effect. It should be remembered that the concept of fraud in Scots law in relation to the annulment of obligations is wide and, as Professor Smith pointed out, can cover not only what Bell in his *Principles* called "a machination or contrivance to deceive", but also conduct inconsistent with bona fides.[7]

9–08

Quite commonly there is no signed document and the trader relies on an unsigned document such as a railway ticket, a receipt for dry cleaning or a notice on the premises. The notice or ticket may itself contain the exclusion clause or it may refer, as for example, railway tickets do, to another document. What is the effect of such documents or notices? It must first be shown that the exclusion clause is contained in a contractual document, as *Taylor v Corporation of the City of Glasgow*[8] demonstrates. Mrs Taylor had gone to public baths run by the corporation. On entering she paid for the facility that she wished to use and was given a ticket. On the front were the words "for conditions see other side" and on the reverse were words excluding the corporation's liability for injury caused to users of the baths. As a result of the negligence of the corporation Mrs Taylor sustained serious injuries in a fall. The corporation sought to rely on the exclusion clause on the ticket. The Inner House held that the clause did not protect the corporation because it was not a contractual document. It was merely:

9–09

"A domestic check on the defenders' running of their establishment, the register and the ticket having taken the place of the old-fashioned turnstile. It also performed the function of a receipt... this voucher aspect of this 'ticket' was the significant aspect."

The court refused to attach the same significance to this kind of ticket as courts have traditionally done to tickets relating to contracts of carriage or deposit.

To be effective the exclusion clause must be brought to the attention of the other party before the contract is made. This is the rationale of *Olley v Marlborough Court*[9] where a couple booked and paid for a room on arriving at the reception desk of a hotel. In their room was a notice exempting the hotel from liability for loss of personal belongings. Some of their belongings were stolen from the room and the hotel sought to rely on the exemption clause. It was held by the English Court of Appeal that the guests' contract had been concluded when

9–10

---

[5] *Henderson v Stevenson* (1875) 2 R. (H.L.) 71 at 74. The English case of *L'Estrange v Graucob* [1934] 2 K.B. 394, provides an example of the harsh consequences of this rule in operation. It has been argued that the case could have been decided differently.

[6] *Curtis v Chemical Cleaning and Dyeing Co* [1951] 1 All E.R. 631.

[7] See TB Smith, *A Short Commentary on the Law of Scotland* (Edinburgh: W. Green, 1962) p.833.

[8] *Taylor v Corporation of the City of Glasgow*, 1952 S.C. 440.

[9] *Olley v Marlborough Court* [1949] 1 K.B. 532.

they booked the room and the notice which they saw subsequently was not part of that contract. This approach was also one reason for the decision in *McCutcheon v MacBrayne*,[10] a Scottish appeal to the House of Lords.

9–11   Where the document containing the exclusion clause can be said to be contractual in nature it is still necessary to show that the party relying on the clause has done, to quote Lord Dunedin in *Hood v Anchor Line (Henderson Brothers) Ltd*, "what was reasonably sufficient to bring to [the other party's] notice the existence of the condition".[11] It was stated in the same case that what is reasonable notice depends on the facts.

9–12   As indicated above, it appears that the courts will be more easily satisfied that reasonable notice has been given where contracts of carriage or deposit are concerned. The high point was probably reached in the English case of *Thompson v London Midland & Scottish Railway Co*,[12] where it was held that an illiterate lady whose niece had bought a ticket for her had been given reasonable notice of a clause by a reference on the ticket to the fact that it was issued subject to the conditions set out in the company's timetable. The conditions could be found on p.552 of that timetable which could be purchased for 6d. The Inner House came to a similar decision in *Gray v London and North Eastern Railway*.[13] Mr Gray had bought his own ticket and admitted that he knew that there was writing on it, though he had not read it.

9–13   The courts have not found notice to be sufficient where a ticket for a ferry crossing contained an exclusion clause on the back but there was no reference to this on the face of the ticket.[14] The same result occurred where the face of the ticket did refer to conditions on the back but the reference was in the smallest known type and presented in such a way as easily to be overlooked.[15]

9–14   In other situations the courts have been less inclined to incorporate exclusion clauses. In *Grayston Plant Ltd v Plean Precast Ltd* it was said in the Inner House that it is wrong to apply

> "the principles of the 'ticket' cases, which are based on matters of practicability and reasonableness peculiar to 'ticket' contracts . . . to a very different kind of case".[16]

The court went on to refer with approval to the dictum of Denning LJ in *Spurling v Bradshaw*,[17] that "the more unreasonable the clause is, the greater the notice which must be given of it". In *Thornton v Shoe Lane Parking Ltd*[18] Lord Denning had suggested that there were some clauses that were so oppressive that they would only be effective if placed in a box in red print with a hand pointing to them.

9–15   In theory it seems that an exclusion clause might be incorporated even though no notice was given on the occasion when a problem arose if it was merely one of

---

[10] *McCutcheon v MacBrayne*, 1964 S.C. (H.L.) 28.

[11] *Hood v Anchor Line (Henderson Brothers) Ltd*, 1918 S.C. (H.L.) 143 at 149.

[12] *Thompson v London Midland & Scottish Railway* [1930] 1 K.B. 141.

[13] *Gray v London and North Eastern Railway*, 1930 S.C. 989.

[14] *Henderson v Stevenson* (1875) 2 R. (H.L.) 17.

[15] *Williamson v North of Scotland and Orkney and Shetland Navigation Co*, 1916 S.C. 554.

[16] *Grayston Plant Ltd v Plean Precast Ltd*, 1976 S.C. 206.

[17] *Spurling v Bradshaw* [1965] 1 W.L.R. 461.

[18] *Thornton v Shoe Lane Parking Ltd* [1971] 2 Q.B. 163. See also *Interfoto Picture Library Ltd v Stiletto Visual Programmes Ltd* [1988] 1 All E.R. 348 CA.

a number of occasions when the parties had contracted. This is referred to as incorporation by means of a course of dealing and might arise where a consumer has frequently contracted with the same trader and their contracts have normally contained an exclusion clause. This argument was put forward in *McCutcheon v MacBrayne*,[19] where the pursuer's car had been lost when MacBrayne's ferry sank. The pursuer was a frequent customer of MacBrayne, both for transporting vehicles and livestock. It was their usual, though not invariable practice, to require the customer to sign a risk note that contained an exclusion clause. They did not do so on the relevant occasion but argued that the pursuer, through a course of dealing with them, knew that goods were shipped on standard terms containing such a clause. This argument failed in the House of Lords. It was accepted that there could be incorporation in this way, but the course of dealing must be both consistent and lengthy. In this case the evidence showed that the pattern of dealings was not consistent, a risk note having to be signed on some occasions but not on others. While there are examples of incorporation by means of a course of dealing in the law reports none concerns a consumer contract.

CONSTRUCTION

If it is established that the clause is part of the contract the next step is to consider whether it protects the party relying on it in the circumstances. Since the passage of the Unfair Contract Terms Act 1977 the courts have not needed to resort to some of the mental gymnastics that were necessary in the past to do justice. However, it is still true that the courts will construe exclusion clauses strictly and against a party seeking to rely on them. The principle, often known by the Latin tag, the *contra proferentem* rule, can be traced back to Stair[20] and has frequently been employed by the courts. In *McKay v Scottish Airways Ltd* it was said in the Outer House in a judgment approved by the Inner House that:

9–16

> "It is well settled that clauses exempting a carrier from liability fall to be construed strictly and *contra proferentem* ... Only clear and unambiguous language will suffice to exclude a common law liability, and as the language used in conditions expressed on a ticket is language framed and devised by the carriers themselves, it will ... fall to be construed in the sense most unfavourable to the carrier who sells the ticket and most favourable to the passenger who buys it."[21]

An example of the principle in operation in a consumer context is *Graham v Shore Porters Society*.[22] Mr Graham arranged to have his belongings moved from Glasgow to Aberdeen by the defenders. While in their custody they were destroyed by fire. The carriers argued that they were protected by the following clause in the contract, "[t]he contractors shall not be responsible for loss and

9–17

---

[19] *McCutcheon v MacBrayne*, 1964 S.C. (H.L.) 28.
[20] *"Verba sunt interpretanda contra proferentem* [words must be construed unfavourably to those who drafted them] where the parties are skilful, or are known to have trusted skilful persons in forming of the writs; and therefore the same should be as much extended in favour of the other party, as their sense can bear", Stair, More's edn, IV, 42, 21.
[21] *McKay v Scottish Airways Ltd*, 1948 S.C. 254 at 256.
[22] *Graham v Shore Porters Society*, 1979 S.L.T. 119.

damage to furniture and effects caused by or incidental to fire or aircraft, but will endeavour to effect insurance on behalf of the customer on receipt of instructions".[23]

9–18 Applying the *contra proferentem* rule, the Court of Session held that this clause did not protect the carriers. They were liable to their customer under the contract to take reasonable care of their goods and also had a statutory duty to them. The court considered that the clause only excluded liability for statutory duty and that the carriers still owed their contractual duty of care to the customer.

9–19 The courts look with particular disfavour on clauses seeking to exempt one party from the consequences of negligence on the ground that it is inherently unlikely that this is what the parties intended. It has, however, always been accepted in Scotland, which did not flirt with the doctrine of fundamental breach as the English courts did, that a properly worded clause could exclude any kind of liability. With the passing of the Unfair Contract Terms Act 1977 the House of Lords made clear that it would approach construction of clauses in a less hostile manner. In particular, it has been stated that clauses limiting liability will be treated less unfavourably than those entirely excluding it.[24] The cases in which this point has been made are commercial cases and may not be relevant to consumer situations.[25]

A wider principle?

9–20 It is arguable that Scots common law had the capacity to control terms in contracts, including exclusion clauses, on more general grounds.[26] In *McKay v Scottish Airways Ltd*[27] Lord Cooper observed that the:

> "Remarkable feature of these conditions is their amazing width, and the effort which has evidently been made to create a leonine bargain under which the aeroplane passenger takes all the risks and the company accepts no obligation, not even to carry the passenger or his baggage nor even to admit him to the aeroplane."

9–21 He went on to note that it had not been

> "argued that the conditions were contrary to public policy nor that they were so extreme as to deprive the contract of all meaning and effect as a contract of carriage".

He reserved his opinion on these matters but was clearly inviting lawyers to develop a wider principle for attacking exclusion clauses. This has not been done and there has been less need or scope for such an approach with the enactment of

---

[23] *Graham v Shore Porters Society*, 1979 S.L.T. 119.

[24] *Ailsa Craig Fishing Ltd v Malvern Fishing Co Ltd*, 1982 S.L.T. 377.

[25] See *Mars Pension Trustees v County Properties and Developments Ltd*, 1999 S.C.L.R. 117 IH, where Lord Prosser considered the proper approach to construing contracts where there was an attempt to exclude liability which would otherwise attach. This was in the context of a case to which the legislative controls did not apply.

[26] See McBryde, "Extortionate Contracts", 1976 J.L.S.S. 322 where a number of cases are referred to.

[27] *McKay v Scottish Airways Ltd*, 1948 S.C. 254 at 263.

the 1977 Act and the Unfair Terms in Consumer Contracts Regulations 1999 (the 1999 Regulations), both replaced by Pt 2 of the Consumer Protection Act 2015.[28]

STATUTORY INTERVENTION

In the absence of some wider principle, such as Lord Cooper appeared to be advocating, the common law controls on exclusion clauses were bound to have limited power to protect consumers even in the hands of the most sympathetic judges. With care, it was possible to ensure that exclusion clauses were incorporated in contracts, and careful drafting could ensure that they were appropriate to exclude or limit the liability of the trader.

9–22

In any event as Lord Reid observed[29]:

> "In the ordinary way the customer has no time to read them, and if he did read them he would probably not understand them. And if he did understand and object to any of them, he would generally be told he could take it or leave it. And if he then went to another supplier the result would be the same."

As Lord Reid recognised,

> "[t]his is a complex problem which intimately affects millions of people and it appears to me that its solution should be left to Parliament".[30]

Parliament has intervened first in 1977 with the enactment of the 1977 Act and then by adding the Unfair Terms in Consumer Contracts Regulations 1994[31] later replaced by regulations with the same title in 1999.[32] This left the law in an unsatisfactory state as the two regimes operated slightly differently. To some extent they overlapped but they had different effects and used different concepts and terminology. In 2001, the Law Commission and Scottish Law Commission were asked to review the law of unfair terms and produced a report, including a draft bill, advocating a harmonised approach. Nothing was done to implement the report but in 2012, the Department for Business, Innovation and Skills (BIS) invited the Commissions to review and update their 2005 Report with respect to consumer contracts as part of a wider plan to clarify consumer law. Their advice to BIS, published in 2013,[33] has informed Pt 2 of the 2015 Act, which now contains the principal statutory controls on unfair terms in consumer contracts.

---

[28] Unfair Terms in Consumer Contracts Regulations 1999 (SI 1999/203), which replaced the original regulations of the same name. See Unfair Terms in Consumer Contracts Regulations 1994 (SI 1994/3159).

[29] *Suisse Atlantique Société d'Armement Maritime SA v Rotterdamsche Kolen Centrale* [1967] 1 A.C. 361 at 406.

[30] *Suisse Atlantique Société d'Armement Maritime SA v Rotterdamsche Kolen Centrale* [1967] 1 A.C. 361.

[31] Unfair Terms in Consumer Contracts Regulations 1994 (SI 1994/3159).

[32] Unfair Terms in Consumer Contracts Regulations 1999 (SI 1999/203).

[33] The Law Commission and the Scottish Law Commission, *Unfair terms in consumer contracts: Advice to the Department for Business, Innovation and Skills* (March 2013).

CONSUMER RIGHTS ACT 2015 PART 2

9–23   Part 2 of the 2015 Act consolidates and clarifies the law relating to unfair terms as it affects consumers. The 1999 Regulations have been repealed as have the provisions of the 1977 Act that relate to consumers. It should be noted that the 1977 Act still applies to contracts between businesses. Part 2 implements the EC Directive on Unfair Contract Terms of 5 April 1993.[34] It is based on art.100a of the Treaty of Rome, which is primarily concerned with the establishment of the single market. As a result it should be borne in mind that where there are difficulties in interpreting any of its provisions resort may be had to the Directive including its recitals. It should also be remembered that the Directive is a form of minimum harmonisation. That means that Members States must ensure that their law at least meets the standards that it sets but they may also provide consumers with greater protection. As will become apparent, Pt 2 does go beyond the Directive's minimum standards.

9–24   The key provisions of the 2015 Act Pt 2 are found in s.62 where subs.(1) states that "an unfair term of a consumer contract is not binding on the consumer" and subs.(2) that "an unfair consumer notice is not binding on the consumer". These brief provisions call for further elucidation. We need to consider who is a consumer for this purpose and how fairness is defined. Further examination of Pt 2 shows that there are limitations on the types of contracts subject to it and to the terms that are subject to the fairness test. There is also the important issue of how Pt 2 is enforced. These issues are discussed in the following pages. Before embarking on that discussion it should be noted that the 2015 Act s.62(3) adds that the preceding subsections do "not prevent the consumer from relying on the term or notice if the consumer chooses to do so".

Coverage

9–25   Part 2 applies to a wide range of contract terms and notices which are dealt with below. Unlike the 1999 Regulations, where Pt 2 of the 2015 Act applies, it matters not whether the terms are part of a standard form contract or have been negotiated. This was the view of the Law Commissions who argued that it would avoid disputes over whether a term had been individually negotiated. However, there are some contracts that are not subject to this part of the Act. The first is the obvious one, contained in s.61(1) that it is only contracts between a trader and a consumer that are affected. "Trader" is defined in s.2 as

> "a person acting for purposes relating to that person's trade, business, craft or profession, whether acting personally or through another person acting in the trader's name or on the trader's behalf".

It is not just natural persons who are included but also companies, charities and arms of government. This is underlined by subs.(7), which makes clear that "'business' includes the activities of any government department or local or public authority". Under the 1999 Regulations, where this part of the definition was not included, it had nevertheless been held in *R (on the application of*

---

[34] Council Directive 93/13/EEC of 5 April 1993 on unfair terms in consumer contracts.

Khatun) v Newham London Borough Council[35] that a local authority when acting as a landlord was carrying on business. "Related to" is much wider than the equivalent phrase in the 1977 Act that was "in the course of a business". In *R & B Customs Brokers Co Ltd*[36] it was held that, to come within that test,

> "the transaction should be an integral part of the business concerned, or one which he or she carries out with sufficient regularity or a one off adventure in the nature of a trade".

"Related to" brings under control transactions such as the isolated sale of a capital item by a business that does not deal in that sort of item.[37] Not-for-profit organisations, such as charities, mutual and cooperatives, may also come within the definition of a trader, for example, if a charity shop sells t-shirts or mugs, they would be acting within the meaning of trader. The latter part of the definition makes clear that a trader acting through another person acting in the trader's name or on the trader's behalf is liable for proper execution of the contract. For example, a trader that subcontracts part of a building contract or a company for which the employees make contracts with customers would be liable to the consumer.

A consumer is defined by the 2015 Act s.2 as "an individual acting for purposes that are wholly or mainly outside that individual's trade, business, craft or profession". So, a consumer must be a natural person thus ruling out businesses, even the so-called one-man company, using a corporate form. In this respect Pt 2 is narrower than the 1977 Act under which, in some circumstances, a company could be regarded as a consumer.[38] On the other hand the consumer need only be acting for purposes that are "mainly" outside their business. This provides more generous protection than the 1999 Regulations did. Thus an employee who has a home computer or mobile phone that are occasionally used for work purposes would not lose the protection of Pt 2.[39]

9–26

Even though the parties fall within the definitions of consumer and trader there are some contracts that are not regulated by the 2015 Act Pt 2. As was recommended by the Law Commissions[40] the 2015 Act s.61(2) provides that it does not apply to contracts of employment or apprenticeship which are regulated by other legislation. Part 2 does not apply to terms that reflect mandatory statutory or regulatory provisions and the provisions or principles of international conventions to which the Member States or the Community are party.[41] The latter would exempt from the controls clauses in transport contracts that comply with

9–27

---

[35] *R (on the application of Khatun) v Newham London Borough Council* [2004] EWCA Civ. 55; [2005] Q.B. 37.
[36] *R & B Customs Brokers Co Ltd v United Dominions Trust Ltd* [1988] 1 All E.R. 847.
[37] cf. *Davies v Sumner* [1984] 1 W.L.R. 1301.
[38] See *R & B Customs Brokers Co Ltd v United Dominions Trust Ltd* [1988] 1 All E.R. 847.
[39] Although decided under the narrower wording of the 1999 Regulations it seems unlikely that the defender in *Prostar Management Ltd v Twaddle*, 2003 S.L.T. (Sh. Ct.) 11 would be regarded as a consumer under the Consumer Rights Act 2015 Pt 2.
[40] The Law Commission and the Scottish Law Commission, *Unfair terms in consumer contracts: Advice to the Department for Business, Innovation and Skills* (March 2013) para.7.127.
[41] Consumer Rights Act 2015 s.73.

the Warsaw Convention. In *RWE Vertrieb AG v Verbraucherzentrale Nordrhein-Westfalen eV*[42] the European Court of Justice (ECJ) indicated that this exception was to be interpreted narrowly. In that case German legislation contained standard terms applicable to certain types of gas contracts with consumers. A gas company applied these terms to gas contracts to which the legislation did not apply. The ECJ held that the terms did not come within the exception. It was legitimate to assume that the national legislature had struck a balance between all the rights and obligations of the parties to certain contracts but that reasoning would not apply to terms in different contracts.

9–28   When the EC Directive was originally implemented there was some doubt as to whether it applied to land transactions and the official view was that they did not. The revised 1999 Regulations indicated a change to a neutral stance as the definitions of seller and supplier followed that in the Directive precisely and made no reference to the supply of goods or services. In *R (on the application of Khatun) v Newham London Borough Council*[43] the English Court of Appeal decided that the 1999 Regulations did apply to contracts relating to land. It now seems clear that Pt 2 of the 2015 Act does apply to land transactions. It is important to emphasise that insurance contracts are subject to Pt 2. They were one of the most important exclusions from the 1977 Act but did not escape the controls in the Directive and so are caught by Pt 2. However, the exclusion of the so-called "core provisions" of a contract[44] from consideration for unfairness means that insurance contracts do get some protection from control under the regulations.

Notices

9–29   Section 61(4) extends Pt 2 to what is termed a "consumer notice"[45] where it relates to rights or obligations between a trader and a consumer or purports to exclude or restrict a trader's liability to a consumer. Like consumer contracts it does not include notices involving employers and employees. To ensure that all sorts of notices are covered the section goes on to state that it applies as long "as it is reasonable to assume it is intended to be seen or heard by a consumer" and "includes an announcement, whether or not in writing, and any other communication or purported communication".[46] This will apply to non-contractual notices such as notices found in car parks purporting to indicate that the owner of the park has no liability to users. The problem with such notices is that though they may have not legal effect they may mislead consumers about their rights. Some notices of this type may, of course, be contractual depending on the factual situation.

9–30   An important reason for the careful definition of consumer notices is the need to apply the fairness controls of Pt 2 of the 2015 Act to a much more modern development, the end user licence agreement (EULA). The Law Commissions found that EULAs commonly accompany contracts for software and other digital

---

[42] *RWE Vertrieb AG v Verbraucherzentrale Nordrhein-Westfalen eV* Case C-92/11.
[43] *R (on the application of Khatun) v Newham London Borough Council* [2004] EWCA Civ. 55; [2005] Q.B. 37.
[44] See para.9–76.
[45] Consumer Rights Act 2015 s.61(7).
[46] Consumer Rights Act 2015 s.61(6) and (8).

products and may also include unfair terms, such as restrictions or exclusions on the suppliers' liability under the law of privacy, negligence or libel.[47] Some, known as "click-wrap licences", which the consumer must explicitly agree to before they are able to download digital content, may have contractual status. These would be consumer contracts and so subject to the provisions of Pt 2 though some dispute this arguing that they are not contracts but merely licences. Other EULAs, referred to as "shrink-wrap" or "browse-wrap" licences state that by downloading material the consumer will be taken to have agreed to the owner's terms and conditions although there is no box or icon to click. The law commissions take the view that such EULAs are void and unenforceable.[48] The provisions on notices are designed to make both forms of EULA subject to Pt 2 and to avoid difficult arguments about their legal status.

The key aspect of the 2015 Act Pt 2 is the meaning of unfairness which is the criterion by which terms are to be judged. Before looking at this concept it should be noted that there are some terms that are not subject to test.　　**9–31**

Core terms

The first terms to which it does not apply are the so-called "core terms" (though this phrase is not used either in the Act or the EC Directive) relating to price and the definition of the main subject matter of the contract. Section 64(1) of the 2015 Act provides that:　　**9–32**

> "A term of a consumer contract may not be assessed for fairness under section 62 to the extent that—
> (a)　it specifies the main subject matter of the contract, or
> (b)　the assessment is of the appropriateness of the price payable under the contract by comparison with the goods, digital content or services supplied under it."

In both cases the terms are excluded only where, to quote s.64(2), they are "transparent and prominent". Section 64(2) goes on to explain that:

> "A term is transparent ... if it is expressed in plain and intelligible language and, in the case of a written term, is legible".

The following subsection provides that:

> "A term is prominent for the purposes of this section if it is brought to the consumer's attention in such a way that an average consumer would be aware of the term."

---

[47] For discussion of the problem see the Law Commission and the Scottish Law Commission, *Unfair terms in consumer contracts: Advice to the Department for Business, Innovation and Skills* (March 2013) Appendix C.

[48] The Law Commission and the Scottish Law Commission, *Unfair terms in consumer contracts: Advice to the Department for Business, Innovation and Skills* (March 2013) para.7.21. But see the Irish High Court decision in *Ryanair Ltd v On The Beach Ltd* [2013] IEHC 124 and the ECJ decision in *El Majdoub v CarsOnTheWeb.Deutschland GmbH* Case C-322/14 (not yet reported).

The "average consumer" test is that taken from EU case law and "means a consumer who is reasonably well-informed, observant and circumspect".[49]

9–33   Transparency is an important concept not only at this point but also more generally. Section 69 of the 2015 Act has a general requirement that terms and notices be transparent and the necessity for this has been underlined in decisions of the ECJ. *Árpad Kásler and Hajnalka Káslerné Rábai v OTP Jelzálogbank ZRT*[50] involved the question whether a clause in a loan agreement was one of the core terms. The ECJ pointed out that for a contractual term to be drafted in plain intelligible language it was necessary not only that it should be grammatically intelligible to the consumer, but also that the contract should set out transparently the specific functioning of the mechanism of conversion for the foreign currency to which the relevant term refers.

9–34   The rationale for these exceptions is that they deal with terms that are subject to competitive forces, unlike terms hidden in the small print which most consumers rarely read. The definition of the subject matter exception is designed to exclude clauses describing what the deal is about. From the recitals to the Directive it can be discovered that insurance contracts are in mind here, though they are not the only possible examples. When the Directive was being drafted the insurance industry argued that because it would be very difficult to distinguish between exclusion clauses and those clauses that defined the insured risk insurance contracts should be exempt from it. The Directive and Pt 2 do not go as far as this. Their approach is to say that terms defining or circumscribing the risk are not, on their own, to be subject to the fairness test. However, contracts of insurance are still subject to the regulations. In *Director General of Fair Trading v First National Bank Plc*[51] the English Court of Appeal held that a term setting out the consequences of default did not define "the main subject matter of the contract" and this was not challenged on appeal to the House of Lords.

9–35   In addition, the "the appropriateness of the price payable under the contract by comparison with the goods, digital content or services supplied under it"[52] is not to be taken into account. However, it clear that these exclusions are to be given a narrow interpretation. On appeal to the House of Lords in *Director General of Fair Trading v First National Bank Plc*[53] it was argued by the bank that the default clause was a "core provision" in that it concerned the adequacy of the price or remuneration, the phrase now drafted slightly differently in the 2015 Act Pt 2. The House of Lords agreed with counsel for the Director General that that this was not so. Lord Bingham emphasised that this aspect of the regulations was to be given a narrow ambit:

> "The object of the Regulations and the Directive is to protect consumers against the inclusion of unfair and prejudicial terms in standard-form contracts into which they enter, and that object would plainly be frustrated if regulation 3(2)(b) [reg.6(2)(b) in the 1999 Regulations] were so broadly interpreted as to cover any terms other than those falling squarely within it. In my opinion the term, as part of a provision

---

[49] Consumer Rights Act 2015 s.64(5).

[50] *Árpad Kásler and Hajnalka Káslerné Rábai v OTP Jelzálogbank ZRT* Case C-26/13; [2014] 2 All E.R. (Comm) 443; [2014] Bus. L.R. 664 and *Matei v SC Volksbank România SA* Case C-143/13 judgment of the Court (Ninth Chamber) of 26 February 2015.

[51] *Director General of Fair Trading v First National Bank Plc* [2000] Q.B. 672.

[52] Consumer Rights Act 2015 s.64(1)(b).

[53] *Director General of Fair Trading v First National Bank Plc* [2002] 1 A.C. 481.

prescribing the consequences of default, plainly does not fall within it. It does not concern the adequacy of the interest earned by the bank as its remuneration but is designed to ensure that the bank's entitlement to interest does not come to an end on the entry of judgment."[54]

This aspect of *First National Bank Plc* has been applied in the English High Court case of *Bairstow Eves London Central Ltd v Smith*.[55] That case involved an agreement between an estate agent and the seller of a flat. The term challenged was one which provided that the commission would be 1.5 per cent of the purchase price but if that sum were not paid in full within 10 days of completion of the transaction the rate of commission was to be 3 per cent. It was held that on a proper construction of the agreement the reference to the 3 per cent rate was a default provision and thus did not fall within the exclusion relating to terms about the adequacy of the price or remuneration.[56]

9–36

The decision of the Supreme Court in *Office of Fair Trading v Abbey National Plc*,[57] the bank charges case, also found that this exemption was a narrow one but held that the relevant charges were part of the price. The case arose when the Office of Fair Trading (OFT) challenged the fairness of charges imposed by banks when a customer draws a cheque which bounces or an overdraft limit is exceeded without prior approval. The OFT was successful in both the English High Court and the Court of Appeal. In the High Court it was found that the charges were in plain and intelligible language and this was not appealed. The Court of Appeal agreed that the charges were not part of the core bargain between the banks and their customers. The Supreme Court disagreed and refused to make a distinction between the core elements of the bargain and incidental or ancillary aspects such as the charges in dispute.

9–37

This decision was controversial and it is possible that it could be overturned by the ECJ.[58]

Part 2 of the 2015 Act does not attempt to do this. Instead Parliament followed the advice of the Law Commissions and clarified the meaning by adding the references to "transparency" set out above. As the case law shows, the exemption is narrowly interpreted so, if a term concerns aspects of the price other than the amount, for example the timing of payment, the term may be assessed for fairness, but the amount of the price cannot be assessed assuming it is transparent and prominent. For example, if an individual contracts with a catering company to provide a buffet lunch, and the contract includes a term that the individual will pay £100 for a three course meal, the court cannot look at whether it is fair to pay £100 for three courses. It may, however, look at other things, such as the rights of the company and the individual to cancel the lunch, and when the price is due to

9–38

[54] *First National Bank Plc* [2002] 1 A.C. 481 at [12].
[55] *Bairstow Eves London Central Ltd v Smith* [2004] EWHC 263 QBD; [2004] All E.R. (D) 354. See also *Office of Fair Trading v Abbey National Plc* [2008] EWCH 875 (the bank charges case).
[56] See also *Office of Fair Trading v Foxtons Ltd* [2009] EWHC 1681.
[57] *Office of Fair Trading v Abbey National Plc* [2009] UKSC 6.
[58] See the Law Commissions, *Unfair Terms in Consumer Contracts: a new approach?* Issues Paper (July 2012) paras 7.56–7.86.

be paid.[59] The importance of transparency has been emphasised by the ECJ in *RWE Vertrieb AG v Verbraucherzentrale Nordrhein-Westfalen eV.*[60]

Negligence liability for death or personal injury

9–39   One of the most important reforms effected by the 1977 Act was the ban on contract terms excluding or restricting liability for death or personal injury resulting from a trader's negligence contained in s.16. Part 2 of the 2015 Act achieves the same result by s.65. It speaks of banning clauses excluding or restricting negligence but it is using an extended meaning of negligence. The first of these is breach of any obligation to take reasonable care or exercise reasonable skill that arises from the express or implied terms of a contract. Thus, exclusion clauses in a wide range of trades and professions are covered. These would include contracts by professional people such as accountants, solicitors or architects, as well as non-professional services provided by garages or dry cleaners. All these service providers have an obligation to perform their services with reasonable skill and care. The definition also applies to any common law duty to take reasonable care or exercise reasonable skill. This covers situations where the delictual duty of care arises as developed in the line of cases originating with *Donoghue v Stevenson*.[61] Finally, it also includes the common law duty to take reasonable care under s.2(1) of the Occupiers Liability (Scotland) Act 1960. In a consumer context this might be relevant where attempts to exclude liability are made at playgrounds, funfairs and other places of amusement or recreation.

9–40   This bar does not apply to a discharge or indemnity given as part of a compensation settlement so it does not apply where litigants settle disputes that have arisen concerning the performance of an earlier contract. It expressly provides that it does not apply to agreements mentioned in s.4(2)(a) of the Damages (Scotland) Act 2011, because not all agreements to discharge liability will include compensation. Section 65 of the 2015 Act does not affect s.5 of the Damages (Scotland) Act 2011, which sets out special rules for settlement of mesothelioma claims in Scotland, and provides that relatives can still claim certain damages in some cases even if the original liability were discharged. The section does not apply to insurance contracts and contracts relating to the creation or transfer of an interest in land.

Contracting out of implied terms

9–41   The 2015 Act provides that certain basic rights of consumers are entrenched when they buy goods, services and digital content. Section 62(8) of the 2015 Act prevents traders from "contracting out" of these statutory rights contained in ss.49, 50, 51 and 52.

---

[59] This example is taken from the explanatory notes to the Bill when it was introduced in the House of Commons: *http://www.publications.parliament.uk/pa/bills/cbill/2013-2014/0161/en/14161en.htm* [Accessed 7 July 2015].

[60] *RWE Vertrieb AG v Verbraucherzentrale Nordrhein-Westfalen eV* Case C-92/11.

[61] *Donoghue v Stevenson*, 1932 S.C. (H.L.) 31.

Unfairness

Assuming that the contract term or notice is one which is subject to the fairness test how will it be applied? Section 62(4) provides that: **9–42**

> "A term... is unfair if, contrary to the requirement of good faith, it causes a significant imbalance in the parties' rights and obligations arising under the contract, to the detriment of the consumer."

The time for applying the test is the time of the conclusion of the contract and a court must also take into account "the nature of the nature of the subject matter of the contract", all the circumstances existing when the term was agreed and all of the other terms of the contract or of any other contract on which it depends.[62]

The last of these criteria, detriment to the consumer, is probably the easiest to explain. It would seem simply to be making the point that only the consumer can take advantage of the regulations.[63] The requirement of "significant imbalance" would seem to mean no more than the application of a de minimis rule eliminating minor imbalances in the rights and obligations of the parties. As Willett has argued,[64] it can hardly mean that the imbalance is particularly extreme. This would run counter to the idea of having an "Indicative and Illustrative List of Terms Which May be Regarded as Unfair" in Sch.2. In *Director General of Fair Trading v First National Bank Plc*[65] Lord Bingham explained: **9–43**

> "The requirement of significant imbalance is met if a term is so weighted in favour of the supplier as to tilt the parties' rights and obligations under the contract significantly in his favour. This may be by the granting to the supplier of a beneficial option or discretion or power, or by the imposing on the consumer of a disadvantageous burden or risk or duty. The illustrative terms set out in Schedule 3 to the regulations provide very good examples of terms which may be regarded as unfair; whether a given term is or is not to be so regarded depends on whether it causes a significant imbalance in the parties' rights and obligations under the contract. This involves looking at the contract as a whole."

Good faith

This brings us to the concept of good faith. The central aspect of unfairness is that the term is "contrary to the requirement of good faith". There has been much comment about the novelty of this is in English and Scots law. Whatever may be the case in English law the fact is that it does have antecedents in Scots law. Professor Smith asserted that it was an underlying feature of the Scots law of obligations. He pointed to the various doctrines such as facility, force and fear, undue influence and control of minors' contracts on what is now the ground of **9–44**

---

[62] Consumer Rights Act 2015 s.62(5).

[63] See "Unfair Contract Terms Directive" in Roger Brownsword, Geraint Howells and Thomas Wilhelmsson (eds), *Welfarism in Contract Law* (Dartmouth: Aldershot, 1994).

[64] C Willett, "Directive on Unfair Terms in Consumer Contracts" (1994) 2 Cons. L.J. 114.

[65] *First National Bank Plc* [2000] 2 All E.R. 759 CA.

prejudice, and argued that these were but specific examples of the wider principle of good faith.[66] Professor Gow notes that "sale is a bargain bonae fidei",[67] and goes on to point out that:

> "Our doctrine of bona fides is of considerable importance *in re mercatoria* [in commercial matters] and its vigorous restatement, especially in an era of instalment credit and buyers, whose pockets appear large enough to impel them into an activity now become essential to the national economy but are not large enough to enable them lightly to embark upon litigations, is urgently required."[68]

9–45   Professor Smith also went on to argue that

> "the principles of bona fides which are latent in the Scottish law of contract could with advantage be resuscitated to deal with problems of the twentieth century".[69]

9–46   Both writers acknowledged that the principle had fallen into disuse. The implementation of the Directive has been an opportunity to begin its revival. Surprisingly, the 2015 Act Pt 2, like the 1999 Regulations give less assistance than the original 1994 Regulations in interpreting the concept of good faith. The original reg.4(3) had directed that in determining whether a term satisfied the good faith requirement regard should be had to the criteria set out in Sch.2. These criteria contained more than a passing similarity to the criteria in Sch.2 of the 1977 Act. They included such matters as the parties' bargaining strength, whether the consumer received an inducement to agree to the term, whether the goods or services were supplied to a special order and the extent to which the supplier had dealt fairly and equitably with the consumer. Their inclusion was clearly intended to placate the fears of English lawyers, in particular, about the use of the unfamiliar concept of good faith so familiar to civil lawyers.[70] In recommending that guidelines should not be reinstated the law commissions observed that:

> "The test is now more familiar to a UK audience, and has acquired a significant body of domestic and European case law to interpret it. It no longer appears to give rise to much confusion."[71]

As the regulations implement an EC Directive it is legitimate, as *Litster v Forth Dry Dock & Engineering Co*[72] demonstrates, to refer to the recitals to assist in interpreting the fairness test.

---

[66] TB Smith, *A Short Commentary on the Law of Scotland* (Edinburgh: W.Green, 1962).

[67] JJ Gow, *Mercantile and Industrial Law of Scotland*(Edinburgh: W.Green, 1964) p.161.

[68] JJ Gow, *Mercantile and Industrial Law of Scotland* (Edinburgh: W.Green, 1964) pp.178 and 179.

[69] TB Smith, *A Short Commentary on the Law of Scotland* (Edinburgh: W.Green, 1962) p.46.

[70] In one of the few reported cases in which the fairness of a term has been raised in litigation between private parties, *Falco Finance Ltd v Gough* [1999] Tr. L. 526 the judge placed considerable emphasis on these criteria. See also *Gosling v Burrard-Lucas*, [1999] 1 C.L. 197; and *Kindlance Ltd v Murphy*, 1997 NI ChD.

[71] The Law Commission and the Scottish Law Commission *Unfair Terms in Consumer Contracts: Advice to the Department for Business, Innovation and Skills* (March 2013), available on Law Commissions website.

[72] *Litster v Forth Dry Dock & Engineering Co* [1990] 1 A.C. 546.

The "grey list"

While there are no guidelines on fairness in the 2015 Act Pt 2, the Directive has a schedule containing a somewhat delphic "indicative and non-exhaustive list of terms which may be regarded as unfair", commonly referred to as "the grey list". This, as s.63(1) provides, is reproduced as Pt 1 of Sch.2 of the 2015 Act with the more helpful title of "Consumer Contract Terms Which May Be Regarded As Unfair". Section 63 and the Schedule are based on a copy-out of art.3(3) and the Annex to the Directive. The terminology has been brought into line with the 2015 Act as a whole and three additional items dealing with early termination charges and terms that grant traders discretion over the price and subject matter have been added to the list as paras 5, 12 and 14 as recommended by the Law Commissions in their report of March 2013. Part 2 of the Schedule qualifies some of the terms in Part by stating that they are not considered as part of the Schedule but are still assessable for fairness unless they are core terms or exempt under s.73 as mandatory terms.

    The grey list includes terms that exclude liability for death or personal injury or the implied terms in contracts for the supply of goods and services, those that give traders the right to end or extend a contract at their discretion or in other ways to alter the terms of the contract. As one might expect, terms imposing harsh obligations to pay compensation in the event of breach as well as barriers to the use of the courts to decide disputes are also in the list. A common characteristic of the list is that the terms included are very much to the advantage of the trader. The terms on the list are not automatically unfair, but may be used to assist a court when considering the application of the fairness test in s.62 to a particular case. Equally, terms not found on the list in the Schedule may be found by a court to be unfair by application of the fairness test.[73] Terms on the grey list are assessable for fairness even if they would otherwise qualify for an exemption under s.64 and are assessable even if they are "transparent" and "prominent" as defined in s.64. While there is no indication that terms appearing in the grey list should be presumed to be unfair, given the nature of many of the terms it will be difficult to show that they pass the fairness test.

9–47

Other aspects of good faith

It was argued in earlier editions of this book that the concept of good faith covered both what is sometimes referred to as procedural good faith and substantive good faith. This was the view of the English Court of Appeal in the first case relating to the regulations to be heard in one of the higher courts in the UK. In *Director General of Fair Trading v First National Bank Plc*[74] they pointed out that "'good faith' has a special meaning in the Regulations, having its conceptual roots in civil law systems". Although the House of Lords in that case

9–48

---

[73] See *Commission v Kingdom of Sweden* Case C 478/99; [2002] E.C.R. I-04147 at [22]; [2004] 2 C.M.L.R. 34; *Nemzeti Fogyasztovedelmi Hatosag v Invitel Tavkozlesi Zrt*, C-472/10; [2012] 3 C.M.L.R. 1.
[74] *First National Bank Plc* [2000] Q.B. 672.

took a different view on the fairness of the term in issue they did not disagree with this approach. Lord Bingham observed that the Directive and the regulations lay

> "down a composite test, covering both the making and the substance of the contract, and must be applied bearing clearly in mind the objective which the Regulations are designed to promote".[75]

He acknowledged that it covered unfairness in the way in which the bargain is arrived at, sometimes referred to as unfair surprise, as well as unfairness because the bargain is very much weighted in favour of the seller or supplier.

9-49   In this case the Director General was challenging the fairness of a term in a loan agreement subject to the Consumer Credit Act 1974 (the 1974 Act). The term provided that if the borrower defaulted on a repayment the bank could demand repayment of the outstanding balance on the customer's account and interest at the rate set out in the loan agreement. It went on to add that where court action was necessary, interest would be payable at this rate on the judgment. The significance of this is that interest on the judgment would not otherwise have been payable. In practice what happens in cases of default is that after a court action has commenced borrowers agree to pay off the debt by instalments and the action is settled without a proper court hearing taking place. Despite making the agreed repayments to pay off the debt the borrower finds that further sums are owed to the bank by way of interest at the contractual rate on the judgment. The Director General's argument was that this rendered the term in the agreement unfair because when a borrower took out a loan it was not made clear that this could be one of its effects. It also meant that, in practice, borrowers did not have an opportunity to avail themselves of the opportunity to apply for time orders under the 1974 Act which could have provided that interest should not be payable. At first instance[76] Evans-Lombe J had considered this term to be fair. The Court of Appeal disagreed and found that it "does create unfair surprise".[77] The House of Lords disagreed with the Court of Appeal and held the term to be fair. They considered that any unfairness flowed, not from the term, but from weaknesses in the procedures of the English county courts which resulted in debtors in default failing to obtain the benefits of those facilities in the 1974 Act designed to protect them.

9-50   In coming to this decision their Lordships gave useful guidance on the meaning of good faith. Lord Bingham observed:

> "The requirement of good faith in this context is one of fair and open dealing. Openness requires that the terms should be expressed fully, clearly and legibly, containing no concealed pitfalls or traps. Appropriate prominence should be given to terms which might operate disadvantageously to the customer. Fair dealing requires that a supplier should not, whether deliberately or unconsciously, take advantage of the consumer's necessity, indigence, lack of experience, unfamiliarity

---

[75] *First National Bank Plc* [2002] 1 A.C. 481 at [17].
[76] *First National Bank Plc* [2000] 1 All E.R. 240.
[77] *First National Bank Plc* [2000] Q.B. 672; [2000] 2 W.L.R. 1353; [2000] 2 All E.R. 759.

with the subject matter of the contract, weak bargaining position or any other factor listed in or analogous to those listed in Schedule 2 to the [1994] Regulations."[78]

Lord Millet suggested a practical way to test fairness:

"There can be no one single test of this. It is obviously useful to assess the impact of an impugned term on the parties' rights and obligations by comparing the effect of the contract with the term and the effect it would have without it. But the inquiry cannot stop there. It may also be necessary to consider the effect of the inclusion of the term on the substance or core of the transaction; whether if it were drawn to his attention the consumer would be likely to be surprised by it; whether the term is a standard term, not merely in similar non-negotiable consumer contracts, but in commercial contracts freely negotiated between parties acting on level terms and at arms' length; and whether, in such cases, the party adversely affected by the inclusion of the term or his lawyer might reasonably be expected to object to its inclusion and press for its deletion. The list is not necessarily exhaustive; other approaches may sometimes be more appropriate."[79]

The fairness test was considered in *Standard Bank London Ltd v Apostolakis (No.2)*[80] where it was decided that a jurisdiction clause which increased the cost and inconvenience of litigation contravened the regulations. In *Picardi v Cuniberti*,[81] the English High Court held that a clause in a contract between an architect and a client which required the client to submit disputes to the adjudication procedure under the Housing Grants, Construction and Regeneration Act 1996, which does not normally apply to residential properties was unfair. In both these cases reference was made to the fact that the clauses fell under one of the headings in the "indicative and non-exhaustive list of the terms which may be regarded as unfair" contained in an annex to the Directive. These are terms that have the object or effect of "excluding or hindering the consumer's right to take legal action or exercise any other legal remedy". Considerable importance was placed by the judge on the failure of the architect to draw the clients' attention to unusual terms and to explain their significance.[82] In *Bryen & Langley Ltd v Boston*,[83] another case arising out of a building dispute the English Court of Appeal held a term to be fair because it had been put forward by the consumer's agent. In *Oceano Grupo Editorial SA v Rocio Murciano Quintero*[84] the ECJ had founded on this paragraph referring to excluding or hindering the consumer's right to take legal action in holding that a jurisdiction clause which confers exclusive jurisdiction on a court in the territorial jurisdiction of which the seller or supplier has his principal place of business must be regarded as unfair. **9–51**

---

[78] *First National Bank Plc* [2002] 1 A.C. 481 at [17]. The factors listed in Sch.2 to the 1994 Regulations can be found in the recitals to the Directive.

[79] *First National Bank Plc* [2002] 1 A.C. 481 at [54].

[80] *Standard Bank London Ltd v Apostolakis (No.2)* [2001] Lloyd's Rep. Bank. 240.

[81] *Picardi v Cuniberti* [2002] EWHC 2923; [2003] B.L.R. 487.

[82] This was also important in *Munkenbeck & Marshall v Harold* [2005] EWHC 356 QBD (TCC).

[83] *Bryen & Langley Ltd v Boston* [2005] EWCA Civ. 973. See also *Lovell Projects Ltd v Legg* [2003] B.L.R. 452 and *Westminster Building Co Ltd v Beckingham* [2004] EWHC 138 QBD (TCC).

[84] *Oceano Grupo Editorial SA v Rocio Murciano Quintero* (C-240/98) [2002] 1 C.M.L.R. 43.

Enforcement

9–52 It is a trite observation that consumer protection laws are of very little value if they cannot be enforced. As we will see in Ch.12 this is a major problem in Scotland, as in many other jurisdictions. Giving individual rights to consumers is of limited value especially where those against whom they must be asserted are much more powerful. Individual consumers can challenge the fairness of terms but this is of limited value. For this reason art.7 of the Directive requires Member States to "ensure that in the interests of consumers and of competitors, adequate and effective means exist to prevent the continued use of unfair terms". It goes on to add that the means referred to:

> "[S]hall include provisions whereby persons or organisations, having a legitimate interest under national law in protecting consumers, may take action according to the national law concerned before the courts or before competent administrative bodies for a decision as to whether contractual terms drawn up for general use are unfair, so that they can apply appropriate and effective means to prevent the continued use of such terms."

9–53 To comply with this aspect of the Directive s.70 and Schedule 3 of the 2015 Act provide that "a regulator may consider a complaint about a term or notice".[85] These regulators are the Competition and Markets Authority (CMA), local weights and measures authorities in Great Britain (i.e. in Scotland district councils), the Financial Conduct Authority, the Office of Communications, the Information Commissioner, the Gas and Electricity Markets Authority, the Water Services Regulation Authority, the Office of Rail Regulation, the Northern Ireland Authority for Utility Regulation, the Department of Enterprise, Trade and Investment in Northern Ireland and the Consumers' Association. These regulators coordinated by CMA may seek interdicts but only after they have given the CMA notice of their intention to do so. This is part of a process of ensuring the co-ordination of action and the avoidance of duplication of effort. A number of these qualifying bodies have used their powers among which local authorities and OFGEM have been prominent.[86]

9–54 The court to which an application for an injunction or interdict may be made is the Court of Session or the sheriff court and, in the rest of the UK, the High Court or the county court. Conferring jurisdiction on the sheriff court and the county court is an innovation which follows the model of Pt 8 of the Enterprise Act 2002, which permits CMA to take action against traders who do not comply with their obligations to consumers. This facility will be particularly useful for trading standards departments who are likely to take action against local traders; and will also be appropriate where other bodies entitled to seek interdicts sue local businesses.

9–55 The CMA is likely to follow the approach of its predecessor, the OFT, and other regulators which has been to seek to persuade traders to remove or amend terms. The OFT put considerable resources into the creation of an unfair terms unit (though it was disbanded some time ago), and its operation must be one of its greatest successes. To see the practical effect of the regulations, it is to the results

---

[85] Consumer Rights Act 2015 Sch.3 para.2.
[86] See OFT, *Unfair Contract Terms Bulletin*, Issues 24 and 25 (December 2003) p.171.

of enforcement by the regulators that one should look rather than the small number of court decisions on individual cases. By the end of September 2003 (the last year when cumulative statistics were published) it had received 8,300 complaints. Approximately 37 per cent of these were not proceeded with either because they were duplicate or defective complaints or could be dealt with more appropriately under other legislation or were not about contract terms. Eight per cent of complaints were about terms which were not considered to be unfair. It was possible to deal with 25 per cent by advice or warning. In 10 per cent, or 888 cases, an informal undertaking to stop using the term was given by a business, and in 27 cases businesses were required to give formal undertakings. In only one case has it been necessary to obtain a court order.[87] Since 2003 the OFT had dealt with approximately 1,000 complaints each year. Two spectacular examples of the benefits of the regulations are contained in a report which shows that the agreement of a mortgage company to remove unfair penalties in its loan agreements has saved consumers £65.2 million and amendments to mobile telephone contracts is estimated to save consumers between £60 and £80 million.[88]

OTHER STATUTORY CONTROLS

Part 2 of the 2015 Act is, undoubtedly, the most important control on exclusion clauses and other unfair terms. Brief mention should be made of some other statutory controls. Section 29 of the Public Passenger Vehicles Act 1981 invalidates a provision in a contract for the conveyance of passengers in a public service vehicle that purports to restrict the liability of a person in respect of death or personal injury. The Warsaw Convention on carriage by air which is given effect to by the Carriage by Air Act 1961 controls their use in contracts of air travel. Section 6(3) of the Defective Premises Act 1972 renders void any attempt to contract out of the provisions of the Act. There are many examples in the 1974 Act of provisions designed to protect debtors and hirers out of which it is not possible to contract as a result of s.173 of that Act. Similarly, s.7 of the Consumer Protection Act 1987 provides that it is not possible to contract out of the strict delictual duty imposed on producers of defective products.

9–56

---

[87] See OFT, *Unfair Contract Terms Bulletin*, Issues 24 and 25 (December 2003) p.155.
[88] See National Audit Office, *The Office of Fair Trading: protecting the consumer from unfair trading practices* (The Stationery Office, 1999), HC Paper No.57 (Session 1999/2000) p.53.

CHAPTER 10

Control of Trade Practices

This chapter deals with the control of unfair trading practices. Some of these will be clearly dishonest practices and others may be simply unfair or confusing rather than clearly illegal. In the former category are practices such as "clocking" cars that is, turning back the mileage recorder in order to obtain a higher price for the vehicle. This is common in the used car trade. In the second category the use of exclusion or exemption clauses would be examples of practices that are not illegal but which can operate to the disadvantage of consumers. In between are practices such as the way in which prices are presented or offers of goods set out. For example, there is a technique known as "bait and switch" advertising where a trader advertises a product at a very favourable price. When customers respond the trader denigrates the advertised product in order to persuade them to purchase another version of the product that sells for a higher price. These and other practices such as pyramid selling are on the margins of legality.

10–01

There are some who argue that intervention by the state to control unfair or deceptive trading practices is unnecessary. They assert that competition will usually ensure that those who promote unfair methods of trading will not flourish and that consumers who have been injured by unfair practices can resort to traditional legal remedies.[1] It is true that there are common law crimes that might be seen as having some role to play and that the common law doctrines of fraud, facility and circumvention, undue influence, and force and fear might have relevance. In practice, such private law remedies are of limited use. The cost of invoking them, if their availability is known, is often prohibitively expensive. In any event, in the more serious cases of malpractice the trader may be difficult to find by the time that the consumer realises that he or she has been the victim of a swindle. This argues for measures which will deter and for institutions with the muscle to police the market.

10–02

Until recently in the UK the usual method of dealing with unfair practices was to use the criminal law. This often involved making specific practices criminal. For example, the now repealed Consumer Transactions (Restrictions on Statements) Order 1976[2] made it a criminal offence to display notices where consumer transactions such as sales of goods are effected which misled purchasers about their rights. Weights and measures and food legislation is sanctioned by many criminal offences. The Trade Descriptions Act 1968 (the 1968 Act) provided wider control by making false or misleading claims about goods and services criminal offences. In some cases the civil law was used, either

10–03

---

[1] See, for example, RA Posner, "The Federal Trade Commission" (1969–1970) 37 U. Chi. L. Rev. 47.
[2] Consumer Transactions (Restrictions on Statements) Order 1976 (SI 1976/1813).

in addition to, or instead of, criminal law. A good example was the control of inertia selling where goods that have not been ordered are sent out in the hope that the recipient will pay for them. Demands for payment of increasing hostility then follow, often alarming recipients, who will frequently be unaware of their legal rights. On general contractual principles no obligation could be created in this way, but whether recipients had any duty to keep the goods safely or any right to appropriate them to their own use was obscure. To combat this problem the Unsolicited Goods and Services Act 1971 was enacted. Similar provisions are now found in the Consumer Protection from Unfair Trading Regulations 2008 (CPR 2008).[3]

10–04   The regulations attack the problem in two ways. First, they clarify the civil law by providing that the recipient of unsolicited[4] goods "may, as between the consumer and the trader, use, deal with or dispose of the goods as if they were an unconditional gift to him".[5] The criminal law is also invoked to control this abuse by making it a criminal offence to demand or assert a right to payment for unsolicited goods.[6]

10–05   A limitation of this approach is that it provides scope for traders to devise methods to circumvent the law. Where criminal sanctions are used to control trade practices it is necessary on grounds of fairness to state clearly what conduct is prohibited and those who are determined to exploit consumers will find ways to operate just within the law. Attempts to control abuses in the timeshare market provide a good example. New products which do not come within the definition of timeshare in the Timeshare Act 1992 but have much the same function have been devised to circumvent the protections provided.

10–06   Over the years this has led to calls for the enactment of a duty to trade fairly or, at least, a duty not to trade unfairly. The idea of a statutory duty to trade fairly was floated by the Office of Fair Trading's (OFT) report on home improvements in 1982[7] and more detailed proposals were set out in 1986.[8] Following consultations with consumer groups and industry the OFT produced new proposals in 1990[9] which advocated the creation of a duty not to trade unfairly. Nothing came of this proposal though it was possible to argue that while there was no general duty not to trade unfairly the combination of a number of pieces of legislation in specific sectors of the market were moving us to that situation. One could point to the fact that the General Product Safety Regulations 2005[10] create a duty to supply safe goods; that legislation on unfair contract terms applies a fairness test to the use of certain terms as well as banning the use of others; and the Consumer Credit Act 1974 (the 1974 Act), in addition to

[3] Consumer Protection from Unfair Trading Regulations 2008 (SI 2008/1277).
[4] Consumer Protection from Unfair Trading Regulations 2008 Sch.1 para.29 describes these as goods there has been a demand for " immediate or deferred payment for or the return or safekeeping of products supplied by the trader, but not solicited by the consumer".
[5] See Consumer Protection from Unfair Trading Regulations 2008 reg.27M(4).
[6] See Consumer Protection from Unfair Trading Regulations 2008 reg.12 and Sch.1 para.29.
[7] Office of Fair Trading, *Home Improvements* (OFT 1982).
[8] Office of Fair Trading, *A General Duty to Trade Fairly* (OFT 1986).
[9] Office of Fair Trading, *Trading Malpractices: A report by the Director-General of Fair Trading following consideration of proposals for a general duty to trade fairly* (OFT 1990) OFTO43a.
[10] General Product Safety Regulations 2005 (SI 2005/1803).

restricting certain practices, came close, through the licensing system it created, to imposing a duty on the credit industry to trade fairly.[11]

This aim of a general duty is now well on the way to being realised with the **10–07** implementation in the UK of the EU Directive on Unfair Commercial Practices (UCPD) by the CPR 2008. Implementation has presented a considerable challenge because, unlike most previous consumer protection Directives, the UCPD is a maximum harmonisation Directive. Previous Directives have been minimum Directives requiring Member States to ensure that their laws provided a minimum level of protection but permitting them to go beyond this and provide greater protection. This is not possible with the UCPD because it is a maximum Directive. Member States in the areas to which it applies must provide the protection that it requires neither falling below that standard nor going beyond it. In the UK that has meant reviewing a large body of legislation to see if it meets these standards. It has been necessary to amend and, in some cases, repeal existing legislation. As a result some well-established pieces of legislation have gone. That cornerstone of consumer protection the 1968 Act has largely been repealed as has Pt III of the Consumer Protection Act 1987 and its associated code of practice on prices. It is possible that there are some pieces of legislation that might be challenged as conflicting with the requirements of the Directive.

It is necessary, because of this background, to explain the scope of the **10–08** Directive because it is only in relation to those matters which it regulates that the UK Parliament's room for manoeuvre is restricted. The Directive covers business-to-consumer, "unfair commercial practices harming consumers' economic interests",[12] commercial practices being defined as:

> "[A]ny act, omission, course of conduct or representation, commercial communication including advertising and marketing, by a trader, directly connected with the promotion, sale or supply of a product to consumers."[13]

Such practices may occur "before, during and after a commercial transaction in relation to a product".[14] This means that issues of taste and decency are not controlled by the Directive that also expressly provides in art.3 that it is without prejudice to contract law. As a result the Directive confers no right of action on consumers affected by an unfair practice. They will still have to rely on existing contractual remedies such as those for misrepresentation. The Directive does not affect health and safety aspects of products though misleading information about these qualities could amount to unfair practices. Neither the laws governing admission to, nor the standards of, regulated professions such as the legal professions nor the standard of fineness of articles of precious metal are affected.[15] In some cases there are already Directives governing unfair practices in particular sectors as in the case of cosmetic products. Where this is so, that legislation takes precedence.

---

[11] The licensing system has been replaced by authorisation under the Financial Services and Markets Act 2000. See Ch.8.
[12] EU Directive on Unfair Commercial Practices art.1.
[13] See EU Directive on Unfair Commercial Practices art.2(d).
[14] See EU Directive on Unfair Commercial Practices art.3(1).
[15] See EU Directive on Unfair Commercial Practices art.3.

10–09   Although the Directive is said to be a maximum Directive this is not entirely accurate because art.3(9) provides that:

> "In relation to 'financial services', as defined in Directive 2002/65/EC, and immovable property, Member States may impose requirements which are more restrictive or prescriptive than this Directive in the field which it approximates."

Also, where existing minimum Directives have been implemented in a way that is "more restrictive or prescriptive than" the UCPD, it was permissible to keep them in force until 12 June 2013, provided that they are "essential to ensure that consumers are adequately protected against unfair commercial practices and [are] proportionate to the attainment of this objective".[16]

THE CONSUMER PROTECTION FROM UNFAIR TRADING REGULATIONS 2008

Overview of the Regulations

10–10   Before dealing in detail with the regulations it may be helpful to outline what they do. The CPR 2008[17] prohibit unfair commercial practices (including advertising and marketing) related to goods and services directed at consumers. There are four categories of unfairness. There is a general category of unfairness designed as a safety net to catch practices not covered by the other three. These three practices, which are defined in detail, are misleading practices, aggressive practices and a group of 31 banned practices set out in a list in Sch.1. Where a practice is prohibited action can be taken against the trader responsible by "enforcement authorities" who are the Competition and Markets Authority (CMA) and local trading standards services. In addition to informal methods of enforcement or reference to established means of control such as the Advertising Standards Authority (ASA), enforcers may resort to civil methods of enforcement. This involves using the powers in Pt 8 of the Enterprise Act 2002 (the 2002 Act) to obtain a court order to prevent the unfair practice continuing. In addition, most unfair practices can also be prosecuted as criminal offences. A new Pt 4A has given individual consumers a private right of redress.

The Regulations in detail

Scope

10–11   The regulations principally protect consumers not businesses against unfair commercial practices. However, the definition of "consumer" has been amended

---

[16] See EU Directive on Unfair Commercial Practices art.3(5).
[17] Consumer Protection from Unfair Trading Regulations 2008 (SI 2008/1277).

to mean "an individual acting for purposes that are wholly or mainly outside that individual's business".[18] The result is that there is some limited protection for sole traders. A commercial practice:

> "[M]eans any act, omission, course of conduct, representation or commercial communication (including advertising and marketing) by a trader, which is directly connected with the promotion, sale or supply of a product to or from a consumer, whether occurring before, during or after a commercial transaction in relation to a product ... "

"Product" in this context has a very wide meaning. It not only means goods, services and immovable property but also digital content as well as rights and obligations and demands for payment. This definition will cover practices occurring before, during and after the purchase of a product. For example, high pressure selling techniques are used by some sellers and will be covered by this definition. It is also necessary to include practices occurring after a product has been acquired in order to include transactions where there is a continuing relationship. An example would be after-sales services promised on the sale of a car. Debt collection also necessarily occurs after the sale. The addition of demands for payment covers practices such as unjustified demands for parking charges. The practice need not be that of the trader who sells to the consumer, it need only be "directly connected" to the promotion, sale or supply of a product. This was emphasised by Davis LJ in *R on the application of Surrey Trading Standards v Scottish and Southern Energy PLC*[19] where he stated that:

> "It is important to bear in mind that 'trader', for the purpose of the 2008 Regulations, extends to any person who in relation to a commercial practice is acting for purposes relating to his business. The words 'any', 'in relation to', 'acting' and 'relating to' are all words of width and elasticity. As to the definition of 'commercial practice' that is likewise broadly framed. It is amply sufficient to cover involvement in or supervision or control of training, in appropriate circumstances, as being directly connected with the promotion or sale or supply of a product; and it is also to be noted that the definition of 'commercial practice' carefully avoids saying that the promotion or sale or supply has to be made by the trader itself."

In that case a holding company was convicted despite the fact that it was employees of one of its subsidiaries who engaged in misleading practices. It also means that the practices of manufacturers may well be caught. For example, manufacturers place labels on the products which they supply to shops who then sell on to customers. The manufacturer's labels must comply with the regulations. In *R v X Ltd*,[20] the English Court of Criminal Appeal stated that "it is clear that a commercial practice can be derived from a single incident. It will depend on the circumstances".

It should be noted that in one respect the definition of commercial practice **10–12** goes further than the similar definition in the Directive. The regulations cover not

---

[18] See Consumer Protection from Unfair Trading Regulations 2008 reg.2 as substituted by reg.2(3) of the Consumer Protection (Amendment) Regulations 2014 (SI 2014/870) in relation to contracts entered into, or payments made, on or after 1 October 2014.

[19] *R on the application of Surrey Trading Standards v Scottish and Southern Energy Plc* [2012] EWCA Crim. 539 at [34].

[20] *R v X Ltd* [2014] 1 W.L.R. 591.

only the sale or supply of a product *to* a consumer they also cover sale or supply *by* a consumer to a trader. This would catch the situation which arose in the 1968 Act case of *Fletcher v Budgen*[21] where a second-hand car dealer made false statements about a car which was traded-in in order to offer a lower price for it.

10–13   Although not explicitly mentioned it is clear from the definitions of unfairness in other parts of the regulations that they protect only the economic interests of consumers and do not relate to taste or decency. As we have seen above, a recital to the Directive itself makes clear that these issues are not covered.

Average consumer

10–14   The consumer protected by the regulations is the "average consumer"[22] and this term is used in the regulations defining when commercial practices are generally unfair or unfair because they are misleading or aggressive. It has no application to the practices in the banned list in Sch.1. The average consumer, according to CPR 2008 reg.2, is one "to whom the commercial practice is addressed or whom the commercial practice reaches". If the practice is directed at a "particular group of consumers", it will be the average member of that group that is relevant. An example of a group to whom a practice was directed might be children in the case of television advertisements during children's programmes. In this case the standard would be that of the average child. Another example of a group might be readers of soccer magazines in which case the test would be that of the average soccer fan.

10–15   The test of who is an average consumer is taken from the case law of the European Court of Justice (ECJ) which has considered this matter in cases dealing with free movement of goods and the Misleading Advertising Directive.[23] In summary, this takes as a benchmark the "consumer, who is reasonably well-informed and reasonably observant and circumspect, taking into account social, cultural and linguistic factors", to quote recital 18 of the Directive. As the same recital goes on to explain:

> "The average consumer test is not a statistical test. National courts and authorities will have to exercise their own faculty of judgement, having regard to the case-law of the Court of Justice, to determine the typical reaction of the average consumer in a given case."

In *Office of Fair Trading v Purely Creative Ltd*, Briggs J, in referring to the test, observed that it reflected

---

[21] *Fletcher v Budgen* [1974] 1 W.L.R. 1056.
[22] For a perceptive analysis of the concept of the "average consumer" see S. Weatherill, "Who is the "Average Consumer"?" in Stephen Weatherill and Ulf Bernitz (eds), *The Regulation of Unfair Commercial Practices under EC Directive 2005/29: new rules and new techniques* (Oxford: Hart Publishing, 2007).
[23] There is an extensive range of cases discussing the "average consumer" of which the most important are *Pall Corp v Dahlhausen* (C-283/89) [1990] E.C.R. I-4827; *Verband Sozialer Wettbewerb e.V v Clinique Laboratoires SNC and Estée Lauder Cosmetics GmbH* (C-315/92) [1994] E.C.R. I-317; *Mars* (C-470/93) [1995] E.C.R. I923; *Commission v Germany (Sauce Hollandaise)* (C-51/94) [1995] E.C.R. I-3299; *Gut Springenheide* (C-210/96) [1998] E.C.R. I-4657; *Estée Lauder Cosmetics GmbH & Co OHG v Lancaster Group GmbH* (C-220/98) [2000] E.C.R. I-117.

" ... the common-sense proposition that the UCPD exists to protect from being misled consumers who take reasonable care of themselves, rather than the ignorant, the careless or the over-hasty consumer".[24]

He went on to find that it should not be assumed that the average consumer would read the entire text of any promotion particularly when it was in very small print.

If the definition went no further it could be criticised for failing to take account of particularly vulnerable members of society. For this reason it goes further and also protects: **10–16**

"[T]he average member of a clearly identifiable group of consumers ... who are particularly vulnerable to the commercial practice or to the underlying product because of their mental or physical infirmity, age or credulity in a way which the trader could reasonably be expected to foresee ... "

However, in deciding whether such a group has been affected the definition in the regulations goes on to say that one should ignore "the common and legitimate advertising practice of making exaggerated statements or statements which are not meant to be taken literally".

The vulnerability group could cover various people. For example, it might be said that the elderly are more vulnerable to claims about home security devices or that young people would be more vulnerable on account of their inexperience. It is, perhaps, surprising that the list of characteristics is so limited. One might have expected factors such as ethnic origin, education and economic circumstances to have appeared on the list as there is empirical evidence that these are relevant.[25] **10–17**

Unfair practices

Regulation 3 is the heart of the regulations as it contains the basic provision that, to quote para.(1), "[u]nfair commercial practices are prohibited". Paragraphs (3)–(5) go on to spell out in detail when a commercial practice is unfair. Paragraph (3) is the safety net provision rendering unfair those practices which do not meet "the requirements of professional diligence" and thus "materially distorts or is likely to materially distort the economic behaviour of the typical consumer ... ". Commercial practices will also be unfair if they amount to misleading actions or omissions as defined by regs 5 and 6, and if they are aggressive as defined by reg.7. Finally, a practice can be unfair if it is one of those listed in Sch.1. In *CHS Tour Services GmbH v Team4 Travel GbmH*,[26] the ECJ pointed out that the various forms of unfair practice are independent of each other and it is not necessary to show that misleading practices or omissions or aggressive practices are also contrary to the requirements of professional diligence. **10–18**

In practice the most common examples of unfair practices are likely to be those appearing in the banned list and those which are either misleading or

[24] *Office of Fair Trading v Purely Creative Ltd* [2011] EWHC 106 (Ch) at [62].
[25] See Stuyck, Terryn and Van Dyck, "Confidence through Fairness? The New Directive on Unfair Business-to-Consumer Commercial Practices in the Internal Market" (2006) 43 C.M.L.R. 107 at pp.121 and 122.
[26] *CHS Tour Services GmbH v Team4 Travel GbmH* (C-435/11) [2014] 1 All E.R. (Comm) 96.

aggressive. For that reason discussion of unfair practices will deal with them in that order leaving the general or safety net provision until last.

Schedule 1 banned practices

10–19   Schedule 1 to the Regulations sets out 31 practices that are considered unfair in all circumstances. Unlike the other kinds of unfair practice there is no need to consider the effects on consumers. The list is rather a rag bag of practices. The first four involve false claims about involvement in trade organisations or schemes such as being a member of a code of conduct, that a code has been endorsed by a public body when it has not or that the trader or its products have been endorsed by someone when they have not. "Bait advertising" where a trader without any reasonable expectation of being able to fulfil likely orders advertises a product and "bait and switch" advertising are also listed. The latter practice is where a trader advertises a product at a very attractive price with the intention of attracting the attention of customers and then, perhaps after denigrating it, a different, probably more profitable, product to them. Also included are false claims that a product can legally be sold,[27] that it will be available for only a limited time, that consumers' legal rights are a distinctive feature of an offer or that the trader is about to close down. Various marketing scams are included such as pyramid schemes, bogus prize schemes, and "free" gifts that involve further payments beyond the cost of responding or collecting the product.[28] False claims that a product can facilitate winning at games of chance, cure illnesses, dysfunctions or malformations or that an after-sales service is available outside the state in which it has been sold or will be available are all banned. So is failing to honour an undertaking to provide after-sales service to consumers in a language other than that in which the trader has communicated with those consumers. Direct exhortations to children to buy advertised products or persuade their parents or other adults to do so are banned. Creating the impression that the consumer cannot leave the premises until a contract is formed, a practice associated with timeshare marketing, conducting personal visits to the consumer's home ignoring the consumer's request to leave or not to return and making persistent and unwanted solicitations by telephone, fax, email or other remote media are also prohibited. The practice criminalised by the Business Advertisements (Disclosure) Order 1976 of pretending not to be selling as a trader when really doing so is also included as are unsolicited product scams, where goods are sent to someone who has not ordered them and then followed up with demands for payment. Using editorial content in the media to promote a product where a trader has paid for the promotion without making that clear, sometimes referred to as "advertorials", and promoting a product of a particular manufacturer in such a way as to mislead consumers to think that it is that of another manufacturer are also on the banned list.

---

[27] In *R (Vuciterni) v Brent Magistrates' Court*[2012] EWHC 2140 (Admin); (2012) 176 J.P. 705 an English divisional court, obiter, expressed doubts about whether this covered civil wrongdoing.

[28] In *Purely Creative Ltd v Office of Fair Trading* [2013] 1 C.M.L.R. 35 the European Court of Justice held that not even a trivial payment to claim a prize such as the price of a phone call or price of a stamp is permissible pursuant to para.31(b), reversing on this point the English High Court's decision, see *Office of Fair Trading v Purely Creative Ltd* [2011] EWHC 106 (Ch).

Misleading practices

Commercial practices can be unfair because they are misleading. Regulations 5   **10–20**
and 6 of CPR 2008 deal respectively with misleading actions and misleading
omissions. There will, of course, be situations that fall under both headings. If
something is misleading because it contains half-truths it could be considered to
be a misleading action or a misleading omission. These two forms of unfair
practice cover things formerly contained in the Misleading Advertising Directive
that was implemented by the Control of Misleading Advertisements Regulations
1984 though they extend much further than advertising.

In each case, as with aggressive practices, it must be shown that the   **10–21**
misleading action caused the consumer

"to take a transactional decision he would not have taken otherwise, taking account
of its factual context and of all its features and circumstances".[29]

"Transactional decision" is defined more fully in CPR 2008 reg.2 as:

"[A]ny decision taken by a consumer whether to act or to refrain from acting
concerning—
(a)   whether, how and on what terms to purchase, make payment in whole or in
part for, retain or dispose of a product; or
(b)   whether, how and on what terms to exercise a contractual right in relation to
a product; . . ."

The definition is wide in scope and can cover decisions taken before, during and
after a purchase such as whether to buy online or over the counter and whether to
pay cash or purchase on credit. Doubts about whether this included a decision to
enter a shop were resolved by the European Court of Justice in *Trento Sviluppo
srl v Autorita Garante della Concorrenza e del Mercato*,[30] which decided that the
concept of 'transactional decision' covered not only the decision whether or not
to purchase a product, but also the decision directly related to that decision, in
particular the decision to enter into the shop.

Misleading actions (reg.5)

There are three ways according to CPR 2008 reg.5 in which a commercial   **10–22**
practice can be unfair because it is a misleading action. It may contain false
information generally; it may create confusion with a competitor's products; or it
may concern the failure of a trader to honour firm commitments made in a code
of conduct.

The first of these three kinds of misleading actions is more fully spelt out in   **10–23**
CPR 2008 reg.2(a) which provides that a practice can be misleading:

"[I]f it contains false information and is therefore untruthful in relation to any of the
matters in paragraph (4) or if it or its overall presentation in any way deceives or is

---

[29] See Consumer Protection from Unfair Trading Regulations 2008 reg.5(3).
[30] *Trento Sviluppo srl v Autorita Garante della Concorrenza e del Mercato* (C-281/12) [2014] 1
W.L.R. 890.

likely to deceive the typical consumer in relation to any of the matters in that paragraph, even if the information is factually correct . . ."

There are thus two subdivisions of this kind of unfair practice: practices containing false information about certain matters; and deceptive practices. The false information must relate to various things set out in CPR 2008 reg.5(4) of which price and the main characteristics of the product will probably be the most important. Price is self-explanatory and will cover a wide range of possible types of unfairness.[31] The main characteristics comprise a long list set out in para.(5) which is not unlike the list of features of a trade description contained in s.2 of the 1968 Act. These include such things as the availability of the product, its benefits, risks, composition and accessories, fitness for purpose, quantity, origin, expected results from use and the results of tests carried out on it. These provisions would, for example, catch the common practice of "clocking" a car, that is, turning back the odometer or mileage recorder. This could come under "usage" in reg.5(5) or could more generally be within the general meaning of "main characteristic" remembering that the list is not exhaustive.

10–24   It should also be noted that although many of the items on the lists in paras (4) and (5) seem to be relevant to goods rather than services commercial practices include services. False information can therefore include difficulties that arise in relation to services such as package holidays. For example, there have been frequent complaints about the failure of holiday companies to provide promised facilities such as air conditioning or swimming pools. False claims about such things could be brought under para.(4)(a) (the existence or nature of the product), (o) the specification of the product or, possibly (e) its composition, though this does seem more likely to relate to goods than services.

10–25   It will be seen that a practice can be unfair under this provision although the information provided is not false if the overall effect is deceptive. An example could be a jar of moisturising cream sold in jars that have false bottoms and are substantially larger in appearance than required to hold the amount of cream. Even though the weight of the contents is accurately printed on the jar it could well be that this form of packaging would amount to a misleading practice.[32]

10–26   The second way in which a practice may amount to a misleading action is where it is marketed in a way which creates confusion with any products, trademarks, trade names or other distinguishing marks of a competitor. This is designed to deal with practices such as copycat marketing where a manufacturer tries to benefit from the popularity of a successful product by producing one that looks similar to it.

10–27   The third kind of misleading action arises where a trader who has undertaken to be bound by a code of conduct indicates that he is bound by it but fails to comply with a firm and verifiable commitment in it. An example given in the OFT's draft guidance on the regulations is of a trader who is a member of a code of practice that promotes the sustainable use of wood and uses the code's logo in an advertising campaign. The code of practice contains a commitment that its members will not use hardwood from unsustainable sources. However, it is found that the product advertised by the trader contains hardwood from endangered

---

[31] The control of price claims is, as ever, rather complex and the CPR interact with other legislation. This is more fully dealt with in Ch.11 on "Advertising".
[32] cf. *R v A & F Pears Ltd* (1982) 90 ITSA MR 142.

rainforests. This practice is a breach of a firm and verifiable commitment. For examples of unfair commercial practices falling under CPR 2008 reg.5 see *Office of Fair Trading v Ashbourne Management Services Ltd*.[33]

Misleading omissions (reg.6)

Practices may be misleading not only because they positively mislead by giving false information but also by failing to give consumers the information they need to make an informed choice. Regulation 6 deals with this aspect of unfair practices and provides that it occurs when practices omit or hide material information, or provide it in an unclear, unintelligible, ambiguous or untimely manner. This might catch the complexity of some promotions or advertisements. Some prize promotions highlight the fact that valuable prizes are being offered but it is only in very small print hidden away on another page that it is possible to find out most winners will obtain only something of little value if anything.[34] A misleading omission can also occur where a trader fails to identify the commercial intent of a practice, if it is not already apparent from the context. An example might be a paid-for feature in a newspaper which could avoid being unfair by having a heading such as "advertising feature". However, these omissions are not enough to render a particular practice unfair for it must also be shown that they would result in the typical consumer taking, or being likely to take, a different decision as a result.   **10–28**

When deciding whether a practice misleads by omission, the courts will take account of the context. In particular reg.6(2) directs that certain factors be taken into account. These are the features and circumstances of the commercial practice, the limitations of the medium used to communicate the commercial practice (including limitations of space or time), and where the medium used to communicate the commercial practice imposes limitations of space or time, any measures taken by the trader to make the information available to consumers by other means. Where, for example, a cereal bar wrapper contained an offer of a t-shirt at a low price as a promotional offer it might be difficult to include comprehensive information. An indication that full details of the offer could be found on the manufacturer's website might prevent a breach of the regulations.   **10–29**

The missing information must be "material" which means information that the typical consumer needs, in the context, to make informed decisions. It includes any information required by European-derived (EC) law, such as the Package Travel, Package Holidays and Package Tours Regulations[35] and the Consumer Contracts (Information, Cancellation and Additional Charges) Regulations 2013.[36] What information is required may range from a very small amount of information for simple products, to more information for complex products. In *Office of Fair Trading v Purely Creative Ltd* Briggs J observed that: **10–30**

---

[33] *Office of Fair Trading v Ashbourne Management Services Ltd* [2011] EWHC 1237.
[34] See *Office of Fair Trading v Purely Creative Ltd*[2011] EWHC 106 at 7.
[35] Package Travel, Package Holidays and Package Tours Regulations 1992 (SI 1992/3288).
[36] Consumer Contracts (Information, Cancellation and Additional Charges) Regulations 2013 (SI 2013/3134) regs 13–16.

> "The question is not whether the omitted information would assist, or be relevant, but whether its provision is necessary to enable the average consumer to take an informed transactional decision."[37]

10–31   The regulations make special provision for certain kinds of commercial practice known as "invitations to purchase". They specify information that traders must provide in invitations to purchase and where such information is not provided, this will be a misleading omission. An "invitation to purchase" is, to quote CPR 2008 reg.2:

> "A commercial communication which indicates characteristics of the product and the price in a way appropriate to the means of that commercial communication and thereby enables the consumer to make a purchase."

It is not to be confused with the idea of an invitation to treat found in contract law though in some circumstances there may be overlap. However, there are obvious differences. For example, an invitation to treat need not contain a price. Advertisements which are one kind of "commercial communication" will often be invitations to purchase.

10–32   There will be many kinds of invitations to purchase. Newspaper advertisements containing prices will be examples as would an interactive TV advertisement through which consumers can place orders. On the other hand many advertisements which are designed to promote the trader's brand will not be. Newspapers, magazines and billboards often contain advertisements which merely draw attention to a product or company without giving specific details about price or the characteristics of products. Such image building advertisements will not be invitations to purchase. Other examples of invitations to purchase might be a restaurant menu or a text message promotion to which consumers can directly respond in order to purchase the promoted product.

10–33   Where the price and characteristics of a product are referred to in a commercial communication, such as an advertisement, and so it is an invitation to purchase, CPR 2008 reg.6(4) requires further information to be provided. Subject to the same considerations about the context and the limitations of the communication medium as we have seen apply to misleading omissions generally, the information must be provided in a clear, unambiguous, intelligible and timely manner.[38]

10–34   The information that is deemed to be material in invitations to purchase is set out in CPR 2008 reg.6(4). It includes the main characteristics of the product, the identity of the trader, the trader's address, the price of the product (including taxes) or, where the price cannot be reasonably calculated in advance, the way it will be calculated and any freight, delivery or postal charges. Also required are any arrangements for payment, delivery, performance and complaint handling that differ from consumers' reasonable expectations.[39] Where products involve a right of withdrawal or cancellation these must be mentioned. As reg.6(3) requires

---

[37] *Office of Fair Trading v Purely Creative Ltd* [2011] EWHC 106 (Ch) at [73].

[38] The application of the concept to advertisements of products which have different versions is discussed in *Konsumentombudsmannen v Ving Sverige AB*, Case C-122/10); [2011] W.L.R. (D) 181.

[39] This is a paraphrase of the term "professional diligence" used in the regulations which is defined as acting in good faith and honestly it would appear that this is a requirement for rogue traders to admit to their shortcomings.

rights contained in existing Directives such as the Consumer Rights Directive[40] to be disclosed in all cases this requirement will only apply to such rights contained in domestic legislation.

Aggressive practices (reg.7)

The regulations extend beyond prohibitions on misleading and deceptive practices to aggressive practices. It is a much broader concept than the traditional view of physical threats and intimidation. There have been many complaints about high pressure selling. Timeshare selling has been notorious for some of its practices, with reports of potential purchasers being compelled to listen to lengthy and very forceful presentations. Some have complained that they agreed to purchase only because they felt that there was no other way to leave the venue. Sellers of products such as double glazing, which often involve visits to consumers' homes by sales persons, have used high pressure sales methods and pressured customers into signing by refusing to leave until they do. These are some examples of practices that might be prohibited by the inclusion of aggressive practices within the meaning of unfair practices.

10–35

CPR 2008 reg.7 sets out the circumstances in which a practice will be regarded as aggressive. There are three requirements: that harassment, coercion or undue influence has been used by a trader; that this has significantly impaired or is likely significantly to impair the typical consumer's freedom of choice or conduct in relation to the product concerned; and that this has caused or is likely to cause the typical consumer to take a transactional decision he would not have taken otherwise.[41]

10–36

Harassment and coercion are not defined in the regulations though coercion "includes the use of physical force".[42] Undue influence:

10–37

> "[M]eans exploiting a position of power in relation to the consumer so as to apply pressure, even without using or threatening to use physical force, in a way which significantly limits the consumer's ability to make an informed decision."[43]

In all three cases the factual context is important and various factors are to be taken into account in deciding whether there has been harassment, coercion or undue influence. These are its timing, location, nature or persistence, the use of threatening or abusive language or behaviour; the exploitation by the trader of any specific misfortune or circumstance of such gravity as to impair the consumer's judgment, any onerous or disproportionate non-contractual barrier imposed by the trader where a consumer wishes to exercise rights under the contract, and any threat to take any action which cannot legally be taken.[44]

It should be noted that it is not enough to show that there has been one of the forms of aggressive practice. It is necessary to show that the practice "significantly impairs or is likely significantly to impair the typical consumer's

10–38

---

[40] Consumer Rights Directive 2011/83/EC dealing with the protection of consumers in relation to distance contracts and contracts negotiated away from trade premises.
[41] See Consumer Protection from Unfair Trading Regulations 2008 reg.7(1).
[42] See Consumer Protection from Unfair Trading Regulations 2008 reg.7(3)(a).
[43] See Consumer Protection from Unfair Trading Regulations 2008 reg.7(3)(b).
[44] See Consumer Protection from Unfair Trading Regulations 2008 reg.7(2).

freedom of choice or conduct in relation to the product"[45] or, as the definition of undue influence puts it, "significantly limits the consumer's ability to make an informed decision". It is, of course, also necessary in all cases to show that as a result the consumer has taken a decision that he or she would not otherwise have taken.

10–39   The practices that might be regarded as aggressive will be numerous and varied. In *Office of Fair Trading v Ashbourne Management Services Ltd*[46] the High Court found that because agreements for gym memberships were not consumer credit agreements the threat to report customers to a credit reference agency could be seen as aggressive because no credit agreement had been breached. The draft guidance on the regulations given by the OFT cites the example of a mechanic who has a consumer's car at their garage and has done more work than agreed, and who refuses to return the car to the consumer until he is paid in full for the work. The mechanic did not check with the consumer before they went ahead with the extra work. As they have the car, they have power over the consumer's decision to pay for the unauthorised work. They have exploited their position of power, by demanding payment for doing more than was agreed and refusing to return the vehicle until the consumer has paid for all the work. The exploitation of specific misfortune referred to above as one of the factors to be taken into account could arise where staff working in a funeral parlour put pressure on a recently bereaved relative, who is deciding on a coffin, to buy a more expensive coffin as a better mark of respect. This could amount to coercion or undue influence. An example of harassment might arise where a debt collector persistently telephones a debtor late at night or telephones the debtor at their workplace. An example of the use of an illegal threat might occur where a tradesman has carried out a repair such as the replacement of slates on a roof and then requested immediate payment. If the customer does not wish to do so for some reason and the tradesman threatens to undo the repair by removing the new slates this would be an example because there are legitimate methods for recovering a debt and their method is illegal.[47]

The general clause

10–40   CPR 2008 regs 3(1) and 3(3) set out the general prohibition on unfair business-to-consumer commercial practices. This can catch practices which are neither misleading nor aggressive and are not on the list of banned practices set out in Sch.1. To quote the senior Commission official in DG Sanco responsible for the Directive:

> "... It serves as a safety net to catch any current or future practices that cannot be categorised as either misleading or aggressive. The primary motivation is to ensure that the Directive is future-proof."[48]

---

[45] See Consumer Protection from Unfair Trading Regulations 2008 reg.7(1)(a).
[46] *Office of Fair Trading v Ashbourne Management Services Ltd* [2011] EWHC 1237.
[47] See the facts of the English Court of Appeal decision in *R v Connolly* [2012] EWCA Crim. 477 for just such a case.
[48] G Abbamonte, "The Unfair Commercial Practices Directive and its General Prohibition" in Weatherill and Bernitz, *The Regulation of Unfair Commercial Practices under EC Directive 2005/29*, pp.20 and 21.

To come within the general prohibition a practice must both contravene the requirements of professional diligence and materially distort the economic behaviour of the typical consumer with regard to the product or be likely to do so. It will be seen that the first test is concerned with the conduct itself, that is, the standards of the trader's practice. The second is concerned with the actual or likely effect the practice has on the typical consumer's economic behaviour.

Professional diligence is defined (in CPR 2008 reg.2) as: **10–41**

> "[T]he standard of special skill and care which a trader may reasonably be expected
> to exercise towards consumers which is commensurate with either
> (a)   honest market practice in the trader's field of activity, or
> (b)   the general principle of good faith in the trader's field of activity, or
> both."

Professional diligence is an objective standard that will vary according to the context. It goes further than simply acting with subjective good faith for it encompasses competence as well as good practice. The word "special" is not intended to require more than would reasonably be expected of traders in their fields of activity. That will not excuse poor practice where low standards are widespread in a particular industry because this is not what a reasonable person would expect from a trader who is acting in accordance with honest market practice and/or good faith. Codes of practice, especially those drawn up in consultation with consumer interests, such as codes approved under the Trading Standards Institute's Consumer Codes Approval Scheme, may be useful in deciding whether the professional diligence standard has been reached.

To be unfair a practice must, in addition to failing to meet the standard of **10–42** professional diligence, also materially distort or be likely to material distort the economic behaviour of the typical consumer. This means:

> "[A]ppreciably to impair the typical consumer's ability to make an informed decision
> thereby causing him to take a transactional decision that he would not have taken
> otherwise."[49]

The emphasis is very much on the economic behaviour of consumers and on practices that distort consumer preferences by affecting the freedom of choice of consumers. It is not necessary to prove that there has been loss to a consumer. It should be noted that the effect must be appreciable so this will rule out situations where there is little impact on the consumer's freedom of action. For example, it is not uncommon for traders to provide refreshments in showrooms and it might be argued that this will have some influence on the decision of consumers. It is unlikely that it would be sufficiently significant to amount to "appreciably" impairing consumers' freedom of choice.

It is not likely that the general clause will often be used to challenge unfair **10–43** practices as most are likely to fall within the list of banned practices in Sch.1 or be misleading or aggressive. There may be some practices which do not fall within these categories and the general clause is designed to catch them. In this way it will be possible for consumer protection agencies to deal with the ingenuity of those traders who choose to sail close to the wind. An example could

---

[49] Consumer Protection from Unfair Trading Regulations 2008 reg.2(1).

be what is known as modem hijacking. This consists of rerouting internet modem connections in a way that causes the consumer to pay high telephone bills. An internet user clicks on a banner to run a program on their computer and, without alerting the consumer, the program disconnects their modem from the local server and reconnects it to a distant server resulting in high telephone charges.[50] *Office of Fair Trading v Ashbourne Management Services Ltd*[51] is an example of a failure to observe the standard of professional diligence. A company that ran gym clubs used unfair terms in its agreements an example being a term which provided that they would receive the whole of a minimum term's subscription which could be for up to three years, in the event of termination for whatever reason.

Enforcement

10–44   The Directive on which the regulations are based gives a good deal of leeway to Member States in how they enforce it. Article 11 directs that "Member States shall ensure that adequate and effective means exist to combat unfair commercial practices". Article 13 adds that:

> "Member States shall lay down penalties for infringements of national provisions adopted in application of this Directive and shall take all necessary measures to ensure that these are enforced."

Such penalties "must be effective, proportionate and dissuasive" but it is clear from comparing the terms used in other languages that this does not mean that the penalties have to be criminal in nature.[52] In *R v Scottish and Southern Energy Plc*[53] the company was fined £1.25 million after conviction of two misleading action offences because many consumers had been the subject of misleading sales scripts delivered by doorstep salesmen selling energy. In other cases such as *R v Rodney Stone and Geoffrey Moore*[54] prison sentences have been imposed.

The duty to enforce is placed on the CMA and local trading standards services.[55] In practice the bulk of enforcement action is likely to be taken at local level with the CMA intervening where wider issues are involved or perhaps where a nationwide trader is concerned.

10–45   The regulations will be enforced using a number of techniques invoking both civil and criminal law. In choosing which method to use enforcers will have in mind the recommendations of the McCrory Review. In the least serious cases no formal action may be necessary and it may be more a matter of guidance and education or issuing warning letters. In more serious cases enforcers have formal options. CPR 2008 reg.20(4) directs enforcers to

---

[50] The example is given in the chapter cited in fn.48.
[51] *Office of Fair Trading v Ashbourne Management Services Ltd* [2011] EWHC 1237.
[52] EU Directive on Unfair Commercial Practices art.13.
[53] *R v Scottish and Southern Energy Plc* [2012] EWCA Crim. 539.
[54] *R v Rodney Stone and Geoffrey Moore* [2012] EWCA Crim. 186.
[55] Consumer Protection from Unfair Trading Regulations 2008 reg.20.

"have regard to the desirability of encouraging control of unfair commercial
practices by such established means as it considers appropriate having regard to all
the circumstances of the particular case".

For example, if an enforcer is satisfied that a problem with an advertisement can
be adequately dealt with by the ASA, which has a well-established record of
dealing with complaints about advertisements, it could refer the complaint to that
body. Similarly complaints about premium rate telephone services could be
referred to PhonepayPlus (formerly ICSTIS, the Independent Committee for the
Supervision of Standards of the Telephone Information Services), the regulator of
premium rate telecommunications.

Where an informal approach or reference to established means is not **10–46**
appropriate enforcers may take civil enforcement action in respect of any breach
of the CPR 2008 as Community infringements under Pt 8 of the 2002 Act.[56]
Under this procedure, enforcers may apply to a court for an enforcement order to
prevent Community or domestic infringements. Breach of an enforcement order
could be contempt of court which could lead to up to two years' imprisonment
and/or an unlimited fine. This procedure is discussed in detail later in this chapter.
As we shall see, enforcers will normally seek to stop an infringement through
consultation with the trader before applying to the court for an enforcement order.
Instead of seeking an order, they may accept an undertaking from the trader not to
continue or repeat the conduct constituting an infringement. The fact that the
CPR 2008 can be enforced using Pt 8 of the 2002 Act means that the range of
organisations that can do so is considerably widened as is essential if the
Directive's requirement in art.11(1), that "persons or organisations regarded
under national law as having a legitimate interest in combating unfair commercial
practices", should be able to take legal action against them.

Breach of the CPR 2008 in almost all cases will be criminal offences. They **10–47**
fall into two broad categories: those involving proof of mens rea and those which
are strict liability offences. Regulation 8 is the mens rea offence making traders
criminally liable for breach of the general duty not to trade unfairly contained in
reg.3. To prove this offence it must be shown that the trader "knowingly or
recklessly" engaged in a commercial practice that contravenes the requirements
of professional diligence; and

"the practice materially distorts or is likely to materially distort the economic
behaviour of the typical consumer (within the meaning of regulation 3(4)) with
regard to the product"[57].

The first part of the test is in similar terms to that in s.14 of the 1968 Act. It
should be noted that reg.8(2) adopts the meaning of "recklessly" advocated by
Widgery LCJ in *MFI Warehouses Ltd v Nattrass*.[58]

---

[56] The EU Directive on Unfair Commercial Practices and the Consumer Protection from Unfair
Trading Regulations 2008 have been added to the list of specified laws in the Enterprise Act 2002
(Part 8 Community Infringements Specified Laws) Order 2003 (SI 2003/1374) by the CPR reg.30(1)
and Sch.2 para.100. An example is the *Office of Fair Trading v Ashbourne Management Services Ltd*
[2011] EWHC 1237 referred to above.
[57] *R v Hamilton* [2015] EWCA Crim. 278 is an example of such a prosecution. The accused pleaded
guilty to an offence stemming from inadequate building work.
[58] *MFI Warehouses v Nattrass* [1973] 1 All E.R. 762 at 768.

10–48   The other offences are strict liability offences of the kind that have been common in consumer protection statutes. All that is required is that the prohibited conduct is proved; it is not necessary to show any form of mens rea or guilty mind. The apparent harshness of this is ameliorated by providing certain due diligence defences. CPR 2008 reg.9 makes it an offence to engage in a commercial practice that is a misleading action under reg.5(1), except for breaches of commitments in codes of conduct referred to in reg.5(3)(b). Misleading omissions as defined by reg.6(1) are offences under reg.10, and reg.11 makes practices which reg.7 defines as aggressive criminal offences as well. Most of the commercial practices listed in Sch.1 are also criminal offences by virtue of reg.12. The exceptions are the practice in para.(11) of the Schedule of promoting a product in editorial content in the media without revealing that the material has been paid for and, somewhat surprisingly, the practice in para.(28) of including in an advertisement a direct exhortation to children to buy advertised products or persuade their parents or other adults to buy advertised products for them.

Defences

10–49   Like other consumer protection measures sanctioning behaviour by means of strict criminal liability, the severity of this approach is mitigated by the defence of due diligence.[59] There is also a defence of innocent publication of advertisements.[60] Although strictly speaking the provision regarding offences due to the fault of another person is not a defence, it is convenient to deal with it here.[61] These defences are in almost identical terms to those in the 1968 Act so it will be appropriate to refer to the case law that built up under that Act. There appears to be one difference between the application of the defences to 1968 Act offences and CPR 2008 offences. In *R v Southwood*[62] it was held that the defences could not be used where the charge was one of applying a false description to goods. In that case a motor trader had "clocked" a car. The invoice given to the purchaser contained a disclaimer on which the defendant relied as demonstrating that he came within the reasonable precautions defence. The English Court of Criminal Appeal found such a course of action illogical and refused to countenance this as a defence. Under the 1968 Act there were two offences one of which involved active falsification and it was to this that the defences did not apply. The CPR 2008 do not have this distinction. In practice there is unlikely to be much change as it will be difficult for a trader who has deliberately provided false information to argue that they should be excused because they have in some way taken reasonable precautions to negate this.

---

[59] See Consumer Protection from Unfair Trading Regulations 2008 reg.17.
[60] See Consumer Protection from Unfair Trading Regulations 2008 reg.18.
[61] See Consumer Protection from Unfair Trading Regulations 2008 reg.16.
[62] *R v Southwood* [1987] 1 W.L.R. 1361.

Defence of due diligence

To establish the defence of due diligence the accused must establish two things: **10–50**
(1) that the commission of the offence was due to their[63] mistake, or reliance on
information supplied to them or to the act or default of another person, an
accident or some other cause beyond their control[64]; and (2) that they took all
reasonable precautions and exercised all due diligence to avoid the commission
of such an offence by themselves or by anyone under their control.[65] Where the
accused is relying on the act or default of, or on information supplied by, another
person they must give, at least seven days before the date of the hearing, written
notice to the prosecution giving such information as they have identifying the
other person.[66]

There is a good deal of case law from the 1968 Act that will still be relevant in **10–51**
construing the CPR 2008. The part of the defence involving ascription of fault to
"another person" revealed a weakness in the 1968 Act where large corporate
traders[67] are concerned. It has been held that a branch manager of a large retailing
chain was "another person", it not being possible to identify them as the alter ego
of the company.[68] Only very senior members of the company could be so
regarded. The extent to which reliance on this defence may undermine the
purpose of the regulations should not be over-emphasised. In another case it was
pointed out that the defence was not available unless all reasonable inquiries had
been made to try to establish the actual person responsible for the offence and
that it was not sufficient simply to produce a list of all the staff who might have
been responsible.[69]

It should also be noted that shifting the blame to another person is only one **10–52**
ingredient of the defence, the other being that the accused took all reasonable
precautions and exercised all due diligence. The courts have not been easily
satisfied on this score. The case law would seem to support the proposition that to
avail themselves of this part of the defence the accused must show that they had
set up a system designed to prevent errors and also that that system was
adequately operated. The two Scottish cases which discuss the reasonableness of
precautions and due diligence certainly set high standards. In one of these cases
the defence was not available, but the High Court of Justiciary would not have
held it to have been satisfied.[70]

The circumstances were that a car sold by the accused company had been **10–53**
serviced by it some months before and the company was not considered to have
taken all reasonable precautions to avoid a misdescription of the car's mileage
because it was proved that it had taken no steps to check its own records. In the
other case the failure of the accused's managing director to check that his

---

[63] *Birkenhead and District Co-operative Society Ltd v Roberts* [1970] 1 W.L.R. 1497; [1970] 3 All
E.R. 391 DC.
[64] See Consumer Protection from Unfair Trading Regulations 2008 reg.17(1)(a).
[65] See Consumer Protection from Unfair Trading Regulations 2008 reg.17(1)(b).
[66] See Consumer Protection from Unfair Trading Regulations 2008 reg.17(2).
[67] As to offences by corporations under the Consumer Protection from Unfair Trading Regulations
2008, see reg.15.
[68] *Tesco Supermarkets Ltd v Nattrass* [1972] A.C. 153; [1971] 2 All E.R. 127 HL.
[69] *McGuire v Sittingbourne Co-operative Society Ltd* [1976] Crim. L.R. 268 DC.
[70] *Macnab v Alexanders of Greenock Ltd*, 1971 S.L.T. 121.

instructions had been carried out showed want of due diligence.[71] It was also stated by the High Court of Justiciary that where auctioneers applied descriptions concerning the condition of cars which they offered for sale it was not sufficient, to meet the reasonableness requirement of the defence, merely to carry out a cursory external examination. The Lord Justice-Clerk (Wheatley) observed that the accused

> "were under no obligation to give any description of the condition of the car, but, if they elected to do so they should have taken some reasonable steps to see that their description was warranted".[72]

10–54   A similarly strict line was taken by the High Court of Justiciary in *Ford v Guild*,[73] in which a motor dealer appealed against a conviction for supplying a car to which a false trade description had been applied. The dealer had bought the car from D, a private individual, who told him that the mileage reading was correct. It was slightly above average for the age of the car but appeared to be consistent with its condition. D gave his name and address and the name and address of B, the previous owner, but could not produce any service documents. The address of B proved to be false and he could not be traced. The appeal was dismissed. Although the dealer had no reason to disbelieve D's information he had made no attempt to confirm that B existed and the sheriff had been entitled to find that he had not established that he could not have ascertained the truth. It seems likely that courts will approach the defence under the CPR 2008 in the same way.

Offence due to the fault of another person

10–55   The regulations incorporate what is sometimes referred to as the "by-pass" provision that appeared in s.23 of the 1968 Act though it was not as well drafted as CPR 2008 reg.16. This enables a prosecution to be brought against a person whose act or default has caused another person to commit an offence, even if that other person has not been prosecuted. It was held in England that a private individual not acting in the course of a business could be prosecuted under s.23[74] and this is made explicit in reg.16.

Civil remedies for misleading and aggressive practices

The background

10–56   The original regulations relied on public enforcement to make them effective: they did not give consumers the right to bring civil actions to obtain compensation or other remedies. It is true that there are common law and statutory doctrines that could be used by victims of misleading and aggressive

---

[71] *Aitchison v Reith and Anderson (Dingwall and Tain) Ltd*, 1974 J.C. 12; 1974 S.L.T. 282.

[72] *Aitchison v Reith and Anderson (Dingwall and Tain) Ltd*, 1974 J.C. 12 at 17 and 18; 1974 S.L.T. 282 at 287.

[73] *Ford v Guild*, 1990 J.C. 55; 1990 S.L.T. 502; 1989 S.C.C.R. 572.

[74] *Olgeirsson v Kitching* [1986] 1 WL.R. 304; [1986] 1 All E.R. 746 DC. See also WCH Ervine, "Private Sellers and the Trade Descriptions Act", 1986 S.L.T. (News) 217.

practices such as the law on misrepresentation, undue influence or duress. In practice these are of little value to consumers. The Law Commissions observed that

> " ... the law appears to give consumers adequate redress for misleading statements, but consumers can become lost in a bewildering array of remedies, all with their own complexities and uncertainties."[75]

They added that:

> "Although aggressive practices are a major problem, often affecting particularly vulnerable consumers, the existing causes of action (duress, undue influence and harassment) provide inadequate protection."[76]

In a report the law commissions recommended that new remedies for misleading and aggressive practices should be created by legislation. Most of their recommendations were enacted by the Consumer Protection (Amendment) Regulations 2014 (2014 Regulations)[77] which inserted a new Pt 4A into the CPR 2008.[78] Civil proceedings to enforce the remedies may be brought in either the sheriff court or the Court of Session.[79]

Scope of the remedies

In summary, consumers who take a relevant "transactional decision" in relation to products following an aggressive or misleading practice by a trader that was a significant factor in their doing so can get civil redress under the new 2014 Regulations. This is the gist of CPR 2008 reg.27A, which speaks of three conditions that must be met before a consumer can seek one of the remedies in Pt 4A. The new remedies apply to most, but not all, of the misleading and aggressive practices that are banned by the CPRs and subject to criminal and other public enforcement. For example, they do not apply to breach of the general clause or to misleading omissions. In the following paragraphs the scope of the new right to redress is examined.   **10–57**

"Products"

Before discussing the three conditions it is important to look at the meaning of "product". CPR 2008 reg.2(1) defines a "product" to mean goods, a service, digital content, immoveable property, rights or obligations, or a product of the kind mentioned in reg.2(1A) and (1B). The last category adds to the definition in a rather artificial way. Regulation (1A) provides that "A trader ("T") who   **10–58**

---

[75] The Law Commission and the Scottish Law Commission, *Consumer Redress for Misleading and Aggressive Practices* (Law Com No.332 and Scot Law Com No.226) (March 2012) Cm.8323 para.4.2.

[76] The Law Commission and the Scottish Law Commission, *Consumer Redress for Misleading and Aggressive Practices* (Law Com No.332 and Scot Law Com No.226) (March 2012) Cm.8323 para.4.3.

[77] Consumer Protection (Amendment) Regulations 2014 (SI 2014/870).

[78] Consumer Protection from Unfair Trading Regulations 2008 (SI 2008/1277).

[79] Consumer Protection from Unfair Trading Regulations 2008 reg.27K(2).

demands payment from a consumer ("C") in full or partial settlement of C's liabilities or purported liabilities to T is to be treated for the purposes of these Regulations as offering to supply a product to C" and reg.2(1B) goes on to state the product that T offers to supply "comprises the full or partial settlement of those liabilities or purported liabilities". The point of these provisions is to bring within the scope of the civil remedy situations where a consumer is faced with demands from a trader to pay which are not based on contract. Examples could include payments made following debt collection activities, online file sharing and illegal downloads.

10–59   In relation to the civil remedies there are exclusions from the definition. CPR 2008 reg.27C(4) excludes immoveable property except an assured tenancy within the meaning of Pt 2 of the Housing (Scotland) Act 1988, i.e. most residential lettings except social housing and student accommodation, and leases of holiday accommodation. In addition, the new rights do not apply to financial services, defined as a regulated activity within s.22 of the Financial Services and Markets Act 2000. This means that pensions, mortgages, insurance and banking are not covered by the civil remedies. Most credit agreements are also excluded with one important exception, a "restricted-use credit agreement".[80] This covers situations where the credit provided is used to finance a specific transaction between the borrower and lender, for example hire-purchase, or to finance a transaction between the borrower and a supplier, other than the lender. The reason for these exclusions is that both areas are already highly regulated and applying the new rights could lead to confusion and inconsistency.

"Consumer" and "trader"

10–60   The definitions of "consumer" and "trader" have been amended in the regulations to bring them into line with the definitions in other consumer protection statutes. Reference should be made to the discussion of these terms in the chapter on the Supply of Goods.

Condition 1

10–61   The first condition is that the consumer has entered into certain sorts of contract with a trader or has made a payment to a trader for the supply of a product. The first of these is where a consumer enters into a contract with a trader for the trader to sell or supply a product.[81] The second situation is the reverse where a consumer contracts with a trader to sell or supply a product to the trader, for example, selling an antique or a second-hand car to a trader.[82] Excluded from this category is a transaction where the trader is also supplying or agreeing to supply a product to the consumer, as well as paying a sum of money for the consumer's product.[83] This would cover transaction where the consumer traded in a car and

---

[80] As defined in the Financial Services and Markets Act 2000 (Regulated Activities) Order 2001 (SI 2001/544) art.60L(1).
[81] Consumer Protection from Unfair Trading Regulations 2008 reg.27A(2)(a).
[82] Consumer Protection from Unfair Trading Regulations 2008 reg.27A(2)(b).
[83] Consumer Protection from Unfair Trading Regulations 2008 reg.27A(3).

in return received another car and cash that was the difference between the value
of the car they had traded in and the new car.

The third situation does not involve a contract. It is the case where a consumer
makes a payment to a trader for the supply of a product. This was the last
category set out in the list of products in the definition discussed above.

Condition 2

Only certain behaviour by traders will allow a consumer a remedy. The consumer   **10–62**
must show that a trader has engaged in a "prohibited practice". This can take two
forms: either the trader has engaged in the practice; or a producer has done so and
the trader is, or could reasonably be expected to be, aware of it. A "prohibited
practice" for the purpose of the civil remedy has a more restricted meaning than
in the rest of the regulations. CPR 2008 reg.27B provides that it means either a
misleading action as defined in reg.5 or an aggressive practice as defined in reg.7.
This means that there is no civil remedy for misleading omissions. This is in line
with the recommendations of the law commissions and the existing civil law on
liability for omissions. In practice it may not matter much as facts that can be
analysed as an omission can also be presented as an implied representation and so
will be caught as a misleading action. The range of behaviour covered by these
practices is more limited than in relation to criminal sanctions. While the general
definitions of misleading actions and aggressive practices is applied it is not so
wide because of the different definition of "transactional decision" that is to be
used in relation to the civil remedy. The consumer's decision must concern the
entry into a contract for the sale or supply of a product from the trader, for the
sale of goods to a trader or making a payment to a trader for the supply of a
product. It does not cover other decisions such as wasted visits to a shop in
response to an advertisement or continuing to spend time browsing on a website
which would be covered under the main version of the definition under reg.2.

The trader's liability extends to things done by a producer. A "producer"[84] is a   **10–63**
manufacturer of goods or digital content, an importer of the goods or digital
content into the European Economic Area (EEA), or a person who purports to be
a producer by placing the person's name, trade mark or other distinctive sign on
the goods or using it in connection with the digital content. It includes a producer
acting personally or through another person acting in the producer's name or on
the producer's behalf. As the definition of producer suggests, this aspect of a
trader's liability only applies to practices connected to goods or digital content.
Services, for example, are excluded. This form of the liability could arise where a
producer undertook a high profile advertising campaign claiming its products had
features that they in fact did not have. If the retailer was aware of this, the
consumer would have a claim against the retailer.

Condition 3

The third condition is that the prohibited practice is a significant factor in the   **10–64**
consumer's decision to enter into the contract or make the payment. The purpose
of this condition is to show that there is some causal link between the trader's

---

[84] Consumer Protection from Unfair Trading Regulations 2008 reg.27A(4)(b).

conduct and the consumer entering into the contract or making the payment. It is not necessary to show that the prohibited behaviour was the only, or even the main, reason for entering into the contract. It must, however, at least be a "significant factor" in the consumer's decision and this is a question of fact.

Remedies

10–65   Assuming that a consumer can show that they have been the victim of a misleading or aggressive practice, what remedies are available under the new regulations? As recommended by the Law Commissions, there are two tiers of remedies: the tier 1 or standard remedies are the right to unwind the transaction or obtain a discount on the price; and the tier 2 remedies are damages for indirect economic losses and distress and inconvenience. The terminology is mostly new, deliberately so, as the Law Commissions wanted to emphasise the contrast with the existing remedies and to use terms "without existing legal baggage".[85] The right to unwind means that the consumer receives a refund of money paid and is released from any future obligations. If unwinding is not possible the consumer may receive a discount on the purchase price depending on the seriousness of the misleading or aggressive practice. The tier 1 remedies apply on a strict liability basis with the amount being based on the price paid and without the need for evidence of loss. This should allow them to be used both in the civil courts and where public enforcement is used, for example, in criminal compensation orders.[86] Tier 2 remedies on the other hand apply only if the consumer proves loss and, unusually, are subject to a due diligence defence for the trader. The remedies as they apply to business to consumer and consumer to business transactions as well as improper payments are discussed in more detail below.

Tier 1

Unwinding business to consumer transactions

10–66   The right to unwind allows the consumers to undo transactions they entered into, restoring them to the position they were in before entering the contract or making the payment. There are two important limits to this right. The consumer must indicate within 90 days ("the relevant period") that they are rejecting the product. There are no formal requirements about how this should be done "but it must be clear".[87] The wisest course would be to do so in some permanent manner such as a letter or email. The 90 day period starts running from the latest of the following alternatives:

- when the goods or digital content are first delivered;
- when the performance of the service begins;

---

[85] The Law Commission and the Scottish Law Commission, Consumer Redress for Misleading and Aggressive Practices (Law Com No.332 and Scot Law Com No.226) (March 2012) Cm.8323 para.8.27.
[86] The Law Commission and the Scottish Law Commission, Consumer Redress for Misleading and Aggressive Practices (Law Com No.332 and Scot Law Com No.226) (March 2012) Cm.8323 para.5.19.
[87] Consumer Protection from Unfair Trading Regulations 2008 reg.27E(2).

- when the lease begins; or
- the right is first exercisable.[88]

If a product contains more than one element (referred to as a "mixed contract") such as a good and a service or digital content, the period will commence on the latest applicable day.[89] There is no discretion to extend the 90 day period though, of course, there will still be the possibility of a discount which could be 100 per cent.

The other limit to the right to unwind is that it can only apply if the product is capable of being rejected. If the goods have been fully consumed, or the service was fully performed, it is no longer possible to restore the parties to the position they were in before the misleading or aggressive practice, and the right to unwind cannot apply. However, it is enough that it is possible to return some element of the product. In respect of services which cannot be returned in a meaningful way it is enough that the consumer rejected some element of the service before it was fully performed and, in the case of a right, that it has not been fully exercised.   **10–67**

Where the right to a refund is established "the contract comes to an end so that the consumer and the trader are released from their obligations under it".[90] If the consumer has paid money the trader has a duty to give the consumer a refund and there is normally no allowance for use of the product that the consumer may have had. However, if the contract was for the continuous or regular supply of goods or services and the consumer has consumed the goods or services for more than one month there can be a deduction reflecting the value that the consumer has received.[91] The market price of what the consumer has used is therefore deducted from the price paid for the product or service. An example might be a situation where a gas company induced a consumer to switch to it as a result of a false claim that it was 10 per cent cheaper than their current supplier when their price was 10 per cent more. If the consumer has used the new supply for more than a month there is a right to a refund but it would be calculated as the difference between what has been paid and the previous supplier's lower price. Even here, it may not be appropriate to apply the deduction when the behaviour of the trader or the impact of the practice on the consumer are taken into account.   **10–68**

Where the contract is for the sale or supply of goods the consumer must make the goods available for collection but does not have to take them back to the trader. In some situations, the trading-in of a car would be a common example, the consumer may have paid over money and transferred non-monetary items. CPR 2008 reg.27F(4) requires the trader, in addition to refunding the money, to return the same amount of non-monetary items transferred to the trader by the consumer prior to the unwinding of the contract. If it is not possible to substitute the same amount of the same thing that was transferred then, under reg.27F(5), the consumer is entitled to receive back whatever they transferred, in its original state, for example a traded-in vehicle. If this is not possible, then the consumer has to be paid the market price of the transferred item when the product was rejected. Thus, if a traded-in vehicle has already been sold on by the trader and so   **10–69**

---

[88] Consumer Protection from Unfair Trading Regulations 2008 reg.27E(4).
[89] Consumer Protection from Unfair Trading Regulations 2008 reg.27E(5).
[90] Consumer Protection from Unfair Trading Regulations 2008 reg.27F(1)(a).
[91] Consumer Protection from Unfair Trading Regulations 2008 reg.27F(7).

cannot be returned to the consumer when the consumer rejects the contract, the consumer is to be paid the market value of the vehicle at the time of rejection.

Unwinding consumer to business contracts

10–70   In some cases the consumer will have sold goods to the trader as a result of a misleading or aggressive practice. There has, for example, been concern about the fairness of cash-for-gold sites that offer to buy consumers' gold or silver jewellery. The remedy of unwinding operates slightly differently in this case. As with business to consumer transactions the consumer has to give a clear indication, by words or actions, to the trader that the contract has ended[92] and both the trader and consumer are released from their obligations.[93] If it is possible for the trader to return the consumer's goods in the same condition as when sold by the consumer, the consumer can get the goods back and has to refund the trader any sum the trader had paid for the goods.[94] If return of the goods, in the same condition, is not possible then, under reg.27F(6), if the market price of the goods sold to the trader exceeds the price paid by the trader, the consumer is entitled to be paid the excess amount. An example would be where a trader has disparaged goods and obtained them below market price. The trader would have to make up the difference between the contract price and the true value of the goods obtained.

10–71   A major difference between consumer to trader and business to consumer transactions lies in the fact that the 90 day time limit for unwinding does not apply to consumer to trader cases. This follows the Law Commissions' recommendation which was based on the fact that unwinding was the only remedy as the idea of a discount could not apply. The right to unwind, therefore, applies at any time within the normal five year period of prescription.[95]

Unwinding improper payments

10–72   There is also a right to unwind where a consumer has made an improper payment as described in reg.2(1A) and (1B). As with consumer to business transactions the 90 day limit does not apply and the time limit for recovery is five years under the same prescription legislation. It must be stressed that the remedy only applies to payments which were not owed either in full or in part. It does not apply to situations where a payment is due, for example, where a consumer has not paid for goods which have been delivered. Even though someone has paid the debt following misleading statements or threats the trader can retain the money. It is always possible that the consumer will have a damages remedies under reg.27J where they can show evidence of distress or other financial loss.

---

[92] Consumer Protection from Unfair Trading Regulations 2008 reg.27G(2) and (3).
[93] Consumer Protection from Unfair Trading Regulations 2008 reg.27G(1)(a).
[94] Consumer Protection from Unfair Trading Regulations 2008 reg.27G(5).
[95] Prescription and Limitation (Scotland) Act 1973 s.6(4).

A discount

The right to a discount applies to cases where there has been a misleading or aggressive practice in relation to a business to consumer transaction. It is available where the right to unwind is no longer available either because the 90 day limit has expired or the product has been consumed. The basic idea is that the consumer can get money compensation. The traditional damages remedy under current law is complex and not well suited to the resolution of consumer disputes. This remedy seeks to offer a simpler alternative that should aid consumers in reaching settlements with traders.
    10–73

Where the cost of the product is not more than £5,000 and the consumer has already paid money they can be refunded "the relevant percentage" of the payments made. If payments have yet to be made, the consumer can reduce some, or all, of them by the "relevant percentage". The relevant percentage is a series of bands: 25 per cent if it is more than minor; 50 per cent if it is significant; 75 per cent if it is serious; and 100 per cent if it is very serious. A minor transgression does not qualify for any reduction. The seriousness of the conduct is a matter of fact but reg.27I(5) provides that the seriousness of the prohibited practice is to be assessed by reference to the behaviour of the person who engaged in the practice, the impact of the practice on the consumer, and the time that has elapsed since the prohibited practice took place. The worse the behaviour of the trader and the greater the impact on the consumer the higher the discount is likely to be.[96]
    10–74

The Law Commissions thought that where higher priced items were concerned the bands might operate unfairly against traders. As a result reg.27I(6) and (7) state that if the amount payable under the contract exceeds £5,000, the consumer paid more than the market price for the product, and there is clear evidence of the difference between the market price and the contract price the discount percentage is the percentage difference between the market price and the contract price. This might apply to that common fraud, the clocked car, where a trader has turned back the odometer on a used car with the result that the consumer pays much more than the proper price. Suppose that the "clocked" car is sold for £10,000 when the market price of the car showing the real mileage would have been £6,000. The percentage difference between these prices is 40 per cent so the consumer would be entitled to a discount of £4,000.[97]
    10–75

Tier 2 remedy: Damages

In addition to the Tier 1 remedies discussed above a consumer may be able to obtain compensation for two other forms of loss which resemble traditional damages. These are consequential financial loss and damages for alarm, distress or physical inconvenience. These second tier remedies for indirect losses are provided only if the consumer can prove that the practice caused actual loss,
    10–76

---

[96] See examples in the Law Commission Consultation Paper No.199 and the Scottish Law Commission Discussion Paper No.149, *Consumer Redress For Misleading and Aggressive Practices: A Joint Consultation Paper (2011)*.

[97] For other examples of the operation of the discount rules see BIS, *Misleading and Aggressive Commercial Practices—New Private Rights For Consumers Guidance on the Consumer Protection (Amendment) Regulations 2014* (August 2014) p.13.

meeting a "but for" test of causation.[98] The consumer must also show that the loss was reasonably foreseeable when the prohibited practice occurred[99] which applies the usual test for the recovery of damages for breach of civil obligations. Compensation for financial loss does not include the right to be paid damages in respect of the difference between the market price of a product and the amount payable for it under a contract as that is covered by the Tier 1 remedy of the discount.[100]

10–77   In their consultation paper the Law Commissions suggested that examples of such indirect financial losses might include the costs of installation or travel, or disposing of an existing product such as where the consumer who is sold a new bed in an aggressive way and then throws away the old bed to make room for it.[101]

10–78   Damages for distress and inconvenience are also available in the same way as they are currently available for breach of contract. It should be stressed that this does not include simply the inevitable hassle of having to obtain redress itself (which applies in every case) but must be related to the experience of the aggressive or misleading practice and the product purchased as a result. The most likely occasion for such damages will be where there has been an aggressive practice. What must be shown is either that an important object of the contract was to give pleasure, relaxation or peace of mind, or that alarm, distress, physical inconvenience or discomfort has been suffered as a result of the practice. Such compensation following a misleading practice should not be ruled out. For example, it is not difficult to imagine circumstances where a misleading statement relating to a holiday could lead to considerable distress and inconvenience. Following various judicial comments in English cases the Law Commissions expected that such damages would be modest.[102] The Department of Business, Innovation and Skill (BIS) guidance echoes this in observing at para.61that such awards,

> "should be restrained and modest, in accordance with the general law in England and Wales and Scotland. Only in exceptional circumstances would these exceed £1,000, and in most cases, a nominal award, or an amount below £1,000 would be appropriate".

A novel feature of the damages remedy is that there is a due diligence defence.[103] Traders will have a defence where they can show two things. First, that the misleading or aggressive practice was due to a mistake, reliance on information supplied to them by another person, the act or default of a person other than the trader, an accident, or another cause beyond their control. Secondly, they must be

---

[98] Consumer Protection from Unfair Trading Regulations 2008 reg.27J(1).
[99] Consumer Protection from Unfair Trading Regulations 2008 reg.21J(2).
[100] Consumer Protection from Unfair Trading Regulations 2008 reg.21J(3).
[101] Law Commission's Consultation Paper, para.14.58.
[102] Law Commission's Consultation Paper, para.14.63 referring to *Milner v Carnival* [2010] EWCA Civ. 389, [2010] 3 All E.R. 701 at [41] by Ward LJ, echoing the words of Lord Steyn in *Farley v Skinner* [2001] UKHL 49; [2002] 2 A.C. 732 at [28] and Bingham LJ in *Watts v Morrow* [1991] 1 W.L.R. 1421, 1445. See also the Law Commission and the Scottish Law Commission, Consumer Redress for Misleading and Aggressive Practices (Law Com No.332 and Scot Law Com No.226) (March 2012) Cm.8323 para.8.164 and the BIS.
[103] Consumer Protection from Unfair Trading Regulations 2008 reg.27J(5).

able to show that they took all reasonable precautions and exercised all due diligence to avoid the occurrence of the prohibited practice. The defence must be established on a balance of probabilities by the trader. It is the same as the defence to a criminal prosecution in CPR 2008 reg.17 and the case law on it discussed earlier in this chapter will be useful in interpreting it. It seems unlikely to have much relevance to aggressive practices.

Other legislation controlling unfair practices

Although the CPR 2008 implement a Directive that set out to create a general duty not to trade unfairly we saw that the Directive did not cover all forms of trade practice. As a result there are other pieces of legislation affecting trade practices and these are discussed below.

10–79

DISTANCE AND DOORSTEP SELLING

Background

Goods and services are sold by a variety of methods. Over the counter sales are still the most common method but doorstep selling has long been used in some sectors and increasing use is being made of electronic methods especially over the internet. Doorstep selling methods have frequently had a bad reputation with allegations of high pressure selling methods, and electronic methods have also attracted a good deal of criticism. As a result, what have usually been referred to as the Doorstep Selling[104] and the Distance Selling[105] Directives were enacted by what is now the European Union and implemented in the UK by regulations.[106] Changes in the consumer market place and technological developments have rendered these measures somewhat dated so, as part of a wider attempt to rationalise consumer protection legislation, the directives have been repealed and replaced by the Consumer Rights Directive 2011.[107] The parts of that Directive relating to doorstep and distance selling have been implemented by the Consumer Contracts (Information, Cancellation and Additional Charges) Regulations 2013 (the 2013 Regulations)[108] which apply to contracts entered into on or after 13 June 2014.

10–80

---

[104] Council Directive 85/577/EEC of 20 December 1985 to protect the consumer in respect of contracts negotiated away from business premises.

[105] Directive 97/7/EC of the European Parliament and of the Council of 20 May 1997 on the protection of consumers in respect of distant contracts.

[106] See the Consumer Protection (Distance Selling) Regulations 2000 (SI 2000/2334), and the Cancellation of Contracts made in a Consumer's Home or Place of Work etc. Regulations 2008 (SI 2008/1816).

[107] Directive 2011/83/EU of the European Parliament and of the Council of 25 October 2011 on consumer rights, OJ. No. L 304, 22.11.2011, p.64.

[108] Consumer Contracts (Information, Cancellation and Additional Charges) Regulations 2013 (SI 2013/3134).

Scope of the regulations

10–81   The Regulations apply to contracts between traders and consumers. A consumer is

> "an individual acting for purposes which are wholly or mainly outside that individual's trade, business, craft or profession".[109]

This is wide enough to cover some businesses but will only apply sole traders and partnerships governed by the Partnership Act 1890 as only "individuals" may be traders. This is more clearly expressed in art.2 of the Consumer Rights Directive, where there is a reference to "any natural person". That article does not make clear that some businesses can be regarded as consumers, but this was the clear intention of the Directive as Recital 17 states that

> "in the case of dual purpose contracts, where the contract is concluded for purposes partly within and partly outside the person's trade and the trade purpose is so limited as not to be predominant in the overall context of the contract, that person should also be considered as a consumer".

This might cover situations such as that in *R & B Customs Brokers Co Ltd v United Dominions Trust Ltd*[110] involving the purchase of a car for use both in the business and as the trader's family car. A trader is

> "a person acting for purposes relating to that person's trade, business, craft or profession, whether acting personally or through another person acting in the trader's name or on the trader's behalf".[111]

It includes the activities of central and local government and public authorities.[112]

10–82   The 2013 Regulations apply to three types of contracts: some to "on-premises contracts", some only to "off-premises contracts", and some only to "distance contracts", terms which are defined in reg.5. A "distance contract" means

> "a contract concluded between a trader and a consumer under an organised distance sales or service-provision scheme without the simultaneous physical presence of the trader and the consumer, with the exclusive use of one or more means of distance communication up to and including the time at which the contract is concluded".[113]

These will include sales conducted via internet sites, by phone, email or by letter. An "off-premises contract" can occur in a number of ways. It covers situations where an offer was made by the consumer, or a contract concluded, in the simultaneous physical presence of the trader and the consumer, in a place which is not the business premises of the trader. The classic example would be where a sales person calls at the home of the consumer and the consumer signs a contract

---

[109] Consumer Contracts (Information, Cancellation and Additional Charges) Regulations 2013 reg.4.
[110] *R & B Customs Brokers Co Ltd. v United Dominions Trust Ltd* [1988] 1 W.L.R. 321.
[111] Consumer Contracts (Information, Cancellation and Additional Charges) Regulations 2013 reg.4.
[112] See definition of "business" in Consumer Contracts (Information, Cancellation and Additional Charges) Regulations 2013 reg.5.
[113] Consumer Contracts (Information, Cancellation and Additional Charges) Regulations 2013 (SI 2013/3134) reg.5.

in their home. To avoid attempts to circumvent these rules it also includes a contract concluded on the business premises of the trader, or through any means of distance communication, immediately after the consumer was personally and individually addressed in a place which is not the business premises of the trader in the simultaneous physical presence of the trader and the consumer. The last version of this type of contract is one concluded during an excursion organised by the trader with the aim or effect of promoting and selling goods or services to the consumer. An "on-premises" contract is one that does not fall within the other two categories.

There is a wide range of contracts to which the regulations do not apply. These include those relating to gambling and lotteries, financial services, immovable property for residential rental and the construction of new buildings and their conversion. Also excluded are contracts or the supply of foodstuffs, beverages or other goods intended for current consumption in the household by regular roundsmen who call at a consumer's home, residence or workplace as well as package holiday and timeshare and related contracts. Sales through automatic vending machines or automated commercial premises are excluded as are those concluded through a telecommunications operator using a public pay phone and those for prescription medicines.[114]   **10–83**

What traders must do

The regulations utilise two main techniques to protect consumers. The first is that traders must provide them with relevant pre-contract information to enable them to make properly informed decisions; and the second, which applies only to distance and off-premises contracts is a right of withdrawal, or cooling-off period, after entering into the contract. The former apply slightly differently to the different types of contract.   **10–84**

Information

Regulation 9 of the 2013 Regulations and Sch.1 specify the information which a trader must provide, in a clear and comprehensible manner, before entering into an on-premises contract. This includes the main characteristics of the goods or service, the identity of the trader and the total price. Such information, by virtue of reg.9(3) becomes a term of the contract and any change to that information is not effective unless expressly agreed between the consumer and the trader. Such information will often be obvious from the context and in this case does not have to be separately provided. An example would be the location of the shop or, often, the characteristics of the goods on sale. However, these requirements do not apply to day-to-day transactions performed immediately the contract is entered into. The rationale for this exemption for things sold on premises is that the consumer will be very familiar with the goods or services, and their cost, so that the level of information required by the 2013 Regulations would be superfluous.   **10–85**

---

[114] See Consumer Contracts (Information, Cancellation and Additional Charges) Regulations 2013 regs 6, 7 and 27.

It will apply to things like buying a cup of coffee, the daily paper, weekly groceries, or a tube of toothpaste which by their nature are likely to be low cost items.

10–86   Regulations 10, 13 and Sch.2 of the 2013 Regulations set out the information required for an off-premises contract or a distance contract. This includes delivery arrangements, the trader's complaint handling policy, if there is one, and cancellation rights together with the cancellation form set out in Sch.3 Pt B. This information and any cancellation form must be given on paper or, if the consumer agrees, on another durable medium and must be legible.[115] Regulations 12 and 16 require the trader to provide the consumer with a copy of the signed contract or confirmation of the contract, within a reasonable time after the conclusion of the contract. These requirements are qualified in the case of small value (i.e. not more than £170) off-premises repair and maintenance services contracts that are to be performed immediately.

10–87   Regulation 18 provides that a term is implied into the contract between the trader and the consumer that the trader has complied with the information requirements in regs 9–14 and 16. Regulation 19 provides that a trader is guilty of a criminal offence if the trader enters into an off-premises contract without having provided the information on cancellation rights specified by reg.10 and Sch.2.

Cancellation rights

10–88   A potentially useful protection for a consumer is the right to cancel a distance or off-premises contract. Regulation 29 of the 2013 Regulations provides such a right to cancel without having to give any reason or incurring any costs other than those specified. It should be noted that it does not apply to contracts relating to prescription medical products, passenger transport services or off-premises contracts under which the payment to be made by the consumer is not more than £42.[116] Consumers must inform traders of the decision to cancel the contract which may be done by making any clear statement or using the model cancellation form in Sch.3 Pt B.[117]

10–89   In some circumstances a right of withdrawal could be inappropriate because of the nature of particular goods or services so reg.28 provides for certain limited exceptions. That is the case for example with goods which will deteriorate or expire rapidly, "investment" type products such as vintage wines, subject to speculative purchase and where the price in the financial market may vary (utilities such as supply of gas are not covered by this exception), personalised goods such as tailor-made curtains, transactions where the consumer has specifically requested a visit from the trader to carry out urgent repairs and contracts for newspapers and magazines except by subscription.

10–90   The cancellation period of 14 days is calculated from the date of conclusion of the contract or the date of delivery, according to the type of contract, and may be extended by up to 12 months if the trader does not provide the consumer with the

---

[115] Consumer Contracts (Information, Cancellation and Additional Charges) Regulations 2013 reg.10(2).
[116] Consumer Contracts (Information, Cancellation and Additional Charges) Regulations 2013 reg.27.
[117] Consumer Contracts (Information, Cancellation and Additional Charges) Regulations 2013 reg.32.

information on cancellation rights specified in Sch.2. Regulation 34 of the 2013 Regulations requires the trader to pay a refund to the consumer within 14 days of being informed of the cancellation or within 14 days of the goods being returned or evidence of return being provided.[118] A trader is entitled to deduct from the refund an amount reflecting the diminished value of the goods caused by unnecessary handling by the consumer. The value of the cancellation rights are reduced by the fact that reg.35 requires the consumer to return any goods to the trader and bear the cost of doing so, unless the trader has agreed to collect the goods or bear the costs of the consumer returning them. There is an exception for goods that cannot by their nature normally be returned by post such as bulky goods. If a service or digital content is supplied during the cancellation period the consumer loses the right to cancel, if the consumer acknowledged that the right would be lost in those circumstances.

In addition to the main contract for the supply of goods or services the consumer may also have entered into what are termed in the regulations, an ancillary contract. Examples would be credit contracts or insurance contracts. Under the regulations, where the consumer cancels the main contract, the ancillary contract is automatically cancelled and it is the trader's responsibility to notify any relevant third party.[119]

10–91

Other issues

A frequent complaint of consumers purchasing goods online has been that they have inadvertently agreed to pay extra charges by failing to untick a pre-ticked box on a website. Some low cost airlines have been notorious for hiding travel insurance in this way. Regulation 40 of the 2013 Regulations is designed to prevent traders from including additional charges, over and above the amount agreed to be paid for the main obligation under the contract, without the consumer expressly consenting to the additional charges. Express consent is no longer inferred from failure to change a default option such as a pre-ticked box on a website. This prevents charges for items such as packaging, delivery, gift wrap or insurance where the costs are automatically added and the consumer has to take positive steps to have such costs removed. This does not mean that pre-ticked boxes, as such, are not prohibited. They can still be used where there is no associated payment, e.g. for signing up to free newsletters, email messages, etc.

10–92

Telephone help lines operated by traders have been a source of annoyance to consumers when they involve premium rates. Under the regulations where a trader operates such a line for the purpose of consumers contacting the trader in relation to contracts, they must not be bound to pay more than the basic rate[120] for such telephone calls though there is no definition of the term "basic rate" either in the regulations or the Directive. The Government guidance states that it means not charging more to phone a trader about something you have bought than to call

10–93

---

[118] Consumer Contracts (Information, Cancellation and Additional Charges) Regulations 2013 reg.34.
[119] Consumer Contracts (Information, Cancellation and Additional Charges) Regulations 2013 reg.38.
[120] Consumer Contracts (Information, Cancellation and Additional Charges) Regulations 2013 reg.41.

a friend or relative, that is to say the simple cost of connection. Premium rate numbers that provide traders with a contribution to their costs are not permissible.[121]

10–94   Other sources of difficulty for consumers purchasing goods have been delay in delivery and a lack of clarity about who bears the risk if something goes wrong during delivery. Unless the trader and consumer have agreed different arrangements, the regulations provide that goods must be delivered without undue delay and in any event not more than 30 days after the date the contract is entered into.[122] The regulations provide that goods sent under a sales contract remain at the seller's risk until they come into the physical possession of either the consumer or someone identified by the consumer to take possession of them, for example, a neighbour or the recipient of a gift. This means that any damage done to, or loss of, the goods in transit to the consumer is the responsibility of the trader contracting to supply the goods, for example if goods are misdelivered, stolen from a doorstep or damaged in transit.[123] If, however, consumers have arranged for their own carrier to deliver the goods (this carrier not being nominated by the trader as a carrier for the consumer to select), then risk in the goods transfers to the consumer when the goods are delivered to that carrier.[124]

10–95   District councils have a duty to consider complaints. They may apply to the sheriff court or the Court of Session for an interdict or order of specific implement against a trader acting in breach of the regulations.

INSURANCE

10–96   Following disquiet about the practices of some insurance salesmen a cooling-off period in respect of ordinary long-term insurance business was introduced by the Insurance Companies Act 1982. This has been repealed and similar protection is now provided by the Conduct of Business Rules made by the Financial Conduct Authority under powers in the Financial Services and Markets Act 2000.[125] A consumer has 30 days in which to cancel a policy.

TIMESHARE AND RELATED PRODUCTS

10–97   Timeshare is a right to use accommodation at a holiday development or resort for a specified number of weeks each year over a specified period of time or in perpetuity. To acquire this right an "owner" pays a lump sum to a "developer". In

---

[121] See Department of Business Innovation and Skills, *Consumer Contracts (Information, Cancellation and Additional Charges) Regulations, Implementing Guidance* (December 2013), available on the BIS website.

[122] Consumer Contracts (Information, Cancellation and Additional Charges) Regulations 2013 reg.42.

[123] Consumer Contracts (Information, Cancellation and Additional Charges) Regulations 2013 reg.43.

[124] Consumer Contracts (Information, Cancellation and Additional Charges) Regulations 2013 reg.43(3) and (4).

[125] See Financial Conduct Authority, *Financial Conduct Authority Handbook* (ICOBS 7.1). Available (and updated on a daily basis) at *http://fshandbook.info/FS/html/FCA/ICOBS*[Accessed 22 June 2015].

addition, there are usually annual service charges and there may also be optional annual fees for participation in a scheme to exchange timeshares with others. A report[126] by the Director General of Fair Trading acknowledged that most timeshare owners were satisfied with their purchases. It also noted that there was also a great deal of evidence to suggest that all too often timeshare was not sold in a healthy market where well-informed consumers dealt with responsible traders. As a result the UK timeshare industry was first specifically regulated by the Timeshare Act 1992 with amending legislation being introduced when the first EC directive (Directive 94/47/EC) provided for the protection of consumers in respect of the sale of timeshare in real property. Given the minimum harmonisation nature of the Directive, a number of states, including the UK, adopted national provisions that went beyond the level of consumer protection required by the Directive. Since then, the provision of timeshare has evolved and new long term holiday products, such as holiday clubs, requiring similar levels of cost and commitment by consumers have appeared on the market. These new holiday products and certain other services related to timeshare, such as resale contracts and exchange contracts were originally not regulated under EU law or domestic law. In addition some areas already covered were in need of updating and clarification to prevent the development of products aimed at circumventing the regulatory regime. The existing regulatory gaps created appreciable distortions of competition and cause serious problems for consumers, hindering the smooth functioning of the internal market.[127] A new Directive was enacted in 2008[128] to create a simplified and coherent framework for the regulation of timeshare and long-term holiday products, as well as exchange and resale. The new Directive, which is a maximum directive, has been implemented in the UK by the Timeshare, Holiday Products, Resale and Exchange Contracts Regulations 2010 (the 2010 Regulations)[129] which came into force on 23 February 2011.

The approach of the regulations, like earlier legislation, is first to try to ensure **10–98** that consumers make a properly informed decision to buy a timeshare or other product, and then to give a period for reflection during which they can cancel the arrangement. Part 2 of the 2010 Regulations contains key definitions and describes the timeshare, long-term holiday product, resale and exchange contracts that are covered by these Regulations. Part 3 sets out the requirements that must be complied with before a trader enters into a regulated contract with a consumer. These include requirements relating to advertising and marketing and the information that must be provided to the consumer in good time before the contract is entered into on standard forms provided in schedules to the regulations.[130] Part 4 sets out requirements relating to the form and content of regulated contracts, including obligations to draw the attention of the consumer to matters relating to the right to withdrawal and the prohibition on advance consideration. Failure to do so will render the contract unenforceable against the

---

[126] Office of Fair Trading, *Timeshare* (OFT 1990) OFTO42.

[127] For example, OFT research on the impact of mass marketed scams found that bogus holiday club scams cost the UK public an estimated £1.17 billion each year, with a mean loss of £3,030 per victim, see Office of Fair Trading, *Research on impact of mass marketed scams*, (December 2006) OFT883.

[128] Directive 2008/122/EC on certain aspects of timeshare and long-term holiday products, 2009 O.J. L 33/10.

[129] Timeshare, Holiday Products, Resale and Exchange Contracts Regulations 2010 (SI 2010/2960).

[130] Timeshare, Holiday Products, Resale and Exchange Contracts Regulations 2010 reg.12(3)–(5).

consumer.[131] Both the pre-contract information and that relating to the contract must be in the language of the state in which the consumer is resident or of which they are a national.[132] Failure to provide such information is a criminal offence.[133] Part 5 makes provisions relating to the termination of a regulated contract, including the consumer's right to withdraw from the contract without penalty during a 14 day withdrawal or "cooling-off" period. Part 6 prohibits a trader from accepting payment from the consumer during the withdrawal period and makes provisions relating to the payment schedule for long-term holiday product contracts. Traders who fails to comply with regs 12, 14, 15 or 17 referred to above may also commit an offence under Pt 2 of the CPR 2008. The regulations are enforced by district councils and their breach can amount to community infringements under the 2002 Act.[134]

ESTATE AGENCY

10–99   Estate agency has been the subject of much criticism over many years because of the sharp practices of a minority of those involved in it.[135] The Estate Agents Act 1979 (the 1979 Act) controls certain aspects of the work of estate agents. Enforcement of the 1979 Act was under the overall supervision of the OFT, but following the recent changes to the consumer landscape, this is now in the hands of a "lead enforcement authority", currently the National Trading Standards Estate Agency Team of Powys County Council.[136] The 1979 Act does not control entry into the profession: instead, it creates a system of negative licensing. The Lead Enforcement Authority is given powers to ban persons from acting as estate agents if it finds that they are unfit to do so. The grounds which may render a person unfit are set out in s.3. They include convictions for fraud, dishonesty or violence; convictions for breach of the 1979 Act; failure to comply with other obligations under the 1979 Act; and discrimination.

10–100   In addition, the 1979 Act ss.12–21 impose duties on estate agents. They must give certain information about their charges and when these are payable. There is a duty to declare any conflict of interest or personal interest in the transaction. Where deposits are taken from a purchaser, there are duties relating to keeping the money in a clients' account. Failure to observe the duty to provide the client with information about charges results in the contract being unenforceable without the approval of the sheriff.[137]

Section 23A of the 1979 Act requires estate agents to be members of a redress scheme approved by the Secretary of State and three such schemes exist.

10–101   The unenforceability of contracts where the duty to provide the client with information about charges was discussed in *Solicitors Estate Agency (Glasgow)*

---

[131] Timeshare, Holiday Products, Resale and Exchange Contracts Regulations 2010 reg.16(4)(b).

[132] Timeshare, Holiday Products, Resale and Exchange Contracts Regulations 2010 regs 12 and 17.

[133] Timeshare, Holiday Products, Resale and Exchange Contracts Regulations 2010 regs 14(5) and 16(4a).

[134] These are discussed later in this chapter.

[135] See Director General of Fair Trading, *Estate Agency: A report by the Director-General of Fair Trading* (OFT 1990).

[136] See Estate Agents Act 1979 ss.3 and 26(1).

[137] Estate Agents Act 1979 s.18(6).

Ltd v MacIver.[138] A client refused to pay his estate agent's fees because an advertising discount obtained by the agent had not been disclosed. This breached both s.18(2)(a) and (d) of the 1979 Act as a failure to give details of any payment which is not part of the agent's remuneration but forms part of the payment to him, and a failure to give details of the method of calculating the advertising charges. The sheriff, before whom the client had argued only that there was a breach of s.18(2)(d), did not think it fair to refuse to enforce the payment but ordered the payment of approximately three-quarters of the fee. On appeal the sheriff principal stated that the deliberate policy of concealing the advertising discount would have justified refusing to enforce the contract but that the sheriff's decision was not such an erroneous exercise of his discretion as to merit being altered. However, as he found that two provisions of the section had been breached he considered that the degree of culpability was so high that it would not be just to enforce the contract at all. On appeal to the Inner House of the Court of Session it was held that the degree to which the sheriff had misdirected himself was not material and that the sheriff principal was not entitled to interfere with the exercise of his discretion. The sheriff's decision was therefore reinstated.

ADMINISTRATIVE METHODS

Traditional methods of consumer protection relying on individual action by consumers or the enforcement of criminal statutes do not always work. Neither the criminal law nor the invocation of the civil law by individual consumers are sufficient deterrents to the unfair conduct of some traders. Relatively small fines lead some traders to ignore criminal sanctions and treat the occasions when they are convicted as minor inconveniences. Some are prone to refuse to honour their civil obligations to consumers knowing that the chances of an action being raised against them are remote.   **10–102**

Since the enactment of the Fair Trading Act 1973 (the 1973 Act) powers have been given to a government agency and some other public bodies to deal with such traders by requiring them to change their behaviour. These powers are now to be found in Pt 8 of the 2002 Act.   **10–103**

ENTERPRISE ACT PART 8—ENFORCEMENT ORDERS

The enforcement order procedure set out in Pt 8[139] of the 2002 Act is designed to improve consumer protection by giving various enforcers strengthened powers to obtain court orders against traders who fail to comply with their legal obligations to consumers. It is important to note that it does not create new legal rights or obligations: it is an enforcement tool. The concept is not new: Pt 3 of the 1973 Act was designed to do something similar. It is nonetheless of great significance because it is designed to create a more consistent enforcement regime and it   **10–104**

---

[138] *Solicitors Estate Agency (Glasgow) Ltd v MacIver*, 1992 S.C. 315. See also the English cases of *Benhams Ltd v Kythira Investments Ltd* [2004] EWHC 2973 (QB) and *MSM Consulting Ltd v Tanzania* [2009] EWHC 121 (QB).
[139] Enterprise Act 2002, in force 20 June 2003.

widens the range of organisations that can use these powers. It is particularly significant that local authorities can exercise these powers and this provides a considerable challenge to trading standards departments, who hitherto have largely been concerned with the enforcement of the criminal law, and their legal advisers in local authorities for whom consumer protection is an unfamiliar area. They have a potentially powerful means of dealing with rogue traders.

10–105   Section 215 may be seen as the central provision of Pt 8 of the 2002 Act. It provides that an enforcer may seek an enforcement order by applying to the Court of Session or the sheriff. This may be done where the enforcer thinks that someone:

> "(a) has engaged or is engaging in conduct which constitutes a domestic or a Community infringement, or (b) is likely to engage in conduct which constitutes a Community infringement."

This raises many questions such as: what is the nature of an enforcement order; what are domestic and Community infringements; and who are "enforcers"?

10–106   Enforcement orders can be obtained to prevent both domestic and Community infringements. A domestic infringement is, to quote s.211(1):

> "[A]n act or omission which—
> (a)   is done or made by a person in the course of a business,
> (b)   falls within subsection (2), and
> (c)   harms the collective interests of consumers."

10–107   The definition has several elements. The first involves the definition of "business" that includes a professional practice, any other undertaking carried on for gain or reward and any undertaking in the course of which goods or services are supplied otherwise than free of charge.[140] The meaning of "consumer" for the purpose of a domestic infringement is slightly different from that in relation to Community infringements. For this purpose a consumer is one to whom:

> "[G]oods are or are sought to be supplied to the individual (whether by way of sale or otherwise) in the course of a business carried on by the person supplying or seeking to supply them, or ... services are or are sought to be supplied to the individual in the course of a business carried on by the person supplying or seeking to supply them."[141]

10–108   In addition, the individual must receive or seek to receive the goods or services otherwise than in the course of a business carried on by them. There is, however, an interesting extension to the range of consumers for this purpose. It also includes those who "receive the goods or services with a view to carrying on a business but not in the course of a business carried on by him".[142] This is designed to catch those who operate fraudulent homeworking schemes and vanity publishers.

10–109   To be a domestic infringement the act or omission must be one which falls within one of the paragraphs of the 2002 Act s.211(2). It sets out a number of

---

[140] See the Enterprise Act 2002 s.210(8).
[141] See the Enterprise Act 2002 s.210(3).
[142] See the Enterprise Act 2002 s.210(4).

kinds of conduct which the secretary of state can specify in more detail in a statutory instrument. These are very wide ranging, including breaches of civil and criminal law both statutory and common law. The current statutory order is the Enterprise Act 2002 (Part 8 Domestic Infringements) Order 2003.[143] It lists a large number of statutes including the familiar consumer protection statutes such as the Consumer Rights Act 2015 (the 2015 Act), the Consumer Protection Act 1987 and the CPR 2008; but also lists under the heading "Rules of Law", "[a]n act done or omission made in breach of contract for the supply of goods or services to a consumer" and, "[a]n act done or omission made in breach of a duty of care owed to a consumer under the law of tort or delict of negligence".[144] The result of this is that a very wide range of conduct can be subject to the controls on domestic infringements. To take a statutory example, breaches of the CPR 2008 which involve criminal offences could found applications for domestic infringements. In the field of civil law failure to observe the obligations in s.9 of the 2015 Act to provide goods of satisfactory quality could also amount to domestic infringements. As pointed out above, it is not only statute that provides examples of possible domestic infringements. Breaches of the common law obligation to carry out work with reasonable skill and care could also amount to domestic infringements.[145]

As the 2002 Act s.211(4) makes clear, the legal obligation breached does not **10–110** have to be one which applies specifically for consumers. For example, the list of statutes includes sections of the Charities Act 1992 that are not specifically consumer protection provisions, and Scots common law on contractual misrepresentation which is a part of the general law and not exclusively for the protection of consumers. The legislation does not have to contain any sanction for the benefit of consumers. It is not necessary for convictions to have been obtained where criminal offences are concerned or for legal proceedings to have been taken in civil cases. Particularly in the former case, an application will be strengthened if there are convictions, though the absence of civil actions by individual consumers will be of less moment as it is well known that there are many factors which deter all but the most determined consumers from resorting to the courts. The fact that a consumer has waived their contractual rights does not prevent reliance being placed on the breach. An example would be where a consumer decides to keep goods despite the fact that they were not supplied in the condition required by the contract.

The third element of the definition of domestic infringement is the meaning of **10–111** "the collective interests of consumers". What is meant by this will be discussed later as it is also relevant to Community infringements.[146]

The other kind of infringement that can justify an enforcement order is a **10–112** Community infringement. This part of the legislation implements the Injunctions

---

[143] Enterprise Act 2002 (Part 8 Domestic Infringements) Order 2003 (SI 2003/1593), in force 20 June 2003.
[144] See Enterprise Act 2002 (Part 8 Domestic Infringements) Order 2003 Sch.1 Pt III para.1.
[145] This was the case in *Office of Fair Trading v MB Designs (Scotland) Ltd*, 2005 S.L.T. 691; 2005 S.C.L.R. 894 which is discussed below.
[146] See para.10–117 and following.

Directive.[147] The Department of Trade and Industry's (a predecessor the BIS) consultation paper on implementation of the Directive explained its purpose succinctly:

"The purpose of the Directive is to permit consumer protection bodies to apply to the courts or competent administrative authorities both in their own and in other Member States for orders to stop traders infringing the legislation implementing ... specific consumer protection directives where these infringements harm the collective interests of consumers. It is not intended as a means of seeking redress for individual consumers."[148]

10–113   Section 212 of the 2002 Act defines a Community infringement. Like a domestic infringement, it is an act or omission which harms the collective interests of consumers. That harm must flow from a contravention of one of the Directives listed in Sch.13 to the 2002 Act as given effect to by the laws of an EEA state. It can also result from the contravention of aspects of these laws which go beyond the requirements of the Directive. This results from the fact that many Directives are what are called "minimum Directives". They provide that a state must ensure that its law reaches a certain minimum level but do not prevent states providing a higher level of protection. The Directive on Certain Aspects of the Sale of Goods and Associated Guarantees was of this kind which was important in the UK as it meant that it was possible to retain our existing level of protection which was, in most respects, better than that mandated by the Directive. Schedule 13 of the 2002 Act lists nine Directives all parts of which are included, and a further two of which parts contain provisions which can be the subject of Community infringements. The legislation implementing these Directives has been listed in an order made by the Secretary of State for Trade and Industry.[149]

10–114   The breach of legislation which may lead to domestic or Community enforcement orders is listed in statutory orders. For the most part legislation appears in one or other order. However, in the case of the Consumer Credit Act 1974 (the 1974 Act) it has been necessary to put the Act in both lists. This has been done because it is not possible to draw a clear distinction between some of the provisions of the Act that implement the Consumer Credit Directive[150] and others that are outside the scope of the Directive. To ensure that there are no omissions which might lead to gaps in the ability to enforce the 1974 Act using Pt 8 of the 2002 Act it appears in both lists. As a result enforcement orders based on either domestic or Community infringements are possible.

10–115   An example of a Community infringement could be misleading advertisements by a trader. This is because one of the Directives listed in the Injunctions

---

[147] Directive 98/27/EC of the Parliament and of the Council of 19 May 1998 on injunctions for the protection of consumers' interests.

[148] Department of Trade and Industry, *Injunctions Directive: Implementation in the UK* (2000).

[149] Enterprise Act 2002 (Part 8, Community Infringements Specified UK Laws) Order 2003 (SI 2003/1374).

[150] Directive 2008/48/EC of the European Parliament and of the Council of 23 April 2008 on credit agreements for consumers and repealing Council Directive 87/102EEC.

Directive[151] is the Unfair Commercial Practices Directive,[152] which was implemented in the UK by the CPR 2008.[153]

In the context of Community infringements "consumer" has a slightly different meaning from that for domestic infringements. Section 210(6) of the 2002 Act says that it means a person who is a consumer for the purpose of the Injunctions Directive[154] and the listed Directive concerned. The reference to the Injunctions Directive is something of a red herring as it contains no formal definition of "consumer" and the only guidance it gives is a reference to a consumer as an individual which is one element of the definition of "consumer" common to the listed Directives. There are slightly different definitions of "consumer" in the Directives. Most define consumer as "any natural person who ... is acting for purposes which are outside his trade, business or profession". The Consumer Sales Directive[155] speaks of a consumer as

> "any natural person who, in the contracts covered by this Directive, is acting for purposes which are not related to his trade, business or profession".

The Package Holiday Directive[156] does not use the term "consumer" but speaks of "any person".

As noted above, common to both types of infringement is the necessity to demonstrate that the "collective interests of consumers" have been harmed. There is no definition of what this phrase means in the 2002 Act but as Pt 8, at least in part, implements the Injunctions Directive[157] from which the phrase is taken it is legitimate to seek help there. Recital 2 does not take matters much further but at least it explains that these interests "do not include the cumulation of interests of individuals who have been harmed by an infringement". This emphasises the fact that enforcement orders are not designed to provide redress in individual cases even where a number of individuals have suffered loss. In other words, it is not intended to be a kind of class action on the American model. What it is intended to do is to provide a mechanism to alter the behaviour of traders which is, or is likely, to harm consumers as a group. It is not to be used against an inadvertent breach of the law, criminal or civil, rather it is intended to discipline those whose conduct is likely to harm all consumers with whom they come in contact.

In the Government's explanatory memorandum to the 2002 Act it was said:

> "For both Community and domestic infringements, the Department does not consider that harming the collective interests of consumers means that a large number of consumers must already have been harmed. The Department believes it simply

10–116

10–117

10–118

---

[151] Directive 98/27/EC of the Parliament and of the Council of 19 May 1998 on injunctions for the protection of consumers' interests.

[152] Directive 2005/29 of the European Parliament and of the Council of 11 May 2005 concerning unfair business-to-consumer commercial practices in the internal market.

[153] Consumer Protection from Unfair Trading Regulations 2008 (SI 2008/1277).

[154] Directive 98/27/EC of the Parliament and of the Council of 19 May 1998 on injunctions for the protection of consumers' interests.

[155] Directive 99/44/EC of the Parliament and of the Council of 25 May 1999 on certain aspects of the sale of consumer goods and associated guarantees.

[156] Directive 90/314/EC of the Parliament and of the Council of 13 June 1990 on package travel, package holidays and package tours.

[157] Directive 90/314/EC of the Parliament and of the Council of 13 June 1990 on package travel, package holidays and package tours, fn.19.

means that a continuation or repetition of an act or omission specified as a Community or domestic infringement could harm the collective interests of consumers, since the interests of future customers of the trader are actually or will potentially be affected."[158]

10–119 It goes on to point out that the fact that the product or service was of interest to only a small minority of consumers would not prevent the test of harm to the collective interests of consumers being met. It gives the example of expensive luxury goods.

10–120 It should be noted that, unlike the former Pt 3 procedure under the 1973 Act, there is no requirement to prove persistence. In practice this will often be the case because Pt 8 of the 2002 Act is not designed to sanction isolated breaches of the law. It will often be impossible to show that there is harm to the collective interests of consumers unless there has been a course of conduct that has been persisted in. This, however, will not always be the case and it will be possible to base an application for an enforcement order on one incident. For example, this might be the case where one complaint to a trading standards department reveals that a credit company is using forms which do not comply with the 1974 Act. This one incident would reveal a breach of the law which could be said to harm the interests of consumers in general. Similarly, where a company offering goods over the internet had a website which showed that it did not comply with the Consumer Contracts (Information, Cancellation and Additional Charges) Regulations 2013[159] this would seem to be enough to demonstrate that there was a Community infringement.

10–121 So far Pt 8 has been considered in only one reported case, *Office of Fair Trading v MB Designs (Scotland) Ltd*,[160] an Outer House decision of Lord Drummond Young. The company against whom an enforcement order was sought was a double glazing company and the OFT stated that in fitting and installing the goods they regularly failed to exercise the requisite level of skill and care of a reasonably competent installer of windows, doors and conservatories. The OFT produced affidavits from an officer of its Consumer Regulation Enforcement Division and a divisional trading standards officer employed by the local council. In a four-year period 299 complaints about the company had been received and a further 47 were recorded by Consumer Direct, the consumer telephone helpline. The company had refused to give an undertaking to the OFT to mend its ways and as a result an order was sought. The OFT contended that the company were guilty of repeated acts of breach of contract in relation to the supply of both goods and services which harmed the collective interests of consumers. Lord Drummond Young's judgment helpfully elucidates the meaning of the legislation especially the key phrase "collective interests of consumers". He found the French version of the Directive helpful and noted that a literal English translation would be that

---

[158] Enterprise Act 2002, explanatory memorandum, para.486. Available at *http://www.legislation. gov.uk/ukpga/2002/40/notes/division/4/8/1/3*[Accessed 22 June 2015].

[159] Consumer Contracts (Information, Cancellation and Additional Charges) Regulations 2013 (SI 2013/3134).

[160] *Office of Fair Trading v MB Designs (Scotland) Ltd*, 2005 S.L.T. 691; 2005 S.C.L.R. 894.

"by collective interests, one means interests which are not a *mere* accumulation of the interests of individuals to whom harm has been caused by an infringement" [emphasis in the original].[161]

He went on to say: **10–122**

"This makes it clear that the expression 'collective interests' is not something wholly separate from the interests of individual consumers who have been harmed by infringements. 'Collective interests' include those interests, but amount to something more than the mere aggregation of those interests. That makes perfectly good sense; it means that the adjective 'collective' denotes the generality of consumers, considered as a body, but at the same time recognises that the interests of individual consumers are part of those collective interests, and that harm to the collective interests will normally be inferred from a number of instances of harm to individual interests."[162]

He went on to add: **10–123**

"The notion of the collective interests of consumers, therefore, indicates that there must be harm or a risk of harm to the public generally, or more precisely to members of the public who may buy the particular goods or services in question. This is distinct from the rights that any particular consumer may have against his or her supplier, whether under the general law of contract or under statutory provisions such as the Supply of Goods and Services Act 1982 or the European directives listed in Schedule 13 to the 2002 Act. The collective interests of consumers, by contrast, are concerned not with the contractual rights of individual consumers but with general trading standards, and in particular with the general standard of goods or services supplied by a particular trader. Part 8 of the 2002 Act is designed to enforce such trading standards."[163]

This case gives useful guidance on the general approach to the interpretation   **10–124**
of "collective interests". The Injunctions Directive and the 2002 Act do not give any examples of interests that are to be protected though one can infer what these are from the list of Directives attached to the Injunctions Directive.[164] These are Directives designed to protect the safety, health and economic interests of consumers, *Office of Fair Trading v MB Designs (Scotland) Ltd* being a good example of a case where economic interests were involved. Health and safety are clearly covered by the Product Liability Directive[165] and the Directive on the Community code relating to medicinal products for human use.[166] The others are largely designed to protect the economic interests of consumers. The Television Advertising Directive[167] appears to extend the concept of collective interests with

---

[161] *MB Designs (Scotland) Ltd*, 2005 S.L.T. 691; 2005 S.C.L.R. 894 at [13].
[162] *MB Designs (Scotland) Ltd*, 2005 S.L.T. 691; 2005 S.C.L.R. 894 at [13].
[163] *MB Designs (Scotland) Ltd*, 2005 S.L.T. 691; 2005 S.C.L.R. 894 at [14].
[164] Directive 98/27/EC of the Parliament and of the Council of 19 May 1998 on injunctions for the protection of consumers' interests.
[165] Directive 85/374/EEC of 25 July 1985 on the approximation of the laws, regulations and administrative provisions of the Member States concerning liability for defective products.
[166] Directive 2001/83 on the Community code relating to medicinal products for human use [2001] O.J. L311/67.
[167] Directive 89/552 on the coordination of certain provisions laid down by law, regulation or administrative action in Member States concerning the pursuit of television broadcasting activities [1989] O.J. L298/23.

its references to ensuring that advertising does not offend human dignity and religious beliefs or involve discrimination. The list of domestic legislation set out in the order amplifying s.211(2) can be said to protect consumers' economic interests as well as their interests in health and safety.[168] The MB Designs case has been applied by the English Court of Appeal in *Office of Fair Trading v Miller*[169] where a six months suspended prison sentence and a fine of £90,000 imposed on a sole trader were considered appropriate.

10–125　　There are three types of enforcer: general, designated and Community. The general enforcers are the CMA, local weights and measures authorities in Great Britain (which means district councils in Scotland), and the Department of Enterprise, Trade and Investment in Northern Ireland. It is general enforcers who have the widest powers as s.215(2) provides that they can apply for enforcement orders in relation to both domestic and Community infringements. A designated enforcer is one which has been designated by the Secretary of State. This can only occur if they think that it has "as one of its purposes the protection of the collective interests of consumers". A public body may only be designated if it is independent. Guidance on designation and the current list of designated public bodies is contained in the Enterprise Act 2002 (Part 8 Designated Enforcers: Criteria for Designation, Designation of Public Bodies as Designated Enforcers and Transitional Provisions) Order 2003.[170] Those who have been designated so far are the Civil Aviation Authority, the Directors General of Electricity Supply and Gas for Northern Ireland, the Office of Communications, the Director General of Water Services, the Gas and Electricity Markets Authority, the Information Commissioner and the Rail Regulator. It is also possible for a person or body which is not a public body to be designated but so far this has not happened. These designated enforcers can only make applications for enforcement orders with respect to those infringements for which they have been designated. As it happens, all the current designated enforcers have been designated to deal with all types of infringements but it is quite possible that others may be given only limited rights.

10–126　　The result of this is that all these enforcers are able to deal with both types of infringement. This means that in addition to taking action in the courts of the UK they may also take action in other EEA states. In practice, it is much more likely that only the CMA will take action abroad as its predecessor, the OFT, did in 2004. It took action in the Belgian courts to stop a mail order company sending what it considered to be misleading mailings to UK consumers, contrary to the 1984 Misleading Advertising Directive.[171]

10–127　　The third type of enforcer is a Community enforcer which is a qualified entity for the purposes of the Injunctions Directive.[172] This means that it is a body listed in the *Official Journal of the European Communities*, but is not a general or a

---

[168] Enterprise Act 2002 (Part 8 Domestic Infringements) Order 2003 (SI 2003/1593).

[169] *Office of Fair Trading v Miller* [2009] EWCA Civ. 34.

[170] Enterprise Act 2002 (Part 8 Designated Enforcers: Criteria for Designation, Designation of Public Bodies as Designated Enforcers and Transitional Provisions) Order 2003 (SI 2003/1399).

[171] Directive 84/450/EEC of 10 September 1984 relating to the approximation of the laws, regulations and administrative provisions of the Member States concerning misleading advertising; OFT press release 6 April 2004.

[172] Directive 98/27/EC of the Parliament and of the Council of 19 May 1998 on injunctions for the protection of consumers' interests.

designated enforcer. It will therefore apply only to enforcers from other EEA states. Community enforcers can apply for enforcement orders only in relation to Community infringements and the court to which they apply "may examine whether the purpose of the enforcer justifies its making the application".[173]

While, ultimately, an enforcer can apply to a court to obtain an enforcement order the legislation is designed to try to ensure that this may not be necessary. Section 214 provides that before making a court application the enforcer must show that appropriate consultation has been engaged in with the trader and the CMA, though this can dispensed with if the CMA thinks that an application should be made without delay. The purpose of this consultation is two-fold. In the case of consultation with the trader the purpose is to seek to resolve the problem without going to court. This might well lead to the matter being resolved by the trader giving the sort of voluntary undertaking envisaged in s.219 of the 2002 Act. Under the Pt 3 procedure under the 1973 Act the Director General of Fair Trading had a duty to consult traders which was one of the problem areas in that scheme. This has been avoided in this procedure by providing that the consultation period need only last 14 days, or seven days in the case of an interim enforcement order. The point of requiring consultation with the CMA is to assist the CMA's co-ordinating role. Section 216 provides that the CMA can direct that only it should make the application or direct which enforcer should make the application. This would avoid multiple applications relating to the same trader. **10–128**

In its guidance on Pt 8 the CMA has stated: **10–129**

> "[I]t will follow the principle that action under Part 8 should be taken by the most appropriate body and will encourage others to do the same. This means that, in nearly all cases, where local or sectoral action is required to prevent what is a local or sectoral problem, the relevant local or sectoral enforcer will take the action. Where the coordination procedure reveals that a number of enforcers are contemplating action against a single business, the OFT may direct which enforcer should bring the proceedings or that only the OFT may do so. This will avoid the possibility of simultaneous multiple actions against a business failing to comply with the relevant legislation."[174]

If it is not possible to resolve the issue informally, s.217 governs the powers of a court to make an enforcement order. There is a slight difference between the requirements for making an order based on a domestic, and one based on a Community, infringement. To make the former it must be shown that the trader "has engaged or is engaging in conduct which constitutes the infringement",[175] whereas in the case of a Community infringement the order can also be granted if the court finds that the trader "is likely to engage in conduct which constitutes the infringement".[176] The legislation was drafted in this way because the Government took the view that this was necessary to comply with the Injunctions Directive.[177] **10–130**

---

[173] Enterprise Act 2002 s.215(6).

[174] The Competition and Market Authority has adopted the OFT's guidance which appears on its website, see Office of Fair Trading, *Enforcement of Consumer Protection Legislation* (OFT 2003) para.3.76.

[175] See Enterprise Act 2002 s.215(1)(a).

[176] See Enterprise Act 2002 s.215(1)(b).

[177] Directive 98/27/EC of the Parliament and of the Council of 19 May 1998 on injunctions for the protection of consumers' interests.

10–131   In deciding whether to make an order a court will take into account whether the trader has given an undertaking or has failed to comply with an undertaking. Instead of making an order the court may accept an undertaking. Both the order and the undertaking can include a requirement that the trader publish a statement about the terms of the order or undertaking or a corrective statement if these are thought necessary for the purpose of eliminating any continuing effects of the infringement.[178] This could be particularly useful where the infringement has taken the form of misleading advertising. In an interesting departure from normal practice s.217(12) provides that an enforcement order made in one part of the UK applies in all other parts. Normally, interdicts or injunctions apply only in the part of the UK in which they are obtained.

10–132   Section 80 of the 2015 Act adds "enhanced consumer measures" (ECMs) to the existing enforcement provisions.[179] They are intended to provide greater flexibility for enforcers investigating suspected breaches of consumer law. They can either be agreed with businesses (by way of an undertaking) or imposed by a court by an enforcement order. The draft Guidance[180] to this part of the Bill states that in many cases the use of ECMs on their own will be sufficient, but enforcers will also be able to bring both criminal and civil proceedings where offences are serious enough to warrant such a "two-pronged" approach.

10–133   There are three types of ECM: redress; compliance; and choice.[181] When deciding which measures to implement, enforcement authorities should give consideration to what measure would be "just, reasonable and proportionate" in the particular circumstances.[182] However, the legislation does not include a list of measures for each of the categories proposed. This is to allow enforcers as much flexibility as possible in devising appropriate measures. Enforcers are expected to work with businesses to agree the appropriate enforcement measure to adopt. In more detail the ECMs are as follows.

Redress

10–134   Measures under this heading are based on the principle of refunding consumers who have suffered a loss due to the actions of a business in breach of consumer law.[183] Such measures will only be available when a consumer has suffered a loss. When considering a redress measure, enforcers must take into account: the likely benefit to the consumer, the cost likely to be incurred by the business in question, and the likely cost to consumers to obtain the benefit of the measure. The redress measures also allow for a group of consumers to be refunded collectively. The BIS guidance note explains that where some consumers cannot

---

[178] Enterprise Act 2002 s.217(9).
[179] The ECMs are not retrospective see Consumer Rights Act 2015 s.80(2).
[180] See Department of Business, Innovation and Skills, *Enhanced Consumer Measures: Guidance for Enforcers of Consumer Law* available on the BIS website. At the time of writing this is in draft on *https://bisgovuk.citizenspace.com/* [Accessed 22 June 2015]. By the time that the Consumer Rights Act 2015 comes into effect in October 2015 a final version will be on the main BIS website.
[181] Enterprise Act 2002 s.219A.
[182] This is the effect of the Enterprise Act 2002 s.219B.
[183] Enterprise Act 2002 s.219A(2).

be identified in such a scenario, an enforcer can seek a measure to require the business to pay the equivalent of the loss suffered to a consumer charity.[184]

Compliance

This type of measure is designed to prevent or reduce the risk of a business committing further breaches of consumer law.[185] Appropriate enforcement measures should take into account factors such as the size of a business, and the impact the measures may have on that business. Examples provided in the guidance include additional training for staff members and appointing a compliance officer to ensure there is no further breach of consumer law.

10–135

Choice

Also termed "information" in the BIS draft guidance, the

10–136

> "measures in the choice category are measures intended to enable consumers to choose more effectively between persons supplying or seeking to supply goods or services".[186]

The BIS guidance indicates that they are intended to enable consumers to access information in relation to a business's past performance and allow enforcers to seek an order requiring a business to give customers greater information on the business's past compliance with consumer law. An example in the BIS Guidance suggests an order could be made against a business requiring it to publish past breaches of consumer law on their website or via social media.

In addition to the person against whom the order is made or an undertaking obtained, which will often be a limited company, someone who consented to or connived at the conduct may also have action taken against them as accessories.[187] Orders against companies can also apply to other companies in the same group.[188] In all these cases failure to obey a court order or undertaking will be contempt of court. This means that a trader will face fines or even imprisonment as occurred in some cases under the old Pt 3 procedure under the 1973 Act.

10–137

The former procedure under the 1973 Act was criticised for not having any provisions enabling the OFT to obtain information. This has been rectified in Pt 8 of the 2002 Act, where s.224 provides powers for the CMA to require a person to provide information. This can be to enable the CMA to exercise or consider whether to exercise its functions under Pt 8 or to enable a Community enforcer or a designated enforcer other than one which is a public body to do so. Other general enforcers and designated enforcers who are public bodies are given similar powers in s.225.

10–138

The *MB Designs (Scotland) Ltd* case gives useful guidance on the nature of an enforcement order. Counsel for the company had argued that if an order were to

10–139

---

[184] Enterprise Act 2002 s.219A(2)(c).
[185] Enterprise Act 2002 s.219A(3).
[186] Enterprise Act 2002 s.219A(4).
[187] See Enterprise Act 2002 s.222.
[188] See Enterprise Act 2002 s.223.

be made against it, it should meet the standards of precision required of interdicts. Lord Drummond Young did not agree, saying:

"That degree of precision is clearly essential in proceedings designed to vindicate a private right, where exact definition of the right is both possible and necessary. Where a trading standard is to be enforced, however, I am of opinion that the same degree of precision is not necessary; nor indeed does it appear possible. The critical point is that the enforcement of provisions such as Pt 8 is not designed to ensure that no defective goods or services are ever supplied; it is rather designed to compel traders to achieve an acceptably low incidence of defects, and to rectify such defects as appear. Any court order of that nature must involve some degree of vagueness about the permissible incidence of defects. The order may also bear some degree of imprecision as to the nature of the defects that are prohibited. This is because the function of trading standards legislation is to minimise defects of every sort, and in cases where management or quality control is poor such defects may take many forms."[189]

10–140   To the argument that an order that was not precise would place the company in danger of inadvertent breach and thus to the penalties for contempt of court the judge pointed out that it would require more than an isolated incident to amount to a breach. In any event, depending on the seriousness of any breach nothing more than a warning might be appropriate.

CONSUMER PROTECTION CO-OPERATION REGULATION

10–141   The Regulation on Consumer Protection Cooperation[190] was adopted by the European Communities in 2004 to stop dishonest practices of traders targeting consumers living in other EU countries. It lays down the framework and general conditions under which Member States are to co-operate. The Regulation sets up an EU-wide network of national enforcement authorities with similar investigation and enforcement powers. Under the new system, each of these authorities is able to call on other members of the network for assistance in investigating possible breaches of consumer laws and in taking action against rogue traders. The network will tackle breaches of consumer law in a variety of areas such as package holidays, timeshares, distance selling and unfair commercial practices. Each Member State must have a single liaison office. This is the public authority in each Member State which has ultimate responsibility for applying the Consumer Protection Co-operation Regulation in their country. In the UK, the CMA will be the single liaison office. In addition, in each Member State there are "competent authorities". These are the public authorities (whether at national, regional or local level) which have specific responsibilities to enforce the laws which protect consumers' interests. In the UK, competent authorities will include the CMA, the Civil Aviation Authority and the Medicines and Health Regulation Authority.

---

[189] *MB Designs (Scotland) Ltd*, 2005 S.L.T. 691; 2005 S.C.L.R. 894 at [16].
[190] Regulation 2006/2004 on cooperation between national authorities responsible for the enforcement of consumer protection laws [2004] O.J. L364/1.

SELF-REGULATION

It has been recognised for some time that law is not the only way in which the goals of consumer protection can be achieved. There has been a good deal of interest in self-regulation by those involved in various industries who agree to take steps to put their own houses in order. It is argued that codes are more flexible than statutes in that they can be altered more easily; those who know the problems of the sector intimately can design them; and they shift the cost of regulation from the state to the private sector. It is also argued that members of a trade association are more likely to comply with rules in a code whose drafting they have been able to influence. On the other hand, they can only affect those who adhere to them through membership of the relevant trade association, and it may well be that the sort of trader who most requires to improve the standards of their business is not likely to be a member of a trade association. Even among members of a trade association it may be difficult to attain high levels of compliance; and it is not always the case that trade associations devote much effort to ensuring compliance with their codes. Enforcement also depends on a willingness to discipline members from time-to-time, and to publicise this. There is also the potentially anti-competitive effect of codes in that where they are most widespread in their coverage they may inhibit consumer choice. It is difficult to know how successful such codes have been. Research carried out for the OFT has suggested that codes do result in a reduction in undesirable trading practices, such as the use of exclusion clauses.[191] However, the achievements of these codes have been limited, as the OFT itself recognised.[192]

10–142

Under the original version of the 1973 Act the OFT was empowered to encourage the development of codes and a number were created. In 2001 the OFT withdrew its support from all existing codes and announced the Consumer Codes Approval Scheme (CCAS), a more rigorous approach to approving codes. This involved a two stage process for approval where stage 1 required the OFT to be convinced by the code sponsor that the code met the core criteria, and would be likely to be of practical benefit to consumers and good traders. Stage 2 required the sponsor to provide evidence that the code was operating effectively after which it would be permitted to use the OFT seal of approval. This process which took about two years did not attract a great deal of interest from industry. In April 2012, the BIS invited the Trading Standards Institute (TSI) to establish a successor to the OFT CCAS on a self-funding basis from April 2013. This they did and management of the scheme has now been transferred to the Consumer Codes Approval Board (CCAB) operated by TSI.

10–143

Like the OFT's scheme there is a two-stage approval process designed to ensure that the code sponsor will adhere to set code criteria including: the provision of clear pre-contractual information; protection of prepayments; dealing with consumers in their own home; monitoring procedures; and independent dispute resolution schemes. A code sponsor is the organisation, firm

10–144

---

[191] JF Pickering and DC Cousins, *The Economic Implications of Codes of Practice* (Manchester: UMIST, 1980).

[192] Office of Fair Trading, *Raising Standards of Consumer Care: Progressing beyond codes of practice* (OFT, 1998) OFT 206; *Review of Impact on business of the Consumer Codes Approval Scheme: A report for the OFT by the Centre for Economics and Business Research Ltd (CEBR) with Opinion Research Business* (OFT 870: London, 2006).

or entity that administers and promotes a voluntary code of practice (as opposed to statutory codes) and can influence and raise standards within its membership. It must be a distinct entity from its membership.[193] Potential sponsors may make an expression of interest and, if the TSI's due diligence procedures are satisfied, they will be given stage one approval if they present a code of practice that is capable of meeting all of the relevant core criteria. At this stage, they will be able to share their "working towards full approval" status with stakeholders (such as government or regulators) but are not permitted to display the TSI approved code logo. Stage two approval is given to sponsors who demonstrate that their code is working well in practice. At this point code sponsors and their members are permitted to display the TSI approved code logo. Currently there are 12 code sponsors of which five relate to aspects of the motor trade and others are the British Association of Removers, British Healthcare Trades Association, Debt Managers Standards Association, Institute of Professional Willwriters, the Carpet Foundation, the Property Ombudsman and the Renewable Energy Consumer Code.

10–145   In addition, some other codes have been developed outwith this scheme by other sectors. Two well-known examples are those of the advertising industry[194] and the Association of British Travel Agents. There are also local schemes such as the Trusted Trader schemes operated by local trading standards departments.

---

[193] See TSI, Consumer Codes Approval Scheme: Core criteria and guidance available on the TSI website *http://www.tradingstandards.gov.uk* [Accessed 22 June 2015].
[194] See, various advertising codes at *https://www.cap.org.uk/Advertising-Codes.aspx* [Accessed 7 July 2015].

CHAPTER 11

Advertising

INTRODUCTION

Much skill and expense is devoted to persuading consumers to purchase goods **11–01**
and services, and the role of advertising in our economic system is recognised as
being important, if controversial. It is essential that advertising be accurate, and
thus there is a good deal of legal regulation of this area. The major problems do
not concern blatant falsehood but the more subtle issues of claims that are
ambiguous or misleading or offend against decency or good taste.

Much of the statutory control of advertising is of a negative character. **11–02**
However, there are a number of Acts which require that advertisers provide
consumers, or potential consumers, with information that will assist them to make
a rational purchasing decision. Examples of such provisions that are discussed
below are to be found in the legislation on food and drugs, weights and measures
and consumer credit legislation.

ROLE OF THE COMMON LAW

The common law has traditionally tended to ignore advertising. The blatantly **11–03**
false advertisement would, almost certainly, involve criminal liability for fraud,
and might give rise to a civil action for fraudulent misrepresentation. This is not,
however, the usual kind of case. The common law has taken a tolerant attitude
towards sellers' statements promoting their products. Its watchwords have been
simplex commendatio non obligat (a mere recommendation does not bind). This
does seem to have been taken too far on occasions.[1] However, the fact is that in
some circumstances a statement will not be regarded as giving rise to legal
consequences.

Despite this laxity in the law, it is possible that statements made about the **11–04**
goods or services by the seller can have legal consequences. As we shall see later,
if the statement is considered to have contractual effect the contractual remedies
for breach will apply. If the offending statement does not form part of the contract
but is what lawyers call a "mere representation" there are still remedies available
to the consumer under the heading of misrepresentation.

To attract legal liability for misrepresentation a statement must be material and **11–05**
made in the course of negotiations. It must also be a statement of fact and not one

---

[1] S Mullins, "An Analysis of Simplex Commendation in Modern Society" (1984) 101 S.A.L.J. 515.

of opinion.[2] Generally, silence will not amount to a misrepresentation but in some circumstances the parties do owe each other a duty to disclose. One of the best known examples of these contracts, uberrimae fidei (of the utmost good faith), arises in insurance where it is the duty of the insured to make full disclosure when requesting insurance.[3]

11–06 The law recognises three types of misrepresentation: fraudulent; negligent; and innocent. Fraudulent misrepresentation occurs where the maker of the statement was aware that their statements were untrue, or made them recklessly, heedless of whether they were true or false, or did not believe them to be true.[4] If fraud can be proved, not only is the contract void, that is, it has no effect, but also the victim may sue for damages.

11–07 Negligent misrepresentations occur where one party has failed to take reasonable care in making a statement in circumstances where the law says that there is a duty of care to do so. This is an area of law which has developed since the House of Lords decision in *Hedley Byrne & Co Ltd v Heller & Partners Ltd*.[5] In Scotland, until the enactment of s.10 of the Law Reform (Miscellaneous Provisions) (Scotland) Act 1985, it was not clear whether damages were available for such misrepresentations. That provision now makes it clear that this is the case.

11–08 An innocent misrepresentation is one that is made in the belief that it is true. The only remedy is to reduce the contract, which can only be done if action is taken without delay and it is possible to restore the parties to their original positions. In addition, the rights of third parties must not have been affected.[6]

11–09 Given the limitations on the remedies relating to misrepresentations, it is better to be able to show that a statement is a term of the contract rather than a representation that induced it. Distinguishing between terms and representations is not easy, but the test is what the parties intended. This in turn appears to depend on the stage at which the statement was made, whether an oral statement was put into writing, and whether the person who made the statement had special knowledge. In *Scott v Steel*[7] a statement about the soundness of a horse made by the seller at the time of sale to clinch the sale was held to be a term of the contract. On the other hand, in *Malcolm v Cross*[8] a gap of almost two months between the statement about the condition of a horse and the making of a contract for its sale resulted in the statement not being regarded as part of the contract.[9]

11–10 In England, the cases of *Oscar Chess Ltd v Williams*[10] and *Dick Bentley Productions Ltd v Harold Smith (Motors) Ltd*[11] have been explained on the basis that in one the maker of the statement was an innocent private individual with no

---

[2] *Bisset v Wilkinson* [1927] A.C. 177.

[3] See *H Demetriodes & Co v Northern Assurance Co Ltd (The Spathari)*, 1925 S.C. (H.L.) 6. For discussion of the concept of unfairness in the legislation on unfair terms in the Consumer Rights Act 2015, see Ch.9.

[4] *Derry v Peek* (1889) 14 App. Cas. 337.

[5] *Hedley Byrne & Co Ltd v Heller & Partners Ltd* [1964] A.C. 465.

[6] See *Boyd & Forest v Glasgow & South-Western Railway*, 1912 S.C. (H.L.) 93.

[7] *Scott v Steel* (1857) 20 D. 253.

[8] *Malcolm v Cross* (1898) 25 R. 389.

[9] See also *Matthew Paul & Co Ltd v Corporation of the City of Glasgow* (1900) 3 F. 119.

[10] *Oscar Chess Ltd v Williams* [1957] 1 W.L.R. 370; [1957] 1 All E.R. 325.

[11] *Dick Bentley Productions Ltd v Harold Smith (Motors) Ltd* [1965] 1 W.L.R. 623; [1965] 2 All E.R. 65.

specialist knowledge of cars, while in the other the statement was made by a motor dealer. The dealer's statement was a term of the contract: the private individual's was not.

As we saw in Ch.10, from October 2014 there are statutory civil remedies available to consumers who lose money because misleading or aggressive practices which are breaches of the Consumer Protection from Unfair Trading Regulations 2008 (CPR 2008). These will often cover the same ground as the common law remedies just discussed and are far preferable as they are much more straightforward. Reference should be made to the earlier discussion. **11–11**

IMPLIED TERMS ABOUT DESCRIPTION

The implied term about description found in the Consumer Rights Act 2015 (the 2015 Act) is relevant to advertising. Section 11 of the 2015 Act provides that where there is a sale by description there is an implied term that the goods will correspond with the description and certain other pre-contract information. If the sale is by sample, as well as by description, it is not sufficient that the bulk of the goods correspond with the sample if the goods do not also correspond with the description. In the case of digital content there is a similar provision in s.38 of the Act. The 2015 Act does not use the terminology of implied terms as the Sale of Goods Acts did for decades. However, the effect is the same. **11–12**

Sales are by description in a wide range of situations. An obvious example, in a consumer context, is provided by mail order purchasing where the buyer relies on the description in a catalogue or an advertisement in a newspaper or magazine. As s.11(3) makes clear, the fact that the goods are seen and selected by the buyer does not prevent the sale being one by description. Many goods are packaged and the buyer relies on the label or packaging for identification of the product. *Beale v Taylor*,[12] a case under the Sale of Goods Act 1979, extended this to a situation where the purchaser had examined the goods. Mr Taylor had placed an advertisement for a car in a newspaper, describing the car as "Herald, convertible, white, 1961". After examining the car, Mr Beale decided to buy it. In fact, the car was an amalgamation of a 1961 Herald and another of a different year which had been welded together and was in a very dangerous condition. As this was a private sale, Mr Beale could not rely on the quality terms in s.14 [ss.9 and 10 of the 2015 Act], so he had to resort to the term about description. The English Court of Appeal held that the words "1961 Herald" formed part of the description which had not been complied with. **11–13**

The modern tendency is to draw a distinction between disputes about quality, which should be reserved for what is now s.9 of the 2015 Act, and those about the identity of the goods, which are appropriate to s.11. This has been asserted in two Scottish decisions; *Britain Steamship Co Ltd v Lithgows Ltd*[13] and *Border Harvesters Ltd v Edwards Engineering (Perth) Ltd*.[14] **11–14**

---

[12] *Beale v Taylor* [1967] 1 W.L.R. 1193.
[13] *British Steamship Co Ltd v Lithgows Ltd*, 1975 S.C. 110.
[14] *Border Harvesters Ltd v Edwards Engineering (Perth) Ltd*, 1985 S.L.T. 128.

11-15 As *Beale v Taylor*[15] demonstrates, almost any words describing the goods will be regarded as part of the description. Strict compliance with description has been enforced in some cases.[16] However, as the unusual facts of *Harlingdon and Leinster Enterprises Ltd v Christopher Hull Fine Art Ltd*[17] demonstrate, there are limits. This case resulted from the sale of a painting which the defendants had purchased some time earlier when it had been described as being by the German artist, Munter. On the plaintiff, a specialist in German art, expressing interest in it the defendant emphasised that he did not know much about it, his particular expertise being in a different school of painting. The Court of Appeal held that it must be the intention of the parties that the description should be relied on. On the facts of this case that could not be said to have occurred.[18]

CONTRACTUAL CONSEQUENCES OF ADVERTISEMENTS AND SHOP DISPLAYS

11-16 The general rule is that advertisements, like shop displays, are regarded as invitations to treat and are not to be considered in contractual terms as offers which, when accepted, give rise to contracts. There does not appear to be any Scottish authority on the status of shop displays. The leading cases are two English cases where, in criminal proceedings, this was the central issue. In *Pharmaceutical Society of Great Britain v Boots Cash Chemists (Southern) Ltd*[19] certain drugs which, under the Pharmacy and Poisons Act 1933 (the 1933 Act), had to be sold by or under the supervision of a registered pharmacist had been sold in a Boots pharmacy that operated a self-service system. Customers selected their purchases from shelves on which the drugs were displayed, put them into a shopping basket supplied by Boots, and took them to a cash desk at one of the two exits. There they paid the price and it was at this stage that a registered pharmacist supervised the transaction. To avoid liability under the 1933 Act, Boots had to prove that supervision took place at the point of sale. It was held by the English Court of Appeal that the contract was made, not when the customer put the goods in the basket, but when the cashier accepted the offer to buy and received the price.

11-17 *Fisher v Bell*[20] involved a shop window display. Mr Bell displayed a "flick knife" in his shop window together with a price ticket. He was charged with the offence of offering the knife for sale contrary to s.1(1) of the Restriction of Offensive Weapons Act 1959. The justices found that no offence had been committed and the prosecutor appealed. It was held that no offence had been committed. The phrase "offer for sale" must be interpreted in the light of the law of contract, and a display in a shop window with a price ticket was an invitation to treat, not an offer to sell which, if accepted, would produce a binding contract.

11-18 There is good reason for this to be the law. Otherwise, if a display were an offer the shop would be bound to supply anyone who offered the price. This

---

[15] *Beale v Taylor* [1967] 1 W.L.R. 1193.
[16] See *Arcos v EA Ronaasen & Son* [1933] A.C. 470.
[17] *Harlingdon and Leinster Enterprises Ltd v Christopher Hull Fine Art Ltd* [1990] 1 All E.R. 737.
[18] Applied in *Drake v T Agnew & Sons Ltd* [2002] EWHC 294.
[19] *Pharmaceutical Society of Great Britain v Boots Cash Chemists (Southern) Ltd* [1952] 2 Q.B. 795.
[20] *Fisher v Bell* [1961] 1 Q.B. 394.

could create problems where the displayed item had been reserved for someone else or its sale was restricted in some way, as is the case with alcohol and cigarettes.

There is a similar rationale behind the rule that advertisements are presumed to be invitations to treat. Were it otherwise, traders who misjudged demand would find themselves in breach of contract. However, it is quite possible for an advertisement to constitute an offer, as Lord Kinnear acknowledged in *Hunter v General Accident Fire and Life Assurance Corporation Ltd* when he said: **11–19**

> "It is suggested that this is making a contract by an advertisement, but it is none the worse for being an advertisement if it is a distinct and definite offer unconditionally accepted."[21]

In that case the defenders had inserted a coupon in a diary, inviting purchasers to avail themselves of accident insurance by completing and returning the coupon together with a small fee. The Inner House and the House of Lords regarded this advertisement as an offer. **11–20**

The classic case of an exception from the rule that advertisements are presumed to be invitations to treat is the English case of *Carlill v Carbolic Smoke Ball Co Ltd*,[22] where a manufacturer placed an advertisement in a newspaper inviting the public to purchase its product, a smoke ball, which, it asserted, would prevent influenza. The advertisement included a promise to pay £100 to anyone who contracted influenza after using the ball as instructed. The advertisement went on to emphasise the company's sincerity by stating that £1,000 had been deposited with a bank. Mrs Carlill used the smoke ball as instructed but contracted influenza. She was held to be entitled to recover £100 from the company because their promise in the advertisement was intended to be legally binding and was sufficiently precise to be enforced. **11–21**

While the facts of *Carlill* may be regarded as highly unusual, the principles underlying it do have modern applications. For example, the not uncommon situation where a retailer offers to refund part of the price if the purchaser discovers that an article could have been purchased more cheaply elsewhere would be decided on similar principles. **11–22**

STATUTORY CONTROL

Until the implementation of the European Communities Directive on Misleading Advertising[23] by the Control of Misleading Advertisements Regulations 1988 (the 1988 Regulations)[24] there was no general prohibition on false or misleading advertising in the UK. Those regulations have now been repealed by the CPR **11–23**

---

[21] *Hunter v General Accident Fire and Life Assurance Corporation Ltd*, 1909 S.C. 344 at 353. This passage was approved by Lord Shaw in *A & G Paterson Ltd v Highland Railway*, 1927 S.C. (H.L.) 32 at 46.

[22] *Carlill v Carbolic Smoke Ball Co Ltd* [1893] 1 Q.B. 256.

[23] Directive 84/450/EEC of 10 September 1984 relating to the approximation of the laws, regulations and administrative provisions of the Member States concerning misleading advertising later amended by the Directive 97/55 to include comparative advertising.

[24] Control of Misleading Advertisements Regulations 1988 (SI 1988/915) as amended.

2008 which implement the Unfair Commercial Practices Directive. The new regulations go much further than regulating advertising but an important part of their function is to control false and misleading advertising. In the previous chapter the CPR 2008 were discussed in detail so at this point only their relevance to the control of advertising will be discussed.

11–24   Their importance in this respect is very considerable. Some idea of this can be gained from noting some of the legislation that they replace. In addition to replacing the 1988 Regulations, both the Trade Descriptions Act 1968 and the price marking provisions contained in Pt 3 of the Consumer Protection Act 1987 (the 1987 Act) are repealed by the CPR 2008. In addition, a number of other statutory provisions have had to be amended. However, it should be remembered that there are limitations on the scope of the Directive and therefore legislation governing some aspects of advertising is not affected. For this reason, having discussed the impact of the CPR 2008, other statutory controls on advertising will be looked at.

11–25   That the CPR 2008 cover advertising is clear from the definition of "commercial practice" in reg.2 which is:

> "[A]ny act, omission, course of conduct, representation or commercial communication (including advertising and marketing) by a trader, which is directly connected with the promotion, sale or supply of a product to or from a consumer, whether occurring before, during or after a commercial transaction in relation to a product ... "

The regulations go on to ban unfair practices generally. This has been referred to as a safety net provision which can regulate practices which are not otherwise controlled. To demonstrate that an advertisement is unfair in this sense it must be shown that "it contravenes the requirements of professional diligence" and "materially distorts or is likely to materially distort the economic behaviour of the average consumer ... ".[25] It is more likely that one of the other controls will normally be invoked. Schedule 1 of the CPR 2008 contains a list of banned practices most of which either directly affect advertising or are capable of doing so. The first four banned practices deal with false claims about membership of codes or practice or endorsements. Such claims could well appear in advertisements. Paragraphs 5 and 6 deal with "bait" and "bait and switch" advertising, CPR 2008 Sch.1 paras (7) with time limited offers, (15) with closing down sales, (16) with claims about games of chance and (17) with claims about illness cures. Claims about "free" gifts are dealt with by CPR 2008 Sch.1 paras (20) and (31) deals false claims that the recipient of the advertisement has won a prize. Paragraph (28) bans a direct exhortation in an advertisement to children to buy an advertised product or persuade their parents or other adults to buy it for them. The advantage of using one of the banned practices to challenge an advertisement from the point of view of an enforcer is that such practices are automatically unfair. There is no need to prove that the average consumer has been deceived or would have acted differently if the claim had not been made.

11–26   An advertisement might constitute an unfair practice because it was an "unfair action" as defined in CPR 2008 reg.5. It will do so if it contains false information about a range of factors set out in paras (4) and (5) such as its existence, price and

---

[25] See discussion at para.10–41 onwards.

main characteristics. Information need not be false: it will be enough if the overall presentation deceives or is likely to deceive the average consumer. The Office of Fair Tradings's (OFT) draft guidance[26] on the regulations gives an example of such an advertisement. A trader advertises televisions for sale stating that the price has been substantially discounted. In fact, they have only been on sale at the non-discounted price in very small numbers for a short time in one of the trader's large chain of shops. The advertisement may be factually correct but it is likely to be considered deceptive. The average consumer would have been deceived about the existence of a specific price advantage in a way that would be likely to cause him or her to take a different decision about it, namely, to buy it.

An unfair action can also occur if the marketing of a product (which includes comparative advertising) creates confusion with another trader's products, trademarks or trade names. In addition, it must be shown that as a result of the unfair action the average consumer would have taken a different decision.

11–27

A practice may be unfair not because it contains some false claim but because of what it does not say. This is covered by reg.6 which deals with practices that are unfair because they contain misleading omissions. Clearly there can be overlap with CPR 2008 reg.5. An advertisement containing a half-truth might be considered a misleading action because the overall impression is misleading or a misleading omission because of what it does not say. Under reg.6 a practice can be unfair because it hides material information, provides material information in a manner that is unclear, unintelligible, ambiguous or untimely, or fails to identify its commercial intent. It must also be shown that this causes the average consumer to make a different decision. What is material will depend on the context of the advertisement. It is easier to include a good deal of information in a full page newspaper advertisement than in the small advertisement columns of a magazine. Where the medium imposes limitations of space and time other measures taken by the advertiser will be relevant to determining whether the information omitted is material. For example, TV advertisements are usually brief and it may not be possible to include all material information. If the advertisement directed viewers to a website where further information could be obtained this might prevent the advertisement being considered unfair.

11–28

Misleading omissions go beyond simply omitting information or presenting it in a way that is unintelligible, ambiguous or unclear. CPR 2008 reg.6 goes some way to prescribing what information must be provided in certain situations. Regulation 6(3), for example, states not only that material information is that which the average consumer needs to make an informed decision but also information that EU law requires them to be given. An example would be the information requirements in the Package Travel, Package Holidays and Package Tours Regulations 1992 (the 1992 Regulations). Where the advertisement is what the 1992 Regulations reg.4 calls an "invitation to purchase" more information must be provided. An "invitation to purchase" is defined by reg.2 as

11–29

> "a commercial communication which indicates characteristics of the product and the price in a way appropriate to the means of that commercial communication and thereby enables the consumer to make a purchase",

---

[26] This is still useful and available on the *http://www.gov.uk* website.

and many advertisements will come within that definition.[27] Where they do the advertisement will have to contain the main characteristics of the product in a way appropriate to that advertisement, the identity of the trader, their geographical address and the price including any taxes. In addition, where appropriate, delivery charges should be included and, if they depart from normal practice, payment, delivery and other arrangements for performing the transaction as well as complaint handling policies. Where products or transactions involve rights of cancellation or withdrawal the existence of these rights must be set out.

Price advertising

11–30   Part 3 of the 1987 Act that contained specific controls on misleading prices supplemented by a statutory code of guidance has been repealed. The CPR 2008 replace these controls but they are more general for the most part. The one exception is para.(20) of the list of banned practices in Sch.1 which outlaws describing a product as

> "'gratis', 'free', 'without charge' or similar if the consumer has to pay anything other than the unavoidable cost of responding to the commercial practice and collecting or paying for delivery of the item".

Otherwise price advertising must avoid infringing the bans on misleading actions and omissions and the general ban on unfair practices. The Department of Business, Innovation and Skills has produced a *Pricing Practices Guide* giving guidance to traders on good practice in giving information about prices.[28] It should also be noted that the Price Marking Order 2004 (the 2004 Order) is still in effect. This is because it gives effect to Directive 98/6/EC of the European Parliament and of the Council of 16 February 1998 on consumer protection in the indication of the prices of products offered to consumers, and thus may continue in operation. For that reason it is the first of the other statutory controls to be discussed below.

OTHER STATUTORY CONTROLS

Price marking of products

11–31   The 2004 Order[29] is intended to increase price transparency in the market, thus enabling consumers to know what the price of goods is and to make comparisons. The Order applies to a wide range of goods for retail sale but not those supplied in the course of the provision of a service, such as food sold in restaurants, hotels, and public houses; auction sales; and sales of antiques and works of art.[30] Where a trader indicates that a product is or may be for sale to a consumer its selling

---

[27] See paras 10–31 to 10–34 for discussion of "invitation to purchase".
[28] Available on the Government website: *http://www.gov.uk*.
[29] Price Marking Order 2004 (SI 2004/102), which replaces the Price Marking Order 1999 (SI 1999/3042).
[30] See Price Marking Order 2004 art.3.

price must be indicated. This does not apply to goods sold from bulk or to advertisements. In certain circumstances the unit price, i.e. the price for one kilogram, litre, metre, square metre or cubic metre or the one item for goods sold by number, must also be indicated. This will be the case where products are sold loose from bulk, as in the case of fruit and vegetables. It also applies to pre-packaged products that are required by weights and measures legislation to be marked with quantity or to be made up in a prescribed quantity. These include most packaged food and drink and a wide range of non-food products such as construction and decorating products, fuel (both solid and liquid), aerosol dispensers, cleaning and toilet preparations, cosmetics and pet foods. The requirement to indicate unit prices does not apply to cinema and television advertisements or, in the case of pre-packaged products, to sales in small shops, by itinerant traders or from vending machines.[31] A small shop is defined in art.1 of the 2004 Order as one with a floor area of less than 280 square metres.

Whatever price must be indicated it must be indicated in a way that is, "unambiguous, easily identifiable and clearly legible", as must any charges for postage, package or delivery. It must be placed in close proximity to the products to which it relates and in such a way as to be available to customers without the need for them to seek assistance from the trader to ascertain it.[32] The latter requirement overrules the decision in *Allen v Redbridge London Borough Council*.[33]   **11–32**

"Selling price" includes VAT and any other taxes,[34] and must be stated in sterling. If a trader is willing to accept payment in foreign currency the price in that currency may also be displayed provided the price in the foreign currency or the conversion rate to be used is indicated together with any commission to be charged.[35]   **11–33**

Comparative advertising

Comparative advertising is now controlled by the CPR 2008 and by the Business Protection from Misleading Marketing Regulations 2008 (the 2008 Regulations).[36] The latter are designed principally to protect traders from misleading advertising and implement Directive 2006/114 concerning misleading and comparative advertising.[37] For the purposes of the regulations comparative advertising "means advertising which in any way, either explicitly or by implication, identifies a competitor or a product offered by a competitor".[38] Regulation 4 of the 2008 Regulations sets out the conditions in which comparative advertising is permissible. These are that: **11–34**

(a) it is not misleading;

---

[31] See Price Marking Order 2004 art.5(3) and Sch.2.
[32] See Price Marking Order 2004 art.7.
[33] *Allen v Redbridge London Borough Council* [1994] 1 W.L.R. 139; [1994] 1 All E.R. 728.
[34] See Price Marking Order 2004 art.1.
[35] See Price Marking Order 2004 art.6.
[36] Business Protection from Misleading Marketing Regulations 2008 (SI 2008/1276).
[37] Directive 2006/114/EC of the European Parliament and of the Council of 12 December 2006 concerning misleading and comparative advertising [2006] O.J. L376/21.
[38] See Business Protection from Misleading Marketing Regulations 2008 reg.2.

(b)   it is not a misleading action or a misleading omission as defined by the Consumer Protection from Unfair Trading Regulations 2008[39];

(c)   it compares products meeting the same needs or intended for the same purpose;

(d)   it objectively compares one or more material, relevant, verifiable and representative features of those products, which may include price;

(e)   it does not create confusion among traders between the advertiser and a competitor or between the trademarks, trade names, other distinguishing marks or products of the advertiser and those of a competitor;

(f)   it does not discredit or denigrate the trademarks, trade names, other distinguishing marks, products, activities, or circumstances of a competitor;

(g)   for products with designation of origin, it relates in each case to products with the same designation;

(h)   it does not take unfair advantage of the reputation of a trade mark, trade name or other distinguishing marks of a competitor or of the designation of origin of competing products; and

(i)   it does not present products as imitations or replicas of products bearing a protected trade mark or trade name.

ADVERTISING FOOD

11–35   Section 15 of the Food Safety Act 1990 (the 1990 Act) provides that it is an offence falsely to describe, advertise or present food. The first of these three offences makes it an offence to sell, offer or expose for sale food which has a label which falsely describes the food or is likely to mislead as to its nature, substance or quality.[40] It is also an offence to publish, or to be a party to the publication of an advertisement which falsely describes any food, or is likely to mislead as to its nature, substance or quality.[41] The 1990 Act defines "advertisement" as including any notice, circular, label, wrapper, invoice or other document, and any public announcement made orally or by any means of producing or transmitting light or sound.[42]

11–36   In relation to both these offences it is no barrier to a conviction that the label or advertisement contains an accurate statement of the composition of the food.[43] This is intended to catch situations where a label or advertisement is literally true but the overall effect is deceptive. For the same reason the 1990 Act s.15(3) creates a new offence of selling, offering or exposing for sale or having in one's possession for the purpose of sale, any food the presentation of which is likely to mislead as to its nature substance or quality. Presentation of the food includes its shape, appearance and packaging as well as the way it is arranged when exposed for sale and the setting in which the food is displayed with a view to sale. Section 53(1) excludes from this definition any form of labelling or advertising.

---

[39] Consumer Protection from Unfair Trading Regulations 2008 (SI 2008/1277).
[40] Food Safety Act 1990 s.15(1). See GG Howells, RJ Bradgate and MS Griffiths, *Blackstone's Guide to the Food Safety Act 1990* (London: Blackstone, 1990) Ch.4.
[41] See Food Safety Act 1990 s.15(2). For defences, see Food Safety Act 1990 s.15(4).
[42] See Food Safety Act 1990 s.53(1).
[43] See Food Safety Act 1990 s.15(4).

In addition to these general prohibitions, there is a considerable body of regulations controlling the labelling, marking or advertising of food for sale for human consumption. As has been traditional in this area, these regulations are made under powers now contained in the 1990 Act. Section 16(1)(e) gives a power to make regulations

> "for imposing requirements or prohibitions as to, or otherwise regulating, the labelling, marking, presenting or advertising of food, and the descriptions which may be applied to food".

Numerous regulations were made under similar powers in previous legislation and these remain in force by virtue of s.59.

11–37

WEIGHTS AND MEASURES

Part 4 of the Weights and Measures Act 1985 (the 1985 Act) regulates the sale of goods by quantity.[44] The 1985 Act, together with a vast corpus of regulations, imposes requirements designed to ensure that consumers are accurately informed about the quantity of goods they are intending to purchase. The CPR 2008 have repealed s.29 of the 1985 Act which made it a criminal offence to misrepresent the quantity of goods being sold or offered for sale. Such activities will now be caught by the CPR 2008 and will be subject to its various enforcement provisions which were discussed in Ch.10.

11–38

ADVERTISING MEDICINAL PRODUCTS

Advertising of medicines for human use is now regulated by Pt 14 of the Human Medicines Regulations 2012 (the 2012 Regulations)[45] which consolidate the law concerning medicinal products and largely replace Pts 5 and 6 of the Medicines Act 1968. "Medicinal product" is defined as a substance for preventing or treating disease in human beings or which may be used by or administered to human beings with a view to affecting a physiological or making a medical diagnosis.[46] Regulation 7 contains a wide definition of "advertisement" to include "anything designed to promote the prescription, supply, sale or use of that product" and explicitly provides that it includes activities such as door-to-door canvassing, visits by medical sales representatives and the supply of samples, though not packaging or packaging leaflets. The regulations deal with the advertising of medicines in general and the specific requirements and restrictions for advertising directed at the public and for advertising directed at healthcare professionals which is not dealt with here. Regulation 279 prohibits the advertisement of medicinal products which do not have a valid licence and the following regulation contains general principles. These are: that advertisements

11–39

---

[44] For example, the Weights and Measures Act 1985 Pt 4 ss.21–46. This area of law is under review, see Department of Trade and Industry, *Fair Measure: a consultation document on modernising the law on the sale of goods sold by quantity* (1999).

[45] Human Medicines Regulations 2012 (SI 2012/1916).

[46] Human Medicines Regulations 2012 (SI 2012/1916) reg.2.

must not be misleading; that products cannot be advertised unless the advertisement encourages the rational use of the product by presenting it objectively and without exaggerating its properties; and the advertisement must comply with the particulars listed in the summary of the product characteristics. Regulations 283–292 contain more specific controls on advertising to the public including bans on advertising certain products such as those for the purpose of inducing an abortions, narcotic and psychotropic substances and prescription only medicines. Breach of the regulations is a criminal offence.[47] Chapter 3 of Pt 14 gives ministers wide powers to monitor advertisements and requires them to consider complaints about advertisements and permits ministers to apply to a court for an injunction prohibiting a particular advertisement. The Broadcast Code of Advertising (BCAP) and the Code of Advertising Practice (CAP) both have special sections containing guidelines as to the making of health claims and the advertising of medicines and treatments. The Proprietary Association of Great Britain's code governs the marketing of over-the-counter (OTC) pharmaceuticals and pre-vets all advertisements of OTC drugs.

TOBACCO PRODUCTS

11–40   The Tobacco Advertising and Promotions Act 2002 bans the advertising of most tobacco product advertising in the UK. It deals with advertising in newspapers and periodicals as well as point of sale advertising which has been strictly limited since December 2004.[48] In Scotland, the Tobacco and Primary Medical Services (Scotland) Act 2010 makes it an offence to display tobacco products or smoking related products in the course of business, subject to certain exceptions and the Supreme Court has upheld the legality of this ban.[49] These restrictions remain in effect as they relate to health and safety which recital 9 and art.3(3) of the Unfair Commercial Practices Directive state are not subject to the Directive.

CONSUMER CREDIT

11–41   Since 1 April 2014, the Financial Conduct Authority (FCA) rather than the OFT is responsible for the regulation of consumer credit, including the regulation of advertisements relating to consumer credit. As a result of the transfer of the regulation of consumer credit from the OFT to the FCA Pt IV of the Credit Consumer Association (CCA) and the subordinate legislation relating to the advertising of consumer credit has been repealed. However, much of the law and the guidance that was issued before 1 April 2014 relating to the advertisement of consumer credit has been replicated by the FCA in Ch.3 of its Consumer Credit sourcebook (CONC3). One notable difference is that, the FCA's considerable enforcement powers apply to the advertising of consumer credit.

---

[47] Human Medicines Regulations 2012 (SI 2012/1916) reg.303.

[48] Tobacco Advertising and Promotion (Point of Sale) (Scotland) Regulations 2004 (SSI 2004/144).

[49] *Imperial Tobacco Ltd v the Lord Advocate* 2013 S.C. (UKSC) 153.

DISTANCE AND OFF-PREMISES SELLING

Consumer Contracts (Information, Cancellation and Additional Charges) Regula-   **11–42**
tions 2013,[50] which implement the Consumer Rights Directive 2011,[51] include
important protections for consumers thinking of buying goods in circumstances
where they and the seller are not in face to face communication or are dealing
away from normal retail premises. They replaced the Consumer Protection
(Distance Selling) Regulations 2000[52] and the Cancellation of Contracts made in
a Consumer's Home or Place of Work etc. Regulations 2008.[53] They apply to
most contracts involving a "means of distance communication" which is defined
as

> "any means which, without the simultaneous physical presence of the supplier and
> the consumer, may be used for the conclusion of a contract between those parties".

They, therefore, covers transactions effected by the internet, digital television,
mail order, including catalogue shopping, telephone and email. In these cases
suppliers must give consumers clear information including details of the goods or
services offered, delivery arrangements and payment, the supplier's details and
the consumer's cancellation right before they buy and this information must be
given in writing The regulations are covered in more detail in Ch.10.

BROADCAST ADVERTISING

Under the terms of its licence the British Broadcasting Corporation is not   **11–43**
permitted to transmit advertisements on its radio and television services. The
broadcasting services regulated by the Office of Communications (Ofcom) which
was set up by the Communications Act 2003 (the 2003 Act) are expressly
permitted to do so. Television, and to a lesser extent commercial radio stations,
are an attractive medium for advertisers. Broadcast advertising is subject to a
range of controls specific to it which encompass an interesting combination of
statutory and self-regulatory methods. Broadcast advertising is, of course, subject
to the various Acts of Parliament which regulate advertising in general.

The 2003 Act provides that, "the inclusion of advertising which may be   **11–44**
misleading, harmful or offensive in television and radio services" must be
prevented,[54] and goes on to provide that Ofcom must ensure "general provision
governing standards and practice in advertising and in the sponsoring of

---

[50] Consumer Contracts (Information, Cancellation, and Additional Charges) Regulations 2013 (SI
2013/3134).
[51] Directive 2011/83/EU of the European Parliament and of the Council of 25 October 2011 on
consumer rights, OJ. No. L 304, 22.11.2011, p.64.
[52] Consumer Protection (Distance Selling) Regulations 2000 (SI 2000/2334).
[53] Cancellation of Contracts made in a Consumer's Home or Place of Work etc. Regulations 2008 (SI
2008/1816).
[54] Communications Act 2003 s.319(2)(h).

programmes",[55] and that this must be done by codes.[56] The 2003 Act also specifically outlaws subliminal advertising techniques.[57]

11–45   Since the beginning of commercial television there have been controls on the amount of advertising that may be shown. These are now found in the *Code on the scheduling of television advertising* (Costa) which sets out the rules with which television broadcasters must comply when carrying advertising. These rules give effect to relevant provisions of the Audio Visual Media Services Directive[58] and policies determined by Ofcom following consultation. Many of the rules apply to both terrestrial channels and cable and satellite channels, but special provision is made for the latter. This is most marked in relation to home shopping channels where up to eight "tele-shopping windows", that is, advertising features of from 15 minutes to three hours in length may be shown. This compares with the rules for terrestrial channels which permit a daily average of seven minutes advertising in each hour and no more than 12 minutes in any one hour.

11–46   Section 321(2) of the 2003 Act has general rules about advertising that prohibit advertisements by any body whose objects are wholly or mainly of a political nature or relate to an industrial dispute. While Ofcom has overall control over the content of all television broadcasting, including control over the content of advertising and has published a Broadcasting Code[59] covering radio and television broadcasting, it has outsourced detailed broadcast advertising regulation to the Advertising Standards Authority (ASA). The ASA operates and enforces the Broadcast Advertising Code (BCAP Code), produced by the BCAP.

11–47   The rules in the BCAP Code, inter alia, require that the advertisements must be clearly distinguishable as such, recognisably separate from programmes, and inserted at the beginning or the end of programmes or in a natural break. They must not be excessively noisy or strident, nor should certain products be advertised in or adjacent to certain programmes. For example, advertisements for alcoholic drinks, liqueur chocolates and pipe tobacco must not be carried in or adjacent to children's programmes.

11–48   The content of BCAP, is very similar to the *CAP Code: The UK Code of Non-broadcast Advertising, Sales Promotion and Direct Marketing Direct Marketing* which applies to print and other media and is discussed below. It shares with that code the same general principles that advertising should be legal, decent, honest and truthful and that its detailed rules are intended to be applied in the spirit as well as the letter. It suffices at this point to draw attention to some features peculiar to broadcasting. The code permits the use of special techniques or substitute materials where technical limitations can make it difficult to portray a subject accurately. However, the resultant picture must present a fair and reasonable impression of the product and must not use unacceptable devices such as glass or plastic sheeting to simulate the effects of floor or furniture polishes. Breath-testing devices and products that are intended to mask the effects of

---

[55] See Communications Act 2003 s.321(1)(a).

[56] See Communications Act 2003 s.319(3).

[57] See Communications Act 2003 s.319(1)(h).

[58] Directive 2010/13/EU of the European Parliament and of the Council of 10 March 2010 on the coordination of certain provisions laid down by law, regulation or administrative action in Member States concerning the provision of audiovisual media services O.J. L 95 15.4.2010, p.1–24.

[59] Available at *http://www.ofcom.org.uk* [Accessed 22 June 2015].

alcohol, betting systems and products that are intended to facilitate winning games of chance, all tobacco products, guns (including replica guns), gun clubs and offensive weapons may not be advertised. Also in the banned category are prostitution and sexual massage services, obscene material, pyramid promotional schemes and, on TV, escort agencies.

Clearcast, a commercial company, pre-vets all UK broadcast advertising on behalf of the commercial television networks who are jointly responsible with advertisers and agencies for ensuring the advertising shown on their networks is compliant. The Radio Advertising Clearance Centre pre-vets advertising for radio. Both organisations will give advice on what is likely to be acceptable advertising content.

11–49

BRITISH CODE OF ADVERTISING PRACTICE

One of the distinctive features of advertising control in the UK is the role of self-regulation. It has already been noted that there is an element of this in broadcast advertising through the BCAP code. It might be argued that this is not pure self-regulation as the code is mandated by statute and drawn up not only by representatives of the advertising industry but also of government and consumers. Self-regulation has an important role to play in the control of advertising standards in media other than broadcasting. This is achieved by means of the CAP *Code: The UK Code of Non-broadcast Advertising, Sales Promotion and Direct Marketing*, the 12th edition of which came into force on 1 September 2010.[60]

11–50

The code was drawn up by the Code of Advertising Practice Committee composed of representatives of the advertising industry in consultation with the ASA and trade and consumer interests. The ASA is a company limited by guarantee set up by the Advertising Association to supervise the code and its enforcement. It is composed of a chairman who, under the terms of the ASA's articles of association, must "not be engaged in the business of advertising" and must be appointed only "after consultation with the Members of the Council of the Authority", a majority of whom must also be independent.[61]

11–51

The ASA receives complaints about advertisements from members of the public and also carries out a limited amount of monitoring of advertisements on its own initiative. Complaints by one advertiser against another are the responsibility of the Code of Advertising Practice Committee. The main sanction available to the ASA is that of adverse publicity, and details of complaints are published by the ASA. One of the criticisms of the self-regulatory system has been the inadequacy of its sanctions. Apart from adverse publicity, its only other sanction is to request those companies controlling the media and which adhere to the *British Code of Advertising, Sales Promotion and Direct Marketing* not to publish advertisements found to be in breach of the code and not to accept advertisements from advertising agencies which do not abide by the code. Since 1999 an independent reviewer has been added to the process of dealing with complaints. In exceptional circumstances, the ASA council can be asked to

11–52

---

[60] Available on the ASA website: *http://www.asa.org.uk* [Accessed 22 June 2015].
[61] For more detail, see Ch.1.

reconsider its adjudication (including a council decision not to investigate a complaint). There are two grounds on which such a request can be made: where additional relevant evidence becomes available; or where there is a substantial flaw in the council's adjudication or in the process by which that adjudication was made.

11–53   In *R v Advertising Standards Authority Ltd, Ex p. Insurance Service Plc*[62] it has been held that the activities of the ASA in adjudicating on complaints against advertisements are subject to judicial review. There have been several applications for judicial review most of which have decided in favour of the ASA. The relevance of the European Convention on Human Rights was considered in *R v Advertising Standards Authority Ltd, Ex p. Matthias Rath BV*.[63] The claimants sought judicial review of the decision by the ASA to publish an adverse adjudication against them regarding a complaint made by a health authority and the refusal of the Independent Reviewer of the ASA to reconsider the adjudication. The claimants argued that the ASA was a public authority for the purposes of the Human Rights Act 1998. The ASA did not argue against this, but wished to preserve the right to argue otherwise in a future case. The claimants claimed that art.10.2 of the Convention permitted interference with freedom of expression only where there were rules prescribed by law and that the *British Codes of Advertising and Sales Promotion* (as they were then known) were not such rules "prescribed by law". The judge referred to the Control of Misleading Advertisements Regulations 1988[64] and concluded that there was:

> "[N]o doubt that the advertising code of practice, which had an underpinning of subordinate legislation and which was readily accessible was prescribed by law. Its provisions were sufficiently clear and precise to enable any person who was minded to place advertisements to know within what limits they were likely to prove acceptable and would also know what were the consequences if he were to infringe its provisions."[65]

Although the codes did not have direct statutory effect, they met the purposive intention of art.10.2.[66]

11–54   The Advertising Code has four general principles: that advertisements should be legal, decent, honest and truthful. It is also stated that it will be "applied in the spirit as well as the letter". In addition to these general principles the code goes into a good deal of detail about various advertising practices and the manner in which certain products and services may be advertised. Advertisements must be clearly distinguished as such and comparative advertising is permissible, although this must be done fairly and without denigrating other products.

---

[62] *R v Advertising Standards Authority Ltd, Ex p. Insurance Service Plc* (1990) 2 Admin. L.R. 77; (1990) 9 Tr. L.R. 169; 133 S.J. 1545 QBD.

[63] *R v Advertising Standards Authority Ltd, Ex p. Matthais Rath BV* [2001] E.M.L.R. 22; [2001] H.R.L.R. 22.

[64] Control of Misleading Advertising Regulations 1988 (SI 1988/915).

[65] *R v Advertising Standards Authority Ltd, Ex p. Matthais Rath BV* [2001] E.M.L.R. 22; [2001] H.R.L.R. 22 at [26]. For the most recent challenge to the Advertising Standards Authority see *R (on the application of Sainsbury's Supermarkets Ltd) v Independent Reviewer of Advertising Standards Authority Adjudications* [2014] EWHC 3680 (Admin).

[66] For another decision raising the question of the applicability of Human Rights Act 1998, see *Buxton (t/a The Jewellery Vault) v Advertising Standards Authority* [2002] EWHC 2433.

A section of the CAP Code sets out rules governing health claims, and there **11–55** are sections devoted specifically to advertisements directed at children, advertisements for slimming and medical products, vitamins, alcohol and cigarettes, as well as mail order advertisements.

Proponents of the self-regulatory system argue that it provides a positive **11–56** approach to advertising control which can deal with matters of taste and decency which it would be impractical to control by statute. It is also argued that the code can be amended more speedily than legislation and that it commands a high degree of commitment from the business community and encourages higher standards in advertising.[67]

Against this, the weakness of the sanctions available to ASA has already been **11–57** noted. It should be added that such sanctions as there are operate only after a breach of the code has taken place. There is no speedy method of taking preventive action against major breaches of the code. Also, as with all voluntary measures, the code only applies to those advertisers and media that subscribe to it. To a limited extent, this criticism of the code lost some of its force with the implementation of the Misleading Advertising Directive.[68] This has now been repealed and replaced by the Unfair Commercial Practices Directive that has been implemented principally by the CPR 2008 which were discussed earlier. Both the broadcast and non-broadcast codes have been revised in the light of this development and the 12th edition came into force on 1 September 2010.

There is a legal backstop if the ASA's non-statutory powers fail to persuade a **11–58** non-broadcast advertiser to change its advertising. The ASA can refer an advertiser, agency or publisher to Convention of Scottish Local Authorities (COSLA) or, in England and Wales, the Trading Standards Service, who took over this role from the OFT in April 2013 as part of the change in the consumer landscape. COSLA and also the CMA can seek an interdict to prevent the same or similar claims being made in future advertisements. In practice, litigation can be avoided by the advertiser giving an undertaking instead. In December 2011, the ASA referred Groupon to the OFT, after it had upheld eleven upheld complaints against it during the year. This resulted in Groupon providing the OFT with undertakings not to continue or repeat the unlawful practices identified by the ASA.

---

[67] See Department of Trade and Industry, *The Self-Regulatory System of Advertising Control: report of the working party* (Burgh Report) (1980) p.3.
[68] Directive 84/450/EEC of 10 September 1984 relating to the approximation of the laws, regulations and administrative provisions of the Member States concerning misleading advertising.

CHAPTER 12

Consumer Redress and Enforcement[1]

INTRODUCTION

As the earlier chapters have shown, there is now an impressive body of law 12–01
protecting the consumer as well as various organisations, notably local authority
trading standards and environmental health departments, who enforce it and
provide advice to consumers. However, in many cases it is up to individual
consumers to take action to assert their rights.

It is a commonplace of debate on consumer protection that settling disputes 12–02
between consumers and traders is a major problem. Much discussion has centred
on this issue. The former Scottish Consumer Council (the SCC), like its parent
body the National Consumer Council (the NCC), devoted considerable resources
to it. The Office of Fair Trading had also been in the van of efforts to deal with
the issue in a number of ways. In 1991 it devoted a major conference to the topic
of redress, the results of which are set out in *Consumer Redress Mechanisms*,[2]
and in its 1998 strategy document[3] it confirmed its continuing commitment to
improving access to redress. Its successor, the Competition and Markets
Authority (CMA), however does not seem to be interested to judge by its Annual
Plan 2015/2016.[4] The Chartered Trading Standards Institute (CTSI), which has
taken over responsibility for consumer codes requires such codes to provide a
conciliation scheme for dealing with consumer complaints and a low-cost,
speedy, responsive, accessible and user-friendly independent redress scheme to
act as an alternative to seeking court action.[5] As one would expect, the consumer
White Paper devoted a chapter to redress and stressed the importance of an
integrated system of information and redress.[6] The follow-up document, *A Fair
Deal for All: Extending Competitive Markets: Empowered Consumers Successful
Businesses*, stated that the government would encourage pilot ADR projects and

---

[1] Some of the material in this chapter, especially that on small claims and alternative dispute
resolution (ADR), first appeared in RE Mackay and R Moody, *Guide to Alternative Dispute
Resolution* (Edinburgh: W.Green, 1995). I am grateful to the editors for permission to use it here.
[2] Office of Fair Trading, *Consumer Redress Mechanisms: A report by the Director-General of Fair
Trading into systems for resolving consumer complaints* (OFT 1991).
[3] Office of Fair Trading, *Consumer Affairs: The way forward* (1998) OFT 241, para.5.11.
[4] See *https://www.gov.uk/government/uploads/system/uploads/attachment_data/file/416433/Annual_
Plan_2015-16.pdf* [Accessed 9 July 2015].
[5] Details of the new Consumer Codes Approval Scheme can be found on the Trading Standards
Institute (TSI) website *http://www.tradingstandards.gov.uk* [Accessed 22 June 2015].
[6] White Papers, *Modern Markets: Confident Consumers*(1999) Cm.4410, Ch.6.

introduce a representative action.[7] The problem is not confined to Scotland or the UK, as the Florence Access to Justice Project amply demonstrated.[8] At European level it has featured prominently in all the consumer protection initiatives of the EU and its *A European Consumer Agenda* in 2012 stressed the importance of adequate redress mechanisms both for individuals and collectively.[9]

12–03 To set the scene for what follows it will be useful to indicate the scale of consumer complaints about goods and services.

The most recent study in 2012 by Consumer Focus[10] which replicated the methodology of the last Office of Fair Trading (OFT) one[11] estimated that consumer detriment over 12 months prior to the study amounted to £3.08bn. This is lower than in 2008, reflecting the lower number of problems and higher proportion incurring no financial detriment over the last 12 months. The mean average amount of financial detriment has stayed at a similar level over the last four years of £376. Problems that cost the consumer more than £20 make up about a quarter (24 per cent) of consumer problems but they comprise 99 per cent of all financial detriment for consumers. It was estimated that a total of 15.7 million problems were experienced with goods and services purchased in the previous 12 months. Regulated services, meaning gas and electricity, water, postal services, and communications caused the highest proportion of problems, but low levels of financial detriment (mean average of £51 per problem compared with £196 for all types of problem). Professional and financial services (£464) and transport (£413) incur the highest levels of financial detriment. Most problems were dealt with fairly quickly. Over half (57 per cent) of problems are dealt with in up to four hours, with a third (34 per cent) taking under an hour. A further 16 per cent of problems take no time, as not all consumers that have a problem about which they can justifiably complain bother to do so. Consumers complained or took further action to try and resolve the problem in two-thirds of all cases (66 per cent) and 69 per cent of problems with regulated services.

12–04 Although surveys show that approximately three out of four consumers take some action about their complaint, few went beyond a complaint to the supplier. Half of problems in the Consumer Focus survey were considered resolved, while over a third (36 per cent) were not. The survey did not reveal how many used dispute resolution mechanisms. An earlier study showed that fewer than one in a thousand of all consumers, or under one-quarter of a per cent of those with complaints, resorted to any kind of redress mechanism[12] though some figures in the 2012 survey suggest that more consumers may be resorting to such organisations. Should it not be possible to reach a settlement what courses are open to the consumer? This is what we investigate below.

---

[7] Department of Trade and Industry, *A Fair Deal for All: Extending Competitive Markets: Empowered Consumers Successful Businesses* (London: June, 2005).

[8] See M Cappelletti and J Weisner, *Access to Justice* (Amsterdam: Sijthoff and Noordhoff, 1978) Vol.11, Bk 1, Pt 4.

[9] Directorate-General for Justice, *A European Consumer Agenda*, COM(2012) 225 final.

[10] TNS BMRB, *Consumer Detriment 2012* (Consumer Focus, 2012).

[11] See Office of Fair Trading, *Consumer Detriment* (April 2008) OFT992.

[12] See Office of Fair Trading, *Consumer Redress Mechanisms: A report by the Director-General of Fair Trading into systems for resolving consumer complaints* (1991); see also Ch.3. This is similar to H Genn and AA Paterson, Paths to Justice in Scotland: What people in Scotland think and do about going to law (Oxford: Hart Publishing, 2001).

COURT PROCEEDINGS

The traditional answer is to point to the courts. In Scotland the appropriate court for most consumer disputes is the sheriff court. There are three main procedures, which may have to be used to resolve a dispute. The ordinary cause will be the appropriate one where the value of the claim is over £5,000. This is a complex procedure which, in practice, requires professional assistance. If the claim is for between £3,001 and £5,000 the summary cause procedure may be used. This was introduced in 1975 in an attempt to provide a simpler and quicker procedure. While it is certainly simpler than the ordinary cause procedure, it has lengthy and complicated rules and does little to provide realistic access to justice for consumers though the most recent revision of the rules has much improved the drafting. To try to create a more user-friendly procedure a small claim procedure was introduced into the sheriff court in 1988.   **12–05**

The legislative basis for the small claims procedure is to be found in s.35 of the Sheriff Courts (Scotland) Act 1971, as amended by s.18 of the Law Reform (Miscellaneous Provisions) (Scotland) Act 1985. The definition of a small claim is to be found in the Small Claims (Scotland) Order 1988.[13] It is wide enough to cover most consumer claims (though it also covers many other types of case) where the amount claimed does not exceed £3,000. The financial limit for small claims was belatedly raised to £3,000 with effect from 14 January 2008, and at the same time personal injuries actions were removed from it. The detailed rules of the procedure are set out in the Act of Sederunt (Small Claim Rules) 2002 (the SCR 2002).[14]   **12–06**

A small claim is begun by filling in a form, known as a summons, setting out the names and addresses of the person making the claim and the person sued, as well as a brief account of what is being claimed. This form, together with the appropriate fee, is lodged with the sheriff clerk who, where the pursuer is an individual,[15] will arrange for it to be served on the defender. Where the defender intends to dispute the claim, this is done by completing and returning the appropriate part of the summons.   **12–07**

In a disputed case under the new rules the next stage is called the "Hearing" and a deliberate attempt has been made to try to resolve most cases at this stage. One of the major criticisms of the original small claim procedure was that preliminary hearings (as this stage was then termed) were not always being conducted as intended or, indeed, as directed by the rules. The Scottish Office research report found that while all sheriffs interviewed noted the defence not all of them went on to discover the issues in dispute as the then rules required.[16] It is not surprising that the same research project revealed that few disputed cases were resolved at that stage, although the rules encouraged the sheriff to effect a settlement at that point. The new rules expand on the guidance in the original   **12–08**

---

[13] Small Claims (Scotland) Order 1988 (SI 1988/1999) as amended by the Small Claims (Scotland) Amendment Order 2007 (SI 2007/496).

[14] Act of Sederunt (Small Claim Rules) 2002 (SSI 2002/133).

[15] This privilege applies to anyone who is not a partnership or company so could be availed of by a one-man business.

[16] Scottish Office, *Small Claims in the Sheriff Court in Scotland* (Central Research Unit Papers, 1991) p.79.

rules in a way which leaves no room for doubt about the purpose of the hearing. SCR 2002 r.9.2 is entitled "Purpose of the Hearing" and directs the sheriff to:

"(a)   ascertain the factual basis of the claim and any defence, and the legal basis on which the claim and defence are proceeding: and

(b)   seek to negotiate and secure settlement of the claim between the parties."[17]

12–09   This clearly indicates a more interventionist role for sheriffs than many have been prepared to contemplate in the past. Particularly where lay litigants are involved it will require a more inquisitorial attitude on the part of the sheriff.

12–10   Where the case is not resolved at the Hearing, a hearing at which evidence is given will be held. Like the Hearing, this is held in public "as informally as the circumstances of the claim permit".[18] To make it more realistic to expect the parties to present their own cases, the legislation dispenses with the rules relating to the admissibility or corroboration of evidence.[19] For those who do not wish to present their own cases, advocates or solicitors are not the only alternatives as lay representatives are permitted. In practice, relatives, citizens advice bureaux staff and trading standards officers have acted in this capacity.

12–11   A major barrier to going to court is expense, or the fear of it, in a system where the losing party will normally have to meet the expenses of the winner. Small claims procedure resolves this problem by providing that in disputed cases involving less than £200 no expenses of any kind are recoverable by the successful party. Where the amount claimed is between £200 and £1,500 expenses are limited to £150 and between £1,500 and £3,000 to 10 per cent of the sum claimed.

12–12   The Scottish small claims procedure has the potential to be a genuinely radical approach to resolving consumer (and other) disputes. The research into its first year of operation showed some positive features. It deals speedily with cases in a way that bears favourable comparison with its English equivalent and trade arbitration schemes; and, as was to be expected, advisers were unanimous in acknowledging the fairness of sheriffs. Court staff were also found to be very helpful to litigants and the explanatory literature was well received. The new rules should improve the operation of the system with its clearer guidance about informality and early resolution of cases. The rules have been more clearly drafted and a glossary added that should make it easier for the lay person to use them. The guidance material available from sheriff clerk's offices has also been improved.

12–13   As has been pointed out more than once,[20] much depends on the approach of the sheriff whose role is central to the operation of the process. Here the limitations of the procedure in practice have been exposed. The research into its operation revealed a variety of approaches in different courts. Variation, while it cannot be entirely eliminated, is inimical to the development of confidence in the system by consumers and, perhaps more importantly, those who frequently provide them with advice. Too often, hearings are held in an atmosphere which

---

[17] Act of Sederunt (Small Claim Rules) 2002 r.9.2(2).

[18] Act of Sederunt (Small Claim Rules) 2002 r.9.2.

[19] See Sheriff Courts (Scotland) Act 1971 s.35; and Civil Evidence (Scotland) Act 1988 ss.1 and 2.

[20] See, e.g. Office of Fair Trading, *Consumer Redress Mechanisms* (1991) p.47; and C Ervine, "The New Small Claims Procedure", 1989 S.L.T. 65.

does not encourage individuals to represent themselves. Commonly, they take place before a sheriff in traditional court dress, in a normal court room where a number of solicitors are waiting to deal with other business. Full hearings tend to be held in less busy surroundings but, again, traditional court rooms are normally used instead of other rooms such as jury rooms. However, there are examples of good practice, such as the "consumer court", as it is commonly termed, in Glasgow which deals with cases involving unrepresented parties.

Insufficient attention seems to have been given to the particular needs of persons bringing small claims on their own. Simple things such as good signposting within court buildings is essential for people who will, in all probability, be making their first and possibly only visit to a court. There is, as the Director-General of Fair Trading has pointed out, scope for improved timetabling of cases to prevent litigants spending long periods waiting for their cases to begin and for experiments with evening or weekend hearings.[21]   **12–14**

The Courts Reform (Scotland) Act 2014 heralds the most significant changes to Scotland's civil justice system in generations and continues the programme of reform of Scotland's courts implementing many of the recommendations of the Scottish Civil Courts Review,[22] led by principal reviewer Lord Gill, commissioned in 2007. For consumers one of the most significant changes which will eventually be made is that summary cause and small claims procedure will cease to exist and be replaced by "simple procedure". This will apply to most claims for up to £5,000 and is expected to be introduced in the spring of 2016. It will be presided over by a new kind of sheriff, the summary sheriff who, in addition to dealing with simple procedure, will hear summary criminal cases.   **12–15**

LEGAL AID

In theory the availability of legal aid should have overcome the problems of lack of access to the courts. There are two forms of assistance in civil matters. Under the Legal Aid (Scotland) Act 1986 it is possible to get advice and assistance from a solicitor on any matter of Scots law and to assert rights in any way short of going to court. In addition, there is a legal aid scheme which funds litigation in the civil courts. In both cases these services are means tested and their availability has diminished in the past few years as a result of the government's policy of reducing public expenditure. The Scottish Government calculates that over 70 per cent of the Scottish population now qualify financially for civil legal aid, albeit applicants with higher levels of disposable income are required to pay contributions to their case.[23]   **12–16**

---

[21] Office of Fair Trading, *Consumer Redress Mechanisms* (1991) p.50, fn.8.

[22] The two volume report of the Review is available on the Scottish Courts website: *http://www.scotcourts.gov.uk* [Accessed 22 June 2015].

[23] Scottish Government, *A Sustainable Future for Legal Aid* (Edinburgh, 2011).

Speculative actions

12–17 On public policy grounds it is illegal for solicitors, though not for others,[24] to pursue a case on the basis that they will be remunerated by a share of any sum recovered. This is often referred to as the contingent fee system and is widely used in the United States. However, the speculative action has a long and honourable history in the Scottish legal system. This is the name given to the practice of solicitors taking on a case on the understanding that they will receive no fee for their services unless they are successful. Section 61A of the Solicitors (Scotland) Act 1980[25] provides a variation of this action. Where a lawyer takes a case on a speculative basis, they can now do so under an agreement with the client that they will receive, if successful, up to twice the normal party and party level of expenses. In the event of failure the solicitor is not entitled to a fee but may recover outlays from the client who is also liable for the other side's legal expenses.[26]

ALTERNATIVE DISPUTE RESOLUTION

12–18 Given the difficulties experienced by consumers in using the courts to resolve disputes, it is not surprising that other avenues have been explored. These are now often known collectively as alternative dispute resolution (or ADR). There is no definitive or agreed definition of ADR, but one that might be used is that it is any means of providing a resolution of a dispute between two or more parties which does not involve traditional court procedures.[27] In this sense the small claims procedure referred to above is a form of ADR. In addition, there have been a number of interesting developments, which are discussed below, involving conciliation, mediation, arbitration and ombudsmen schemes. Both the general consumer White Paper, *Modern Markets: Confident Consumers*[28] and the consumer credit White Paper[29] advocated the use of ADR and one of the central features of the CTSI Consumer Code Approval Scheme is the need for codes to include ADR mechanisms. The Consumer Credit Act 2006 (the 2006 Act) added credit disputes to the range of cases that can be taken to the Financial Ombudsman Service and the Consumers, Estate Agents and Redress Act 2007 has a power to require estate agents to belong to an approved redress scheme.[30]

---

[24] *Quantum Claims Compensation Specialists Ltd v Powell*, 1998 S.C. 316; 1998 S.L.T. 228; 1998 S.C.C.R. 173.

[25] Solicitors (Scotland) Act 1980 s.61A was inserted in the Act by s.36 of the Law Reform (Miscellaneous Provisions) (Scotland) Act 1990.

[26] For detailed discussion of speculative actions see *Review of Expenses and Funding of Civil Litigation In Scotland* (The Taylor Review) (September 2013), available at *http://www.scotland. gov.uk/About/Review/taylor-review/Report* [Accessed 22 June 2015].

[27] WCH Ervine, *Settling Consumer Disputes: A review of alternative dispute resolution* (National Consumer Council, 1993) pp.2 and 3. See also Ervine, "ADR in Consumer Disputes" in *Alternative Dispute Resolution in Scotland*, S Moody and RE MacKay (eds) (Edinburgh: W.Green, 1995).

[28] White Papers, *Modern Markets: Confident Consumers*(1999) Cm.4410, fn.4.

[29] Department of Trade and Industry, *Fair, Clear and Competitive: The consumer credit market in the 21st century*(2003) Cm.6040, Ch.3.

[30] See the Estate Agents Act 1979 s.23A, inserted by the Consumers, Estates Agents and Redress Act 2007 Sch.6 para.2.

Both the Scottish Legal Aid Board and the Scottish Civil Justice Council have been exploring ADR.[31] In June 2013, the EU published new legislation on ADR and online dispute resolution (ODR). This comprises a Directive[32] on consumer ADR and a Regulation[33] on consumer ODR. This legislation will allow consumers and traders to solve their disputes without going to court, in a quick, low-cost and simple way. The ADR Directive will ensure that consumers can turn to quality alternative dispute resolution entities for all kinds of contractual disputes that they have with traders; no matter what they purchased (excluding disputes regarding health and higher education)and whether they purchased it online or offline, domestically or across borders. According to the ODR Regulation, an EU-wide online platform will be set up for disputes that arise from online transactions. The platform will link all the national alternative dispute resolution entities and will operate in all official EU languages. Member States have to implement the ADR/ODR rules by July 2015 and the ODR platform will be operational in January 2016.

The Directive will mainly be implemented by the Alternative Dispute Resolution for Consumer Disputes (Competent Authorities and Information) Regulations 2015 (the 2015 Regulations).[34] The Government has decided not at this stage to pursue the suggestions raised in its consultation regarding the possible overall rationalisation of the ADR landscape by creating a single consumer ombudsman.[35] The regulations create "competent authorities" who oversee the activities of "ADR entities", i.e organisations that provide ADR services. In the case of the Financial Ombudsman Scheme the competent authority is the Financial Conduct Authority (FCA) and for the English Office for Legal Complaints it is the Legal Services Board.[36] The Civil Aviation Authority, the Gambling Commission, the Gas and Electricity Markets Authority, the Office of Communications and the lead enforcement authority for the purposes of the Estate Agents Act 1979 are the competent authorities for ADR entities in their areas.[37] The Secretary of State for Department of Business, Innovation and Skills (BIS) is the competent authority in relation to the Pensions Ombudsman and for any other organisation that becomes an ADR entity.[38] In the latter case BIS has subcontracted this task to the CTSI. The role of competent authorities is to assess applications to become ADR providers following the criteria set out in the

12–19

---

[31] See, Scottish Legal Aid Board, *Making Justice Work, Enabling Access to Justice Project— Overview report of Alternative Dispute Resolution in Scotland* (November 2014) and the Scottish Government and The Scottish Civil Justice Council, *Access to Justice Literature Review: Alternative Dispute Resolution in Scotland and Other Jurisdictions* (2014).

[32] Directive 2013/11/EU of the European Parliament and of the Council of 21 May 2013 on alternative dispute resolution for consumer disputes.

[33] Regulation (EU) No.524/2013 of the European Parliament and of the Council of 21 May 2013 on online dispute resolution for consumer disputes.

[34] Consumer Disputes (Competent Authorities and Information) Regulations 2015 (SI 2015/542).

[35] See Department of Business, Innovation and Skills, *Alternative Dispute Resolution for Consumers, Government response to the consultation on implementing the Alternative Dispute Resolution Directive and the Online Dispute Resolution Regulation* (November 2014), available on the BIS website.

[36] Consumer Disputes (Competent Authorities and Information) Regulations 2015 reg.8 and Sch.1 Pt 1.

[37] Consumer Disputes (Competent Authorities and Information) Regulations 2015 reg.8 and Sch.1 Pt 2.

[38] Consumer Disputes (Competent Authorities and Information) Regulations 2015 reg.4.

regulations.[39] These set out the criteria in the Directive such as expertise, independence, impartiality, fairness and effectiveness. They also maintain lists of ADR providers and monitor the operation of schemes under their jurisdiction.

12–20   Apart from the areas of business where membership of an ADR scheme is a statutory requirement, such as financial services or estate agency, the regulations do not impose a requirement on any business to be a member of such a scheme. What they do is set up a structure for creating schemes. Having considered various options, the Government has decided not to establish a "residual" ADR scheme, which would have been available where businesses are not obliged or committed to using another ADR scheme. This is because the emergence of a private sector organisation, Ombudsman Services, is thought to be capable of fulfilling this role.

12–21   ADR entities, once approved, must keep their competent authority informed of any changes in relation to them and publish each year on their website "an annual activity report" setting out the numbers and types of complaints they have dealt with and what the outcomes were. Every two years they must provide a more detailed report reflecting on issues that have arisen and assessing the effectiveness of their scheme.

12–22   The regulations also impose obligations on traders who are obliged to use an ADR scheme by statute, as is the case with financial services, or under the rules of their trade association. Such a trader must provide the name and website address of the ADR scheme on its own website if it has one and in its general contractual terms. Regulation 19(2) of the 2015 Regulations requires every trader to provide a consumer with information regarding the availability of ADR when the trader has exhausted its internal complaint handling process in relation to a complaint brought by that consumer. They must also indicate whether they are obliged, or prepared, to submit to an ADR scheme.

MEDIATION

12–23   Mediation or conciliation of consumer disputes commonly takes place under the provisions of codes of conduct governing a particular trade sector. Many of these codes were drawn up by trade associations in consultation with the OFT when the Director-General of Fair Trading had a duty to encourage the creation of such codes. Approval has now been withdrawn from these codes and a new procedure, discussed in Ch.10, is in place to produce more effective codes. It is believed that several of the codes are still in operation and that their conciliation schemes operate. The NCC pointed out that little is known about how conciliation operates in practice and that consumers tended to perceive conciliation as biased towards the trader.[40] A Scottish example is the Scottish Motor Trade Association (SMTA) whose code provides a conciliation service whereby members of the public who have a complaint against a member of the SMTA can put forward written representations to a committee. These representations together with the written

---

[39] Consumer Disputes (Competent Authorities and Information) Regulations 2015 reg.9 and Schs 2 and 3.

[40] National Consumer Council, *Out of Court: A consumer view of three low-cost trade arbitration schemes* (1991).

responses of the SMTA member are placed before a complaints committee who will make a recommendation to resolve the complaint and reconcile the differences between the member and the customer. In 2012/2013 27 complaints were dealt with of which 40 per cent were resolved in favour of the consumer. This masks the fact that 431 consumers had contacted the Association which was able to resolve all but 27 by advice over the telephone.

In addition to the sector specific schemes there is an interesting development in Scotland. Consumer Advice Scotland launched a pilot mediation project in February 1995, which was not limited to consumer cases. It now runs in Edinburgh Sheriff Court with funding provided by the Justice Department of the Scottish Government and deals with an average of about 90 cases per year. It accepts cases referred by a sheriff within the small claims and summary cause limits. Mediation is undertaken by qualified mediators nominated by the Centre for Dispute Resolution and is free to both parties. Of the 77 mediations in 2013/2014 84 per cent were successful.[41]

12–24

ARBITRATION

Arbitration as a method of private dispute resolution has a long history and is widely used in commercial disputes. Its advantages are that disputes can be decided by an adjudicator who is an expert in the subject-matter of the dispute and that they are held in private. Speed and cheapness are not necessarily characteristics of arbitration.[42] Scotland has a long history of arbitration which was eventually modernised by the Arbitration (Scotland) Act 2010. For reasons of cost, arbitration, until relatively recently, has not been a realistic option for consumers.

12–25

Most consumer arbitrations take place as a result of arbitration schemes contained in codes of practice originally drawn up by trade associations in consultation with the OFT and now under the Chartered Trading Standards Institute Consumer Codes Approval Scheme. Their approval criteria state that dispute resolution schemes should be free for the consumer if possible. One of the most widely used consumer arbitration schemes in the UK is that of the Association of British Travel Agents (ABTA) though it is not part of the Consumer Codes Approval Scheme. In most cases the arbitration service is operated by the Independent Dispute Resolution Service, an arm of the Chartered Institute of Arbitrators.

12–26

Originally, the Consumer Arbitration Agreements Act 1988 sought to ensure that arbitration was a genuine alternative to the courts in cases involving consumers and that they were not forced to submit to arbitration. That Act has now been repealed and replaced by provisions in the Arbitration Act 1996 ss.89–91. These extend the unfair terms provisions in Pt 2 of the Consumer

12–27

---

[41] The Scottish Civil Justice Council, *Access to Justice Literature Review: Alternative Dispute Resolution in Scotland and Other Jurisdictions* (2014) p.58.

[42] Indeed, some types of arbitration may be more expensive than using the courts as the parties have to meet not only the costs of their lawyers but also the costs of the arbitrator and the venue.

Rights Act 2015 to arbitration agreements. Section 91 provides that for the purposes of the Regulations such agreements are deemed to be unfair where the amount claimed is up to £5,000.[43]

12–28   The former OFT approved arbitration schemes required the consumer to pay a registration fee, usually of the order of £40, though it was refunded where the consumer was successful. The arbiter under most schemes was appointed by the Chartered Institute of Arbitrators. To reduce costs, arbitrations are almost invariably on a documents only basis. Each side provides the arbiter with its written submissions and relevant documents. Normally, the parties have no direct contact with the arbiter except in the case of the Glass and Glazing Federation's (GGF) scheme (which still operates) where site visits are quite common. It seems likely that this pattern will continue to be the case under new codes drawn up under the new procedure.

12–29   In addition to the schemes approved by the OFT or the new Consumer Codes Approval scheme operated by the CTSI there are a number of other low cost schemes, such as those of Virgin Trains and the National Association of Funeral Directors. The settling of cross-border disputes could be particularly difficult using the traditional court procedures. The EU attempts to assist consumers by providing information and advice through the EEJ-Net scheme which has offices in all member countries. It is hosted in the UK by the CTSI.

12–30   Not a great deal is known about the operation of these various arbitration schemes. Only with the publication of the NCC's study, *Out of Court*,[44] did empirical evidence about any of them become widely available. This study looked at the three most heavily used schemes, those of the ABTA, the GGF and British Telecom (BT). Unfortunately, the schemes do not keep statistics on a regional basis so it has not proved possible to produce figures relating to Scotland. In the course of the study the researchers learnt that many of the schemes operating under codes of practice are hardly ever used. At the date of the study the funeral scheme had never been used and the photography scheme only once. The main reason for this is probably consumer ignorance of their existence, which is related to under-resourcing of the schemes.[45] This study is now rather dated—BT, for example is now a member of an ombudsman scheme instead of an arbitration one. However, the findings of *Seeking Resolution*[46] suggests that the general picture may not now be all that different.

OMBUDSMEN

12–31   One of the most interesting additions to the range of redress mechanisms available to consumers in the UK over the past generation has been the ombudsman. The concept has been borrowed from the public sector which, in its

---

[43] Unfair Arbitration Agreements (Specified Amount) Order 1999 (SI 1999/2167).

[44] National Consumer Council, *Out of Court: A consumer view of three low-cost trade arbitration schemes* (1991).

[45] See Office of Fair Trading, *Consumer Redress Mechanisms* (1991) pp.31 and 32.

[46] Department of Trade and Industry, *Seeking Resolution; the availability and usage of consumer-to-business alternative dispute resolution in the United Kingdom* (URN 03/1616); research conducted by independent consultants Margaret Doyle and Katrina Ritters, and Steve Brooker of the National Consumer Council. It was published in January 2004.

turn, had adapted an institution that originated in Scandinavia. A Parliamentary Commissioner for Administration, more commonly referred to as "the Ombudsman", was first appointed in 1967 to investigate allegations by individuals of maladministration by central government. This was followed by the creation of a Health Services Ombudsman in 1973 and local government ombudsmen, or Commissioners for Local Administration, to give them their official title, in 1974. The Scottish Public Services Ombudsman Act 2002[47] reorganised the Scottish ombudsmen. A Scottish Public Services Ombudsman took over the functions of the Scottish Parliamentary Ombudsmen, the Health Services Ombudsman for Scotland, the Local Government Ombudsman for Scotland and the Housing Ombudsman for Scotland.

In response to increasing number of consumer complaints, first the insurance industry and then the banks and building societies created ombudsmen, as did the former Personal Investment Authority which was the self-regulatory organisation for retail investment. Following the creation of the Financial Services Authority (FSA), now the FCA, by the Financial Services and Markets Act 2000, the financial ombudsmen have been amalgamated in the Financial Ombudsman Service. In the private sector there is an ombudsman for corporate estate agents and, between 1994 and 2002, there was a Funeral Ombudsman. The Pensions Ombudsman was created by the Social Security Act 1990 and differs from the other ombudsmen in that investigations can be carried out into maladministration in both the private and the public sectors. All these ombudsmen have jurisdiction throughout the UK. So common have ombudsmen become that they have set up an association, the British and Irish Ombudsman Association (BIOS), one of whose functions is to try enable the public to distinguish between independent ombudsmen and schemes using the title but not operated by an independent person.

12–32

The ombudsmen in the financial services sector proved very popular and this continues to be the case with the new Financial Ombudsman Service (the FOS). In the year to March 2014 it resolved 518,778 cases, 31,029 being settled by an ombudsman.[48] It is thought to be the largest ombudsman scheme in the world, with 3,256 staff, 10,000 member firms within its jurisdiction and a budget of approximately £223 million. The FOS is operated by a company, FOS Ltd, set up by the FSA, though it is operationally independent of it. The independence of its ombudsmen is assured by the fact that they are appointed by FOS Ltd not the FSA.

12–33

Like its private sector predecessors, there is no fee to use the FOS, the danger of frivolous complaints being dealt with by the power to make awards against claimants in favour of the FOS where they have acted unreasonably, improperly or have been responsible for unreasonable delay.[49] The running costs of the FOS are provided by a levy on firms subject to its jurisdiction and fees paid by firms involved in complaints. The ombudsman can require parties to provide it with information and member firms are required by the FCA to co-operate with them. Awards are binding on firms but not on complainants who may elect to pursue alternative means of redress. This is one way in which the ombudsman differs

12–34

---

[47] Scottish Public Services Ombudsman Act 2002.
[48] Financial Ombudsman Service, *Annual Review* 2013–2014.
[49] Financial Services and Markets Act 2000 s.234(4).

from arbitration. Another is that they can base judgments on what is fair, just and reasonable in the circumstances rather than on purely legal considerations. A shortcoming of arbitration schemes is sometimes said to be that their findings are not published and thus it is difficult to know how they are applying the law and whether a pattern of complaints is building up against particular firms. While the FOS scheme does not publicise the names of parties it can consider whether the conduct complained of merits regulatory action and refer the matter to the FSA.

12–35   The Scottish Legal Complaints Commission replaced the Scottish Legal Services Ombudsman in 2008 but operates in a way that parallels other ombudsmen. It deals with complaints against solicitors, advocates, commercial attorneys, conveyancing and executry practitioners. The Commission deals only with what it terms service complaints which are complaints about the quality of a practitioner's work. It does not deal with conduct complaints that are about a practitioner's behaviour, their fitness to carry out work and how they have behaved either in carrying out a transaction or outside of business. Such complaints are referred to the relevant professional organisation. Where a client has made an eligible service complaint the Commission first offers a free mediation service conducted by independent mediators and this resolves 80 per cent of cases. If mediation does not resolve the complaint it is referred to a case investigator who, after examining the complaint, will made recommendations for its resolution. If these are not accepted by the parties the case is resolved by a "determination" by members of the Commission. The Annual Report Commission for 2013–2014 shows that 1,024 complaints were received all but 19, which involved advocates, relating to solicitors. 257 of these were found to be eligible service complaints and 62 conduct complaints which were passed to the relevant professional body. During the year 62 complaints were resolved by mediation and 210 went to the determination process. Of these 118 were upheld and 92 rejected.

OTHER METHODS OF OBTAINING REDRESS

12–36   Most methods of obtaining redress place the onus on the consumer to take action. There are various reasons why consumers may not do so. They may not be aware of their rights; and, if they are, they may be inhibited by the cost of litigation or fears about going to the alien environment of a court. In addition, if the loss is small, it may not be thought worthwhile to seek redress, although it is realised that the individual consumer is but one of a large number who has been the victim of a legal wrong. Professor Cappelletti in his major study of these problems has argued:

> "It is necessary to abandon the individualistic, essentially laissez-faire, 19th century concept of litigation, a concept which awards the right to sue, if at all, solely to the subject personally aggrieved in his own narrowly-defined individual rights for example, to the owner of a neighbouring property in a case of pollution or of a zoning violation. The new social, collective, 'diffuse' rights and interests can be protected only by new social, collective, 'diffuse' remedies and procedures. Indeed,

the quest for these new remedies and procedures is, in my judgment, the most fascinating feature in the modem evolution of judicial law."[50]

Scots law has not gone far in the direction of meeting these concerns but there have been a number of steps and these are discussed below.   **12–37**

Where a consumer suffers loss which also results in a criminal conviction, the Criminal Procedure (Scotland) Act 1995 (the 1995 Act) provides a procedure designed to remove the need for separate civil proceedings. The criminal court may make a compensation order directing the offender to pay compensation to the victim. If made by a judge, other than a stipendiary magistrate in the district court, these are limited to level 4 on the standard scale, currently £2,500, and to £5,000 in summary proceedings if made by a sheriff or stipendiary magistrate.[51] In solemn proceedings there is no limit on the amount that may be awarded. Orders should take precedence over fines[52] but may not be made in respect of death or of injury, loss or damage due to an accident arising out of the presence of a motor vehicle on a road, except damage treated as caused by the convicted person's acts.[53] Section 302A of the 1995 Act permits procurators fiscal to issue compensation offers to an alleged offenders where it seems an offence which could be tried summarily had been committed. The maximum amount of a compensation offer is £5,000[54] and if the alleged offender accepts the offer no prosecution follows.   **12–38**

Like the equivalent English scheme, the procedure is designed to apply to fairly clear cases where no great amount is at stake and the compensation can be assessed easily and quickly. An obvious example in a consumer context where orders have been made is following a conviction under the CPR 2008 for "clocking", i.e. turning back the odometer of a car. A weakness of the procedure, apart from an apparent unwillingness of some sheriffs to apply it in what seem to be appropriate circumstances, lies in the fact that there is no formal procedure for invoking it. The victim has no standing to make an application and much depends on the procurator fiscal raising the matter and having some evidence on which the sheriff can base a compensation order.   **12–39**

In earlier chapters we have already seen a number of examples of a government official having power to take action for the benefit of consumers as a whole. The enforcement order procedure under Pt 8 of the Enterprise Act 2002 (the 2002 Act), designed to allow the OFT (now the CMA) and other regulators to curb illegal conduct, is one. The Enhanced Consumer Measures that have been added to this procedure envisage more use being made of compensation as a means of providing redress.[55] The CMA also has powers to seek an interdict where it considers that a contract term is unfair,[56] a power which has been extended to other bodies.[57] The consumer credit White Paper has also recognised   **12–40**

---

[50] M Cappelletti and J Weisner, *Access to Justice*(Amsterdam: Sijthoff and Noordhoff, 1978) Vol.111, pp.519 and 520.
[51] See Criminal Procedure (Scotland) Act 1995 s.249.
[52] Criminal Procedure (Scotland) Act 1995 s.250(1).
[53] Criminal Procedure (Scotland) Act 1995 s.249(4)(b).
[54] Criminal Procedure (Scotland) Act 1995 Compensation Offer (Maximum Amount) Order 2008 (SSI 2008/7).
[55] See para.10–132.
[56] Unfair Terms in Consumer Contracts Regulations 1999 (SI 1999/2083) reg.10. See Ch.10.
[57] See Ch.9.

the importance of this kind of action in making private law rights effective in its proposals for reforming unjust credit transactions. It proposed that named third parties could bring a group-claim against a trader engaged in rogue trading practices.[58] This idea was not proceeded within the 2006 Act, though unfair credit relationships could be dealt with by the powers in Pt 8 of the 2002 Act.

12–41   Beyond these examples there are few other methods by which one or a small number of persons may take action to benefit a larger class, or the public at large. An action by one individual may, incidentally, benefit a large number of other people as where one person who is affected by a nuisance obtains an interdict to put an end to it and thereby improves matters for all those living in the vicinity.[59] Scots law does have the *actio popularis* and the possibility of action by the Lord Advocate or a local authority in certain circumstances, but these seem to have fallen into disuse.[60]

12–42   Where a number of individuals are affected by the same wrong it is possible to deal more efficiently with litigation by the use of a test case or, if several actions have been raised, these may be heard at the same time or may even be formally conjoined. Beyond the special circumstances of unincorporated societies, Scots civil procedure does not permit a representative action such as is available in limited circumstances in England and Wales. In the United States and some Commonwealth countries a special procedure, known as a class action, exists permitting one or more people to raise an action on behalf of a larger number who have been affected by the same wrong. A widely quoted example from California, *Daar v Yellow Cab Co*,[61] involved one pursuer taking action for the benefit of all those who had been overcharged by a taxi company. In the Canadian case of *Naken v General Motors of Canada Ltd*[62] four plaintiffs sued on behalf of all those who had purchased new 1971 or 1972 Firenzas, claiming $1,000 for each as damages for misrepresentations contained in advertising.

12–43   In 1982 the SCC produced a report of a working party which it set up recommending the introduction of class actions into the Scottish legal system.[63] In 2013 this recommendation was endorsed by the Gill Review, which contains a full discussion of the issues.[64] Following some high profile disasters such as the Lockerbie bombing and the Piper Alpha disaster which produced multiple claims, the issue was referred to the Scottish Law Commission which published a report advocating the introduction of class actions.[65] A class action is a court procedure that enables a number of individuals with similar complaints against the same defender to seek a judicial remedy in one action instead of each raising separate actions. It is important to note that it is a legal procedure only: it does not give claimants any new substantive rights. There are many situations where such a

---

[58] Department of Trade and Industry, *Fair, Clear and Competitive: The consumer credit market in the 21st century* (2003) Cm.6040, para.3.41.

[59] An example is *Webster v Lord Advocate*, 1985 S.L.T. 361.

[60] See Scottish Consumer Council, *Class Action in the Scottish Court* (1982) Ch.2.

[61] *Daar v Yellow Cab Co* 433 P. 2d. 732 (1967).

[62] *Naken v General Motors of Canada Ltd* [1983] 144 D.L.R. (3d.) 385.

[63] See Scottish Consumer Council, *Class Action in the Scottish Court* (1982). The council have recently returned to this subject, see C Ervine, *A Class of Their Own: Why Scotland needs a class actions procedure* (SCC, 2003).

[64] See Scottish Civil Courts Review, *Report of the Scottish Civil Courts Review* (September 2009) Vol.2, Ch.13.

[65] Scottish Law Commission, *Multi-Party Actions* (Scot Law Com. No.154, 1996).

procedure might be appropriate. In the so-called mass disaster cases where many people are killed or injured as a result of, for example, a rail accident at least some of the legal issues could be dealt with by such a procedure. It might also be of use in "creeping" disasters, of which claims for damages in respect of allegedly defective drugs such as tranquillisers are examples. In these cases there is no connection between the victims except that they have all suffered from the same drug though at different times and, possibly, in different ways. Claims falling within these two categories will often arise in consumer situations but it is also usual to refer to a third category more specifically as "consumer claims". These are cases where a large number of consumers of goods or services claim relatively small amounts of money which, individually, it might not be economic to recover through litigation. Examples could be found in cases where a number of holidaymakers are misled by the same error in a package holiday brochure or many people purchase the same shoddy product.

The class action is a subset of the group or multi-party action. The other kind **12–44** of group action may be termed the "public interest action". The public interest action is one where a public official takes action for the benefit of the public at large or a section of it; or one brought by an organisation, such as a consumer protection or environmental organisation, on behalf of its members and the public. The SCC Class Actions report,[66] in addition to advocating the introduction of a class actions procedure, envisaged further reforms which would develop group actions. Ironically, while no progress has yet been made on class actions, considerable progress has been made in relation to the other type of group action.

The overriding reason for advocating the introduction of class actions is that it **12–45** is essential in the interests of upholding the rule of law. It is unacceptable that consumers or others should be given rights which they cannot effectively enjoy. Such a situation is a reproach to a legal system. The importance of a remedy has been recognised in the introduction of small claims procedures and other methods of improving access to justice. The class action is but one more way of doing so. There is also the deterrent argument in favour of the class action. To quote an Australian judge:

> "Why should a defendant secure benefits by unlawful conduct, relying on the inadequacy of the legal system and the timidity and lack of organisation of those wronged?"[67]

Not infrequently, there are situations where many individuals lose small **12–46** amounts as the result of unlawful actions by traders but few find it worthwhile to take action. The result is that the wrongdoer makes a windfall profit. An example of this kind of situation was the Hoover flights saga in the early 1990s, when the company failed to honour an offer in a marketing promotion to provide free flights. Many thousands of consumers appear to have been disappointed but few seem to have resorted to the small claim courts. That few of those disappointed in the Hoover case took their cases to court is not surprising. The amounts were not large and many may not have thought it worthwhile to do so. One may also

---

[66] Scottish Law Commission, *Multi-Party Actions* (Scot Law Com. No.154, 1996).
[67] Kirby J (then chairman of the Australian Law Reform Commission), "Class Actions: A panacea or disaster?" 1978 *The Australian Director*, 25 at 33.

speculate that fear and ignorance of the workings of the legal system may also have played a part. Research on small claims both in Scotland and England demonstrates that many potential litigants are reluctant to embark even on the simplified procedures offered by the small claims courts.

12–47   Where larger sums are at stake, as there will usually be in the mass disaster and creeping disaster cases, there are other factors to be taken into account. In these cases the claims may involve considerable difficulty. In many product liability cases, especially those involving drugs, the evidence required is elaborate and controversial. Much research is required and expert evidence will be needed to assess the viability of the claims. These claims can also involve considerable legal complexity and areas of law with which few lawyers are familiar. For cases to be litigated separately is inefficient where similar issues arise in many aspects of the case. It makes much more sense for claimants to band together. Common issues can be explored on behalf of a group of potential claimants and the cost of doing so can be spread over the whole group. In this way the unequal struggle between the individual victim and the well-resourced corporation can be made fairer. Dealing with similar disputes against the same defender in one litigation also prevents inconsistency. If individual cases are dealt with in different courts there is the possibility that different judges will arrive at different conclusions.

12–48   It is not only victims who benefit from the more efficient handling of litigation by means of group procedures. Defendants can benefit also through fighting only one action rather than a series of actions. Not only may there be a saving in litigation costs for companies in such situations but also other savings in less loss of management time to the unproductive business of dealing with litigation. The courts too may benefit. The Ontario Law Reform Commission[68] noted that one benefit that is commonly attributed to class actions is judicial economy in that they may benefit both the parties and the courts by diminishing the total amount of litigation and thus reduce the total cost of settling disputes arising from mass wrongs.

12–49   Having recommended that class actions should be included in the Scottish legal system, the SCC Class Actions report[69] concluded with a perceptive chapter looking further ahead. Further steps were envisaged, though it was not thought appropriate to recommend these steps at the time because they went well beyond procedural reform and required reform of substantive law. Ironically, two of the steps envisaged have been adopted by government, one with conspicuous success. The first step beyond class actions was labelled the "external pursuer class action" or "public interest class action". The main type of class action recommended by the report is sometimes referred to as an "internal pursuer class action" because one or more people take action on behalf of themselves and others who have suffered harm. In the external pursuer action a group or association would be granted standing to sue on behalf of consumers for damages suffered by them. A tentative step in this direction has recently been taken with an interesting change to the Competition Act 1998 made by the Enterprise Act 2002. This permits bodies approved by the Secretary of State to bring claims for damages before the Competition Appeal Tribunal on behalf of consumers of

---

[68] Ontario Law Reform Commission, *Report on Class Actions* (1982).
[69] Scottish Consumer Council, *Class Action in the Scottish Court* (1982) fn.53.

goods and services.[70] This has not worked well and in January 2013 the BIS announced proposals for a new form of "collective" action before the Tribunal.[71] These claims will be particularly difficult and expensive and there is little incentive for organisations to become involved, particularly as the normal legal expenses rules will apply and will probably leave them out of pocket even if the action is successful. To make this kind of action more attractive probably needs some financial incentive such as the treble damages actions available in American anti-trust law or, at least, some enhancement of the legal expenses normally awarded to a successful party.

The second recommended step beyond the traditional class action was to allow consumer groups to seek remedies by way of interdict or declarator. It was argued that this was a particularly appropriate method as consumers face suppliers on unequal terms. The report noted that the powers of the Director-General of Fair Trading to take action under Pt 3 of the Fair Trading Act 1973 against traders who persistently treat consumers unfairly provided a model. This suggestion has proved to be extraordinarily prescient. The Pt 3 model has not proved as effective as had once been hoped, but has been replaced by the Enforcement Order procedure under Pt 8 of the 2002 Act. This permits the CMA and various other organisations to take action on behalf of consumers against infringements of a wide range of laws. The Enforcement Order procedure is similar to other more specific procedures such as that under the Unfair Terms legislation.[72] This is an excellent example of the value of the public interest class action. The regulations supplement the traditional means of redress through individual litigation by giving the CMA and a number of other organisations, including the Consumers' Association, power to require traders to remove unfair terms from their contracts. This has the great benefit not only of making the new legislation effective, but also of operating on the principle that prevention is better than cure. These regulations have been very successful in dealing with almost 7,000 cases, with very few exceptions, without having to take court action. Two spectacular examples of the benefits of the regulations are contained in a recent report by the Comptroller and Auditor General that shows the agreement of a mortgage company to remove unfair penalties from their loan agreements has saved consumers £65.2 million and amendments to mobile telephone contracts are estimated to be saving consumers between £60 and £80 million each year.

12–50

As Cranston has pointed out, "[c]lass actions are not a universal panacea for consumers".[73] Indeed, it must be remembered that redress procedures are only one aspect of consumer protection. It must be seen as part of an overall strategy involving the enforcement work of the OFT and trading standards departments. Just as important is the provision of advice and information for consumers. Without this they may never learn of their rights or be able to avail themselves of the redress procedures that exist. The importance of an integrated network of

12–51

---

[70] In 2008 *Which?* successfully brought an action on behalf of 600 of consumers who had been the victims of a cartel of retailers of replica soccer kit.

[71] Department for Business Innovation and Skills, *Private actions in competition law: a consultation on options for reform—government response* (2013).

[72] Now in Pt 2 of the Consumer Rights Act 2015.

[73] R Cranston, *Consumers and the Law*, 2nd edn (London: Weidenfeld and Nicolson, 1984) p.98.

advice agencies was emphasised by the now defunct SCC.[74] This was recognised in the 1999 consumer White Paper and, after research was carried out Consumer Direct, a new national telephone and online consumer advice and information service was launched. One of the first areas to benefit is Scotland, where the scheme was launched in July 2004. It is aimed to provide consumers with the knowledge, tools and confidence to resolve their consumer problems themselves. Following the reorganisation of the consumer landscape it is now operated by Consumer Advice Scotland. It works in partnership with a network of national organisations allowing it to provide advice quickly and easily on a wide range of issues such as debt, employment and welfare as well as consumer issues. As well as offering traditional telephone based advice, it uses a website, webforms and a chat service.

---

[74] See Scottish Consumer Council, *Let the People Know: A report on local advice services in Scotland* (1977); and Scottish Consumer Council, *Following Our Advice: A review of advice services in Scotland* (1988).

INDEX

All references are to paragraph number

Acquiring goods
becoming owner
  generally, 3–16—3–17
  Rule 1, 3–20
  Rule 2, 3–21
  Rule 3, 3–22
  Rule 4, 3–23
  specific goods, 3–18—3–19
contracts for supply of goods
  contracts for transfer of goods, 3–13
  contracts of hire, 3–11
  fitness for purpose (s.10), 4–37—4–44
  generally, 3–05
  goods covered, 3–06—3–09
  hire purchase, 3–12
  sales contracts, 3–10
delivery and risk
  digital content, 3–59—3–64
  generally, 3–54—3–58
deposits, 3–15
digital content
  generally, 3–59—3–60
  meaning, 3–61
  pre-contract information, 3–64
  trader's right to supply, 3–62—3–63
generally, 3–01—3–04
nemo dat quod non habet
  conditional sale agreements, 3–38—3–43
  generally, 3–37
  hire purchase, 3–38—3–43
  motor vehicles, 3–38—3–43
  personal bar exception, 3–44—3–46
price, 3–14—3–15
unascertained goods
  contracts for transfer of goods, 3–33—3–35
  generally, 3–24—3–27
  sales contracts, 3–36
  transfer of ownership, 3–28—3–36
voidable title
  buyer or seller in possession, 3–49—3–53
  generally, 3–47—3–48
Advertising
bait advertising, 11–25
British Code of Advertising Practice,
  11–50—11–58
children, 11–25
common law, 11–03—11–11
comparative advertising, 11–34
consumer credit, 11–41
distance selling, 11–42—11–49
false claims, 11–28
food, 11–35—11–37
free gifts, 11–15
implied terms re description, 11–12—11–15
introduction, 11–01—11–02
invitations to purchase, 11–29
invitations to treat, 11–19—11–22
medicinal products, 11–39
misleading omissions, 11–28—11–29
off-premises selling, 11–42—11–49
OFT draft guidance, 11–26
price marking, 11–31—11–33
prices, 11–30
statutory control, 11–23—11–34
tobacco products, 11–40
unfair commercial practices
  bait advertising, 11–25
  banned practices, 11–25
  children, 11–25
  "commercial practices", 11–25
  comparative advertising, 11–34
  confusion with another trader's products,
    11–27
  false claims, 11–28
  free gifts, 11–15
  invitations to purchase, 11–29
  legislation, 11–23—11–24
  misleading omissions, 11–28—11–29
  OFT draft guidance, 11–26
  price marking, 11–31—11–33
  prices, 11–30
  unfair practices, 11–26
weights and measures, 11–38
Advertising Standards Authority
role of, 1–52—1–53

293